THE BRIDGE
TO AIRPOWER

The History of Military Aviation
Paul J. Springer, editor

This series is designed to explore previously ignored facets of the history of air-power. It includes a wide variety of disciplinary approaches, scholarly perspectives, and argumentative styles. Its fundamental goal is to analyze the past, present, and potential future utility of airpower and to enhance our understanding of the changing roles played by aerial assets in the formulation and execution of national military strategies. It encompasses the incredibly diverse roles played by airpower, which include but are not limited to efforts to achieve air superiority; strategic attack; intelligence, surveillance, and reconnaissance missions; airlift operations; close-air support; and more. Of course, airpower does not exist in a vacuum. There are myriad terrestrial support operations required to make airpower functional, and examinations of these missions is also a goal of this series.

In less than a century, airpower developed from flights measured in minutes to the ability to circumnavigate the globe without landing. Airpower has become the military tool of choice for rapid responses to enemy activity, the primary deterrent to aggression by peer competitors, and a key enabler to military missions on the land and sea. This series provides an opportunity to examine many of the key issues associated with its usage in the past and present, and to influence its development for the future.

THE BRIDGE TO AIRPOWER

LOGISTICS SUPPORT FOR ROYAL FLYING CORPS OPERATIONS ON THE WESTERN FRONT, 1914–18

PETER DYE

Naval Institute Press
Annapolis, Maryland

Naval Institute Press
291 Wood Road
Annapolis, MD 21402

Library of Congress Cataloging-in-Publication Data
Dye, Peter.
  The bridge to airpower : logistics support for Royal Flying Corps operations on
the Western Front, 1914–18 / Peter Dye.
      pages cm. — (The history of military aviation)
  Includes bibliographical references and index.
    ISBN 978-1-61251-839-8 (alk. paper) — ISBN 978-1-61251-840-4 (ebook) 1.
World War, 1914–1918—Logistics—Great Britain. 2. World War, 1914–1918—
Aerial operations, British. 3. Great Britain. Royal Flying Corps—History. I. Title.
II. Title: Logistics support for Royal Flying Corps operations on the Western Front,
1914-18.

  D530.D93 2015
  940.4'4941—dc23

                                                                    2015012372

23 22 21 20 19 18 17 16 15   9 8 7 6 5 4 3 2 1
First printing

All photographs are courtesy of the Royal Air Force Museum.
Map created by Bobby Wright.

TO MY FAMILY,
who waited patiently

CONTENTS

⊙ TABLES, MAPS, AND FIGURES

Tables

Map

Figure

PREFACE

M Y INTEREST IN THE LOGISTIC ARRANGEMENTS THAT UNDERPINNED ROYAL FLYING Corps (RFC) and Royal Air Force (RAF) operations on the western front is long standing and driven by both professional and personal motives. Employed as an aviation logistician for more than thirty years, and with a grandfather who served in the Royal Naval Air Service (RNAS) and the RAF during the First World War, I have been intrigued by the way that the airplane, a prewar novelty, was transformed within just a few years into a practical weapon. Indeed, the more I have understood the complex and diverse challenges involved in maintaining aircraft, in war and peace, the more impressed I have been by the RFC's ability to sustain air operations under the extraordinary conditions represented by the western front—in the absence of any body of experience or an existing model. This has provided the genesis for a series of papers and articles in which I have explored the origins of aviation logistics doctrine and the contribution of support activities to British airpower in both world wars.[1] Through this process of analysis and reflection, various threads have emerged that suggest substantial continuity in aviation logistic principles (if not practice). I have argued elsewhere that the logistic arrangements developed on the western front provided the foundation for strategic success in the Second World War, as well as demonstrating the interdependence of logistics—in the form of its enabling systems and processes—and airpower.[2] A detailed examination of the effectiveness of the RFC's logistic system provides an opportunity to explore the nature of this conti- nuity and to highlight enduring principles.

I must admit to a further motive. The more I have read and researched, the clearer it has become that the strategic and operational dimensions of logistics have been neglected by military historians. The critical role of production, supply, main- tenance, and repair in the birth of three-dimensional warfare remains unexplored, even though the "modern style of warfare"—in the form of indirect, predicted artillery fire—only emerged because the RFC was able to secure and sustain air superiority.[3] The ability of the RFC's logistic system to keep sufficient numbers of artillery cooperation aircraft above the trenches in face of combat attrition, high wastage rates, and rapid technological change (J. F. C. Fuller's "constant tactical fac- tor") was the precondition for what is argued by some to have been *the* First World War Revolution in Military Affairs (RMA).[4] The RMA is not without its critics and has suffered at the hands of those wishing to argue for a "new" (post–Cold War) style of warfare. It can certainly be argued that the concept has evolved in a way that was neither anticipated nor necessarily welcome.[5] The effort to identify specific turning points and to create a persuasive narrative built around a definitive chronology can result in selective analysis and superficial conclusions that ignore the ebb and flow of military practice and the influence of retrograde as well as progressive thinking. Jeremy Black has been one of the more trenchant critics, pointing out the fallacy of believing that great events have great causes.[6] These aspects will be touched on later, but for the present it is sufficient to say that the First World War brought about radical changes in the scale, intensity, and breadth of warfare that were both unprecedented and "modern" in their conduct and style.

There is a long tradition of military men writing military history. Professional knowledge and personal interest have lent their efforts substantial credibility, even where the results could be viewed as "myth-making."[7] It might be imagined that logistics is not a subject to excite the emotions. But, like any other aspect of history involving complex human activity, objectivity can prove elusive. Logistic "truth"— in the form of dispassionate and unassailable evidence—is no easier to find than military "truth." The ability to measure component activities, such as production and supply, does not mean that logistics is simply a matter of computation. The logistic profession is as prey to misconceptions, prejudice, and passion as every other aspect of military affairs. Important as it is to discover and record what really happened, there is a further obstacle to overcome. According to Hans Delbrück, "The military man who turns to history transfers phenomena from contemporary practice to the past without taking adequate account of the difference in circumstances."[8] Long practice may qualify me to examine the history of military logistics, but it could equally impose a mindset that distorts and blinds, particularly in the effort to demonstrate contemporary relevance. Finally, logistics is a subject that can only be understood in context. As Colin Gray has warned, "They cannot know logistics who only logistics know."[9] My approach in this study will be to understand the landscape before looking at the detail—while always remembering the circumstances of the time. In other words—to paraphrase Michael Howard's three general rules—to study the width, depth, and context.[10]

● ACKNOWLEDGMENTS

THIS BOOK COULD NOT HAVE BEEN WRITTEN WITHOUT THE GENEROUS SUPPORT OF the Royal Air Force through the award of a Portal Fellowship. I am also grateful for the encouragement of the Royal Air Force Museum and, in particular, Matt George, Andy Renwick, and Andrew Cormack. Finally, I must acknowledge the encouragement and advice provided by Gary Sheffield, chair of War Studies in the Department of History, Politics, and War Studies at Wolverhampton University. The original thesis that provided the basis for this book can be found at the Birmingham University eTheses Repository.

ACRONYMS AND ABBREVIATIONS

AAC	Air Ammunition Column
AAP	Aircraft Acceptance Park
AD	Aircraft Depot
AEF	American Expeditionary Force
AFC	Air Force Cross
AG	Adjutant General
AGS	Aeroplane General Sundries
AID	Aeronautical Inspection Department
AOD	Army Ordnance Department
AP	Army Air Park
AQMG	Assistant Quartermaster General
ASC	Army Service Corps
ASD	Aeroplane Supply Depot
BEF	British Expeditionary Force
CAS	Chief of the Air Staff
CB	Companion of the Most Honourable Order of the Bath
CinC	Commander in Chief
CMG	Companion of the Order of St. Michael and St. George
DAA & QMG	Deputy Assistant Adjutant & Quartermaster General
DAG	Deputy Adjutant General
DA & QMG	Deputy Adjutant & Quartermaster General
DMA	Directorate of Military Aeronautics
DQMG	Deputy Quartermaster General
EO	Equipment Officer
ERS	Engine Repair Shops
FAA	Fleet Air Arm
GAS	German Air Service
GHQ	General Headquarters
GOC	General Officer Commanding

HQ RAF	Headquarters Royal Air Force
HQ RFC	Headquarters Royal Flying Corps
IGC	Inspector General Communications
MOD	Ministry of Defence
MT	Motor Transport
NAO	National Audit Office
NATO	North Atlantic Treaty Organization
OASD	Ordnance Aeronautical Stores Department
OC	Officer Commanding
POL	Petrol, Oil & Lubricants
QMG	Quartermaster General
RAF	Royal Air Force
RE	Royal Engineers
RFC	Royal Flying Corps
RLP	Reserve Lorry Park
RMA	Revolution in Military Affairs
RNAS	Royal Naval Air Service
SARD	Southern Aircraft Repair Depot
TNA	The National Archives
USAF	United States Air Force
USAS	United States Air Services

THE BRIDGE
TO AIRPOWER

INTRODUCTION

T HERE HAS ALWAYS BEEN A DEGREE OF VAGUENESS ABOUT WHAT LOGISTICS actually comprises. This has arisen partly because of a confused etymology, and partly because it has proved a convenient term to encapsulate the varied activities that control the "means of war."[1] Nevertheless, to understand the contribution made by aviation logistics to RFC operations on the western front we need a working definition that makes clear what activities are included and (just as importantly) what activities are not.

Responsibility for coining the word logistics has been credited to Antoine-Henri Jomini, who introduced it in his treatise on military strategy, first published in the mid-nineteenth century.[2] Jomini is somewhat catholic in his definition, embracing virtually all military activities (including staff duties and intelligence) other than tactics and operations. His contemporary, Carl von Clausewitz, does not employ the term, although the latter does briefly touch on some roles traditionally associated with logistics (such as provisioning, supply, and the functioning of depots).[3] The importance of logistics in modern warfare has encouraged speculation that Clausewitz might have written more about the subject, and with a different emphasis, had he had the time.[4] This is more than stretching a point. All the evidence indicates that Clausewitz consciously excluded the logistic dimension of warfare, insisting that "it stood in about the same relationship to combat as the craft of the swordsmith to the art of fencing."[5] In subordinating the logistic to the operational, Clausewitz made clear his break with previous writing on the theory of war.[6]

The emergence of large citizen armies, and the need to sustain them continuously in the field, demanded unprecedented national economic effort and created an interest in the systems, practices, and organization that made this possible. But it took much longer for logistics to be recognized as central to military operations and even longer to be viewed as a suitable employment for officers. Edward Luttwak has argued that the lack of writing on the subject—at least in the premodern era—was driven by a disdain for "grubby sutlers," rather than ignorance about the importance of supply.[7] He goes on to observe that "while the class that would have been interested to read about logistics was not a reading class at all until the modern era, the class that did the writing regarded logistics as undignified, the province of its social inferiors." Luttwak exaggerates to make a point, but there is a kernel of truth. According to Shaw, "Although British methods of supply towards the close of the Napoleonic wars became more efficient, its servants and their work were generally despised by the combatant whose one remedy for failure was to suggest shooting or hanging the commissary."[8]

As late as the 1970s it was still possible for a respected senior officer, described by *The Times* as doing more than any man to dispel the widely held belief that most generals were ignorant fools, to write about the "profession of arms" while entirely excluding the subject of logistics.[9] This is not simply a generational issue but reflects a deep-seated cultural tradition that is still prevalent. "Logistics and supply chain management are rarely mentioned when countries expound upon their military achievements."[10] Nor should it be thought that this is a peculiarly military perspective—in the commercial world logistics has never been regarded as the fast track to a top management position, an indifference that led Peter Drucker to declare over forty years ago that "logistics was like Africa—the last great unexplored continent of business."[11]

British Defence Doctrine states that logistics is "the means by which force is materially sustained."[12] However, as the North Atlantic Treaty Organization (NATO) *Logistics Handbook* explains, there are actually many definitions—each placing a slightly different emphasis on the relationship between logistics, strategy, tactics, movement, and production.[13] There is also the question of scope—and in particular the extent to which finance and procurement are included. For example, Kenneth Macksey has defined logistics as "the ways and means of financing and procuring war resources, in conjunction with the supply and transport of men and materials."[14] This broader and more inclusive approach provides an appropriate model for studying the many and varied activities that aviation logistics comprises— arguably the most complex of military logistic activities.[15] For the purpose of this study, therefore, "aviation logistics" is defined as: the varied activities that procure, store, move, sustain, maintain, and repair the systems, associated components, and equipment employed by air forces.

These processes include technical development, manufacture, testing, modification, and salvage as well as the building of airfields and the recruiting and training of technical personnel, with the product known as a "supply chain." The United States Air Force (USAF) describes the supply chain as the cycle comprising: funding, requirement setting, determining stock levels, purchasing, repairing, and moving assets.[16] Although it is tempting to regard this as a linear process, in reality there is no particular sequence. The National Audit Office (NAO), in assessing the Ministry of Defence (MOD) logistic performance in Afghanistan, has adopted a similar definition, describing the supply chain as "the processes involved in the availability, storage and distribution of materiel."[17] The performance of the supply chain is a key driver in operational capability, ensuring that the right equipment reaches the right place at the right time.

The genesis of modern logistic studies is trans-Atlantic. This is not to suggest that the British Army has consciously ignored "administration" (the term traditionally employed in the UK to describe those activities supplying the army's daily needs). Maintaining secure lines of communication and ensuring adequate provisions has been an abiding concern for British generals, whether it be Marlborough and his march to the Danube or Wellington's operations in the Peninsula.[18] To some extent, however, logistic competence has been instinctive rather than inspired. Geography, politics, and economic necessity demanded that careful attention be paid to the supply aspects of expeditionary warfare. As a result, an emphasis on logistics has characterized the British way of war for centuries. However, the opposition to standing armies ensured that there was no established supply chain and hence greater reliance had to be placed on contractors compared to other nations. Rather than weaken military capability, this arrangement offered an efficient and effective system that in many ways was more responsive to the Army's needs than a permanent supply organization.[19] It has been argued that the British Army's failure in the American War of Independence was largely owed to logistic shortcomings, but closer examination suggests that this was essentially a problem about continuity of supply and the difficulty of coordinating army and navy arrangements rather than a lack of effort or inadequate logistic processes.[20] By contrast, the logistic arrangements for the First Fleet to Australia in 1787 demonstrated "Britain's superior administrative capability and its accumulated experience of sending large expeditions into distant seas."[21]

There was never any prospect that a British general operating on a foreign shore would ignore supply in the way that Napoleon was able to abandon some of the more static aspects of the line of communication and free himself (to a degree) from reliance on depots and distribution centers.[22] On the other hand, it has been a long-standing tradition to separate command from logistics. The catastrophic administrative failures experienced in the Crimea led to a blurring of these boundaries, but the Army continued to try to sustain the distinction and avoid distracting commanders with supply issues. *British Army Field Service Regulations (Part II)* (1909) reinforced this Clausewitzian perspective by endeavoring to disassociate senior officers from matters of administration.[23] Even after the First World War, a commander could bemoan changes that meant "attention was more concentrated on such matters as the correct counting of canteen takings and the price of necessities than on training."[24] The British Army and logistics was a relationship where familiarity bred contempt. Professional competence in the fields of supply and administration was the foundation for successful campaigns throughout the nineteenth and twentieth centuries, yet rarely featured in British military histories. It is no surprise, therefore, to find that two out of the ten volumes covering U.S. Army operations in the European theater, 1941–45, are dedicated to logistic issues, whereas none of the thirty-seven volumes that form the UK Military Series within the *History of the Second World War* specifically addresses logistic or supply issues.[25]

The work frequently credited as the watershed in American logistic studies is George Thorpe's *Pure Logistics: The Science of War Preparation* (1917).[26] Penned at a time when the United States was attempting to mobilize its industrial capacity to create a modern army (from what was in effect a standing start), this modest book of less than eighty pages is regarded as marking the birth of "modern" logistics. Thorpe drew on a long tradition of logistic writing, including William Kobbe, who was one of the first to recognize that "strategy in modern war was intimately connected with logistics."[27] However, it was Alfred Thayer Mahan who was the most influential of his predecessors. In a series of books and lectures at the Naval Academy between 1885 and 1911, Mahan introduced the term logistics into United States Navy usage and incorporated the concept within his theory of sea power.[28] He himself had been greatly influenced by the American Civil War—the first major war of the industrial age and generally regarded as the first "modern" war. The use of railroads, the widespread employment of new technology (including military aeronautics in the form of observation balloons), and the dominance of firepower marked a sharp break with the Napoleonic tradition and pushed the American soldier over the "critical threshold of modern war."[29] The employment of mass armies equipped and sustained by the mobilization of industry and standardized production ensured that logistics emerged at the forefront of military art such that "logistical capabilities shaped the plans and sometimes the outcomes of campaigns."[30] The North's victory also demonstrated that logistic superiority could overcome an enemy equally or better skilled in the operational art. Although a strategy built on attrition rather than annihilation favored the North, with its greater natural resources and manufacturing capacity, this did not mean that the North was necessarily profligate in how these advantages were employed, as Sherman's march to the sea amply demonstrated. The success of the operation was underpinned by careful planning, allied to efficient tactical execution, and represented "a logistic achievement of unparalleled accomplishment."[31] Thorpe argued for a broad understanding of logistics that recognized the industrial and economic aspects—beyond the previous narrow focus on supply and transportation. He highlighted the long neglect of the subject and offered a theory, together with a set of principles, for its organization and direction. At its heart was a holistic approach that allowed the strategic dimension to be managed through a professionally educated logistic staff. These ideas were well ahead of their time but are now recognized as entirely sound. Contemporary military logistic organizations very much follow Thorpe's model.

The catalyst for the latest upsurge in logistic studies was Martin van Creveld's *Logistics from Wallenstein to Patton* (1977).[32] This important and influential study made logistics a "reputable" academic subject and unleashed a tide of logistic-centered books ranging from Donald W. Engels' *Alexander the Great and the Logistics of the Macedonian Army* (1978) to Steve R. Waddell's *United States Army Logistics—The*

Normandy Campaign (1994).[33] The breadth of this activity is reflected in John A. Lynn's *Feeding Mars* (1993), which presents a collection of twelve essays addressing logistics in Western warfare from the Middle Ages to the present day.[34] The new-found enthusiasm for logistics triggered a successful crossover from academia into the commercial world and, ultimately, military terminology. By the late 1980s, it looked as if every self-respecting hauler using Britain's motorways had decided that their professional aspirations were better served by claiming to be "International Logistic Specialists." The subsequent emergence of the Royal Logistic Corps (1993) and RAF Logistic Command (1994) indicated that the military had not been slow to recognize the benefits of rebranding their supply and transportation activities.

The most recent survey of military logistics from ancient to modern times is Julian Thompson's *Lifeblood of War* (1991).[35] The author makes clear his debt to van Creveld, but the analysis is thinner and the writing more pedestrian. It is also weakened by its ambition— forty pages suffice to cover the period 700 BC to AD 1918. Inevitably, the narrative dwells lightly on the First World War. It also largely excludes any discussion of naval or aviation logistics—on the (debatable) grounds that logistics in land warfare are distinctive and the challenges inherently more difficult than those faced by a naval or air force logistician. A slightly earlier overview of logistics by Kenneth Macksey, *For Want of a Nail* (1989), is in many ways a more polished, albeit shorter, work that addresses the logistic aspects of the First World War in some detail.[36]

The relationship between logistics and airpower has been little explored. The most comprehensive survey of the history of airpower writing, Phillip Meilinger's "The Historiography of Airpower: Theory and Doctrine" (2000), does not touch on the subject.[37] To be fair, Meilinger's focus is on the theory of airpower and the evolution of doctrine, but it is still striking that the existing literature largely ignores the substantial technological, economic, and industrial foundations required by air forces. There are honorable exceptions such as Robin Higham, who has argued over a number of years about the wider "invisible" architecture essential to devel-oping an effective air weapon. Many of the areas he has identified and analyzed—infrastructure, spares, administration, management, maintenance, training, and personnel—are embraced by the term "logistics."[38] Higham's *Bases of Air Strategy: Building Airfields for the RAF, 1914–1945* (1998) and "Revolutionary Innovation and the Invisible Architecture" (1999) represent good examples of his ideas.[39] The latter article attempts to build a coherent picture from the earliest days of aviation, provid-ing coverage of the First World War and the detailed organizational arrangements needed to support air operations. Notwithstanding their leadership in thinking and writing about logistics, American studies on the subject of aviation logistics have been thin on the ground. Roger Miller, employed by the United States Air Force History Program, has proved the exception and provided some important articles over recent years.[40] The other notable author to explore the logistic underpinnings of airpower is Richard Overy. In his highly regarded and groundbreaking work *The*

Air War 1939–1945 (1980), Overy argues that the air war was a test of "modernity," based on organization, strategy, industrial potential, social structure, administrative competence, and the integration of science—merely possessing aircraft was insufficient for success.[41] This paradigm is equally relevant to the western front, where the logistic system developed by the RFC drew on all these themes, exhibiting a high degree of agility and adaptability to achieve, and sustain, operational relevance and military effect. Producing ever greater numbers of aircraft and aero-engines was insufficient—it was how these were integrated with training, maintenance, supply, modification, and repair that delivered battlefield success. Beyond Overy, however, there has been little exploration of the enabling aspects of airpower. The lack of academic interest in aviation logistics is not entirely surprising. J. F. C. Fuller observed that "one of the strangest things in military history is the almost complete silence upon the problems of supply."[42] Basil Liddell Hart, in discussing this indictment, commented that "the treatment which the subject has received has been slight in comparison with its importance and almost in inverse ratio to its growing importance."[43]

The performance of the British Expeditionary Force (BEF) on the western front has been the subject of considerable debate over the last thirty years. Putting to one side the sometimes ill-tempered argument about Douglas Haig's role, new insights and perspectives have emerged that have thrown important light on the British Army's style of command and its attitude to technology. Tim Travers has been in the vanguard of this effort, notably in *The Killing Ground* (1987) and *How the War Was Won* (1992).[44] Both books are insightful, although both sometimes verge on the polemical. In essence, Travers argues that command was poor, particularly at the highest levels, and that it stumbled into a war-winning strategy (attrition). Victory was achieved against an increasingly exhausted German army by employing infantry-centric tactics supported by massed artillery fire, even though new technology (in the form of tanks) offered a less expensive solution. These conclusions have been vigorously challenged by other historians, notably Gary Sheffield and John Bourne, concerned by the use of selective evidence and the overly negative view of the contribution of senior commanders.[45] Travers also fails to consider whether the logistic difficulties faced by the BEF after August 1918 (when attrition, unreliability, and an extended supply chain greatly diminished the number of tanks available) might have constrained the tactical options available.[46]

An earlier but more balanced study, and one that looks like standing the test of time, is Shelford Bidwell and Dominick Graham's *Fire-Power: British Army Weapons and Theories of War 1904–1945* (1982).[47] The authors focus on the role of artillery in both world wars. This wider tapestry provides an effective context for the five chapters that address the First World War. Unlike Travers, who is clearly intrigued by the nascent RAF's experiments in tank cooperation but little else, Bidwell and Graham highlight the central role of aircraft in the new artillery techniques that formed the basis for operational success in 1918. As they succinctly point out, "their starting point and pivot was the RFC pilot," adding that the prerequisite was air superiority, "one of the fruits of RFC persistence."

This more objective and inclusive approach is mirrored in Paddy Griffith's *Battle Tactics of the Western Front: The British Army's Art of Attack 1916–1918* (1994).[48] This is an impressive book (although the title is slightly misleading as it describes the evolution and success of the British Army's operational art rather than simply explaining how tactics changed during the last two years of the war) that gives full credit for the RFC's contribution in dramatically improving artillery firepower, not just by observation and control but also through photography and mapping. Until recently, there has been no comprehensive study of the development of aerial photography but this has been partly redressed by Terrence Finnegan's *Shooting the Front*.[49] Mapping has also been largely neglected by historians—other than Peter Chasseaud, who has produced a series of studies including *Artillery's Astrologers: A History of the British Survey and Mapping on the Western Front 1914–1918* (1999).[50] This is a long and detailed work, clearly a labor of love, which describes the immense effort required to produce the detail needed to locate and destroy enemy batteries and strong points. The narrative largely concentrates on the efforts of the Royal Engineers (RE), but it does not ignore the work of the RFC. In describing the survey and mapping tasks undertaken in preparation for the Somme, Chasseaud notes the official historian's comment that "the air co-operation upon which the artillery so much depended was invaluable; air photos had become almost indispensable for mapping purposes." Chasseaud then adds, "One wonders why he qualified this statement with the word 'almost,' as mapping the enemy defences was simply impossible without air photos!"[51] Unfortunately, the decision to employ a chronological rather than thematic approach makes it difficult to draw conclusions or to understand the relative contribution between, for example, flash-spotting, sound-ranging, and aerial survey. The latter activity, however, is well described in Peter Mead's *The Eye in the Air* (1983), which covers the history of air reconnaissance and observation up to 1945.[52] It is particularly strong in explaining how air observation solved the "artillery problem" (achieving accurate, predicted, indirect fire).

What is clear from all of these varied narratives is that airpower and logistics are integral to modern warfare. It is also evident that they are inextricably linked—in that both draw on the same dynamic mix of technology and mass production that has shaped two world wars. The critical role of logistics in creating airpower echoes the part played by logistics in previous periods of significant military change. Admittedly, it can be difficult to distinguish between continuity and change and, sometimes, to separate preconditions from precipitants, but what emerged on the western front was very different from what had gone before, driven by qualitative and quantitative changes in technology, standardization, administration, and supply. Modern warfare was also expensive—in terms of the resources consumed or discarded. The history of airpower on the western front is essentially a story about ever-greater capabilities allied to an insatiable need for more men and matériel.

By the armistice, the RAF's manpower was 137 times greater than the combined strength of the RNAS and RFC at the outbreak of war. Daily expenditure had risen by a factor of two hundred, while the number of aircraft on strength was over ninety times the prewar figure.[53]

The birth of three-dimensional warfare—the integration of artillery, armor, and aircraft—allowed firepower to dominate the battlefield. In operational terms, the RFC's main contribution on the western front was undoubtedly artillery coop-eration.[54] The deployment of new, war-winning firepower techniques depended entirely on aircraft operating in conjunction with the artillery, using maps produced from aerial photography.[55] Other than the need to solve a number of technical and procedural issues, the only significant constraint on progress was the number of frontline aircraft available for cooperation duties. It is hardly surprising, therefore, to find that the proportional increase in resources committed to the air services was significantly greater than that expended on the Army. From the Third Battle of Ypres onwards, the RFC was able to sustain sufficient numbers of aircraft in the air (weather permitting) to allow artillery cooperation to be provided on a continuous basis, where and when required.[56] The critical development in this achievement was the creation of a system that enabled delicate, often temperamental, and constantly evolving machinery to be supported under the most testing operational conditions and in the face of wastage that averaged more than 50 percent of frontline strength per month. In addressing these problems, the RFC found innovative solutions that provided a template for other air services and established best practice that continues to be relevant in the delivery of contemporary airpower.

It was rapidly discovered that the tempo of air operations and the key logistic drivers were quite different from all that had gone before. Squadrons were constantly in action—there were no rest days unless the weather intervened—no routine rota-tion in and out of the line and often no pause at nightfall. Aircraft demanded con-tinuous maintenance, ideally conducted under cover, while attrition was extremely high—as a result of accidents and low reliability as much as from enemy action—necessitating a constant supply of new aircraft and aircrew. The disparity between production and supply, particularly in aero-engines, meant that salvage and repair made a significant contribution to sustaining operational availability. Obsolescence, design flaws, manufacturing shortcomings, and shortages of critical equipment necessitated a high level of modification and rework—all to be undertaken in the field. A wide range of transportable accommodation, special equipment, tools, and a myriad of individual parts and components had to be readily available to support these activities as well as routine maintenance.

All of this required the creation of an extensive ground organization, employ-ing large numbers of skilled and semi-skilled personnel, underpinned by a supply chain that stretched from the front line, via the repair depots and air parks, to the factories at home. Aircraft and their component parts largely populated this pipe-line, together with a constant flow of technical information, spares, equipment, and personnel. However, unlike previous logistic systems, it was not one dominated by consumables but by scarce, high-value items that flowed to *and from* the front line.[57] Finally, the entire system, including the depots, had to be mobile to allow airpower to be concentrated at specific parts of the front. As a result, and unlike any previous army or arm, noncombatants hugely outnumbered combatants. This was no subtle shift in the balance of roles but a step change in the "teeth-to-tail" ratio.[58] Thus, of the 50,000 RAF uniformed personnel serving in France by November 1918, only 8 percent were classed as combatants (pilots, observers, air gunners, etc.) while the majority, some 29,000 (57 percent) were technicians.[59] By comparison, 896,000 personnel (65 percent of other ranks) of the British Army present in France in 1918 were categorized as combatants.[60] According to Brigadier-General Robert Brooke-Popham, "In an air force the fighting man is largely replaced by the machine." It would perhaps have been more accurate to have said that, in an air force, the fighting man is largely *displaced* by the machine.[61]

Profligate as airpower was in manpower, particularly in its appetite for scarce technical skills, the real cost lay in matériel. During the course of the war over 50,000 aircraft were delivered to the British air services of which only 36 percent remained on charge by the Armistice.[62] Between 50 percent and 60 percent of the budget allocated to the air services was expended on equipment—a consistent and defining characteristic of airpower.[63] Van Creveld has written of "the logistic revolution of 1914," by which he means the transformation in the supply needs of armies that occurred during the course of the First World War.[64] He argues that this was driven by three interlinked developments. First, the huge increase in the quantity and range of military supplies such that food and fodder, which previously formed the greater proportion, represented a rapidly reducing share. Second, these supplies by their very nature could not be found locally, they had to be brought into the theater of operations (the result was that an army that remained stationary was easier to sustain than one that moved—a reversal of all previous experience).[65] Third, not only did consumption far exceed expectations (which itself created an armaments production crisis) but it demanded a transportation system with a capacity that could never be met by the horse-drawn arrangements that had sufficed for centuries. As a result, to an extent far larger than in any previous age, "strategy had become an appendage of logistics."[66]

Notwithstanding van Creveld's promptings, little has been written about logistics on the western front. One exception is Roger Miller's "The Logistics of the British Expeditionary Force: 4 August to 5 September 1914" (1979), which considers the effectiveness of the supply arrangements supporting the BEF during its retreat from Mons.[67] In this brief article Miller proposes that the measure of logistical success is "whether the system proves capable of meeting the physical needs of the army without reducing operational efficiency and mobility of the field forces." The most important recent book on First World War logistics has been I. M. Brown's *British Logistics on the Western Front 1914–1919* (1998).[68] It is significant, not only because it tackles a largely neglected subject, but also because it provides a comprehensive and well-argued analysis of how Sir Eric Geddes transformed the transportation arrangements on the western front and provided the foundation for operational success. The focus is very much on the transportation system—production, salvage, and repair are effectively outside the study's scope. There is little or no mention of aviation (perhaps not too surprising given the small fraction of the British Army's daily supply needs represented by the RFC). However, it provides a sound basis for further work and a welcome backdrop for this study, as is Keith Grieves' *Sir Eric Geddes*.[69]

Although embedded within the wider BEF supply system, the RFC logistic organization created to support air operations on the western front was quite distinct from any previous military enterprise. It was built around a series of close-knit processes, interlinked and interdependent, with matériel moving continuously forwards and backwards at a tempo determined by wastage, operational intensity, and technological change. Unprecedented in complexity, cost, and in the balance between combatants and noncombatants, it demanded a sustained level of "industrial mobilization" that firmly connected the front line with the nation's manufacturing and technological base.[70] There has been no detailed investigation of how this system, which supported a largely immobile front line for nearly four years, adjusted to the changed circumstances of 1918 and the need to function as a dynamic supply chain. The ability of the RFC's logistic organization to respond to these changed circumstances and to evolve will be explored in detail.[71]

While the capabilities of the RAF were relatively modest by the armistice, in comparison to the Second World War, the potential for airpower to shape the battlefield at the tactical, operational, and strategic levels was evident from 1916 onwards. It was also clear that the effective deployment of airpower depended on the enabling logistic arrangements. An understanding of the development of British airpower on the western front, and the associated technical, industrial, and operational challenges is essential in assessing logistic effectiveness. This can only be achieved by examining the organizational and economic context and the role of key personalities—not just those that led and managed the RFC, such as Major-General Hugh Trenchard, Brigadier-General Sefton Brancker, and Brigadier-General Robert Brooke-Popham, but also those politicians and civil servants who mobilized the nation's industrial effort, such as Lloyd George and William Weir.

The RFC/RAF official history, *The War in the Air*, which also covers the work of the RNAS, draws heavily on wartime records, material supplied by the Reichsarchiv, interviews, and personal reminiscences (including the war experiences of officers attending the RAF Staff Course at Andover).[72] The first volume, written by Sir Walter Raleigh, sometime professor of English at Oxford University, appeared in 1922. After his untimely death, H. A. Jones was appointed as official historian, writing the remaining six volumes (including Appendices), the last published in 1937. Despite the difference in style—Raleigh, as perhaps befits a professor of English, employs a somewhat richer and more languid prose—all seven volumes sit well together. There has been criticism that Raleigh and Jones could not have escaped the influence of the air romantics and that both historians reiterated the extravagant claims made for the air weapon and airmen.[73] Contemporary correspondence between Jones and the RAF staffs indicates that there was no overt attempt to influence or to otherwise constrain the narrative—the only concern appears to have been how to expedite publication.[74] On the other hand, recent studies indicate that the efficacy of strategic bombing was certainly exaggerated, or at least not subject to adequate scrutiny.[75] Pending a deeper study, such as David French's "Official but Not History?" (1986), which provides a critical analysis of the approach taken by Sir James Edmonds, or Andrew Green's *Writing the Great War* (2003), which argues that the Army's official historians were able to place honesty and objectivity above personal reputation and sectional interest, there is no reason to regard *The War in the Air* as other than an authoritative and balanced account of air/land operations.[76] The German official history generally supports this view, especially in its description of the RFC/RAF's artillery cooperation activities.[77] It would certainly be wrong to simply write off *The War in the Air* as a propaganda tool in the RAF's interwar struggle to survive as an independent service.

The British official histories of military operations in the First World War, published between 1922 and 1949, usefully supplement *The War in the Air*. There is (understandably) no substantial coverage of aviation, other than to provide essential context for the narrative. Nevertheless, the twelve volumes covering the western front are essential reading in understanding the wider conduct of the war and the role of the RFC in supporting the British Army. Thus, volume 1 of Edmonds' *Military Operations France and Belgium, 1916* (1932), provides an excellent account of the preparations for the Battle of the Somme, including a detailed picture of the logistic aspects and the RFC's buildup.[78] Logistics does not attract specific coverage in this series, although Henniker's *Transportation on the Western Front* (1937) provides an important overview of the role of transportation and how it evolved to meet the British Army's supply needs during the course of the war.[79] While no history of the overall Allied logistic effort was ever produced, the *Report of the Military Board of Allied Supply* (1924–26), published in three volumes, provides an important overview of the supply arrangements in place during the last year of the war.[80] The Military Board came into existence in June 1918 and spent much of its time addressing the logistic needs of the American Expeditionary Force (AEF). In the process, the opportunity was taken to describe the logistic systems of each of the Allies, including details of the arrangements for aviation supply.

An important source of information on aircraft production, and associated manufacturing activities, is provided by the *Official History of the Ministry of Munitions* (1919–22).[81] This work appeared in twelve volumes covering, inter alia, administration, finance, labor, materials, and munitions. The chapters on aircraft manufacture, ancillary components, aero-engines, and ordnance are particularly helpful. The writing of the history actually commenced before the armistice but, as detailed as it is, somehow lacks substance. There is no real thread to the story or any obvious effort to identify key themes. The story of how the history came to be commissioned, and the manner of its writing, explains much of the problem, although it should be stressed that it remains an invaluable, if not unique, source of information.[82]

The official history of the United States Air Services (USAS) should also not be overlooked. Produced in the form of a "lessons learned" exercise shortly after the end of the war, the four-volume history of the United States Air Services in World War I was not actually published until 1978. There is much that is of interest to the British historian. Although the French provided the bulk of the aeronautical material supplied to the AEF, there was an extremely close relationship between senior officers in the USAS and RFC. USAS doctrine was largely drawn from the RFC, as was their logistic model. Of the four books, volume 1 is probably the most useful, describing American supply and maintenance arrangements in some detail.

The official records covering the operations of the RFC and RAF on the western front are to be found in The National Archives (TNA)—largely in the AIR1 and AIR2 series. These documents were originally collected by the Air Historical Branch in support of the official history. Indeed, working drafts for many of the constituent sections are to be found among the files. TNA also holds Army records detailing supplies provided to the frontline squadrons in France and Belgium—as part of their wider logistic responsibilities (for ordnance, fuel, clothing, etc.), and the work of the RE in building airfields and aircraft depots. The records of the Ministry of Munitions are also valuable from both the production and disposal perspective. Robin Higham has suggested that the RFC and RAF depot records were thrown away as of no interest after the war.[83] It is true that some may have been lost or disposed of, but a huge number of primary and secondary documents remain that detail aviation logistic activities on the western front.[84] The archives reveal that the RFC responded enthusiastically to the administrative demands of maintaining a modern army in the field. The hand-written single-page reports of 1914 (sometimes apparently torn from school-issue writing books) rapidly give way to typed, multi-copy reports on a wide range of standard printed forms. The desire for detail seems to have been insatiable, requiring squadron commanders to spend a considerable amount of their time preparing and reviewing daily and weekly reports for forwarding up the chain of command. This reflects yet another aspect of logistics—the need for information and, in turn, for control systems.

At the center of the RFC's logistic system was a bureaucracy of trained staff recording and reporting on every activity and the fate of every item. This was not simply a concern for the proper management of expensive and scarce resources—it was also recognition that the efficient management of the supply chain required timely, comprehensive, and accurate data. The resulting archive meticulously details the daily minutiae of the RFC's operations on the western front. If there was substantial weeding out of records at the end of the war, and in the succeeding years, it

has still left a mountain of paper. Each squadron produced a daily war diary recording activities by aircraft and crew. Separate reports were provided on specific operations such as air combats, reconnaissance, photographic sorties, and bomb dropping.
Reports were also required on casualties to personnel and aircraft, as well as requests
for authority to strike off equipment (including machines and aero-engines). All of
these documents were seen by superior formations, which added additional obser-
vations together with summary reports. These wing and brigade records exist for
most of, if not the entire, war.[85] The detail is extensive, allowing the availability of
aircraft to be plotted day by day across the entire western front, together with the
number of enemy batteries targeted, destroyed, or neutralized. The amount of data
presents a substantial challenge in its own right, but it also provides an opportunity
to assemble an authoritative picture of the logistic arrangements that sustained RFC
operations. There are inevitably gaps—particularly the April after the German 1918
offensive when the frequency and detail of reporting requirements were relaxed—
but the requirement for multiple copies of most forms has meant that missing documents can often be found in files held by intermediate authorities, including wings
and brigades, or Headquarters RFC (HQ RFC).[86] A further complication is the
data hiatus that arose during the transition from a well-established Army system
to new RAF forms and different reporting requirements. In some ways, however,
there is too much information and too many locations. As a result, the trees can
sometimes obscure the forest.

The private papers of a number of key individuals involved in the creation,
development, and management of the RFC's logistic system provide invaluable
firsthand testimony on its day-to-day functioning. The papers of Air Chief Marshal
Sir Robert Brooke-Popham, who as a brigadier-general headed up the logistic organization on the western front for much of the war, are available in the Liddell Hart
Centre for Military Archives.[87] Other relevant papers are held by the Imperial War
Museum, including those of Sir Sefton Brancker, who as a colonel played a central role in planning the RFC's expansion and later, as a brigadier-general, leading
its training activities. TNA holds a number of relevant personal papers, including Brooke-Popham's personal overview of the RFC supply system—penned in
response to a query by the official historian of the Allied Board of Supply.[88] Lord
Trenchard's personal papers, held by the RAF Museum, provide considerable detail
on the day-to-day management of aircraft in the field, reflecting his personal interest in supply issues and the technological challenges faced by the flying squadrons.

Much of the published literature about the air war concentrates on operations,
and, largely (if not disproportionately) on air combat. The personal experiences of
those who served behind the lines, or in support activities, have attracted little interest and few, if any, publishers. The majority of firsthand accounts have been written
by pilots. Few books have been published about the experiences of those RFC
personnel (the majority) who were employed on logistic duties. Fortunately, some

personal testimonies have emerged through the efforts of volunteer organizations and initiatives, such as those mounted by the Liddle Collection at the University of Leeds, the Department of Records and Information Services at the RAF Museum, and the Imperial War Museum Department of Documents, designed to preserve individual war experiences in all forms.[89] This analysis draws on these archives to bring some color as well as context to the description of the RFC's logistic system and to provide an immediacy and authority that the "official" records often lack. After all, without the many thousands of equipment officers, skilled technicians, and support staffs, employed at home and overseas, the RFC simply could not have functioned.

If logistics is the lifeblood of war, then industry is the heart of modern warfare. In this sense, logistics provides the connection between economic and military affairs. "As the link between the war front and the home front, the logistics process is at once the military element in the nation's economy and the economic element in its military operations."[90] Without economic strength to nurture and sustain armaments—through innovation, development, and production—there can be no military logistic system. In the years following the armistice there was a considerable output of articles and books on the economic and financial aspects of the conflict. Most notable was the Carnegie Endowment series on the *Economic and Social History of the World War* (over fifty volumes published from 1921 to 1937). However, the advent of the Second World War and its aftermath meant that there was no sustained interest in the economic history of the First World War. A collection of writing on *War Finance*, edited by Larry Neal and published in 1994, includes eight articles, the majority published in the period 1919–22 and the most recent in 1931.[91] More recently, the situation has been reversed and a number of insightful studies, based on considerable research and careful analysis of the available data, have been published. David Stevenson's *Armaments and the Coming of War* (1996) led the way, followed by Niall Ferguson's *The Pity of War* (1999), which explored the financing of the First World War, and Kevin Stubbs' *Race to the Front* (2002), which focused on the Allied effort to mobilize their economic resources.[92] Hew Strachan's *Financing the First World War* (2004) has brought together much of this original research.[93]

By the armistice, the total cost of British military aviation, in matériel and human terms, amounted to £200 million per year (equivalent to 4 percent of gross domestic product) or 7 percent of Britain's total daily war expenditure. This was set to rise still further with some £165 million of outstanding aviation orders, more than half the production commitments of the Ministry of Munitions.[94] Even so, there has been no dedicated study of the cost of airpower in the First World War or any effort to determine the proportion of Britain's national resources allocated to the air services. One of the criticisms of Allied strategy in the Second World War has been that it was based on "brute force"—in the form of overwhelming industrial capacity and logistic affluence.[95] Regardless of whether this argument has any validity, it is sensible to consider whether the effectiveness of the RFC's logistic arrangements was achieved through profligate expenditure in men and machines rather than the efficient management of scarce national resources.

Availability of skilled manpower was essential to the expansion of the RFC. Identifying those with the necessary skills (sometimes already serving in the Army) was only one of the many challenges to be overcome. A greater difficulty was establishing sufficient priority to obtain these individuals in the face of competing demands from industry and the other services (a situation made all the more difficult as the RFC came late to the game). The RFC's support to the BEF depended on the rapid expansion of a training system that was under constant pressure to provide as many qualified personnel as quickly as possible—while still maintaining standards. In a declining manpower pool these were likely to be the same individuals needed to build the aircraft and aero-engines required by the expanded training schools and the new frontline squadrons. The inherent tension in this situation was never satisfactorily resolved, largely because of the government's failure to recognize "the close inter-relationship between economic activity on the home front and the enlargement of British forces at war."[96]

Although the majority of RFC personnel were employed in support activities, the availability of trained pilots was a key constraint in determining operational performance. Some understanding of this aspect is needed if the effectiveness of the RFC's logistic arrangements is to be adequately assessed. When, in June 1917, the War Cabinet decided on a substantial expansion of the RFC, it was stated that the two main constraints on any great increase were the supply of aero-engines and the supply of pilots.[97] Exemplary logistic performance could achieve little without a continuous supply of trained and capable pilots. The RFC's flying training system improved significantly during the course of the war, both in standards and in scale (this included dedicated flying training schools in Canada, Egypt, and the United States). Nevertheless, a shortage of pilots continued to delay the planned growth in frontline squadrons. A proper understanding of this subject, and its actual influence on the RFC's contribution to the western front, has been impeded by a degree of misrepresentation and confusion. Denis Winter, in *The First of the Few* (1982), exaggerates the losses in training fourfold and states that they exceeded those suffered in combat. He is also in error over the total number of casualties suffered by the RFC.[98] Unfortunately, these claims have been repeated in subsequent studies and appear to have become part of the mythology of the air war.[99]

One study of battlefield success has concluded that, of all the possible predictors, "logistics capacity appears to be the most powerful and important."[100] Aviation logistic capacity comprises not just the physical ability to satisfy the supply needs of an air force but also its ability to adapt and change. The pervasive problem faced by all logistic systems, particularly in wartime, is uncertainty. Predicting demand levels is fraught with difficulty. Analysis of aviation logistic systems deployed in the Second World War suggests that logistic planning, however detailed, cannot anticipate the changes brought about by new tactics, new weapons, technological shifts, or altered strategic circumstance.[101] The characteristics of a responsive logistic system, capable of managing uncertainty, include:[102]

- Coherence (alignment with operations)
- Flexibility (the ability to change)
- Learning (the ability to acquire, review, and adapt to new developments)
- Technological competence (the constant tactical factor)
- Administrative excellence (pipeline management)
- Information-driven (timely, accurate, and comprehensive)

The degree to which the RFC's logistic system was able to function according to these principles provides a measure of its responsiveness. However, these are not the only criteria for logistic success. Modern supply chain management identifies a wide range of ways to measure performance, including the size and cost of the inventory, how quickly demand can be met, and productivity (in manpower and assets).[103] Bachrach has observed that "all study of logistics must begin with numbers."[104] The question of how to measure operational output will be addressed shortly, but, to provide the necessary context, strategic success for the RFC's logistic system is defined—paraphrasing Roger Miller—as meeting the physical needs of the air services without reducing operational efficiency and mobility.[105]

Assessing the RFC's performance against this definition requires both a qualitative and a quantitative approach. Moreover, inputs (resources) as well as outputs (operational effort) need to be considered, although care has to be taken to distinguish between logistic drivers and other factors (such as poor weather) that might also affect operational performance. The practical workings of the RFC's logistic system can be determined through a review of unit records, reports, and personal testimony. Analysis will show the scale and tempo (in terms of the rate of consumption and sustained maximum effort) of the support activities involved—both on the western front and at home. In this process, an attempt will be made to assess the decision-making cycle and the speed of response to changed circumstances. A key theme will be the degree of integration achieved by the RFC in managing strategy, science, engineering, supply, and organization (Richard Overy's test of "modernity"). Other aspects to be considered include the level of agility and organizational resilience in face of unexpected or unprecedented demands.

The consumption of matériel provides a good indicator of input efficiency—particularly manpower employed. For example, the resources needed to keep a single airplane on service at the front in 1917 were calculated to be the equivalent of forty-seven men. This was a significant drain on military manpower and skilled technicians but the full cost was even higher. The total labor required (when production was included) was closer to 160 men.[106] Other important indicators include the flying hours generated by each tradesman and the hours flown by each aircraft available. In addition, the way that these ratios changed over time will indicate whether the RFC's logistic arrangements improved during the course of the war. Engineering efficiency can be judged from the level of serviceability achieved, while the ability to sustain the flying squadrons at an agreed establishment provides an indicator of overall logistic effectiveness, including the speed and responsiveness of the supply chain. The engineering outputs of the RFC's depots also provide relevant performance metrics, including the number of aero-engines salvaged and the number of aircraft repaired or reconstructed. Operational output can be measured in a number of ways, such as total sorties generated or enemy aircraft destroyed. A particular focus, however, will be those outputs that contributed most to the advent of three-dimensional warfare—such as photographs taken and enemy batteries neutralized. The performance of the corps squadrons and their contribution to the "artillery revolution" will be central, therefore, to this analysis. The U.S. Air Force (USAF) has made a particular effort over recent years to develop a set of metrics to allow an organization's overall logistic performance to be gauged.[107] Key activity areas measured include: work force management, sortie generation, maintenance performance, mission analysis, and fleet availability. Using these metrics as a model for organizational efficiency and effectiveness, a potential matrix of RFC performance indicators can be mapped.

To determine the effectiveness of the RFC's logistic arrangements and to understand how this changed over time, three specific periods will be examined: the Somme, where the RFC achieved substantial operational success but did not face

TABLE 1. RFC PERFORMANCE INDICATORS

USAF LOGISTIC METRICS	RFC LOGISTIC PERFORMANCE INDICATORS
WORK FORCE MANAGEMENT	Total manpower employed
	Tradesmen per aircraft
	Flying hours per tradesman
SORTIE GENERATION	Total sorties generated
	Monthly flying hours
	Flying hours per aircraft
MAINTENANCE PERFORMANCE	Daily & monthly serviceability rates
	Aircraft & aero-engines salvaged
	Aircraft repaired & reconstructed
	Aero-engines repaired
MISSION ANALYSIS	Enemy batteries destroyed
	Photographs taken
FLEET AVAILABILITY	Frontline strength
	Squadron strength as percent of establishment

serious opposition from the German Air Services (GAS); Arras and Third Ypres (where the RFC operated on a much larger scale but had to fight hard to achieve air superiority); and the Hundred Days (where the RAF had to adapt to mobile warfare). The analysis will focus on the RFC as a whole rather than just those squadrons directly assigned to the offensive. It is neither practicable nor appropriate to regard the RFC and its supporting logistic system as other than a single entity—particularly as squadrons were rotated between armies as required, while others undertook diversionary attacks well outside the immediate battle zone. It should also be noted that the scope of this study has been deliberately restricted to aircraft and excludes kite balloons. Although the latter grew in number and importance during the course of the war, their supply needs were relatively modest and drew on the same system of parks and depots as did the frontline squadrons. There were some unique aspects to kite balloon operations, such as the need to manufacture hydrogen, but the logistic challenges involved were insignificant compared to aircraft operations. Finally, to simplify matters, the term RFC is generally employed throughout this study, rather than RFC/RAF.

Three preliminary chapters will provide the context for these case studies: the evolution of the RFC's operations on the western front, including the formative years 1914–16; the logistic arrangements that developed over the course of the war at home and in France; and the supply of aircraft and aero-engines (the raw material of airpower). A concluding chapter will address the enduring lessons and the degree to which the logistic principles established in the First World War influenced RAF planning for the Second World War as well as presaging the global supply chain and best practice in contemporary logistic management. The opportunity will also be taken to evaluate the RFC's logistic arrangements against an external comparator—in the form of the logistic principles first articulated by James Huston as part of his highly regarded review of U.S. Army logistics.[108] These principles offer a framework for assessing the RFC's performance, as well as highlighting the differences between land and aviation logistic practices:

- *Equivalence*: Logistics should be given equivalent status to strategy and tactics in planning, organization and execution.
- *Feasibility*: Strategy cannot be divorced from logistic feasibility.
- *Unity of Command*: Logistics is a function of command and within a given area logistic responsibility should be identical to command authority.
- *Matériel Precedence*: The mobilization of matériel should precede manpower.
- *Forward Impetus*: The impetus of supply should be from the rear, relieving commanders of detailed involvement.
- *Economy*: The ratio of secondary requirements (those necessary for the means used to meet the primary requirements) to primary requirements (those for direct support of tactical units) should be kept as low as possible.

- *Mobility*: The mobility of the logistic organization is essential to achieving the greatest possible military flexibility.
- *Dispersion*: Storage and other logistic activities should be dispersed (within reason).
- *Flexibility*: Since war changes plans there must be flexibility in logistic arrangements to meet the unexpected.
- *Information*: Accurate, up-to-date information is essential to logistic planning.
- *Simplicity*: Simplicity is essential at all levels of the logistic system. Complexity should be avoided in the planning and execution of logistic activities.
- *Relativity*: All logistics is relative to time, to place, and to circumstances. As logistic resources are limited, decisions in one area affect those in another.
- *Continuity*: Arrangements and organization should not change between peace and war.
- *Timeliness*: The timely provision of resources is as important as quantity.
- *Responsibility*: Procurement activity must be coordinated with the needs of the civilian economy and the chief reliance for the production of military goods must rest with private industry.
- *Quality*: Equipment quality has to be balanced against wider factors including political, industrial, and financial, as well as production, supply, and maintenance.

The development and effective employment of the air weapon on the western front required a radical and unprecedented change in the way that national resources were employed (in exploiting a technological opportunity), to achieve tactical and operational advantage. It also established an interdependence between logistics and airpower that has profoundly shaped the activities and culture of the RAF.

CHAPTER 1

ROYAL FLYING CORPS OPERATIONS ON THE WESTERN FRONT

T HE RFC's SUBSTANTIAL CONTRIBUTION TO OPERATIONS ON THE WESTERN front has been both distorted and diminished by an enduring public fascination with air combat and, in particular, the deeds of individual fighter aces. Film, television, and popular literature have given this aspect of the first air war an undeserved prominence and an element of glamor—while largely ignoring the genuine achievements of the air services and their significant role in the BEF's success. Specialist literature has been equally at fault, often preferring the detailed analysis of the victories claimed by single-seat pilots rather than an assessment of the operational impact made by the more pedestrian two-seater artillery cooperation machines.[1] Military historians have not been immune from this cultural and professional myopia. Indeed, even when the wider aspects of the air war are addressed it is often through the prism of subsequent events, such as the Battle of Britain or the Strategic Air Offensive. John Terraine noted more than twenty years ago that the RFC's greatest contribution to victory was the support it provided to the BEF—yet these efforts have otherwise attracted little academic attention.[2]

Between 1914 and 1918 the air arms of all the major belligerents, with the exception of the Ottoman Empire, underwent an immense transformation, but none more so than the British Air Services. By the armistice, the RAF possessed 22,171 aircraft and boasted a total strength of 274,494 personnel compared to the 270 aircraft and 2,073 personnel available on the outbreak of war—shared between the RFC and RNAS.[3] The RAF was the second largest (if not the largest) air force in the world and the first independent air arm.[4] This was only achieved through the commitment of substantial national resources—both human and matériel, total industrial mobilization, strong political commitment, and energetic military leadership. It also required, as will be shown, persistent logistic excellence. According to a postwar study on interallied supply, the RAF enjoyed the most fully developed system of aviation supply among the Allies.[5]

Well before powered flight was possible, command of the air and its potential in warfare had been the subject of speculation and passionate advocacy by "airpower" visionaries.[6] While it is possible to trace the origins of this debate to the early nineteenth century, it was the development of a practical heavier-than-air machine by the Wright brothers, and their successful demonstration of controlled flight at Kitty Hawk in December 1903, that fired the imagination of the public and started the debate on the role of aviation in future wars.[7] Those searching for an early description of airpower will find it a frustrating exercise. The term arose as a natural sister to sea and land power and was commonly employed before there had been an opportunity to define it in any detail. Given that the capabilities of the early aircraft consistently lagged behind popular imagination, it is hardly surprising to find a lack of rigor in explaining exactly what airpower comprised. While the military staffs of all nations remained skeptical, the popular press and crusading politicians experienced no hesitation in arguing for greater national investment in a weapon that would transform warfare.[8] Unfortunately, there was little about aviation that was settled—a situation epitomized by the lengthy and intense debate about the relative advantages of the airplane and the airship.[9] It was only Wilbur and Orville Wright's flights in France and Germany during 1908 and 1909 (drawing huge crowds) that forced the Great Powers to take the technology seriously.[10]

Although it is often asserted that Edwardian Britain, or at least the ruling class, was oblivious to the potential of military aviation, the picture is more complicated than suggested.[11] For a start, the British Army had experimented with aviation, in the form of tethered balloons, since well before the turn of the century, commissioning its first balloon in 1878.[12] Balloons were successfully employed in the Army maneuvers of 1880 and 1882, and by 1890 had been accepted as an important reconnaissance aid. During 1897 the RE Balloon School (responsible for the development of balloons) was renamed the Balloon Factory and placed under the direct control of the War Office.[13] Over the next few years experiments were conducted with man-lifting kites and, increasingly, with powered balloons (dirigibles). Following a committee of enquiry on the future of aeronautics in 1904, the Balloon Factory moved to a more open site at Farnborough. Concurrent with the development of the first British airship, the Balloon Factory began to interest itself in airplanes. Experiments were conducted with gliding machines designed by Lieutenant J. W. Dunne, but at the same time the potential of Samuel Cody's kites was investigated. By 1907 experiments with Dunne's tailless glider, Cody's new Powered Kite running along an aerial, horizontal wire, and the first airship, *Nulli Secundus*, were all under way.[14] On 1 April 1908, the Factory became His Majesty's Balloon Factory in recognition of its achievements. The great success of the year was the flight of British Army Airplane No. 1 (designed by Cody) on 16 October. Although it ended in a crash, this was a significant "first" for a British-designed and -built powered airplane, albeit equipped with a French engine.[15]

In the month of Cody's successful flight, a subcommittee of the Committee of Imperial Defence had been constituted to look into the whole subject of aerial navigation. It reported in early 1909 and effectively condemned the efforts of the Balloon Factory to design an airplane of its own, recommending that private enterprise should be left to undertake such development. The employment of Dunne and Cody was to be terminated in favor of a more disciplined, scientific approach to aeronautical research. The driving force behind these changes was Richard Haldane, secretary of state for war.[16] Haldane has been criticized over his perceived lack of interest in military aviation but, on the whole, he was supportive if somewhat cautious.[17] In May 1909 a new scientific body, the Advisory Committee for Aeronautics, was formed under the chairmanship of Lord Rayleigh and, after an inspection of the almost idle Balloon Factory, recommended that "instruction" should be divorced from "construction."[18] The link between the Balloon School and the Factory was formally broken, with the School remaining a military unit and the Factory becoming a civilian research establishment under the control of a superintendent reporting directly to the War Office. These Haldane-inspired changes would prove highly influential in shaping the development of British aviation. Indeed, Farnborough and the Royal Aircraft Establishment would not have existed without his influence. On the other hand, Haldane's measured approach meant that aeronautical research progressed more rapidly than military aviation. "The policy was to go slow in the acquisition of aeroplanes, and to gain experience as to the nature and scope of the air units and equipment suitable and necessary for war before purchasing aeroplanes on a large scale, organising in detail and expanding appreciably."[19]

Haldane remained of the view that aeronautics could not be effectively employed for military purposes until the essential principles underlying the new technology were fully understood. Further trials of army airplanes were halted, although an increasing number of individuals, both private and military, continued to experiment. Several private airplanes participated in the 1910 summer maneuvers and, although the results were not particularly successful, the ban on army airplane trials was rescinded shortly afterwards.[20] The change of heart was partly the result of the Army's recognition that airplanes would inevitably play a part in future warfare, and partly the result of the rapid progress being made by the French and Germans. This more positive mood was reflected in the decision to expand the existing Balloon School into an Air Battalion comprising airplanes as well as kites, balloons, and airships, although it was not until March 1911 (when the War Office formally authorized the purchase of four Bristol Boxkites), that the matériel basis for military aviation was established. Under the command of Major Sir Alexander Bannerman, the Air Battalion "would push on with the practical study of the military use of aircraft in the field."[21] The organization enjoyed a relatively brief existence, but this was sufficient to demonstrate that airplanes offered greater military potential than airships—at least for the Army. The creation of the Air Battalion was more than a transitional step, it was tangible evidence that the War Office had started to take aviation seriously.[22] The Army's increasingly positive view of military aviation was reinforced by the valuable contribution made by aircraft and airships in the 1912 and 1913 maneuvers.

In parallel with these developments, there had been growing disquiet that military aviation remained in the hands of the RE. A number of officers expressed the view that a separate branch of the Army was required in order to create an efficient fighting force, able to draw on the wide experience available across the services. A particular concern was that aviation was under the control of staff officers, who did not fly and had conflicting responsibilities. These complaints coincided with the prime minister's direction to the Committee of Imperial Defence to identify what further measures were needed to secure "an efficient aerial service" for the armed forces. Without seeking to predetermine the outcome, First Lord of the Admiralty Winston Churchill urged that "whatever happens, the RE must have nothing to do with HM's Corps of Airmen, which should be a new and separate organization drawing from civilian, as well as military and naval sources."[23] The necessary work, undertaken by a technical subcommittee, commenced in December 1911 and included, under the chairmanship of Colonel John Seely (undersecretary of state for war and Haldane's deputy), Brigadier-General David Henderson (director, Military Training), Commander Charles Samson of the Royal Navy (RN), and Mervyn O'Gorman, superintendent of the Aircraft Factory. Their report was actually the work of a smaller specialist group under Henderson that included Captain Frederick Sykes, a general staff officer and recently graduated pilot. Sykes had recently been sent to France by Brigadier-General Henry Wilson, director of Military Operations, to study French military aviation. His report, produced in November 1911, and titled *Notes on Aviation in France*, outlined the value of airplanes in war and the importance of strategic reconnaissance, raids against vital points, and tactical reconnaissance, including finding targets for the artillery and facilitating intercommunication between forces.[24] Sykes' tour of French military aviation establishments would soon provide the organizational blueprint for the RFC.[25] "Before the war, France was the recognized world leader in flying and hence Sykes' report from France could be considered one of the most important pre-war organizational influences on British aviation."[26]

Henderson's report was accepted by the technical subcommittee in February 1912. With the energetic support of the Admiralty, and the War Office, the Royal Flying Corps was constituted on 13 April, although it did not become an entity until 13 May, when it absorbed the Air Battalion. The RFC was the very first British joint military organization, comprising an Army Wing, commanded by (the recently promoted) Lieutenant-Colonel Frederick Sykes, and a Naval Wing commanded by Commander Charles Samson—with a Central Flying School (commanded by Captain Godfrey Paine, RN) tasked with training the pilots of both wings. Overall responsibility for the RFC fell to Henderson, as director of Military Training. In September 1913 these duties were transferred to a new Directorate of Military

Aeronautics (DMA), with Henderson as its first director. Various subdepartments of the DMA were tasked with the policy, finance, procurement, recruiting, and personnel aspects of the RFC.[27] The work of these staffs would later prove critical in the development of the air arm.

Even from this distance the creation of the RFC was ambitious and achieved at breakneck speed. It belies the popular story of official indifference and the skepticism attributed to senior army officers, fixated by concerns about the role of cavalry. Nevertheless, it was the French that set the pace in the race to forge an effective air weapon. It was the French army that took the first practical steps to create an aviation organization capable of keeping up with an advancing army and adequately self-sufficient to provide the necessary technical and logistic support to operate aircraft in the field. Some forty-six aircraft participated in the 1912 French military maneuvers, organized into eight escadrilles, each provided with two motor vehicles capable of carrying ten men and towing a two-wheeled float for carrying a crated or dismounted airplane. Additional vehicles were provided to carry an airplane directly as well as serving as dedicated workshops.[28] French influence was physical as well as spiritual. The RFC relied on French industry to provide many of its aircraft and most of its aero-engines while drawing on the French military for its organization and doctrine. This close relationship would continue, and even strengthen, during the First World War when the RFC's operational doctrine would be influenced by French wartime experience, particularly the contribution of airplanes to the defense of Verdun.

British expenditure on military aviation prior to the First World War has usually been compared unfavorably to other nations. On the other hand, it has been argued that the number of aircraft employed was actually proportionally higher (noting that the British Army was considerably smaller than its European rivals).[29] Taken as a whole, however, the share of expenditure allocated in 1913–14 to military aviation in Britain (1.8 percent) was lower than in France (2.6 percent) and in Germany (2.7 percent) and grew at a slower rate in the years immediately before the outbreak of war.[30] This reflects the degree of skepticism that existed about aviation among naval and military authorities as well as politicians.[31] John Moore-Brabazon, holder of the first British pilot's license, had written in 1909: "I have known the difficulties of constructing a machine in England, where everybody is so ready to discourage one, ridicule one, and look upon one as an amiable idiot. . . . [M]y advice to anyone about to build a machine is to do it in France: there he will find the enthusiasm without which it is so difficult to really make a machine fly."[32]

The development of British military aviation was also influenced by reports of Germany's aeronautical progress—particularly Count Ferdinand von Zeppelin's pioneering achievements—and growing concerns about Imperial Germany's ambitions. These two themes, ever closer working with France and the belief that war with Germany was inevitable, dominated public discussion in the years before the outbreak of war, driven by the view that Britain had fallen behind France and

Germany in aeronautical achievement.[33] "I ask you to give publicity to the success of aviation as adapted to military purposes because it is high time that our authorities took some steps to follow the example of the French."[34] Although much was achieved in the next few years, British aviation continued to lag behind both France and Germany. By the end of 1911, France had issued more than five hundred pilot's certificates compared to just 110 in Great Britain. On the outbreak of war, the five most important aviation records (including distance, duration, height, and speed) were all held by either France or Germany. No British pilot held a world record of any sort.[35]

From the beginning, however, Britain's aeronautical efforts were handicapped by the lack of reliable aero-engines of adequate power. This single problem effectively constrained the development of the British aviation industry, both before and during the war. In August 1914 there was no aircraft or aero-engine industry to speak of, while a number of key components—such as magnetos—could only be obtained abroad.[36] The pressure of war overcame most of these problems but the supply of aero-engines continued to compromise aviation planning right up to the armistice. Part of the difficulty was that it was easier to purchase aero-engines in France (such as the Gnome with its outstanding power-to-weight ratio) than to develop British alternatives. British aviation came to rely almost exclusively on French aero-engines and French aircraft. When the RFC was first formed, it was able to boast an establishment of just fewer than two hundred personnel and seventeen machines, with another thirty-six on order—but half of these were to be supplied by France and all would be powered by French aero-engines. In comparison, l'Aéronautique Militaire already possessed at least one hundred aircraft and the German Air Service (GAS) a similar number.[37] "The French authorities, who were naturally gifted with more imagination than our own politicians, had grasped the potentialities of aircraft very early in their development, and had spent large sums of money in order to encourage their experimenters. The results had far exceeded their expectations and the French pilots and constructors were far ahead of the rest of the world in every branch of aviation."[38]

Sykes, as head of the RFC's Military Wing, rapidly set about creating an effective air service, drawing heavily on French aviation practice. Many of these principles would later be incorporated in the RFC's *Training Manual*, first published in 1914, which provided the foundation for all future British airpower doctrine.[39] A steady stream of officers visited France over the next few years, either to observe army maneuvers or to inspect factories and flying fields.[40] "In aeronautical matters France is without doubt far ahead of any other country, and we must therefore look to her for hints as to the manner in which we may best augment our own resources in this direction."[41]

Although the RFC possessed just sixty-three frontline aircraft at the outbreak of war, it grew rapidly as the utility of military aviation became clearer.[42] This was only feasible, however, because it was possible to procure additional aircraft and aero-engines in France. The French contribution to the British air effort was timely, substantial, and essential. As the *History of the Ministry of Munitions* observed:

> French assistance was of peculiar value in that it was rendered in the first months of the war, when home industry was incapable of supplying the Services with the necessary equipment. The French rotary engines alone enabled the two Services to carry on through the first two years of the war, and such were the qualities of these engines that they were used in increasing quantities throughout the war. French aeroplanes were also invaluable during the first two years of the war and the Maurice Farman was the standard training machine until nearly the end of 1917.[43]

Britain did supply some aeronautical material to France, including aircraft and machine guns, but this was a fraction of what was provided in return.[44] Entire front-line squadrons were equipped with French aircraft, as were a large proportion of the training units supplying pilots to the western front—where the strength of the RFC increased from just five squadrons in 1914 to twenty-nine by 1916, and nearly ninety by the Armistice.[45] Although the direct procurement of aircraft from France became less important as the war progressed, the supply of aero-engines remained vital in powering British-manufactured machines. The supply of aircraft from overseas (largely France) represented 5 percent of total wartime production but nearly 40 percent of production in 1915. The supply of aero-engines from overseas (again largely France) represented some 40 percent of total wartime production and over 50 percent of production in 1915.[46]

Although the provision of adequate quantities of aeronautical matériel was a major challenge for the RFC, there were many other problems to be overcome before military aviation could make an effective contribution to the war. The RFC and l'Aéronautique Militaire were partners in the struggle to develop a conceptual model for military aviation and, just as importantly, to gain the understanding of army commanders and the support of politicians. In this process the RFC was not necessarily the junior partner, although it soon found that there was much to be learned from the French, including their approach to aerial photography and map-making. By December 1914, the RFC's photographic organization had been remodeled entirely along French lines and, when this was changed to a more decentralized arrangement in early 1916, the RFC followed suit.[47] In a similar way, the RFC's procedures for army cooperation, notably the employment of contact patrols to support infantry attacks, was largely drawn from French practice.[48]

While Trenchard is commonly regarded as the father of the RAF, it is often overlooked that he initially resisted the idea of an independent air service.[49] Moreover, his views on airpower and the importance of strategic bombing only emerged over time, evolving as the war progressed. Central to this process was his relationship with Commandant Paul du Peuty.[50] Both Trenchard's personal papers and the

RFC/RAF official history describe the importance of the French in the development of his thinking on operational and tactical matters.[51] Neither Trenchard nor du Peuty was fluent in the other's language but, through Maurice Baring (Trenchard's liaison officer), they were able to develop a shared view of how airpower should be employed in support of the ground battle. In the autumn of 1915, Trenchard and du Peuty met to distill their collective experience into fundamental principles governing the employment of aircraft in war. The need to coordinate the French Tenth Army's air activities with adjacent RFC formations may have been the instigation for this debate but there were matters of real substance to be addressed, which would have long-lasting implications for British airpower doctrine. "This policy [the strategic offensive] was thrashed out in the autumn of 1915 in many conversations between General Trenchard and Commandant du Peuty, talking and arguing over the experiences of the two air services."[52]

It has been suggested that the concept of the "strategic offensive" was uniquely Trenchard's, not least by Trenchard's biographer, and that in turn it shaped the French response to the German air effort at Verdun.[53] The evidence is far from conclusive. What seems more likely is that the two airmen contributed to a process in which theory, experience, and analysis were woven into a new orthodoxy that employed aircraft as a weapon of attack rather than of defense.[54] Just as importantly, they both concluded that the effective employment of military aviation was only possible through centralized control and decentralized execution.[55]

With the move of the French Tenth Army, in early March 1916, both Trenchard and du Peuty were determined to establish liaison officers in the other's headquarters to facilitate their continued communications.[56] Du Peuty was now based on the Verdun front from where he provided regular reports, willingly sharing his experience and reinforcing Trenchard's views about the need for a continuous offensive in the air. According to du Peuty, there were clear organizational as well as operational lessons to be drawn, including the necessity of grouping, in each army, the fighting machines employed on offensive duties under a single commander; the primary importance of the work done for the higher command; and the need for great adaptability in the organization as well as the necessity of a high degree of training.[57] These lessons were incorporated in the RFC's planning for the Somme, including the decision to withdraw the fighter aircraft provided to the corps (army cooperation) squadrons for self-defense and organize them into dedicated fighter squadrons.[58]

It should not be assumed, however, that Trenchard was without criticism of l'Aéronautique Militaire. While he acknowledged their innovation and leadership, he also felt that they lacked something in delivery:

> Generally speaking, I would say that the French Air Service excels in conception, but to a certain extent fails in execution. The development of aerial methods especially in the case of aerial fighting owes a very great deal to French thought and initiative and we have based

our tactics largely on their teaching. Their organisation for making use of aerial information, studying photographs, reporting the result of bombardments, keeping the command in touch with the advance of their troops is extremely good. Its execution, in my opinion, leaves something to be desired and this is principally due I think to a lack of real discipline.[59]

This more nuanced view of the relationship between the two air services may be closer to the truth than the somewhat formulaic expressions of appreciation provided by Trenchard when he left France in 1918:

I would be grateful if you could express to all those involved with the French Air Services the heartfelt debt and gratitude that I feel towards them for all the assistance that they gave me whilst in command of the Air Services in France. I can state categorically that it was the example shown by the French aviators at Verdun and at other important battles that influenced me directly. I also wanted to learn from the French Air Service's modus operandi; the perfection they demonstrated whist undertaking artillery and photographic missions were the benchmarks that I applied to our own artillery missions.[60]

From its creation, the RFC was focused on supporting the British Army in the field. Since the Army's main effort was the western front, so too was the RFC's. There were of course the "sideshows" (including the Dardanelles, Middle East, and Italy) and a great deal of activity directed at home defense and training (at home and overseas), but the RFC's main resources, most of its planning effort, and many of its best people were committed to the fighting in France and Belgium. Organizational changes, including the creation of the RAF on 1 April 1918 and the establishment of the Independent Force (to undertake the strategic bombing of Germany), did not substantially weaken this resolve. Although the proportion of forces employed on the western front fell over time, from 61 percent of RFC service (frontline) squadrons in May 1917 to 49 percent of RAF service squadrons in May 1918, supporting the BEF remained the "main effort" throughout the war.[61] This commitment was not only substantial but also unmatched by any other arm. The number of guns, particularly heavy artillery, has been represented as the greatest transformation in the BEF's firepower during the war, yet the ratio of aircraft to divisions serving on the western front increased by over 400 percent between 1916 and 1918, while the number of guns grew by just 62 percent.[62] As the war progressed, it became clear that the RFC's most important contribution to victory would be through artillery cooperation and reconnaissance (including photography and contact patrols). "The War of 1914 to 1918 in the air was, for obvious reasons, an 'Army co-operation' war in the narrow technical sense of the term."[63]

At the start of the war, the potential to gain information through air observation was substantial while the potential for offensive capabilities was slight. In time, air bombardment would emerge as an important role—once the RFC had the appropriate bombs and equipment.[64] Over time, further roles emerged but all remained subordinate to the task of supporting the BEF. Even air fighting was regarded as part of the cooperation with the army, "as it was carried out mainly with the object of rendering reconnaissance and observing possible."[65]

When the first four RFC squadrons arrived in France in August 1914, under the command of Brigadier-General David Henderson, they were employed exclusively on reconnaissance tasks at the direction of General Headquarters (GHQ).[66] Although the RFC has been famously credited with bringing the first news that the Germans had swung to the southeast, making possible the Battle of the Marne, the efforts of its aircraft and crews had limited impact. The frequent changes in location and the difficulties in moving aircraft, men, and support equipment across a poorly mapped landscape meant that the squadrons were hard pressed simply to continue flying.[67]

While the RFC's main role in the opening months of the war was reconnaissance, the potential for artillery cooperation was understood—even though the practical arrangements had yet to be properly developed. The possibility of directing artillery fire from the air had been explored as early as 1912, but the lack of funds for artillery ammunition and a shortage of equipment (particularly wireless sets) restricted what could be achieved.[68] The first practical employment of wireless to control artillery fire took place during the Battle of the Aisne. By December, a dedicated wireless unit (No. 9 Squadron) had been formed to help develop the technique.[69] At the Battle of Festubert, all the RFC's aircraft employed on artillery cooperation were equipped with wireless and, with the introduction of the clock code and the employment of squared maps, the basic principles were in place that would provide the foundation for the RFC's artillery cooperation efforts. "From the Battle of Loos to the end of the war, great improvements were made in the execution of the policy, details of the procedure were perfected, and a few special calls were introduced, but there was no general change in method."[70]

Parallel improvements in aerial photography, both in the development of cameras and in the printing and analysis of photographs, provided the timely intelligence needed to identify the precise location of enemy positions well beyond the front line. "Air photos became the principal intelligence tool of the counter-battery staffs, and furnished a link between the artillery staffs and the General Staffs."[71] On average, one thousand photographs were taken daily in 1918—with as many as six thousand prints produced.[72] By 1916 individual batteries were provided with dedicated RFC wireless operators, while each corps squadron had one or more artillery liaison officers with landlines to the divisional artillery staffs. Nearly all (90 percent) counter-battery observation was done by airmen using wireless and, as a result, "the success of the artillery battle had come to depend on the weather being suitable for flying."[73] Even so, it took until 1917 to develop the necessary equipment and provide the mapmakers with the quality of photographs they needed. The 1:20,000 and 1:10,000 maps covering the entire western front, produced by the RE Survey

Sections, together with daily air photography, offered the precision needed by the garrison and field artillery in the short, intensive bombardment that was the foundation for British success in 1918.

Of course, the RFC's ability to provide the required level and quality of observation did not of necessity deliver a war-winning strategy. The BEF's artillery techniques and policies progressed through several stages and not always for the better.[74] The artillery plan at the Battle of Neuve Chapelle demonstrated the value of a short, concentrated, and intensive bombardment to neutralize (rather than destroy) the enemy's defenses. In retrospect, the wrong deductions were drawn about the benefits of destructive fire and subsequent offensives (including the Somme and Third Ypres) sought to destroy the enemy's defenses and artillery positions through a prolonged bombardment.[75] It was not until the Battle of Cambrai that the advantages of neutralizing fire were "rediscovered." At the same time, however, the absence of a preliminary bombardment placed even greater importance on the accuracy of air observation, before and during the assault, to help neutralize counter-battery fire and locate silent hostile batteries and anti-tank guns.[76] In enabling artillery to engage with targets that could not be seen from the ground, the RFC created both the precondition for three-dimensional warfare and a radical change in the way that firepower shaped the battlefield. Jonathan Bailey has argued that this represented the birth of the "modern style of warfare," but fails to add that, without the RFC's ability to operate in the third dimension, warfare would have remained (self-evidently) two-dimensional.[77] Unfortunately, the "ability to operate" could not be taken for granted. It required the RFC to overcome the enemy, the weather, and unreliable machinery in equal measure.

Air superiority, the ability to operate in the third dimension as and when desired—and without interference—was not a permanent state but had to be continuously reestablished. The airspace over the western front was permeable. The RFC could no more occupy aerial vantage points than the GAS could create aerial barriers. Trenchard's doctrine of the "strategic offensive" (sometimes characterized as a visceral attempt to demonstrate the warrior ethos of the RFC) was aimed at securing and maintaining the ability to operate at will across the battlefield while denying the GAS the same advantage. This was not an outcome that the GAS was willing to concede. The RFC's offensive strategy had to be resisted "as it was of outstanding importance that we should hold mastery of the air over the battlefield, if we were to succeed either in offensive or defensive operations."[78] The result was an air war in which both qualitative and quantitative factors played a part. Above all, however, it was a continuous effort in which there were no operational pauses, no periods of recuperation, and no armistice. Aircraft and crews were lost daily, through enemy action, unreliable aero-engines, landing accidents, or simply bad weather. Achieving air superiority was in essence an attritional struggle. Under these circumstances, the RFC's logistic efficiency—and the ability to make good the losses—became a key factor in the mathematics of three-dimensional warfare and a question of strategic importance. As Peter Hart has succinctly observed, when discussing the RFC's experience during "Bloody April:" "Although casualties rose sharply, the RFC still managed to deliver the services that Trenchard and Haig required. One of the great lessons of aerial warfare had been learnt. Supremacy in the air meant the ability to keep army photographic reconnaissance and artillery observation aircraft above the front and the question of casualties incurred in doing so was almost immaterial."[79]

The RFC's operational contribution to the western front was not restricted solely to improving the effectiveness of the BEF's artillery fire, important though this was. The ability to achieve effect at distance, day and night, and through air reconnaissance to anticipate and counter the enemy's actions, enabled the BEF's commanders to achieve greater operational tempo as the war progressed. Improvements in airborne communications, in the form of wireless telegraphy and, toward the end of the war, wireless telephony, offered a more comprehensive, detailed, and timely picture of the battlefield than ever previously available. During the Hundred Days offensive, the RAF was increasingly able to provide real-time intelligence, including direct liaison with tanks. The rapid growth in the RAF's capabilities meant that airpower could be readily deployed to specific effect as the operational situation demanded. The fighter squadrons that machine-gunned and bombed advancing German columns in March and April 1918 were the same that had previously protected the corps squadrons in their artillery cooperation duties, and the same that a few months later flew close air support against German anti-tank guns during the Battle of Amiens. None of this is particularly novel or contentious. It has been well described by John Terraine, Shelford Bidwell, and Dominick Graham among others:

> The most momentous contribution—greater than the tank—was from the maturing air force, the RFC/RAF, on its own initiative developing tactical air support and later strategic support, feeding reliable information to the intelligence staff and also enhancing the scope and accuracy of artillery fire. Improvements in radio telegraphy and the invention of the thermionic valve benefitted the air arm, leading to the first steps towards revolution in what we now call C^3I.[80]

However, everything hinged on the ability of the RFC to achieve air superiority.[81] The GAS fully understood the threat that this represented, as a postwar assessment of the air war observed:

> Whenever we succeeded in holding off the enemy's reconnaissance machines, their artillery became practically blind. Another point of equal importance was the necessity of possessing the mastery of the air during infantry offensives over those places where the fighting was the hottest, in order that a close watch could be kept on the development of the attack. When telephone wires were cut as a result of the preliminary bombardment, the infantry contact machines became the

sole reliable means of communication between the fighting troops and the higher command. Should the enemy manage to disperse our contact patrols, no communication existed to the rear of our lines, and if this happened when the enemy's fighting machines had succeeded in chasing away our artillery observation machines which were directing the fire of our guns against the enemy's barrage, it was impossible for us to send up reserves without a terrible loss of life and waste of time.[82]

Winning the air battle depended on: quality (relative to the enemy), capability (the deployment of effective tactics and systems), and persistence (providing sufficient aircraft in the right place at the right time). The RFC's logistic organization played a vital role in meeting each of these requirements but, by enabling continued operations in the face of combat attrition and high wastage, it also endowed the RFC with a fundamental advantage. The relative technical efficiency between the RFC and the GAS waxed and waned over time. In general, no side ever enjoyed an overwhelming advantage such that they could operate with impunity. The RFC's ability to consistently field more aircraft than the enemy, irrespective of wastage, offered a decisive edge over the GAS. Although the proportion of resources directed at army cooperation diminished over the course of the war, particularly during the period 1916–1918, the weight of effort remained constant—matching the size of the BEF.[83] The operational focus, and highest priority, remained the BEF throughout the war.[84] The RFC's logistic competence meant that sufficient aircraft were always available to meet this requirement.

The organizational changes that emerged on 1 April 1918, with the creation of the RAF, did not weaken the focus on supporting the ground war: "Right up to the Armistice, the RAF remained overwhelmingly committed to the support of the army on the Western Front, functioning as the RFC before it as a tactical ancillary of the service from which it had sprung."[85]

There was certainly no reduction in the level of artillery cooperation (indeed, the number of aircraft available steadily grew as unit establishments were increased). On the other hand, more and more fighter squadrons were required to allow the army cooperation task to function with minimum interference from the enemy. The other key change over the same period was the sharp rise in the number of bombing squadrons.[86] Political necessity, military ambition, and technical development all played a part in ensuring that an ever-larger share of the RFC's growing resources was committed to operations well beyond the front line. This period also saw an increase in the range of roles undertaken as innovation created new possibilities and as the military potential of airpower was better understood. Ammunition dropping, smoke laying, and massed airfield attacks were just some of the new tasks that emerged in the last year of the war.

The importance of army cooperation is best illustrated by considering the evolution in the employment of the corps squadrons. No. 9 Squadron was employed continuously on artillery cooperation and army support from early 1916 until the armistice. Analysis of the squadron war diary (which is complete for the entire period) indicates how the balance of employment changed as well as the different roles that emerged as the war progressed. During the Somme, No. 9 Squadron's B.E.2c aircraft were largely used for artillery cooperation tasks (74 percent of all sorties), both patrol and observation, with less than 11 percent of sorties dedicated to reconnaissance, photographic or bombing.[87] The remainder of the squadron's operational effort was dedicated to contact patrols. A year later, at Third Ypres, the overall proportion of activities had changed very little.[88] Now operating the R.E.8, the majority of the squadron's sorties (70 percent) were still committed to artillery cooperation (through a mixture of patrols, observation, and registration). Contact patrols, photography, and reconnaissance continued to feature strongly but dedicated bombing missions no longer featured. On the other hand, and reflecting the BEF's greater operational maturity, some 6 percent of the squadron's efforts were directed at defeating German counterattacks. The Hundred Days offensive saw a radical change in the pattern of combat operations. Artillery cooperation formed a much smaller proportion of the squadron's sorties (less than 10 percent), whereas 60 percent were allocated to low bombing and offensive patrols. In undertaking these more general tasks, the squadron was still able to direct fire at unregistered locations and targets of opportunity, but there was no requirement for the intensive artillery registration and observation that had characterized Third Ypres. Although artillery cooperation was more problematic during mobile operations, air observation still allowed targets to be identified and engaged. On the other hand, sound ranging and flash spotting were largely ineffective during this period, having been optimized for static warfare.[89] More "exotic" activities (such as smoke laying and ammunition drops) now featured in the squadron's daily tasks—reflecting the increasing complexity of the RAF's activities and the flexibility of the army cooperation squadrons in responding to changing threats and exploiting new opportunities.

Reviewing the RFC's overall contribution to the western front, it is evident that by 1916 the RFC had the technology, resources, and operational art necessary to achieve air superiority, although this came at significant cost—in both personnel and matériel. By the armistice, just over three thousand members of the British Air Services had been killed on the western front, equivalent to losing the establishment of about one hundred single-seat fighter squadrons.[90] These casualties were a fraction of those suffered by the BEF as a whole, but still represented a heavy drain on the front line and the training system. Just over 13,000 aircraft were "consumed" on the western front during the last three years of the war.[91] Some 36 percent of this total represented combat attrition; the remainder were struck off in accidents, as time-expired or simply obsolescent.[92] This placed a heavy burden on the fledgling British aircraft and aero-engine industry—as we will see in the next chapters.

The RFC's operational performance turned on the ability to develop (and sustain) the capabilities needed to conduct three-dimensional warfare. These comprised: comprehensive and timely photographic coverage of the front line, accurate target registration, and effective artillery cooperation. In as much as the conditions of static warfare were initially produced through a deficiency in offensive firepower, it can be argued that the RFC provided the foundation for a return to mobile warfare—and an Allied victory—in enabling the BEF to achieve overwhelming kinetic effect through accurate, unregistered, and unobserved fire.[93] It is little wonder, therefore, that John Terraine was moved to claim that artillery cooperation was "probably the RFC's most important contribution of the whole war."[94]

Everything depended, however, on sustaining operations. Air superiority had to be fought for every day and demanded a ready supply of replacement aircraft and crews. For the RFC, this challenge was all the greater because the prevalent winds (blowing from the west), coupled with persistent German tactical superiority and frequent technological advantage, produced a higher loss rate than that experienced by the GAS. The latter operated largely over its own territory, where an aircraft forced to land because of a wounded pilot or a faulty engine could be retrieved along with its crew to fight another day. In sustaining the front line, while maintaining technical parity and continuing to deliver effective artillery cooperation, the performance of the RFC's logistic system became a matter of strategic importance.

The First World War initiated a radical change in warfare that was unprecedented in scale, intensity, and the widespread employment of technology.[95] The role of aviation in the conflict has sometimes been regarded as marginal, or at least no more than an interesting indication of what might be achieved in the future. According to Robin Prior and Trevor Wilson, "The air war of 1914–1918 only managed one cost-effective purpose: observation of the battlefield and its environs. This purpose, if noteworthy and of value, was less than crucial to victory and defeat."[96] Colin Gray, who otherwise enthusiastically supports the argument for an artillery-centric RMA during the First World War, prefers to credit the BEF's map, topographic, flash-spotting, and sound-ranging sections for this achievement, rather than the RFC.[97] These views are not supported by the evidence. They reflect, however, a failure to understand the role of airpower in creating and sustaining three-dimensional warfare, and the attritional struggle that lies at the heart of air operations. Moreover, because air superiority is by its nature transient, and is as much about indirect as direct action—through deterrence and denial, the importance of the enabling processes and systems required to support the RFC has neither been recognized nor properly investigated. This is to be regretted as the RFC's logistic system not only laid the foundation for achieving air superiority on the western front and the "modern style of warfare," but also (as we will see) introduced logistic practices that underpin the global supply chain.

THE ROYAL FLYING CORPS' LOGISTIC SYSTEM, 1914–18

CHAPTER

ROM ITS INCEPTION, THE RFC WAS DESIGNED TO OPERATE IN DIRECT SUPPORT of the Army and the Royal Navy.[1] The organization of the Military Wing of the RFC was tailored for deployment with the BEF and the flight and squadron system selected to provide for flexibility and ease of handling in the field.[2] Each squadron—comprising three flights of four airplanes and a headquarters flight—was to be a self-contained, homogeneous unit with its own field repair, stores, and transport services capable of operating on a detached basis for short periods.[3] This model, with variations, survived the test of two world wars, although "centralization" (the pooling of engineering activities to support several squadrons on a collective basis) was found to offer greater efficiency during the Second World War when a high degree of mobility was required.

The early airplanes were delicate, fragile, and unreliable. Their integrity deteriorated rapidly when exposed to the elements such that hangs—in the form of aircraft sheds (either wooden or canvas)—was essential to provide protection for both machines and mechanics. The technologies involved were extremely high for the time, demanding skills and equipment that were not readily available. Engine lives were short, requiring thorough overhaul after a comparatively brief period. Effective support was made all the more difficult by the proliferation of aircraft and aero-engine types and the lack of standard components. To enable the squadrons to function effectively in the field, the engineering organization had to be mobile yet also offer a wide range of specialist facilities. As a result, it was recognized that only a proportion of aircraft would be available for operations.[4] This was underscored in the draft *Training Manual* issued in May 1914 to all officers of the RFC. Under the section titled "General System of Maintenance," it was stated that:

> Aircraft are delicate machines and will be subjected to rough treatment on service. In war it is doubtful whether more than half of the total numbers of airships or one third of the total number of aeroplanes

will be available for use at any one time, even provided that repairs and replacements can be effected rapidly. It is essential, therefore, that any aircraft capable of flying shall not be kept on the ground for any avoidable cause such as want of petrol, and that as little delay as possible shall be caused by want of material for repairing damaged machines. As little reliance can be placed on local resources, replenishments must be sent up from the rear.[5]

The key to maintaining aircraft in the field was motor transport—itself a fledgling technology. Following a series of trials conducted in 1912 under the auspices of the War Office's Mechanical Transport Committee, the RFC was allotted a range of standard vehicles including: Leyland three-ton lorries, Crossley light tenders, and Phelan & Moore motor cycles.[6] By the time of the Military Wing's Concentration Camp at Netheravon in June 1914, each squadron had an establishment of twenty-six lorries and tenders, together with six motorcycles and six trailers.[7] The Army's need for motor vehicles had been demonstrated in successive exercises but peacetime affordability was a major concern.[8] The War Office had introduced a novel scheme in 1911, at the urging of the Treasury, under which participating firms could claim a subsidy equal to half the cost of a lorry.[9] This operated on the basis of a grant (£50 toward purchase and £20 per annum for maintenance to agreed standards) paid on the understanding that in an emergency the vehicle could be purchased by the War Office for full-time use. When war was declared, there were over one thousand vehicles registered under the scheme, many of which were destined for the RFC and subsequently appeared in France still sporting their commercial colors, such as No. 5 Squadron's brilliant scarlet lorry, previously operated by Maple's Store, advertising "HP Sauce—The World's Appetiser."[10] Not surprisingly, such incongruous sights fostered a belief that the RFC was woefully unprepared for war. In fact, it was evidence of an innovative and pragmatic solution to that perennial problem—matching limited national resources to limitless military needs.[11] The RFC was, in effect, the first fully motorized organization in the British Army.[12] By October 1917 just over 2,700 vehicles were employed on the western front in support of air operations—equivalent to one vehicle for every ten personnel or approximately three vehicles for every frontline aircraft.[13] The largest single group (2,533) comprised heavy and light tenders—including specialist repair vehicles—approximately 10 percent of all lorries employed by the BEF, even though the RFC represented just 1.1 percent of the BEF's total manpower.[14] In September 1916 the Ministry of Munitions assessed that the Army required 245 three-ton lorries each week, of which forty-five (18 percent of new production) were for the RFC.[15] The number of vehicles operated by the RFC kept pace with the expansion of the overall organization and, although the ratio of vehicles to personnel gradually fell over the course of the war, it remained an order of magnitude higher than the BEF as a whole, where the ratio of vehicles to personnel also fell over time.[16]

The RFC ratio of one vehicle for every ten personnel on the western front was also five times better than that of the American Expeditionary Force (AEF), which relied largely on trucks rather than horses to meet its transportation needs, the most heavily motorized of the Allied armies. Moreover, in standardizing on just four vehicle types the RFC enjoyed a significant advantage over the AEF, which operated thirty-four different makes.[17] In as much as mobility on the western front depended on the availability of lorries and other forms of mechanical transport, the Allies had a substantial advantage with about 100,000 lorries in March 1918 compared to just 23,000 available to the Germans.[18] Such was the ready availability of motor vehicles that Maurice Baring, temporarily billeted at Headquarters First Division in 1915, noted in his diary, "The first thing that struck one after living with the RFC was the absence of transport."[19] According to Liddell Hart, while motor vehicles multiplied by the thousand in the First World War, "this acceleration of movement only improved the capacity of supply; it did not markedly affect strategy since it could not alter the immobility of fighting troops."[20] This observation may have been valid for the BEF as a whole, but it was certainly not true of the RFC, where the substantial investment in motor transport imbued the organization with a natural agility and resilience, permitting squadrons to redeploy quickly over substantial distances without disrupting the supply chain and without weakening operational capability.

The creation of the RFC coincided with significant changes in the organization of Army transportation that saw greater authority pass to the Inspector General of Communications (IGC) for supply in the field, relieving divisions of some of their existing responsibilities. The combination of motor transport and railways meant that the front line was no longer entirely dependent on what it could carry. Motor transport operating from parks located at the nearest railhead offered a greater level of support and wider freedom of action by removing the horse-drawn divisional baggage train.[21] The new arrangements were tested during the 1911 maneuvers and proved sufficiently successful to be formally adopted the next year. The RFC's supply arrangements were built around this system from the very beginning but, unlike the BEF, where the Army Service Corps (ASC) operated motor transport on behalf of IGC and the Quartermaster General (QMG), the RFC managed its own vehicles and carried out minor repairs.[22] This had the considerable advantage of allowing squadrons to function largely independently, although the heavy reliance on organic transport did give rise to some concerns about the availability of vehicles in war and the level of spares required.[23]

Even before the war, it was recognized that squadrons could not support themselves for more than a limited period in the field and that a facility was required—close to the Army's main operations—capable of undertaking a greater depth of repair and holding a wide range of spares and equipment. These needs were met by a Line of Communications Workshop, which became known as the Flying Depot, and later the Aircraft Park, based at Farnborough and comprising separate stores and workshop sections capable of packing up and moving in twenty-four hours.[24] On the outbreak of war, the Aircraft Park deployed to France to support the squadrons in the field, arriving at Boulogne on 18 August 1914.[25] The RFC/RAF official history records that, on disembarkation, the port landing officer sent an urgent wire to General Headquarters: "An unnumbered unit without aeroplanes which calls itself an Aircraft Park has arrived. What are we to do with it?"[26] Despite this initial hiccup, the Aircraft Park proved itself invaluable in sustaining the four RFC squadrons initially sent to France. It was, in effect, their travelling base and as such was constantly on the move. Eventually, at the end of October, after five changes in location, the Aircraft Park found itself at St-Omer, where it would remain for much of the war.[27]

The mobilization of the RFC had been rapid and thorough, but the failure to leave any substantial core of trained staff in the War Office, or to retain functioning squadrons that could provide the basis for new units, slowed any immediate expansion. It also created difficulties in procuring replacement aircraft and spares—although this was partly disguised by purchasing much of what was needed directly from French sources. Henderson's decision to abandon the War Office for France (with many other senior staff officers) compromised the higher direction of the air arm at a critical moment. Henderson would continue to act as the RFC's field commander for the next year while (notionally) continuing to serve as the director-general of Military Aeronautics, overseeing the rapid expansion of the organization and resolving all the varied administrative, procurement, and policy issues that arose. This was an unsustainable situation that placed a huge burden on a single individual, who wilted "under the impossible load of responsibility for both the operation and supply of the Royal Flying Corps."[28] As Sefton Brancker observed, "this crippling of the General Staff on mobilisation was really the only amateurish feature in the whole original plan of campaign—it was illogical, unpardonable, and had bad results later on."[29]

In defense of the RFC, it should be noted that the air arms of all the belligerents suffered significant logistic problems during this period. The failure of the GAS to make any significant military contribution in the first year of the war has been attributed to confused support arrangements. "The lack of organisation and of the service of supply in the GAS was almost unbelievable."[30] The output of new aircraft was far lower than operational losses and quite incapable of meeting the demand for new flying units. Rather than supplying each aviation section with two airplanes daily, the supply system could only offer one replacement every two weeks. As a result flying units would visit factories to commandeer aircraft, while support units tasked with supplying aircraft to the front line had no liaison with the sections they were meant to serve.[31] L'Aéronautique Militaire also struggled with the demands of supporting aircraft in the field. Aviation supply was disrupted under the strain of the retreat prior to the Battle of the Marne, while the decision to close all the aviation schools (and draft the ground crews into the infantry) severely restricted air operations.[32]

By the end of 1914 a modest but effective logistic system was in place to support the RFC in France. Supplies from England were sent via Rouen to the Aircraft Park and then onwards to the frontline squadrons.[33] Two particular aspects are worthy of comment. First, a considerable quantity of matériel was purchased in France and delivered directly to the Air Park for formal acceptance and issue. This included complete machines as well as aero-engines, wireless equipment, and a wide range of aeronautical stores. Such was the urgency of the RFC's needs that one hundred aircraft were purchased from French manufacturers during the first six months of the war. Their employment, while of significant operational benefit, considerably complicated the Aircraft Park's logistic efforts, particularly the challenge of maintaining machines manufactured to metric rather than imperial measurements and the lack of interchangeability between British- and French-sourced components of identical design.[34]

Second, aside from local purchase, all stores for the Air Park were issued by the Ordnance Aeronautical Stores Department (OASD), part of the Army Ordnance Department (AOD), based at Farnborough.[35] Their supplies were obtained either by direct purchase from manufacturers or from the Royal Aircraft Factory.[36] The increasing range and quantities of matériel that had to be handled by the OASD led to the setting up of a dedicated stores depot at Farnborough in October 1914 to hold aircraft, aero-engines, pyrotechnics, and all stores special to the RFC.[37] Almost immediately, the buildings allocated proved inadequate to the task and additional stores were established at Greenwich and Didcot, the first elements in a stores distribution system that would ultimately comprise seven main depots and ten distributing parks in the United Kingdom alone. The situation at Farnborough was not made any easier by the requirement that all aircraft purchased for the RFC had to be flown there, or delivered crated and then erected, for inspection and flight testing by the Aeronautical Inspection Department (AID). This potential bottleneck remained until March 1915 when regional delivery centers were opened.[38]

The stores section of the Aircraft Park at St-Omer was responsible for requisitions ranging from complete aircraft to lawnmowers for keeping aerodromes trim. As a result, the depot came to resemble, in the words of its commander, "a gigantic factory and emporium," repairing everything from aircraft to wireless equipment.[39] By July 1915, the organization had become just too unwieldy to satisfy the demands placed upon it and a second park was established at Candas, to cater for those squadrons working directly for the newly formed Third Army.[40] Both parks were supplied by rail from separate port depots, based respectively at Boulogne and Rouen, which received all the RFC's stores from England.[41] In due course, the Rouen base would become a huge engineering complex that included the Engine Repair Shops (ERS) at Pont de l'Arche. The latter steadily grew in size such that by the summer of 1917 it comprised over 1,700 personnel employed in the overhaul and repair of engines from every squadron on the western front.[42] Repairs were also carried out by civilian contractors, but the bulk of arisings (engines made unserviceable by air combat, accidental damage, failure, or simple wear and tear) were allocated to Service-manned repair shops in order to avoid persistent labor and production problems in the United Kingdom.[43]

Even with these changes, it was evident that unless the parks were relieved of some of their heavy repair work, and the increasing size and range of stores they were required to hold, there was little possibility they could sustain a mobile role. The solution—credited by Maurice Baring to Trenchard—was to create air parks for each RFC brigade and to convert the existing parks at St-Omer and Candas into fixed Aircraft Depots (AD) comprising some five hundred to one thousand personnel, depending upon the number of squadrons to be supported, organized into a wide range of specialist shops (including wireless, instruments, and photographic), together with airframe and component repair sections.[44] The new Army Air Parks (AP) came into being on 15 December 1915 and were kept as small as possible, comprising some 150 personnel organized into separate repair, stores, and transport sections, and based in the rear of the army area, adjacent to a railhead to enable a rapid move if required.[45] "The object in forming Army Aircraft Parks is to have a mobile unit of supply for the RFC and mobility must always be the first consideration."[46] Consumables, such as ordnance, petrol, rations, clothing, and so on, would continue to be provided by a combination of Army supply, specific RFC arrangements, and local purchase.[47] For example, aviation spirit was supplied in two- and four-gallon cans direct from England, using the Army supply system (although the quantities, 600,000 gallons per month by early 1918, eventually required that dedicated filling arrangements be provided in France).[48] Ammunition was provided direct to squadrons by the Army Ordnance Services but aerial bombs were supplied by the Air Parks. The transportation of bombs presented an increasing challenge during 1915 as the quantity, size, and range of ordnance rapidly grew.[49] Approval was given in June 1915 for the creation of an Air Ammunition Column (AAC) for each RFC wing, tasked with moving bombs from the parks to the squadrons. By April 1916 each brigade had a dedicated AAC comprising six three-ton lorries and sixteen staff (largely drivers).[50] As the war grew in scale and intensity, ever greater human and matériel resources were needed to sustain the RFC. On the eve of the Battle of the Somme, the logistic organization had expanded to support over four hundred aircraft in the field. The operational squadrons were based six to eight miles from the front line while the parks, holding one month's supply of aeronautical stores, were positioned at railheads some five to ten miles further back. Stock holdings were strictly controlled to ensure mobility was not impaired and all stores were packed in specially constructed cases that could be readily loaded onto lorries and issued, if necessary, "on the move." Minor facilities, for example to conduct wing repairs, were provided, but the AP was first and foremost an issuing center supplied (usually by rail) from one of the two main depots, up to forty miles from the front line, that held up to three months' stock of aeronautical and transport stores. The main depots (No. 1 AD at St-Omer and No. 2 AD at Candas) also received, and issued, stores and aircraft direct to the individual squadrons, maintained an attrition reserve, and over-hauled and rebuilt aircraft, balloons, transport, and associated equipment. All air-craft and engines requiring repair outside squadron capabilities (assessed as in excess of thirty-six hours) were returned direct to the depots, as were all wrecked aircraft.[51]

In parallel with these developments, it had become clear that specialist officers were required to oversee the RFC's technical needs, both to supervise stores and to manage the repair and overhaul of aircraft and equipment. The initial solution was to employ a fourth flight commander on each squadron but this proved unsatisfac-tory.[52] To employ flying officers for such duties, when the lack of trained pilots was a severe constraint on the RFC's expansion plans, was simply not realistic. As a result, equipment officers (EOs) were introduced from early 1915 and by July were to be found in all wings and squadrons in France.[53] Their duties embraced what would now be called the engineer and supply disciplines (including transport, armament, photographic, wireless, and maintenance). The EOs took much of the technical burden off the squadron commanders, giving them more time to concentrate on operational matters. In each corps squadron there were eventually up to four EOs on the establishment.[54] Their overall importance is indicated by the fact that, in a little over a year (that is by July 1916), nearly four hundred officers in the RFC were graded as EOs—about 20 percent of the total officer strength.[55]

Although the purchase of aeronautical equipment from France, particularly aero-engines, continued throughout the war, the mobilization of the British air-craft industry saw increasing numbers of aircraft produced in the UK. Deliveries reached 120 aircraft per month by July 1916, rising to an average of 1,300 per month in 1917 and 2,700 in 1918.[56] Completed aircraft were sent directly from the manufacturer to a system of Aircraft Acceptance Parks (AAPs), developed from the regional delivery centers, but controlled by the RFC from March 1917 onwards. Ultimately there would be sixteen AAPs, but their existence was largely owed to continuing failures in supply, not only of aero-engines but also of components such as crankshafts, magnetos, and ball-bearings. Although the government took upon itself responsibility for the production and allocation of these critical items, it was found much easier to increase the rate of manufacture of airframes using a wide range of contractors—many of which had not produced aircraft before. As a result, there was a rapid buildup in stocks of aircraft pending availability of what would now be termed government-furnished equipment. The AAPs allowed airframes to be accepted formally from the manufacturers, pending completion, so avoiding the possibility of congested factories and production bottlenecks.[57]

In the event, this system worked remarkably well, although it would clearly have been preferable, and more efficient, to deliver aircraft and equipment direct to the RFC's depots for allocation to the frontline squadrons. When a new airframe was ready it was inspected by the AID and, once passed, delivered (generally by road) to the appropriate AAP for completion and onward dispatch. For example, Armstrong Whitworth FK8 (Serial No. B273) was passed by the AID, less its engine, at

Newcastle on 21 June 1917 and dispatched to No. 8 AAP at Lympne on 25 June. The aircraft was successfully flight-tested on 12 July, after engine installation, and delivered to No. 1 AD at St-Omer on the same day for the fitting of wireless equipment, guns, and other accessories. The completed airframe was then transferred to No. 2 AD at Candas on 31 July, where it remained in store until issued, as received, to No. 2 Squadron on 1 September 1917—nine weeks after it first left the manufacturer.[58] It should be noted that this process was not always so trouble-free and the DMA routinely planned on the basis of 10 percent wastage in moving aircraft from the manufacturer to France.[59]

The logistic system in place by Third Ypres had evolved substantially since 1916. The depots were by now fixed, with the parks and squadrons comprising the mobile element. The OASD had been absorbed in January 1917 when the RFC took responsibility for the supply and storage of all aeronautical matériel. The network of parks and squadrons had grown substantially to support over eight hundred aircraft— double the RFC's frontline strength in 1916. The division of work between the various elements of this system was designed to ensure the flying squadrons could meet their operational task, yet not be encumbered with excessive equipment and personnel that would limit their mobility. Given the common perception that warfare on the western front was a static affair, this might seem an unnecessary concern, but the RFC's squadrons moved frequently—very much as the operational situation dictated. Thus, No. 9 Squadron, employed on the western front from December 1915 until the armistice, was based at twenty different airfields in France and Belgium, roughly a move every two months.[60] Some of these deployments were major relocations to a different army area, up to seventy miles away, while others were successive moves to keep in touch with the changing front, as in the last few months of the war. In all cases, the squadron was able to conduct operational sorties within forty-eight hours of leaving its previous location—an impressive achievement.[61]

It is appropriate at this stage to look at the squadron logistic organization in a little more detail. The RFC squadrons in France nominally retained the prewar establishment of twelve aircraft, but this was usually augmented during active operations, in the case of the corps squadrons up to a total strength of twenty-one or even twenty-four machines by 1918 (subject to sufficient aircraft and crews being available). This had the effect of increasing the operational output of an individual frontline squadron, although it made it less easy to manage and diluted supervision levels. Brooke-Popham commented after the war that twenty-four machines were probably too many for corps squadrons to handle effectively.[62] Each flight had its own flight sergeant responsible for some thirty-five or so mechanics, allocated in small groups to specific aircraft. The flight fitters carried out daily servicing and minor adjustments (such as valve grinding) on their own aircraft, while the headquarters flight undertook deeper maintenance and rectification (effectively, the equivalent of what would today be called "second line").[63] The mechanics' working hours reflected the operational tempo. Poor weather reduced the engineering task

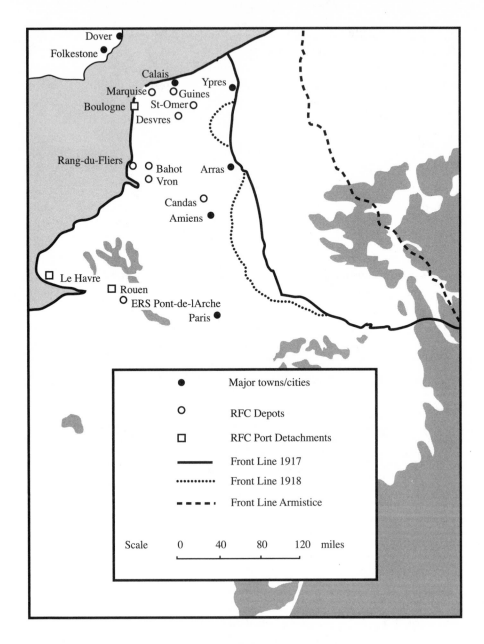

Major towns/cities
○ RFC Depots
□ RFC Port Detachments
——— Front Line 1917
············· Front Line 1918
– – – – Front Line Armistice

Scale 0 40 80 120 miles

MAP 1
ROYAL FLYING CORPS DEPOT LOCATIONS, WESTERN FRONT

but there was always routine maintenance to be undertaken. During active operations the ground crew might work through the night to prepare aircraft for the next
day. The following description, provided by an engine fitter of No. 60 Squadron,
operating Nieuport 17 Scouts, gives some feel for the working environment and the
functioning of the logistic system in the field:

> Normal battle damage to airframes, requiring wing patching, strut
> replacement, etc., would be repaired in the flights. The equipment
> store in Headquarters Flight carried a considerable range of spares;
> I think it would have been possible to build a complete machine from
> them. A set of planes was stocked for each flight, but not unpacked
> until needed. The Equipment Officer was responsible for running the
> store and was assisted by a technical stores sergeant, a sergeant, a cor-
> poral and two airmen. The headquarters stores' lorries were available
> for moving all the gear. Each flight carried two spare engines, making
> six in all for the squadron. We were expected to keep at least four of
> them completely serviceable, which meant they were going through
> the station workshop all the time. Of course, in France they were
> only temporary workshops made up from the workshop lorries allo-
> cated to each flight, including the Headquarters. I used to park the
> four in a square and work in the centre; the sailmakers made a huge
> tent which completely covered the enclosed area. Each lorry had a ten
> horse power motor, driving a generator, with an output of 110 volts.
> We also had a lathe and a grinder, together with a little hand-operated
> shaping machine that we managed to "scrounge" in France.[64]

The highest stores priority was reserved for items needed for immediate minor
repairs on unserviceable airplanes, engines or motor vehicles. These were ordered
from the APs (via the Wing) by telegram and had priority over all other demands,
generally being delivered direct to the squadron. Components to repair damaged
aircraft were provided from squadron stores or, if not available, from the AP and
collected by the squadron. Ordinary stores and spare parts (to bring the squadron
equipment up to scale) were ordered on a fortnightly basis.[65] Together with the
inevitable specialist sections (wireless, photographic, armament, stores, and so on)
and support staff, each squadron needed some 190 ground personnel and forty-
five vehicles to keep it in the field.[66] The latter included provision not only for the
transportation of tents and hangars, but also for a wide range of mobile facilities,
including machine shops, wireless vans, generators, darkrooms, and so on. Moving
this number of personnel and their specialist equipment safely across the poor roads
of northern France presented a significant challenge, but the RFC demonstrated a
high degree of mobility in routinely relocating its squadrons, notwithstanding the
lack of prepared airfields and the limited availability of suitable accommodation and
other infrastructure.

The flexibility of the overall system was such that it was able to take on additional responsibilities, including the supply of air ammunition from 1917 onwards, as well as greatly expanded salvage, stores, and transportation capabilities. This was achieved by the simple expedient of adding individual specialist sections to the depots. Thus, in October 1917, when the volume of new aircraft deliveries (then averaging four hundred a month) and the quantity of repair and salvage work were beyond the capabilities of the depots, the existing repair sections were separated from their parent aircraft depots and expanded into Airplane Supply Depots (ASDs) responsible solely for aircraft receipt, issues, and repairs. This left the depots to concentrate purely on the receipt and issue of aeronautical spares and the reception, repair, and issue of motor transport.[67]

At the same time, it was decided to create a strategic transport reserve by withdrawing a proportion of the vehicles issued to the APs and squadrons to form a Reserve Lorry Park (RLP) attached to each brigade—arrangements that more than proved their worth during the RFC's desperate but largely successful redeployment in the face of the German 1918 offensive.[68] These developments marked the last significant changes to the logistic system before the creation of the RAF. By August 1918 and the final Allied offensives, the RAF's logistic arrangements had evolved significantly since 1917. The most notable changes were the introduction of the ASD and RLP, but just as importantly the organization had expanded to support almost twice as many aircraft.

To enable a better understanding of the role of the RFC's logistic system on the western front, four aspects will be examined more closely: the issue of aircraft; the salvage of aircraft and aero-engines; stores management, including the supply of aviation fuel; and the role of the headquarters staffs. Other functions will be addressed in subsequent chapters—in the context of the logistic system's contribution to the RFC's operational effectiveness.

The issue of airplanes was arranged directly between HQ RFC and the frontline squadrons. This procedure saved time, but it relied on the ability of the headquarters staffs to maintain an accurate and comprehensive picture of the disposition and state of every aircraft and aero-engine on the western front. This in turn depended on collecting and updating copious amounts of data. A card index was created for every individual aircraft or engine issued to the BEF. It was the sole task of a clerk to keep this up to date. Each card recorded the detailed movement of the item, including arrival from England, issue to a squadron or move to a depot. It also included the date of striking off from squadron strength (as a result of air combat, accident, and transfer to a depot or return to England).[69] By the armistice, this system provided a detailed picture of more than 3,500 aircraft and 5,500 engines, but it depended entirely on the receipt of daily returns from the depots, identifying aircraft on charge and their state ("serviceable," "ready in three days," "ready in seven days," and "still under repair"), fortnightly returns from squadrons recording the serial number and status of every airplane and engine on charge, daily casualty returns from squadrons, and fortnightly returns from the ERS. Detailed instructions were provided to squadrons, wings, and brigades on the proper compilation of casualty reports with a particular emphasis on accuracy and timeliness.[70] Separate arrangements were also made to record the substantial number of engines in transit.[71] During offensive operations, the task of issuing replacement aircraft became a fulltime job for the relevant staff officer, who had little time to leave his office.[72]

> When a squadron had a machine damaged or missing, they telegraphed or telephoned direct to QA1 [who] had a table in front of him showing exactly what aeroplanes were serviceable in each ASD [and] would then allot an aeroplane by number as a replacement, decide whether it should be fetched by the squadron or flown out by one of the ASD pilots, and, in any case, inform the squadron what he had done, issue orders to the depot and confirm by telegram, a copy of this telegram being sent to the Brigade Equipment Officer. This method worked exceedingly quickly and machines frequently arrived at squadrons three to four hours after their original one had been damaged or was known to be missing. When there was no fighting going on, this system was conducted by ordinary letter correspondence in which case machines generally took about 48 hours to get to squadrons after the casualty had occurred.[73]

A critical element in responding rapidly to engineering problems or incipient spares shortages was the proactive work of the headquarters logistic staffs in identifying issues as early as possible. Squadrons were encouraged not only to provide detailed information on faults and breakages, but also to suggest modifications (where possible accompanied by sketches and the particulars of any tests carried out).[74] The general officer commanding (GOC) led from the front in this respect. Maurice Baring's diary reveals that, during his frequent tours of the front line, Trenchard was concerned as much about logistic problems as operational matters. For example, on 17 May 1916 Trenchard travelled to both No. 1 AD at St-Omer and several frontline squadrons.[75] Among the topics discussed was the shortage of interrupter gear, the fitting of wireless sets, alterations to the pilot's seat in the Nieuport, and difficulties with the Monosoupape engine. A flurry of wires and instructions followed detailing corrective actions to be taken or engineering investigations to be put in hand. Reading Maurice Baring's diary, it is difficult not to feel a sense of urgency and energy generated by Trenchard—directed at any and every technical problem encountered in France. This very visible intervention in the logistic process was echoed by regular liaison between the depots and the squadrons, as well as visits from technical officers working for the War Office and Ministry of Munitions seeking feedback on production standards and possible modifications.

> During the greater part of the year [1916], and in addition to my duties at the depot, I acted as a liaison officer between headquarters of

formations, aircraft parks, squadrons and the depot. I visited these regularly and thus the depot was in regular touch with any difficulties or
shortages which existed at a time when new types and modifications
were so frequent that supply was more complicated than at present. At
the depot we were able to realise the difficulties and needs of the units
and to make provision accordingly. Ideas were exchanged on all matters of equipment, improvements suggested and we were able to more
accurately gauge future requirements and forestall possible shortages.[76]

A visit to Nos. 1 and 2 ADs in France and the Southern Aircraft Repair Depot
(SARD) at Farnborough, carried out between April and May 1917 by the deputy assistant director of Military Aeronautics, resulted in a twenty-page report that
identified five improvements, which would increase the number of machines available in the field:

- Reducing the time elapsed between the issue of a modification and its
  introduction.
- Providing early advice to the depots and squadrons on the extent to
  which a modification would affect interchangeability.
- Providing feedback to designers on defective construction.
- Preparing interchangeability lists between different machines.
- Establishing stock and an "odd job" capability within the depot airplane
  repair sections.[77]

The effectiveness of these visits led to the establishment of a Liaison Branch at the
War Office (and subsequently the Air Ministry) tasked with expediting the supply
of stores and other equipment. Outstanding demands for urgently required stores
were subject to a special "War Office Hastener." When a specific spare was needed
to make an aircraft or motor vehicle serviceable in the field, the depots were able to
indent directly through the War Office. A dedicated liaison officer maintained daily
contact by telephone with the equipment staffs at HQ RFC and also visited in person
fortnightly to discuss the progression of demands.[78] The functioning of the various
depots and their contribution to the RFC's operational effectiveness will be assessed
in later chapters. However, it is sufficient to say that the depots represented the logistic
system's center of gravity. They operated as strategic warehouses within an integrated
supply chain, providing the vital link between industry and the front line, preparing
aircraft for the squadrons, and incorporating the latest modifications while allowing
the Ministry of Munitions' production lines to operate at maximum efficiency. "In
France we would continually be finding some essential or desirable alteration to aeroplanes or engines. But if this was introduced during the process of manufacture, much
delay in output would be caused, because the factories concerned being laid out on a
production basis could not make any change rapidly. We got over this to some extent
by making modifications at our own depots in England or in France."[79]

This process of "standardization" was the foundation of operational capability in that it allowed the RFC to sustain a fighting edge in the face of the rapid tactical and technical evolution experienced on the western front. The utility of the depots was such that they continued to grow in scale and capability as the RFC's frontline strength expanded. Indeed, new depots and air parks were being created right up to the armistice.

Battlefields have always been scoured for booty but with war being waged on an industrial scale, employing valuable materials that could be recycled, this process became a more serious and systematic enterprise, driven by both opportunity and necessity. The importance of salvage and repair to the RFC cannot be exaggerated. The wastage rate at the beginning of the war was relatively low but by June 1916 it had reached 37 percent per month, rising to 58 percent during the Hundred Days.[80] In July 1917, it was calculated that to keep 1,800 aircraft in the field (approximately the size of the RAF in France at the armistice), 1,500 aircraft would have to be provided each month.[81] Every aircraft that could be repaired or rebuilt and every component or engine that could be salvaged helped to offset these massive losses and sustain operations.[82]

Over the seven months May–November 1917 a total of 3,160 RFC aircraft were struck off on the western front, while nearly 2,500 aircraft wrecks were received by the depots at Candas and St-Omer from their respective salvage sections (some 79 percent of all aircraft casualties).[83] In the same seven-month period of 1918, 5,300 aircraft were struck off but nearly 4,000 wrecks were received by the depots, 75 percent of the total. This is an impressive achievement, particularly as a substantial proportion of combat losses occurred east of the lines—literally beyond the reach of the salvage sections. In 1917, 20 percent of all aircraft were lost in enemy territory and 22 percent in 1918.[84] In other words, over the two years (1917–1918), 97–99 percent of all aircraft that were physically accessible to the salvage teams were retrieved.

Salvaging a wrecked machine—or at least its remains—was a relatively straight-forward exercise, as long as sufficient vehicles and labor were available. Processing the tons of assorted wreckage that accumulated at the depots was more difficult. Stripping, sorting, cleaning, identifying, assessing, repairing, refinishing, reassembling, and packing the thousands of individual components and piece parts that emerged represented a major industrial enterprise demanding careful management. For example, it required at least 135 man-hours to dismantle a R.E.8, including cleaning and packing into boxes.[85] Reference has already been made to the difficulties of obtaining sufficient spares for machines early in their operational life. Salvage offered one way to counter this deficiency. On the other hand, there was a balance to be struck between reducing a machine to spares and rebuilding it. Reconstruction consumed substantial effort and tied up spares that might otherwise be employed to repair many more aircraft:

> The rebuilding of machines of a new type for which there is a serious
> shortage of spares would appear to be entirely opposed to the interests

of the Service in as much as with a definite and serious shortage of spares the position is aggravated by increasing the number of machines, and consequently the demand for spares. More particularly is this so when it is remembered that the rebuilt machines are largely comprised of spares which should have been available for replacements, and that each machine so rebuilt would if disassembled have provided spares for a large number of machines. For with a given quantity of spares available only a certain number of machines can be kept in the air, and this number can only be increased by increasing the supply of spares.[86]

Salvage needed to be managed, therefore, as part of the wider supply chain. Spares recovery also had its limitations—some components were more easily reused than others. Engines were an obvious example, but there was always a ready supply of mainplane and fuselage struts as these suffered little damage in crashes. Shorter bolts survived better than longer ones, while nuts were obtained in roughly a two to one proportion against bolts because of damage to the threads. Metal fittings (spar boxes, wiring plates, joint sockets, etc.) were also recoverable in significant quantities, together with iron and brass wood screws. As a result, it was assessed that up to 25 percent of all demands for metal fittings could be met by a determined spares recovery program.[87]

The scale of the operation is reflected in the monthly production reports. In September 1918, the Salvage Section of No. 2 ASD received 121 wrecked aircraft (handing 62 over for reconstruction and dismantling 34) while sending 12,000 unserviceable fittings to England and 6,579 serviceable fittings to the Repair Park. It also provided 79,982 serviceable shackles, bolts, nuts, and turnbuckles together with 285 engine parts to the Repair Park and transferred 3,012 instruments, 355 guns, and 72 magnetos for repair by other specialist sections. In the same month, some 57 hundredweight of scrap aluminum and 18 hundredweight of copper was sent to England.[88] The salvage section of No. 1 ASD received 274 wrecks in the same month, handing 98 over for reconstruction and dismantling 47. Some 30,000 fittings and parts (both serviceable and unserviceable) were sent to the Repair Park or England, together with 23,000 turnbuckles, shackles, and bolts.[89]

Notwithstanding the RFC's comprehensive salvage and spares recovery program, the demand for new aircraft parts grew steadily throughout the war. By the beginning of September 1916, just over 20,000 tons of aircraft stores had been dispatched to France since the beginning of the war. This had risen to 34,000 tons by the end of 1916.[90] Speaking in 1920, Air Commodore Robert Brooke-Popham stressed that the single most important element in the upkeep of aircraft was the provision of spares. He drew a parallel with the Army where the loss of equipment did not necessarily impair efficiency, whereas "the failure of one small bolt, even the absence of a washer or split pin, may convert a whole aeroplane from a valuable weapon of war to a useless encumbrance on the ground."[91]

This was no sudden revelation. The RFC had understood well before the war that the provision of spares was a key driver in determining operational availability. In 1913, Mervyn O'Gorman, superintendent of the Royal Aircraft Factory at Farnborough, had written to the director of Military Training, seeking a weekly report on spares consumption to enable his staffs to forecast future demand.[92] To do so, however, the respective squadron commanders needed an "approved" list of spares, employing standard nomenclature and unique identification numbers. Drawings were prepared, therefore, that showed the standard parts for all aircraft currently in use. The schedule for the B.E.2 (a single page) totaled sixty-seven parts—excluding the engine and stay and control wires. By 1917, the equivalent schedule for the R.E.8 ran to forty pages and identified some two thousand separate line items of which about 20 percent were Aeroplane General Sundries (AGS).[93] This reflected not only increasing complexity but also the need (for reasons of efficiency and economy) to identify piece parts as well as parent assemblies. Aircraft-related spares did not make up the entire RFC inventory. The 1913 Mobilisation Stores Table identified a wide range of general equipment, tools, consumables, and motor transport spares to be held by a flying squadron. These items were issued on mobilization in addition to any "special to type" spares—relating to the particular aircraft design. The prewar stores table comprised 700 separate items, but had risen by October 1915 to some 2,400 items, of which 1,300 were for motor transport alone. By July 1917, the number had crept slightly higher to around 2,700 items.[94]

Over the course of the war, a total of 131,339 tons of aircraft stores were shipped to the BEF.[95] This included disassembled aircraft and aero-engines, although the majority of aircraft were flown to the depots. Even excluding these direct deliveries, the actual tonnage needed to support the flying squadrons in the field was greater than indicated because consumables, including ordnance, petrol, rations, clothing, and so on, were not recorded. The bulk of these items were provided by Army supply, augmented by specific arrangements for specialist stores together with local purchase.[96] Roughly two thirds of the RFC's supplies were landed via Rouen (including all airplanes) while the remainder were shipped via Boulogne.[97] The pattern of deliveries indicates that the logistic staffs at HQ RFC and the DMA were increasingly able to anticipate the consumption of aviation matériel. The opening of the Somme offensive was followed by a rapid increase in the flow of aviation stores, but thereafter the evidence suggests a conscious effort to pre-position spares and replacement aircraft. These buffer stocks meant that there was no surge in shipments following the opening of Third Ypres.[98] There is no direct evidence that these developments came about because of the changes wrought by Sir Eric Geddes in the management of the BEF's transportation but there seems little doubt that the introduction of statistical forecasting transformed the supply chain.[99] From late 1916, the RFC's logistic staffs set about calculating their supply needs in a methodical manner, using historic information and planned activity levels to predict wastage rates and likely spares demands—echoing the scientific management ("American practice") that underpinned the work of the Transport Mission to GHQ in 1916.[100] It does not appear that the RFC deliberately recruited those with experience in managing modern transportation systems—as did GHQ—but the logistic staffs undoubtedly included many individuals from an engineering or technical background likely to be comfortable with scientific methods. "The various Aircraft Depots and Aircraft Supply Depots in France number among their personnel some of the cleverest engineers yet produced in connection with aeronautics. Many of them were professional engineers before the war, though some were not, and they have learned all that is worth knowing about aircraft in the hard school of active-service experience."[101]

Some 26,000 tons (an average of five hundred tons per week) of aviation stores were delivered to the RFC during the course of 1917 (excluding food, clothing, armaments, and vehicles).[102] This total also excludes 1,079 aircraft delivered from England in crates, although at an average (dead) weight of 2.5 tons per machine, they represented the equivalent of just 10 percent of weekly deliveries.[103] There was a marked increase in the shipping tonnage allocated to the RFC in the months prior to Third Ypres (even allowing for the fact that some stores were carried in barges that travelled directly to the depots).[104] Starting in late April 1917, aviation stores received in France rose from 200 tons per week to a maximum for the year of 1,174 tons during the week ending 19/20 May 1917. The level fell thereafter (although rising immediately after Messines) until August 1917, when it stabilized at roughly 400 tons per week. There was a further rise during late October and early November—possibly reflecting the need to replace the stores dispatched at short notice to Italy to support the RFC squadrons redeployed to the Italian front. However, the overall pattern strongly suggests a concerted effort to prepare for the wastage and high consumption of Third Ypres. Although the surge in stores deliveries commenced during "Bloody April," it cannot be explained by the need to replace the losses in matériel experienced during the fighting. In the three months April–June 1917, just over two hundred aircraft were shipped to France in crates, equivalent to 40 tons per week or 5 percent of the total stores shipped.[105] The steady fall in stores shipped to France as the fighting progressed (and wastage grew) tends to support this analysis. By comparison, the tonnage of aviation stores received in 1916 rose week by week for the duration of the Somme fighting—suggesting that stocks required continuous replenishment.

The tonnage of aviation stores delivered in 1918 gradually increased through the course of the year, although there was a significant, but brief, hiatus in April as a result of the German 1918 offensive when shipments through Boulogne virtually ceased. During 1916, the weekly tonnage never exceeded 1,000 (deadweight) tons—a level reached only once in 1917. However, from June 1918 until the armistice weekly tonnage never fell below 1,000 tons. Indeed, in the week ending 26–27 October 1918 nearly 3,500 tons of aviation stores were shipped to France, compared to an average of 200 tons per week between August 1914 and August 1916.

Toward the end of the war, the stores handled by the RAF Port Detachments at Rouen, Le Havre, and Boulogne amounted to over 5,000 tons per month.[106] Some idea of the range and scale of the supplies required can be gained from the items handled by Rouen during the week ending 4 October 1918. A total of 737 tons (deadweight) was discharged, comprising tools, aero-engines, spares, instruments, ground equipment, machine tools, planes, propellers, vehicles, and crated aircraft. The latter included thirteen R.E.8s, ten DH9s, eight Sopwith Dolphins, four DH4s, and three S.E.5s. Onward shipping to the depots was either by canal or rail. Thus, 85 tons of spares and aero-engines were shipped by barge to Pont de l'Arche while a total of 158 (rail) trucks were dispatched to No. 1 AD and No. 2 AD, as well as to the Independent Force in the form of No. 3 AD (the latter comprising 126 trucks in three special trains).[107] It is also important to recognize that the RFC relied almost entirely on the BEF's transportation system within France to move its stores—at least from the ports to the railheads—irrespective of origin. Benefitting from an abundance of motor transport, but requiring a fraction of the daily tonnage needed to sustain the BEF, the RFC was well positioned to exploit the increasing capacity provided by the Transport Directorate under Geddes. The RFC's weekly shipments (in 1917) represented barely 0.3 percent of the weekly tonnage carried by the Northern Line of Communications and less than 1.3 percent of that carried by the Southern Line.[108]

While the armistice brought a cessation of hostilities, day-to-day requirements for stores and general supplies still had to be met. It was clearly impracticable to recover personnel and equipment rapidly to the United Kingdom, particularly while a final treaty was awaited. Indeed, the continuing advance into Germany over ever-lengthening lines of communication posed special difficulties for the RAF as well as the BEF.[109] Not surprisingly, the last overseas elements of the logistic organization to remain in place were the port depots. Rouen was still receiving stores as late as May 1919, although the bulk of shipments were in the other direction (from France to Southern England).[110] General salvage and repair work also continued well into 1919. No. 1 ASD received 146 aircraft and issued 145 in March, received 52 wrecks, dismantled 99 (salving the components and AGS such as turnbuckles, shackles, and bolts) and dispatched 23 tons of aluminum, 5 tons of brass, 110 tons of iron, and 2 tons of copper. Similar activities were under way at No. 2 ASD and the Base Motor Transport (MT) Repair depot.[111] Gradually, however, the great machine that had supported the RAF on the western front was dismantled, but not before every effort had been made to recover from the Continent some of the immense matériel resources that had been committed to the war.

The supply of aviation spirit presented particular problems. The increasing power of aero-engines demanded tight specifications as well as extreme care to avoid contamination, notably by water.[112] It was also discovered that only some sources were suitable for aviation use. The provision of sufficient quantities of petroleum products presented a significant obstacle in the planned expansion of the British Air

Services. Although the consumption of aviation spirit never matched the volume of petroleum products required by the British Army and the Royal Navy, it did provide a distinct challenge as a result of its special characteristics.[113] Responsibility for provision and distribution for all petrol, both for land and aviation use, fell to the ASC. The BEF's initial consumption of petrol was modest—around 250,000 gallons per month of which 10,000 gallons (or 4 percent) was for aviation purposes. However, the increase in motor transport on the western front saw consumption grow rapidly until, by the autumn of 1918, the BEF required in excess of 12 million gallons per month—of which some 1.5 million gallons (12.5 percent) comprised aviation spirit, all transported to France in two- and four-gallon tins.[114] The evident practical difficulties led to the decision to set up filling plants at Rouen and Calais in 1916—with petrol supplied in bulk from England.[115] Once the filling sites were in operation, the shipment of petrol in cans practically ceased, other than for aviation spirit which, because of quality issues, continued to be filled in England (at Portishead) until the spring of 1918, when this responsibility was also transferred to France, under AID supervision.[116] From early 1917, 3,000-gallon railway tank wagons and 600-gallon tank lorries were introduced for the larger fuel consuming units, although as it was rarely practicable to fill vehicles directly from the tank lorries, transport to the receiving units still required the employment of tins.[117] The only exception to this system was the provision of aviation fuel for the Independent Force. The average fuel load of the Handley Page 0/400 bomber was 1,400 gallons, and the 700 tins required to fill it occupied twenty men for no less than eight hours. Special arrangements were put in place that included inland tank storage, at aerodromes and railheads, and overhead tanks to fill aircraft rapidly under gravity—the whole operation taking less than an hour.[118] By the armistice, the RAF's monthly petrol consumption in the United Kingdom was averaging 1.2 million to 1.4 million gallons. Total consumption was, therefore, in excess of 9,500 tons per month, or £2–3 million a year.[119]

As engine power grew and aircraft operated under a wider range of conditions, so quality became a more problematic issue. At the beginning of the war, there was no specification for aviation spirit—normal motor gasoline was employed (the Air Board only issued a formal specification for aviation spirit in January 1918). Petrol supply to the western front was initially contracted through the Asiatic Petroleum Company until 1917, when the government assumed control of all petrol imports. In the latter part of the war, an increasing proportion of supplies came from America, although it was subsequently determined that aviation spirit from this source caused overheating of engines—through preignition and detonation. Petrol for other theaters was obtained from either the Asiatic Petroleum Company or the Anglo-Persian Oil Company. Unfortunately, the aviation spirit required in Mesopotamia had to be shipped in from either Egypt or Burma as the petrol distilled at Abadan, while entirely adequate for motor vehicles, caused aero-engines to run hot and seize up. As a result, over 10,000 gallons a month had to be imported

solely for use by the RFC.[120] The supply of aircraft lubricating oils presented an easier challenge, although the significant growth in the demand for castor oil for use in
rotary engines meant that by the middle of 1917 consumption had largely absorbed
the world's prewar output of castor seed. Additional production had to be developed in India and new sources created in America and the French colonies. While
never on the same scale as petrol, production of aircraft lubricating oil had reached
750,000 gallons per month by the armistice.[121]

The scale and expense involved in supplying the RFC, particularly when there
were competing demands for scarce resources, created a degree of organizational
sensitivity, exacerbated by the air agitation of 1916 that alleged incompetence and
waste in the administration of the RFC.[122] Maurice Baring clearly felt it important
to defend the RFC against such allegations. His comments, following a visit made by
Trenchard to No. 1 AD at St-Omer on 25 November 1916, are particularly reveal-
ing. After detailing more than forty technical issues addressed by the GOC, he adds:

> I have written down all these technical details, not from any hope that
> the reader will keep them clear in his mind, but because people used
> to talk glibly, and still do talk glibly, of the extravagance of the Flying
> Corps. The RFC were extravagant no doubt. Flying and everything
> to do with it is an extravagant matter. The pilot is extravagant, the
> squadron is extravagant, even the Equipment Officer, even the tech-
> nical Sergeant-Major was sometimes found to be extravagant, but a lot
> of this extravagance is inevitable; what nobody knew or realised was
> that a perpetual effort was being made to check useless extravagance;
> and that even superfluous magneto boxes and an unnecessary indent
> for lorry cushions were noted.[123]

Notwithstanding his role in stimulating many of the allegations regarding the
poor administration of the RFC, Charles Grey was particularly fulsome about the
efficient recycling of material in France:

> Those who regard the Army as purely wasteful may be interested
> to know that one part of the duties of certain equipment officers on
> active service is to collect all the components of wrecked aeroplanes,
> to sort them out into bins according to their various uses, to inspect
> them in detail to see whether they are fit for re-use, and to re-issue
> them as spares to the various squadrons. In this way some thousands of
> pounds worth of stuff is saved per week; let alone much valuable time
> which would otherwise be wasted in getting supplies from England
> to replace parts which, under a less efficient Service, would simply be
> scrapped.[124]

The overall management of the RFC and RAF logistic system on the western front for much of the war fell to Brigadier-General Robert Brooke-Popham,

universally known to friends and acquaintances as "Brookham."[125] Brooke-Popham, who had been attached to the Air Battalion in 1911 and was therefore a founder-member of the RFC, had rapidly grasped the attritional nature of air operations: "In war we must expect a casualty list of 100 percent every three months in men and material and must be prepared to replace all our pilots, observers and machines at this rate. . . . On service, it is doubtful if more than half the machines would be in a condition to go up at any one time."[126]

On the mobilization of the BEF, Brooke-Popham, who had commanded No. 3 Squadron since 1912, was appointed deputy assistant adjutant and quartermaster general (DAA & QMG). During the next few months he laid the foundations for the RFC's logistic organization in France while coping with unprecedented rates of consumption. Within three days of landing in France there had been nineteen crashes, leaving one pilot to wonder: "If we have all these accidents now what will it be like when we go into action?"[127] Major (later Air Chief Marshal Sir) John Salmond, who replaced Brooke-Popham in command of No. 3 Squadron, was fulsome about the "miracles" Brooke-Popham had performed in 1914 by ensuring the retreating squadrons were never short of spares or ammunition.[128] The difficulties of maintaining the RFC's aircraft serviceable during this period of constant movement, when aircraft and lorries became separated for days at a time, cannot be overestimated. On occasions it was only the presence of mechanics that flew with the pilots that allowed operations to continue.[129] Brooke-Popham's logistic baptism was relatively short—he left HQ RFC in November to take over the newly formed Third Wing; however, his period in frontline command was equally brief and he returned to the staff in May 1915.[130] Promoted to brigadier-general on 12 March 1916 and appointed deputy adjutant and quartermaster general (DA & QMG), Brooke-Popham was responsible for the RFC's combined logistic and personnel needs for the next eighteen months, until it became evident that the task was too great for a single individual.[131] From October 1917 the role was split, with Brooke-Popham focusing on supply issues—as deputy quartermaster general (DQMG)—and his erstwhile deputy, Colonel Francis Festing, promoted to brigadier-general with responsibility for personnel matters—as deputy adjutant general (DAG).[132] On the formation of the RAF, the QMG staffs became known as the "Equipment Branch" and the Adjutant General (AG) staffs the "Personnel Branch," the former comprising over twenty officers organized into seven sections with duties ranging from the allotment and repair of airplanes to motor transport, stationery, the supply of petrol, and technical matters of kites and parachutes.[133]

Brooke-Popham was due to return to London as controller of aircraft production in April 1918, but this move was postponed following the German offensive when his experience was urgently needed in France. In the event, he remained as DQMG until after the armistice, working alongside Festing to ensure the continued supply of men and machines to the front line.[134] An administrator of considerable ability, Robert Brooke-Popham enjoyed the trust of Trenchard and his successor

John Salmond.[135] The latter was particularly grateful for his achievements when the RAF's supply bases were threatened in 1918:

> The sagacity and foresight of Brigadier-General Brooke-Popham was equal to the emergency. The two offensives had led him to make arrangements in case a rapid evacuation became necessary. At the beginning of April all supplies for one month necessary to two brigades at our depot at St-Omer were made ready for immediate evacuation to Guines near Calais. Thus Guines would be in a position to supply all their demands without interruption. The final evacuation of St-Omer was completed by the middle of May and two nights later on the 18th it was bombed to destruction—although empty of stores.[136]

These views were echoed by J. M. Bruce in his authoritative study of the RFC. Noting the importance of Robert Brooke-Popham's prewar pronouncements on the potential for air warfare, he added: "Of incomparably greater historic significance was the profound but unrecognised influence he was to exert on the RFC in France during the 1914–1918 war. Just how greatly the RFC benefited from Brooke-Popham's incisive and intuitive grasp of its needs, his instinctive, intelligent and seemingly instantaneous reactions in dealing with the multitudinous problems and difficulties that were his inescapable portion as Deputy Adjutant and Quartermaster General, above all from his total devotion to these duties, has never been assessed or acknowledged."[137]

Brooke-Popham's involvement in the loss of Singapore in 1942 has colored subsequent assessments of his abilities—a process hastened by Duff Cooper's casual aside that "Brooke-Popham was sent out as a sort of buffer between the Services and the politicians, and he was a nice old buffer."[138] Contemporary press reports, even if well intentioned, were also less than flattering. "The tall, somewhat humourless officer with the high falsetto voice belying his virile organisational genius became a warning figure among the feather-pated statesmen of the day." "An administrator well known for the fiery chits in which he speaks his mind, but they never carry ill-will."[139] The same article added that "he was simply a man who will not tolerate slackness or inefficiency." Brooke-Popham's entry in the *Dictionary of National Biography* is also critical, observing that "his cautious, reserved, dreamy, though somewhat cold personality made him an intellectual rather than an inspirational leader." On the other hand, credit is given for his ferocious energy, industry, and administrative competence before concluding: "An able and sometimes brilliant professional officer, and a talented amateur diplomat, it was tragic for him that after his active career should have ended his reputation became closely linked with the greatest calamity ever to strike British arms. This was evidently unjust since he was allowed neither the time nor the power to solve a problem already beyond solution."[140]

Charles Grey, who knew Brooke-Popham better than most, was generous in his praise. "He was very successful in what is known today as 'procurement,' but I fancy that what puzzled most of those who worked with him was how he escaped working himself to death," adding that "no-one could have called Brookham a popular man. He would have hated to be considered so. But I have known few senior officers in the RFC or RAF who inspired so much affection or carried so much influence as he did, both with officers and men."[141] If there was any individual who can claim to have transformed the RFC's logistics in the way that Eric Geddes transformed the BEF's transportation arrangements it was Robert Brooke-Popham. His energy and grasp of detail fitted him to the role he had to play—qualities that were still apparent more than twenty years later. He served in France continuously from 12 August 1914 to the armistice, returning for a week in May 1915 for a tour of RFC stations.[142] For over three years he had sole responsibility for the RFC's logistic arrangements—during the critical formative months of 1914 and the great battles of the Somme, Third Ypres, and the Hundred Days campaign. Public recognition followed with the award of the Air Force Cross (AFC) (January 1919), Companion of the Order of St. Michael and St. George (CMG) (January 1919), and Companion of the Most Honourable Order of the Bath (CB) (June 1919). Equally telling, however, is the personal testimony of those that served with him. Lieutenant-Colonel L. F. R. Fell, chief engineer at the ERS, who joined the RFC as an EO in 1915, recalled fifty years later that: "It must not be overlooked that we had no opposition from anybody in authority. Brigadier-General Brooke-Popham did everything he could to encourage us and make sure that if we asked for anything it was provided without question and with the absolute minimum of delay."[143]

Major G. P. Bulman joined the Engine Branch of the AID in 1915 and remained with the organization throughout the war, responsible for improving the quality and speed of aero-engine production as well resolving reliability problems experienced on the western front. During this period he worked closely with Brooke-Popham:

> "Brookham" used to fly in every few weeks and from the pockets of his British Warm strewed our tables with bits of broken engine, recalling in that high pitched voice the number of the engine, how long it had run, the circumstances of the failure, and such ideas as he might have as to the cause, especially if it were the first of the kind. For that might mark the start of an epidemic demanding immediate investigation; or it might just be a freak. Thus failures which otherwise would have taken reams of Army forms and months of time to arrive, and possibly have been disregarded, were dealt with "forthwith," and sometimes remedial action taken within hours. What a grand man "Brookham" was. We were understanding friends until he died, almost forgotten in his last few years, and rejected.[144]

Wing Commander E. W. Havers also joined the RFC in 1915 as an EO, and was initially employed in the Aeroplane Repair Section of No. 1 AD at St-Omer, receiving and issuing aircraft. By the time he returned home in September 1919 he could claim to have commanded every type of RAF supply unit in France (including No. 10 AP, Advanced No. 2 AD, and No. 2 AD at Vron).[145] His views represent an experienced and authoritative perspective, based on four years of personal experience managing key elements in the RFC/RAF logistic system:

> Summarising my impressions [of the Equipment Supply Organisation in France] I feel the main one is the absolute excellence of the whole of the Stores and Equipment organisation at the head of which was Brigadier-General Brooke-Popham at HQ RFC. Under him at the various depots and parks were many officers, who had made their mark in civil life and brought a wide experience and judgment to bear. As a result, the whole system was sound, elastic, economical and never failed, so far as I am aware, to cater for every need. Moreover, efficiency marched with economy. Records were excellent and there was little waste. Only at the demobilisation periods did records break down, but under the circumstances then obtaining, the multiplication of work manifold whilst personnel were fast being demobilised, any system was bound to break down. Bearing in mind the complexity of the problem beyond any previously encountered in war, the enormous variety and type of spares ever changing and growing, and the necessity of hastily moving both depots in 1918, the smooth and efficient working of the whole must reflect the highest credit on those who devised, organised and developed it, and forms a model for future campaigns.[146]

Nearly ninety years have passed since these words were written, but there seems no reason to argue with their sentiments. The chapters that follow will demonstrate that the RFC's logistic organization was not only effective in delivering airpower on the western front but also established the basis for the support organization that sustained RAF operations throughout the Second World War.

THE SUPPLY OF AIRCRAFT AND AERO-ENGINES, 1914–18

CHAPTER 3

ACONTINUOUS SUPPLY OF AIRCRAFT AND AERO-ENGINES WAS FUNDAMENTAL TO the RFC's operational contribution to the western front. At one level, this was an issue of industrial capacity. At another, it was a question of political will. The rapid growth of the RFC, and the allocation of the resources required to sustain this expansion, represented an unprecedented national commitment to airpower. Although these ambitious plans were never fully realized, this was largely because of problems with the supply of raw materials, and the failure of the aero-engine industry to provide reliable engines of adequate power, rather than any lack of confidence in the air weapon or political concerns about affordability.

The expansion of the British aircraft industry between 1914 and 1918 is a story of mixed success. Substantial overseas purchases were required in the early years of the war but, by 1917, British companies were producing aircraft types, such as the Sopwith Camel and the Royal Aircraft Factory S.E.5a fighters, which were as good as any employed on the western front and in quantities that matched if not exceeded German production.[1]

Over the course of the war, more than 55,000 airframes and 41,000 aero-engines were produced, primarily for use by the RFC and RNAS, an impressive achievement given that in 1914 there was practically no aero-engine industry and a total of only eight aircraft contractors. This massive expansion in production inevitably

TABLE 2. BRITISH AIRCRAFT PRODUCTION, 1914–18

	1914	1915	1916	1917	1918
HOME AIRCRAFT PRODUCTION	245	1,933	6,149	14,748	32,018
OVERSEAS AIRCRAFT PURCHASES	11	748	938	1,141	213
PERCENTAGE FROM OVERSEAS	4%	28%	13%	7%	1%
GERMAN AIRCRAFT PRODUCTION	694	2,950	7,112	13,977	17,000

created problems, ranging from dilution of skilled labor to shortages of critical components. Even so, deliveries to the RFC had reached 120 aircraft per month by July 1916, rising to an average of 1,300 per month in 1917 and 2,700 per month in 1918.[2]

The aero-engine position was less happy. The provision of engines represented the most problematic logistic challenge faced by the RFC. The reasons were complex, but ultimately arose from the failure to develop any significant design and production capability in the years preceding the First World War. The majority of aero-engines, and ancillary components such as magnetos, in use with the RFC on the outbreak of war were either foreign-built or licensed foreign designs. Indeed, all of the aircraft that accompanied the BEF in August 1914 were powered by French engines. This legacy constrained the RFC's expansion and impeded operations. Ambitious plans for large quantities of more powerful and reliable aero-engines depended on a narrow industrial base, untested designs, and limited experience. Because it generally took twice as long to develop a new engine as a new aircraft, it was much more difficult to recover from the failure of the former. Unfortunately, an inability to produce sufficient quantities of powerful aero-engines characterized the British aircraft industry until the end of the war.[3]

The shortfall was partly made up by overseas purchases (largely from France) and partly by licensed manufacture of foreign designs, although this was still insufficient to achieve the planned expansion in the number of frontline squadrons and forced the RFC to employ aircraft types well beyond their planned out-of-service date. As a result, a significant proportion of aero-engines used by the RFC were foreign-sourced (never less than 25 percent), further complicating maintenance and supply arrangements.[4] At one stage, the difficulty in sourcing spares for French engines forced the Engine Repair Shops (ERS) at Pont de l'Arche to cannibalize defective engines in order to repair others.[5]

The history of the design and supply of aeronautical material for the RFC during the First World War can be divided into two distinct periods. During the first phase, from August 1914 to February 1917, the design of aircraft and aero-engines was the responsibility of the War Office, while during the second phase, from March 1917 until the armistice, design and production for both services was the responsibility of the Ministry of Munitions.[6] Prior to March 1917, aircraft and aero-engines were produced under two systems: either official designs (provided by the Royal

TABLE 3. BRITISH AERO-ENGINE PRODUCTION, 1914–18

	1914	1915	1916	1917	1918
HOME AIRCRAFT PRODUCTION	99	1,721	5,363	11,763	22,098
OVERSEAS AIRCRAFT PURCHASES	39	911	1,864	4,902	9,181
PERCENTAGE FROM OVERSEAS	28%	35%	26%	29%	29%
GERMAN AIRCRAFT PRODUCTION	848	5,037	7,822	11,200	15,542

Aircraft Factory) manufactured by contractors and subcontractors, or private designs produced in some instances with the assistance of technical officers provided by the Admiralty and War Office respectively.[7] When the RFC (and its constituent Naval and Military Wings) was formed, the Army already had the capability (in the form of the Royal Aircraft Factory) to design and build experimental aircraft. The Factory became accountable to the Equipment Branch of the DMA while its inspection and testing roles were transferred to the newly formed Aeronautical Inspection Department (AID). The Factory played a central role in the development of aircraft for the RFC, particularly the B.E.2 series, which was ordered in substantial numbers in the early years of the war. In the last three months of 1916 over 30 percent of the total aircraft produced for the RFC were of this type, while the B.E.2c (equipped with the Factory's RAF1a engine) provided nearly 50 percent of airplanes in service on the western front in the summer of 1916.[8] It should be stressed that the Factory manufactured only a very few aircraft—the majority of its designs were built by contractors employing drawings and parts provided by the Factory. From the beginning of the war up to May 1916 the Factory produced just seventy-seven machines of its own design, whereas private contractors delivered over 2,100.[9]

While the Factory was dominant in the design of aircraft and aero-engines for the RFC, the Admiralty had successfully encouraged private enterprise. This ultimately led to complaints that the Factory was competing unfairly and impeding the development of effective fighting machines. These concerns, coupled with agitation about the high losses experienced in France, led to the establishment in March 1916 of a committee of inquiry into the organization and management of the Royal Aircraft Factory.[10] Before it had completed its work a further committee was established into the administration and command of the RFC.[11] The subsequent reports from both committees made it clear that there were few substantive concerns with either the Royal Aircraft Factory or the RFC.[12] Indeed, it was recognized how difficult it was to determine the equipment needs of such a young organization and that, while the B.E.2c and the RAF1a engine had their faults, they formed a valuable combination.[13] On the other hand, both reports criticized the failure to develop more powerful aero-engines. The Factory had in fact started to design a range of aero-engines immediately prior to the war, following the failure of a naval and military competition intended to foster private designs. One of these designs developed into the RAF1a and RAF4a series of engines while the others were handed over to civilian contractors to develop. Rolls Royce decided instead to develop its own design, which eventually led to the "Eagle" engine employed successfully later in the war. Nevertheless, a substantial proportion of British aircraft production continued to rely on French-supplied or French-designed engines, while efforts to develop more powerful British aero-engines were characterized by false optimism, delay, and failure.

Managing the supply requirements of the RFC proved to be a complex and challenging task from the very start of the war. Sefton Brancker, who served as director of air organization in the DMA, commented that it was "a story of a service whose function it was to keep pace with demands which increasingly expanded and deviated from their expected path."[14] The task in the early months was quite clear: there were insufficient airplanes and aero-engines, a shortage only matched by the shortage of pilots. The general position improved through 1915 with an increasing number of contractors able to undertake the manufacture of aircraft and aero-engines supported by a rapidly growing pool of subcontractors, although there was a continuing concern about manufacturing standards. In the case of Daimler, the War Office was able to source for the first time both the aircraft (B.E.2c) and the engine (RAF1a) from a single contractor.[15] Even so, there were never enough aircraft or pilots to sustain the planned expansion of the RFC or, as 1916 progressed, sufficient numbers of modern types capable of meeting the improved machines being deployed by the GAS. In early January 1917, Trenchard made representations to Brancker about the vital necessity of more and better aircraft. "Day after day, during the spring of 1917, I [Brancker] wrote giving him some fresh disappointment through our failures to come up to the programme."[16] Unfortunately, the very process of moving to new and improved designs slowed manufacturing output. It generally took three and a half to five months to change a factory over from one type to another. "No one who has not had actual experience of aeroplane production under pressure can even begin to grasp the endless troubles which must be faced in the development of each new type. Each slight failure or unexpected trouble brought in its train long lists of irksome modifications which irritated the manufacturer and held up output terribly. When these difficulties were intensified by labour troubles, as they often were, the responsibility of aircraft production was enough to drive anyone crazy."[17]

As already mentioned, the Admiralty had a rather different approach to procuring aircraft and aero-engines. Not only did they make greater use of private design, employing production officers based at the contractor's works, but they also employed a more relaxed system of inspection—relying largely on the contractor's own inspectors rather than an external, independent body such as the AID.[18] Competition between the Admiralty and the War Office over resources, conflicting priorities, and the failure to meet the growing needs of the Air Services led to the creation of an Air Board in May 1916 responsible, inter alia, for the coordination of the supply of aircraft material. This was followed, in November 1916, by the decision to allocate responsibility for aeronautical supply to the Ministry of Munitions (leaving design under the Air Board). Aircraft and aero-engine production became the responsibility of the controller of aeronautical supplies (Sir William Weir), who introduced significant changes in the system of procurement. The Army method of inspection was adopted together with the Admiralty preference for placing design responsibility on the contractors. The most important development, however, was the concentration on larger production facilities and the creation of national factories. However, the main obstacle still remained aero-engine capacity. An increase in production was facilitated by the Air Board's decision to reduce the number of different aero-engine and aircraft types through standardization, although this was not without risks—as the failure of the "Puma," "Arab," and "Dragonfly" engines demonstrated. Excessive reliance on these few untested designs resulted in severe delays to the replacement program and ultimately to the planned expansion of the RFC on the western front.

In June 1917 the War Cabinet sanctioned the increase of the RFC to two hundred service squadrons.[19] This came on top of an existing program, agreed in the summer of 1916, to expand the RFC to 106 service squadrons from the seventy service squadrons previously authorized.[20] The latter program had required the production of at least two thousand engines each month—an increase of 200 percent over existing production levels. It was recognized that the supply of aero-engines and the availability of skilled manpower remained problematic, but it was hoped that the increase in production rates already achieved by the Ministry of Munitions could be sustained through 1918 and that the necessary engines would be forthcoming. Plans were drawn up, therefore, for a monthly output of 3,500 aircraft and 4,000 aero-engines to allow for the increased size of the front line (and the higher wastage this would bring), together with an expanded flying training system to provide the additional pilots needed.[21] This program placed a premium on skilled labor at the very time that manpower was in ever greater demand and dilution levels (the proportion of unskilled to skilled labor) were already increasing.[22] It also exacerbated existing problems with the supply of components, such as magnetos and ball bearings, essential to aero-engine production. In the event, engine production would continue to lag behind the expansion in aircraft production, and the planned increase in service squadrons would not be achieved. As with aircraft, therefore, the repair of aero-engines became of the utmost importance in reducing the supply shortfall. Nevertheless, by August 1918 there were 4,200 aircraft in store without engines.[23]

The rapid expansion in aircraft production made quality control in materials and construction all the more important. The AID was critical to maintaining the required manufacturing standards, especially among the many new contractors and subcontractors. By the end of 1918 the organization had grown to over ten thousand strong, with staff employed at every major manufacturing works (including the Royal Aircraft Factory), depot, and park.[24] The scope of the AID's work included all aircraft and aero-engines produced for the British Air Services as well as supplies such as balloons, hangars, tools, raw materials, and fabrics. The AID also played an important role, together with the Factory, in creating a range of spares, known as Aeroplane General Sundries (AGS)—based around standard parts—designed by the Royal Aircraft Factory. The provision of AGS facilitated mass production and enhanced interchangeability—to the benefit of maintenance and repair.[25] The AID was proactive in assessing its contribution to the war effort—at home and abroad. For example, the AID's chief examiner for the Midland District, working closely with staff at Daimler responsible for the license-production of the RAF1a engine installed in the B.E.2c, visited five squadrons on the western front in April 1916 to determine whether the inspection methods employed by contractors were effective.[26] The answer was generally affirmative, although it was also clear that poor design, defective lubrication, and inadequate technical information adversely affected aero-engine availability and made the replacement of engines in the field more difficult than planned.

To understand how these supply issues impacted on the RFC's logistic system, the remainder of this chapter will focus on two case studies: the development and production of the R.E.8 two-seater artillery cooperation aircraft, and the development and production of the (French) Hispano-Suiza aero-engine and its employment in the Sopwith Dolphin single-seat fighter.

The design, development, and deployment of the Royal Aircraft Factory R.E.8 provides an instructive example of the challenges faced by industry in the effort to achieve mass production while meeting the RFC's need for reliable, efficient fighting machines. As the R.E.8 provided the mainstay of the corps reconnaissance and artillery cooperation squadrons from Third Ypres to the armistice, its availability and performance had a direct bearing on the RFC's support to the BEF at the most critical periods of the war. The R.E.8 was also the most numerous type supplied to the RFC on the western front—a total of 2,139 machines being delivered in 1917 and 1918.[27]

The operational requirement for the R.E.8 first emerged in the autumn of 1915 when HQ RFC formulated a request for a new aircraft type to replace the B.E.2c.[28] The design was allocated to the Royal Aircraft Factory, partly because of the limited capabilities then existing in the private sector and partly because it was felt that Farnborough was best placed to develop a successor machine using the Factory's new 12-cylinder, 140-hp RAF4a engine. It has been argued that had the aero-engine position been better, the Armstrong Whitworth FK8 design (powered by the 6-cylinder, 160-hp Beardmore engine) might have been preferred to the R.E.8 on the basis of its better flying characteristics.[29] Under operational conditions there was actually little to choose between the two types.

Basic design work on the R.E.8 was completed early in 1916, with the initial machines being ordered on 25 March 1916. The first two examples flew on 17 June and 5 July respectively.[30] The second prototype was rapidly dispatched to France where it was extensively tested at No. 2 Aircraft Depot (Candas) using frontline crews. These trials revealed the need to incorporate a number of modifications, some being undertaken by the depot's engineers and the details passed to the War Office and Farnborough where the aircraft returned on 12 August 1916.[31] Because of the urgency in finding a replacement for the B.E.2c, the initial production batch of fifty R.E.8s had been ordered from the Factory in April 1916—before the prototypes had flown.[32] Delivery of the first production machines was delayed, however, by the need to incorporate the modifications identified in France. As a result, the first R.E.8 was not submitted for acceptance by the AID until 13 September 1916.

Meanwhile, orders for 1,200 aircraft had been placed with three manufacturers—suggesting considerable faith in a type that had not yet seen operational service.[33]

Notwithstanding the controversy over the Factory's role in undertaking production as well as design, there is little doubt that contract aircraft could never have reached the western front as quickly as Factory-built machines. Even without this contribution, the Factory's efforts were essential in supporting the contractors' production lines, either through the provision of drawings, tooling, and spares or the supply of modification kits.[34] By early 1917 the rapidly growing inferiority of the B.E.2c was such that HQ RFC agreed to waive the need to incorporate all the required modifications prior to delivery. Even so, by 24 February 1917, there were only nine R.E.8s in France (of which five were still in cases), with fourteen en route and fifteen ready to fly out. On the other hand, a further forty machines were expected to be ready in fourteen days.[35] The planned schedule of R.E.8 deliveries continued to prove optimistic. A combination of factors was to blame, including a shortage of raw materials, delays in the supply of components, industrial action, and essential modifications—operational service had revealed that the undercarriage needed strengthening (new drawings were completed by the Factory in May 1917), as did the center-section struts.[36] Even so, the number of R.E.8-equipped artillery observation and army cooperation squadrons grew rapidly through 1917 and the type was able to play a decisive role in the Third Battle of Ypres (sixteen squadrons by August 1917).[37]

Once again, however, it was the supply of aero-engines that proved most troublesome. As a rule of thumb, twice as many aero-engines as aircraft were required in an operational theater. A pool of surplus aero-engines was essential to provide immediate replacements and to make up for engines unavailable because of scheduled maintenance or repairs (engine repairs also took much longer to complete than aircraft repairs). This was counterbalanced by the fact that aero-engines were more likely to survive crashes and other causes of wastage. Even where an airframe was totally written off, it was often possible to salvage the engine for repair and reissue.[38] It is significant that of the 174 RAF4a engines received by the ERS between February and August 1917, 70 percent (121 engines) had failed as a result of crashes.[39]

The paradox was that while the overall pool of aero-engines needed to be larger than the pool of airframes—to sustain a given number of frontline squadrons—the replenishment rate was substantially less. It was assessed in early 1917 (for planning purposes) that eighty aero-engines were required for each squadron sent to France (employing air-cooled engines) with a subsequent wastage rate of 7 percent per month. The equivalent figures for aircraft were 100 percent of establishment (eighteen to twenty-four aircraft per squadron) with a wastage rate of 50 percent per month.[40] On this basis, an individual frontline squadron required approximately ten aircraft and six engines each month to make good wastage.[41] These predictions proved to be a reasonable approximation to the actual position, with an average of forty to sixty engines on charge for each squadron through most of 1917 and 1918.

At the time of the armistice, fifty-four RAF4a engines were held on the western front for each R.E.8 squadron.[42] In effect, there were as many RAF4a engines in store or in the repair pipeline as fitted to frontline aircraft.

The overall availability of the RAF4a (from a manufacturing perspective) was generally good for all of 1916 and well into 1917.[43] Substantial numbers of engines had been ordered as early as 1915 from Daimler and Siddeley-Deasy. However, toward the end of 1917 production delays were being reported by both contractors as a result of aero-engine shortages.[44] By the end of 1917, cumulative airframe production was approaching total engine production—a situation that would worsen through the remainder of 1918. This position had come about because of continuing delays with the Bristol Fighter, the planned successor to the R.E.8 (and FK8), created by problems with the former's Sunbeam Arab engine.[45] Considerable faith had been placed in this new design and major orders (over two thousand machines by February 1918) had been placed in the belief that substantial quantities of the Arab would be available from late 1917 onwards (although just a handful had been built by Christmas 1917 rather than the scheduled 1,800). In the event, quantity production did not begin until spring 1918. During the early summer of 1917 there was no desire to order further aircraft that would likely prove surplus to the needs of the western front. Indeed, such was the general optimism regarding the Bristol Fighter that some existing R.E.8 contracts were cut back. For example, an order for two hundred R.E.8s, placed with Siddeley-Deasy on 1 May 1917, was reduced to only 150 machines just three weeks later.[46] In reality, all two hundred would be required from the company, who would then be asked to build a further 550 R.E.8s by the armistice.

It had been hoped by the Air Board that the Bristol Fighter could take on the corps squadron role from the spring of 1918. Indeed, it was still being argued— as late as summer 1917—that retention of the R.E.8 could not be justified, even though it would create a surplus of 1,500 RAF4a engines that had no airplanes to take them.[47] As the weeks passed, this timetable became increasingly improbable and by 29 August 1917 it had been agreed to defer replacement of the R.E.8 squadrons in France from March until September 1918 (while still replacing the five Armstrong Whitworth FK8 squadrons). This eased the aero-engine position (freeing up Sunbeam Arabs for other programs), but it also meant that new production would be needed to sustain the R.E.8 on the western front—to make good attrition and general wastage. Urgent contracts had to be placed—and in significantly greater quantities than the previous year—including over 1,200 machines ordered from three manufacturers in September alone.[48] Such was the continuing uncertainty, however, that a number of the contracts were described as "similar to the R.E.8 type," presumably anticipating a decision to change production to the Bristol Fighter if the engine position improved.[49]

Further difficulties arose from the shortage of raw materials, particularly wood. Once the United States entered the war, much of the timber previously obtained from

North America was diverted to support the expansion of the American Air Services. A great deal of effort was expended to secure alternative sources of good quality, dry timber—not always successfully. For example, some two thousand replacement wooden undercarriages for the R.E.8 were scrapped because AID inspectors found them deficient—a problem exacerbated by the kiln-drying process employed to "season" the timber. Eventually, the problem was resolved by employing ash rather than silver spruce.[50] A few weeks later, there was concern about the delivery of self-sealing petrol tanks—orders for one thousand had been placed in April and May yet only nine had been delivered by the beginning of July. In this instance, it turned out that the delays had partly been caused by the need to prepare new drawings incorporating essential modifications.[51] Coordinating the myriad contracts and subcontracts presented the Ministry of Munitions and the Air Board with a difficult juggling act, made worse by the number and pace of modifications driven by operational experience, design flaws, and material shortcomings. The scale of the modification program was such that a formal system was introduced from April 1917 to enable the necessary work to be prioritized on the basis of urgency (ranging from vital through essential to desirable). For the R.E.8, the relevant modification sheets, issued to the depots by the DMA, record seventy-four separate modifications (up to June 1918), evenly balanced between essential and desirable.[52]

The 1917 planning calculations had anticipated monthly wastage on a 24-aircraft corps reconnaissance squadron of 50 percent, meaning that 160–180 replacement R.E.8s would be needed each month (depending on actual squadron strength), beyond those required to form new squadrons.[53] Average wastage between March and September 1918 was actually closer to 130 machines per month (excluding May).[54] With new deliveries averaging only one hundred aircraft each month, this left a deficit of thirty aircraft per month.[55] In the event, frontline strength was successfully maintained at a little over three hundred machines throughout 1918—but only because the depots were able to reconstruct sufficient numbers of damaged and salvaged aircraft.

The depots' aircraft reconstruction program was to some extent preplanned—in that it was prioritized to address anticipated shortfalls in new production. This "rough-cut" plan would be successively refined as the actual position became clearer. Thus, in June 1918 the Air Ministry's director of aeronautical equipment (Brigadier-General Cecil H. Whittington) wrote to Brigadier-General Brooke-Popham at HQ RFC proposing adjustments to the program of reconstruction at the depots in the coming six months. One of the changes was to increase the planned monthly reconstructions of the R.E.8 because of the "grave uncertainty in regard to the Bristol Fighter Arab."[56] The depots' role as a flexible and responsive tool to overcome logistic uncertainty was articulated by Brooke-Popham in a note circulated in early 1918: "It should be impressed on all ranks that the object of a Repair Park is not merely to produce a big total of machines, but to turn out the greatest possible number of the particular types which are short, either owing to excessive casualties, or a shortage from England. It is therefore often necessary for the Repair Park to leave machines half-finished and turn over and concentrate on one or two particular types, thereby upsetting the whole of the Repair Park programme. It is quite realised that this reduces the total output of machines."[57]

The R.E.8 has subsequently gained an unfortunate reputation yet it is clear that those who flew the machine regarded it highly. The qualities of the aircraft were later debated in the pages of *Popular Flying* (under its editor W. E. Johns) where it was ultimately conceded that the aircraft's good points outweighed its vices.[58] There is no doubt, however, that the R.E.8 was ill-suited to the training role when it was prone to stall in the hands of an inexperienced pilot. Modifications to the rudder and improved fire protection largely obviated the more obvious faults and thereafter the type gave excellent service until the very end of the war. However, if it had not been for the failure of the Arab-powered Bristol Fighter, the R.E.8 would have been replaced in the corps squadrons during the spring of 1918. As it was, the R.E.8 soldiered on until the armistice, even though its performance was increasingly pedestrian in the face of faster and more maneuverable German fighters. The general shortage of aero-engines and the belated decision to extend the operational life of the R.E.8 (and other types) had a major impact on the RFC's logistic system. The salvage and repair of aero-engines became an imperative rather than simply desirable—if the corps squadrons were to continue to operate. Although efforts were made to expand engine repair in the UK by employing civilian firms, the output fell short of expectations, forcing greater reliance to be placed on repairs carried out by service units.[59] In response, in-theatre engine repair facilities were expanded and the number of salvage parties increased.

> Every time a machine crashed near the lines a party had to be taken up to get it. This job always fell to the poor old Technical Sergeant Major. More often than not the machine turned out to be actually between the lines, in no-man's land! We used to have to get a rope attached to the aircraft and then drag it into our trenches, with the infantry cursing us for drawing the Hun's attention. By this time the plane was a bit of a mess but it wasn't the airframe we were interested in: it was the engine.[60]

In-theatre repair capacity was increased substantially by expanding ERS facilities and manpower. Whereas a total of 2,561 aero-engines were repaired in 1917, a total of 3,320 were repaired in the subsequent ten months (up to the armistice).[61] Coincidentally, operational wastage also fell—at least for the corps squadrons. The proportion of combat losses suffered by the latter fell from 30 percent in 1917 to 17 percent in 1918.[62] Even so, the supply position of the RAF4a continued to be finely balanced. When Brigadier-General Brooke-Popham proposed in June 1918 to give up repair of the engine in France he was advised by Brigadier-General Alfred Huggins, controller aircraft at the Air Ministry, that "I do not like the idea of being solely dependent on one source of supply for an engine which is required in such large numbers. If there is any other engine the repair of which you could reduce, instead of the RAF4a, I should prefer you to continue on the latter type."[63] In the absence of a replacement for the R.E.8, the RAF4a engine would remain in large-scale use on the western front until the end of the war.

The importance of foreign aero-engines in sustaining British aircraft production has already been mentioned. The most significant of these was the Hispano-Suiza. The story of its development and production illustrates the particular problems encountered in providing reliable, high-power aero-engines. The failure of the British aero-engine industry had a direct impact on operations but the purchase of foreign aero-engines was not without its own problems. The RFC had high hopes of the Hispano-Suiza, especially when installed in the Sopwith Dolphin, but the potential benefits were compromised by a series of shortcomings.[64]

The adoption of a foreign design by the RFC reflected the French engine's remarkable performance as much as the parlous state of the British aero-engine industry. The Hispano-Suiza offered a significant improvement in power-to-weight ratio compared to existing water-cooled aero-engines, including those still in development, as well as better fuel consumption and sustained performance over a wider flight envelope—particularly at altitude.[65] Ultimately, over seven thousand examples of the Hispano-Suiza (including the Wolseley-built Adder, Python, and Viper versions) were purchased for use by the British Air Services.[66] The predominance of the Hispano-Suiza and the importance of its operational contribution can be judged from the number used on the western front and the range of aircraft types it powered. In June 1917 the RFC's aero-engine holdings in France consisted of some 2,100 aero-engines, of which just 5 percent were Hispano-Suizas. A year later the Hispano-Suiza (and its variants) represented nearly 30 percent of all frontline aero-engines.[67] By the armistice, the RAF held nearly four thousand examples on charge of which 1,250 were on the western front and a further one thousand under repair.[68]

The 8-cylinder water-cooled Hispano-Suiza first ran in early 1915. Its very high power to weight ratio was the result of employing cast aluminum. Porosity problems with the aluminum were resolved by enameling inside and out.[69] The first RFC order (for fifty engines) was placed in August 1915 on the recommendation of Lieutenant Colonel (later Brigadier-General) Brooke-Popham.[70] The engine's innovative design meant that volume production did not get under way for some time, the first engines from the RFC's order not being delivered until August 1916. The initial version was rated at 140 hp, but this was soon raised to 150 hp. Admiralty officials were so impressed with early examples that they argued for the purchase of eight thousand engines to be split between Britain, France, and Russia, with Britain providing the raw materials.[71] The Air Board was initially reluctant but eventually agreed, advancing the necessary funding (£2 million) for the construction of a new factory to be managed by the French manufacturer Emile Mayen. Meanwhile, Wolseley obtained a license to build a development—the Python. Fitting higher-compression pistons allowed power to be increased to 180 hp at 2,100 rpm (license-built by Wolseley as the Python II).[72]

The most widely produced Hispano-Suiza was the 200 hp type 8B, which featured high-compression pistons and a geared drive.[73] It was this engine and its sub-types that were fitted to the Dolphin, although difficulty in obtaining the necessary aero-engines from France meant it was initially proposed that the prototypes be fitted with the Wolseley version. The slow supply of aero-engines from France—only five were available by 25 September 1917—delayed production deliveries still further such that the first machines were not with the RFC until November 1917. Continuing delays in the supply of aero-engines constrained production rates throughout 1918 such that the deliveries peaked in May (224 machines) and fell in the following months, delaying the planned deployment of new squadrons.[74]

Persistent manufacturing problems with the gear train—in part due to the use of air-hardened steel coupled with high tooth pressure—led to the development of a de-geared version (type 8Ba) early in 1918. This removed the gear drive but required a modified crankshaft. Other changes involved a different radiator intake, repositioned propeller, and a modified gun bracket. In light of the problems experienced with the type 8B, the Ministry of Munitions' Progress and Allocation Committee (chaired personally by Sir William Weir) expressed early interest in acquiring examples of the de-geared engine.[75] Machines fitted with this version would become known as the Dolphin III, although production delays meant that most Sopwith Dolphins employed on the western front were fitted with the geared type 8B engine.

More than 49,000 engines were built by Hispano-Suiza and its licensed manufacturers in England, France, Italy, and Russia. It was one of the most important aero-engines produced during the First World War and was undoubtedly the bedrock of Allied airpower for the last eighteen months of the war. According to the RFC/RAF official history, the decision to order large numbers of the Hispano-Suiza from both British and French sources saved the supply situation in 1918.[76] Nevertheless, the high compression ratio and geared drive of the type 8B created significant reliability problems. This manifested itself in many ways—necessitating considerable care in the operation of the engine by pilots and ground crews. Frequent removals were common and the time between overhauls was often less than the sixty hours advertised—compared to the one hundred hours of the Rolls Royce Eagle.[77]

The National Archives holds a lengthy series of files (twenty-three in total, more than any other engine type) detailing the problems faced by squadrons operating the Hispano-Suiza (including the Wolseley-built Viper).[78] The difficulties recorded are numerous, as are the modifications and alterations that followed. Changes made to improve performance and reliability included: revised test procedures; different metal specifications; better build standards; improved quality control; employment of special tools; modified oil, fuel, and water filters; and stricter manufacturing and overhaul clearances. Many of these issues appear to have stemmed from the large number of firms involved in license production. The scale of the problem led Headquarters RAF (HQ RAF) to initiate a series of monthly meetings, attended by representatives from the ERS—responsible for the repair and overhaul of aero-engines in France—and from the depots, brigades, and frontline squadrons operating the Hispano-Suiza or Viper.[79] In opening the inaugural meeting on 18 June 1918, Brigadier-General Brooke-Popham commented that "like other engines the Hispano has its faults—faults in design, faults in manufacture, and faults arising in use," but he then went on to add that "with all its faults the Hispano was a really good engine. . . . If anyone got despondent about the Hispano they had only got to look at other engines."[80]

The defects experienced largely arose from excessive vibration and poor or faulty lubrication. In view of the engine's light weight and high power it was possible to overstress the components by operating at high rpm or tolerating irregular running. Low oil pressure was often an early warning that all was not well. Special pressure checks were therefore instituted for engines when taken on charge. Other measures involved daily oil changes and careful inspection of filters for signs of incipient failure. A report issued in April 1918 by HQ RAF stated that the type 8B continued to be the most troublesome of the Hispano-Suiza engines and was inclined to shake to pieces due to the harsh running of the reduction gear. As a result, it averaged a very short life and required a large amount of attention to keep serviceable.[81]

A number of modifications were introduced to overcome these problems. Some changes could be implemented on the squadrons, but many could only be incorporated at the ERS. By 30 May 1918 the latter had overhauled nearly one thousand Hispano-Suiza engines. More rigorous pass-off tests were also introduced to ensure that engines were not released to the squadrons where there was any sign of vibration, knocking, misfiring, oil leaks, overheating, air leaks, bad carburetion, or a drop in oil pressure. As a result the front line came to regard ERS-supplied engines as being as good as, if not better, than those supplied by the manufacturers.[82]

All of this may seem a significant burden, but a report describing a visit to squadrons on the western front in August 1918 reveals a more positive side to the picture.[83] Compared with No. 40 Squadron operating the S.E.5a (fitted with the Viper), No. 79 Squadron seemed largely content with the Hispano-Suiza in its Dolphins, stating that the troubles they had previously experienced were being overcome by experience or by modifications introduced by the ERS. The squadron had issued instructions that, if followed, offered one hundred hours between overhauls. Special procedures had also been instituted on a daily and post-flight basis, while further checks were carried out after every six hours' flying, including the emptying and thorough cleaning of the tank and sump of old oil, changing the plugs, and cleaning the distributor leads. Checks were also conducted after twenty and fifty hours respectively. Finally, the engine of every new machine that was received was subject to an extensive inspection program that included checking the filters and ignition timing, changing the oil and sparking plugs, and replacing the carburetor.[84]

Effective as these measures were, there is no doubt that the Hispano-Suiza caused the frontline squadrons significant problems and required substantial engineering effort to maintain serviceability. Simply fitting the engine required greater effort than earlier types. For example, it took 55–60 man-hours to install, run up, and test the 80 hp Le Rhone fitted to the Sopwith Pup, compared with 120 man-hours for the 200 hp Hispano-Suiza fitted to the Sopwith Dolphin. Another difficulty was that the lack of special tools and parts necessitated the return to the ERS of engines that might otherwise have been repaired on the front line.[85] In 1918 (up to the armistice) ERS repaired some 1,196 Hispano-Suizas, 36 percent of the year's total output, even though it represented just 28 percent of the total aero-engines on charge.[86] The overall result was to increase the number of engines in the repair pipeline and to require the front line to hold a larger stock of reserve engines.[87] Ultimately this slowed the planned increase in the number of squadrons at the front as well as the introduction of new aircraft types.

A further difficulty faced by the Dolphin squadrons was the impact on engine reliability of defective engine accessories or associated systems—such as oil tank breakages, debris from poorly enameled water jackets, or inadequate radiators.[88] Other problems included the positioning of the petrol gauge and the Constantinesco gear, as well as the operation of the radiator shutter control levers.[89] Finally, the supply system had to contend with a large number of French manufacturers, often working to different tolerances, and varying quality standards, producing sub-components that were not always interchangeable. For example, the crankcases of Peugeot, Brasier, and Hispano-built engines were not interchangeable whereas the crankshaft was exchangeable between Peugeot and Hispano-built engines (but not Brasier). On the other hand, the propeller shaft was interchangeable between the Peugeot and Brasier but not the Hispano.[90] Ultimately, it was found necessary to place AID officers at the French manufacturers to improve quality and ensure that the completed engines met acceptance standards.[91]

An analysis of the War Diary of No. 87 Squadron (newly equipped with Sopwith Dolphins in May 1918) gives some feel for the impact of these factors on operations.[92] From its very first month on the western front the squadron faced a series of aborted sorties or forced-landings arising from engine or engine-related defects. Although the squadron's average serviceability gradually improved, from 76 percent in May to 85 percent in October, some 26 percent of all war sorties flown that month had to be curtailed because of engine problems or engine-related defects. This compares to an average of over 90 percent serviceability for the other RAF squadrons on the western front. There is little doubt that these varied problems made operating the Sopwith Dolphin more difficult than many other types but it is also clear that, with care and discipline on the part of its pilots and engineers, the Hispano-Suiza gave good service and endowed the Dolphin with excellent performance, particularly at altitude. The large number of Hispano-Suiza engines produced and their wide employment suggests that these problems were seen as a fair price to pay for the high performance enjoyed when the engine was running well.

Had the war continued beyond 1918 the RAF would have benefitted from two further developments: the introduction of the de-geared Hispano-Suiza 8Ba and the more powerful Hispano-Suiza 8Fb (rated at 300 hp). The first 8Ba engines were available from early 1918. The removal of the reduction gear offered improved reliability and better performance. According to Brigadier-General Brooke-Popham, "The performance is better than the geared engine and it is certainly the fact that pilots with the ungeared engine when flying at 18,000 ft, in formation, have to throttle their engines down to prevent them running away from pilots with machines having the geared engine."[93] Such was the success of the installation that instructions were issued for the modification work to proceed as fast as possible. However, in view of the large numbers of Dolphins fitted with geared engines, it was advised that it would take some time for ungeared machines (to be known as the Dolphin III) to be issued to the western front. As a result, it was estimated that no more than thirty would be delivered in November 1918.[94]

The Dolphin II, fitted with the 300 hp Hispano-Suiza 8Fb, offered a substantial improvement in performance, as well as better reliability. The 8F was in essence an enlarged direct-drive version of the 8B. The Dolphin II offered a greater top speed (140 mph) and a higher service ceiling (26,000 ft) compared to the Dolphin I and III. It also offered a faster rate of climb, reaching 10,000 ft three minutes quicker. By 18 October 1918 a total of eighteen Hispano-built 8F engines had been dispatched to England. Their immediate use was limited, however, by the need for them to be reworked before issue.[95] A further 250 engines were to be delivered direct from French stocks, while Mayen was contracted to provide several thousand more, although only eighty-two of these were delivered by the armistice.[96] There seems little doubt that the Dolphin II would have given a very good account of itself had the war continued into 1919.

Perhaps the last word on the Hispano-Suiza should be left to the Royal Aircraft Establishment (RAE). A report published in 1968, based on several contemporary articles, noted German respect for the very advanced techniques employed in the construction of the engine. It went on to comment that the design was highly successful, but suffered "as most projects do, from development problems." These included: torsional vibration caused by the 8-cylinder configuration resulting in extensive fretting between the propeller hub and the airscrew shaft; reduction gear failures caused by poor heat treatment; broken crankshafts; and oil system malfunctions. It concluded that: "Despite these setbacks, the advanced techniques employed in this design enabled the manufacturers to produce an aero-engine with an installed power weight ratio of 3.5 lb/hp, a considerable improvement over any other aero-engine of the period."[97]

The manufacture of large quantities of advanced combat aircraft stretched British (and Allied) industrial capacity, particularly in the development of reliable, high-powered aero-engines. Just as importantly, however, the ability to employ these machines on operational tasks depended on the subsequent ability to provide adequate logistic support—including modifications. The RFC was largely successful in meeting this challenge for the R.E.8, but was less successful with the Sopwith Dolphin. Over the period 31 October 1917 to 31 March 1918 (when deliveries had grown to more than 1,500 machines), total wastage amounted to 483 machines, meaning that 59 percent of all R.E.8s produced were still effective (that is employed on operational duties either in France, Italy or the Middle East).[98] An average monthly production rate of some two hundred aircraft proved adequate to sustaining an operating fleet of nine hundred aircraft (410 in France, 210 in the Middle East and Italy and 280 in the Training Division). The Dolphin position was less happy. Delays in engine deliveries meant that many newly manufactured machines went straight to store. By 31 March 1918, nearly five hundred Dolphins had been produced but at least 280 were either in Storage Depots or at Acceptance Parks, leaving less than one hundred machines for the western front. As a result, only 23 percent of Dolphins manufactured up to 31 March 1918 were judged to be "effective," compared to 75 percent of F.E.2s, 60 percent of Armstrong Whitworth FK8s, and 58 percent of Sopwith Camels.[99] These ratios obviously varied over time depending on the size of the front line (if the number of squadrons remained stable, the number of "effective" aircraft would naturally fall with growing wastage), but the Dolphin production rate of some 180 new machines per month should have been able to support an operating fleet of 850 rather than the 140 achieved by 31 March 1918—if sufficient engines had been available. In the event, the number of Dolphins employed on the western front would never rise above one hundred machines.

In reviewing this position, Brigadier-General Cecil Whittington, director of aeronautical equipment at the Air Ministry, observed that the AAP holdings should be seen as the final stage of manufacture—awaiting auxiliary equipment such as magnetos, carburetors, and so forth—and should normally amount to a third of a month's output.[100] On the other hand, machines in store were generally only awaiting engines, and the failure of Hispano-Suiza deliveries was shown very effectively in the case of the Dolphin. He went on to add: "In the case of the Dolphin, there were nearly twice as many machines in store as there were in service, while the chart if brought up to date would show the position to be considerably worse," concluding that the R.E.8 was probably the best example of a machine well in production and following a normal course.[101]

These two case studies have illustrated the range of logistic problems faced in operating combat aircraft on the western front. The quest for more and better performance aircraft created unrealistic expectations and production plans that were never fulfilled. All too often, the RFC either found itself struggling to maintain older types that were no longer combat effective or trying to support newer types that were unreliable or required extensive modifications to make them fit for service. The lack of sufficient numbers of aero-engines made repair and salvage a major preoccupation, while the high proportion of French-sourced engines complicated maintenance and impeded the supply of spares. Nevertheless, these challenges were overcome by a logistic system that exhibited sufficient flexibility to make good the shortages in supply, as well as the resilience to continue to support aircraft types beyond their expected out-of-service date. It is all the more significant that this was achieved under both static and mobile conditions—suggesting an inherent responsiveness and an ability to cope not only with the peaks and troughs of operational demand but also the dislocation and disruption of both rapid retreat and steady advance.

1916—THE SOMME

The RFC's performance during the Battle of the Somme has been widely portrayed as a success.[1] This was certainly the German Army's view—recorded in a wide range of contemporary documents. The diary of an unknown soldier of 8th Company, 28 Infantry Regiment, is typical of these accounts. "16 August 1916. Everybody is wishing for rain or at least bad weather so that we may have some degree of safety from the English aviators. One daren't leave one's hole all day or else one immediately gets artillery fire on the trench for half-an-hour."[2] The RFC's superiority led some Germans in the trenches to feel they had been betrayed by their airmen.[3] Corporal Klier, 76 Infantry Regiment, recorded on 25 August 1916: "The aviators descend to a height of 80 metres and fire on the garrison with machine guns and signal with horns. The enemy's airmen are far superior, especially in numbers. Our airmen are powerless and are put to flight as soon as the enemy machines approach our trench line."[4] The German official history repeats these views, commenting that this was "the characteristic feature of the Battle of the Somme and influences all combat operations to a decided degree."[5]

The rapid and extensive reorganization of the GAS in September 1916 reflected the scale of the RFC's initial success and its enduring impact.[6] The German First Army's post-battle analysis was unequivocal, concluding that "the beginning and first weeks of the Somme battle were marked by a complete inferiority of our own air forces." It went on to describe how "heavy losses in personnel and matériel were inflicted on our artillery by the enemy's guns, assisted by excellent air observation without our being able to have recourse to the same methods. Besides this, both arms were exposed to attacks from the air by the enemy's battle planes, the moral [sic] effect of which could not be ignored."[7]

The British official history, in detailing the RFC's achievements, went as far as describing German accounts of the RFC's success as "monotonous." Subsequent historians have largely echoed this theme.[8] The only dissenting voice has been the Smithsonian's 1992 exhibition *Legend, Memory, and the Great War in the Air*, which blamed the British Army's failure at the Somme on an exaggerated confidence in airpower and, in particular, on deficiencies with the RFC's B.E.2c artillery observation aircraft that caused a breakdown in air to ground communication and prevented accurate artillery fire. In the words of the Smithsonian's curators, "The failure of aviation at the Somme led to carnage on the ground."[9] This perspective caused controversy at the time and, although the exhibition remains on public view, it has not been supported by subsequent historians who continue to portray the RFC's participation as a success.[10] There is, however, a grain of truth in the Smithsonian's criticisms. The direction of artillery fire did falter in the early weeks—largely due to the weather—while contact patrols initially had difficulty communicating with the infantry; although the situation later improved. On the other hand, even without these problems, the weight of artillery fire would still have been insufficient to cut the barbed wire that impeded the initial infantry assault or to destroy the deep bunkers that protected so many of the defenders. Poor artillery tactics and the failure to concentrate fire on a narrow front, rather than the RFC's limitations, were the fundamental causes of the BEF's failure.[11]

Planning for the British attack on the Somme started in earnest during January 1916, following agreement the previous month on the Allied strategy for the coming year.[12] For the RFC, the offensive presented the first operational test of an organization that had more than doubled in size since the Battle of Loos and was now regarded as indispensable in the planning, preparation, and conduct of trench warfare. Given the rapid growth in the resources allocated to the RFC, and the substantial increase in the number of aircraft employed on the western front (a seven-fold rise since August 1914), there was both a need and an opportunity for the new arm to prove itself. The expansion of the RFC on the western front coincided with the appointment of Brigadier-General Hugh Trenchard as GOC on 19 August 1915, following the return of David Henderson (who had commanded the RFC in France since August 1914) to the Military Aeronautics Department at the War Office. In a matter of days, Trenchard was arguing for an immediate increase of four squadrons to support the continuing growth in the size of the BEF and to counter the rise in the number of German aircraft.[13] Within the month, he wrote proposing a further increase to meet the needs of the soon-to-be-formed Fourth Army. The War Office was supportive but, by the New Year, it was evident that the planned expansion would be constrained by the limited availability of new machines and trained pilots. Nevertheless, the RFC was able to deploy some twenty-six service (frontline) squadrons on the western front by the eve of the Somme and thirty-five squadrons by the end of the year.[14] Not only were there more squadrons but they were also 50 percent bigger (with eighteen rather than twelve aircraft each). Trenchard's argument for more machines and pilots was undoubtedly helped by the good working relationship he forged with Douglas Haig, who took over as commander in chief BEF in December 1915. The latter's support was hugely influential in the subsequent growth of the RFC and its expanding role.[15]

The scale of effort involved in equipping, training, and supporting these additional squadrons was unprecedented—in cost, matériel, and manpower. An entire industry had to be created to design, develop, and produce the required quantities of aircraft, aero-engines, and support equipment. Much of this output had to be directed at expanding the training base to provide the pilots and observers needed to operate the new machines (and to make good the losses from flying accidents), as well as the technicians to maintain and repair them. This was part of the wider process of war mobilization, which saw the nation's industrial capacity focused on meeting the demands of the western front.

Notwithstanding these obstacles, the growth in the size of the RFC was continuous through 1916, the total number of officers and other ranks rising from just over 16,000 in January to almost 55,000 by December. Although the force deployed on the western front grew rapidly, it actually represented a declining share of the RFC's overall manpower, falling from 44 percent of total strength in January 1915 to just 32 percent by the end of 1916—reflecting the increasing level of investment in the training system.[16] By the end of the year, the western front still represented approximately half of the RFC's operational effort (in terms of service squadrons available) but the support "tail" had grown substantially. The growth of the RFC's operational capability was not simply a matter of frontline numbers; it also required new and better types of aircraft. It generally took some six months for a design to move from the drawing board to production. This created a lag in the mobilization process, which, coupled with the need to train substantially more pilots (despite the abbreviated training regimes of the period), meant that new squadrons continued to arrive on the western front during the course of the fighting. It should also be remembered that the RFC's expansion echoed an equally rapid growth in the size of the BEF—creating severe competition for finite resources. Even so, the increase in the number of RFC aircraft on the western front was rapid, rising from a little under 230 in January 1916 to more than nine hundred by the end of the year.[17] Given the problems faced by the British aircraft and aero-engine industry, this was an impressive achievement. However, it masked a reality that would undermine successive plans to expand the British air effort on the western front: the substantial number of "inactive" aircraft required to sustain a service squadron. If one takes into account aircraft unserviceable, or under repair, together with those held in reserve, the actual number of machines available for operational flying was much lower than the headline total would indicate. For example, of the 229 aircraft held on charge by the RFC on the western front as of 1 January 1916, only 191 were with the frontline squadrons.[18] Over the course of 1916 the proportion of "inactive" aircraft grew from approximately 16 percent to over 30 percent.[19] The reasons were various, but included the need to hold a higher level of immediate reserves (to match increased wastage levels), a larger pool of damaged machines awaiting repair, and increased wear and tear from more intensive flying rates. The fragility of aircraft exposed to the elements and the poor condition of many landing fields also ensured that there was a regular demand for replacement machines—even when the RFC was not engaged in operations. It took some time for the War Office staffs to recognize this reality, although GOC RFC endeavored to explain why the total number of aircraft recorded as being in France was not the same as frontline strength.[20]

These factors had been recognized before the war, but the western front revealed the sheer scale of the problem.[21] In 1914, new aircraft had to be supplied to the squadrons in France at the rate of 33 percent (of squadron establishment) per month. By 1916 the replacement rate had reached 37 percent and would subsequently rise to 47 percent in 1917 and finally 52 percent in 1918.[22] In effect, the greater the RFC's operational effort (in terms of flying hours generated), the greater the consumption of aircraft and the greater the burden on the engineering and supply organization. Getting new squadrons to France also proved problematic because of the difficulties of coordinating production and training programs. Planned movement dates consistently slipped, leading to increasingly querulous letters from Trenchard to Brancker (at the War Office) seeking confirmation as to when reinforcements could be expected.[23] Alan Bott, who served as an observer on 70 Squadron, equipped with Sopwith 1½ Strutters, summed up the experience in a light-hearted but perceptive account:

> The machines comprise a less straightforward problem. The new service squadron is probably formed to fly a recently adopted type of aeroplane, of which the early production in quantities is hounded by difficulty. The engine and its parts, the various sections of the machine itself, the guns, the synchronising gear, all these are made in separate factories, after standardisation, and must then be co-ordinated before the craft is ready for its test. If the output of any one part falls below what was expected, the whole is kept waiting; and invariably the quantity or quality of output is at first below expectation in some particular. Adding to the delays of supply, of others due to the most urgent claims of squadrons at the front for machines to replace those lost or damaged, it can easily be seen that a new squadron will have a succession of dates.[24]

The first flight of No. 70 Squadron arrived in France on 31 May 1916, the next on 3 July, and the third on 1 August. The two-month delay in deploying the full squadron was caused by a combination of supply delays, spares shortages, and inclement weather. Its experience was not untypical of the time. The move of No. 29 Squadron to France became infamous as a result of the high wastage suffered during the outward journey, and the significant delays encountered because of weather and sickness. The unit had received its full complement of twenty DH2 single-seat scouts by the end of January 1916. After familiarization and further training the squadron (less the ground crew and transport, which had travelled ahead) moved to Dover on 24 March. The loss of their experienced tradesmen led to technical delays, while poor weather and accidents created further problems. As a result, only twelve machines had actually reached France by the second week in April. The attrition was even worse than at first appeared since additional machines had been delivered direct to the squadron from the factory during the course of the deployment. A frustrated HQ RFC later declared that "the total number of machines consumed in order to deliver at St-Omer twelve serviceable was 27."[25] The majority of these were to be found scattered around southern England while the remainder had either ditched in the Channel or crash-landed on arrival in France.

From the start of the war a substantial proportion of aircraft was delivered to France by sea or in crates, thus avoiding the problems caused by poor weather or flying accidents, although this strategy created its own difficulties. The more aircraft that needed to be erected before they could be employed the less repair or reconstruction that could be undertaken by the depots. Trenchard was so concerned about this situation that he asked only a month later for a greater proportion of replacement aircraft to be flown out. The problem from the War Office's perspective was that flying aircraft to France demanded more pilots than were available, which in turn depended on providing more aircraft for the training schools. The DMA was acutely aware that it was not possible to separate the supply needs of the western front from those of the Home Establishment—especially the flying training schools.[26] In essence, the expansion of the RFC in France could only occur if further resources were allocated to the home base.

The RFC's requirement for additional manpower was a matter of enduring concern, given its appetite for specialist skills and the immense pressure on manpower supply resulting from the creation of the New Armies. The RFC's overall needs were modest compared to the BEF's, but this did not make them any easier to satisfy. Maintaining aircraft in the field demanded experienced wood and metal workers, as well as welders, tinsmiths, fabric workers, and engine mechanics—skills that were also required by the aircraft and aero-engine industry as it struggled to meet ever larger production orders. In early 1916, it needed just over twenty-five men on the western front to support each frontline aircraft. This remained fairly constant over the next twelve months, indicating little progress along the learning curve.[27] However, if all aircraft on the western front are considered (that is inclusive of those held at the depots), a more positive picture emerges that suggests a gradual but slow improvement through most of 1916. Greater engine reliability, faster repairs, and better salvage rates for damaged aircraft and engines all played their part in this process. On the other hand, overall RFC manpower efficiency—the number of personnel (less officers) supporting each frontline aircraft at home and overseas—did not reflect the same steady progress, remaining somewhere between forty and fifty men throughout 1916.[28]

The War Cabinet was acutely aware of the resource implications when considering the future expansion of the RFC.[29] As a result, Trenchard, as GOC RFC, spent a great deal of his time addressing logistic-related issues and exploring ways of improving the overall efficiency of the system. Indeed, the bulk of his correspondence with the War Office over this period relates to the supply of equipment and manpower (particularly pilots).[30] He would later write that:

> Many people fail to realise what a large number of men, and what a large number of machines are required to keep a certain number of machines going at the front. If 1,000 machines are to be kept serviceable and be available to cross the line each day, this result can be secured only by having a large reserve of machines which can be available in depots, a large number of repair shops kept manned and at work, and a system of training for pilots at home kept continually going. The training of these pilots uses up more machines for which there must be reserve depots and more repair shops. Then, each of the separate services, such as wireless, need training establishments to be kept up and the whole of the equipment needs to be provided and replaced to keep the system going.[31]

The growth of the RFC necessitated substantial organizational changes involving both command and logistic arrangements. As the number of frontline squadrons grew it became necessary to create a higher formation in the form of brigades, each comprising an army and corps wing, to meet their administrative and functional needs. This change came about on 30 January 1916, together with the creation of a dedicated AP to support each brigade.[32] The AP was responsible for supplying the logistic needs of some six squadrons, although this would later grow. Each air park held two to four weeks' stock of aeronautical stores, drawn from the depot, and also offered some limited repair capabilities—where this would not impair the park's mobility.

These important changes were reflected at HQ RFC where a new post, DA & QMG, was created, responsible for all technical and supply matters on the western front. As the next most senior officer to Trenchard (operations was headed by a lieutenant-colonel), this one-star appointment placed logistics at the very heart of the planning and direction of RFC operations. The first incumbent was Brigadier-General Robert Brooke-Popham, who would remain in the post for the remainder of the war, and was largely responsible for developing the RFC's logistic system such that it was able to sustain some 1,800 frontline aircraft by the armistice—nearly nine times the number available for operations in January 1916.[33] Other significant developments, intended to improve the performance of the overall logistic system, included the creation of an additional depot at Candas (the single depot at St-Omer had grown too unwieldy and could not adequately support the RFC's southern squadrons) and a new port depot at Rouen (Boulogne rapidly proved incapable of handling the increased volume of stores). A further development, and one that would later prove hugely significant, was the expansion of the engine repair facility at Rouen. The ERS had emerged from the original RFC aircraft park that had moved to France from Farnborough in August 1914. This organization would eventually grow into a major industrial facility that by the armistice was the largest single RAF unit operating on the western front. In January 1916, however, it comprised just five officers and 147 men, tasked with repairing engines that would otherwise have had to be returned to England.[34]

It should not be thought that the functioning of the expanded supply system was without difficulty or that the relationship between the logistic units in France and the home base was either easy or without rancor. Toward the end of 1916, both depots forwarded a list of concerns via DA & QMG at HQ RFC to the War Office regarding the supply of stores.[35] Problems identified included: an inadequate supply of ash in the required sizes, deficient information on what stores were being delivered, poor marking of case contents, rusting of metal parts due to no protective finish being applied, and a range of difficulties with Motor Transport (MT) and motorcycle spares. It was noted, however, that the supply of airplane spares had improved recently, although there were continuing shortages of some engine spares. The response from the assistant director of Stores at the OASD was helpful, but not entirely sympathetic, leading Lieutenant-Colonel Ralph Donaldson-Hudson, commanding No. 2 Aircraft Depot at Candas, to minute that: "I have gone carefully through this correspondence and have come to the conclusion that no useful purpose will be served by making any remarks thereon. Until the authorities in England will cease siding with the manufacturers against the BEF, a cause doubtless pursued by them to avoid rippling the surface of their present placid existence, it hardly seems worthwhile drawing their attention to irregularity, however glaring, as their replies are always to the effect that the BEF is incompetent to judge."[36]

The demise of the OASD in January 1917, when the RFC took direct responsibility for the supply and storage of all aeronautical matériel (although consumables and general stores remained with the Army), is unlikely to have caused Donaldson-Hudson to shed any tears.

The increasing number of frontline squadrons not only placed an increasing demand on the RFC's logistic system, but also required a matching investment in airfields and infrastructure. While the aircraft of the period could safely operate from a grass field, the ground had to be clear of obstructions and well drained. The area also had to be sufficiently large to allow for changes in wind direction, and the approaches free of obstructions such as buildings or trees. The selection, acquisition, and preparation of airfields (and temporary operating strips) were a major undertaking. A similar investment was needed in technical and domestic accommodation. Aircrew and ground crew needed billets close to the airfield, while hangars (increasingly wooden or steel-framed) were required for overnight storage and rectification. Although the frontline squadrons were mobile—in the sense that all their specialist equipment could be moved by lorry—this did not obviate the need for a substantial range of facilities. Tired pilots or sodden aircraft could reduce the RFC's operational tempo as quickly as a shortage of spares or a lack of fuel.

Men and machines were very much on the input side of the RFC logistic equation—the real test of this investment was, of course, operational output. The RFC's contribution to the Somme offensive started well before the initial assault on 1 July 1916. The effort, in terms of flying hours expended and sorties undertaken, was substantial, both during the battle and in the preparatory phases.[37] By now, both sides had realized the importance of directed artillery fire and the critical role of air observation both for mapping the front and accurately targeting the guns. Much of the RFC's work in the months preceding the battle was allocated to photography and reconnaissance tasks intended to help inform the planning of the assault and pinpoint the German defenses and artillery positions. Following French experience at Verdun, this period was also used to establish air superiority, enabling the RFC to operate largely as it wished while denying the Germans the same advantage. However, air superiority could only be sustained through continuous effort. While artillery cooperation lay at the heart of the RFC's operational contribution, the bulk of its effort lay in offensive combat patrols designed to protect the army cooperation machines from enemy interference and to push the engagement line between the opposing air forces well to the east of the battle zone. As a result, artillery cooperation sorties represented fewer than 40 percent of all sorties conducted throughout 1916 and approximately 30 percent of the operational effort during the offensive itself.[38]

The first photographs of the German defenses on the Somme were taken by the RFC in October 1915 as part of a continuing task to build a detailed picture of the front line. This effort intensified in March 1916 when Fourth Army took over the sector between Curlu and Gommecourt, north of the Somme River, where the main British assault was to be launched. The area was subject to regular photography over the next few months, growing in scope and frequency as the Germans rushed to extend their defenses behind the Somme front. The initial attack was planned for 29 June but was postponed until 1 July to allow for a supporting French attack immediately north and south of the river.[39]

The RFC allocated six corps squadrons for counter-battery work, contact patrols, and trench flights (close reconnaissance and bombardment) in support of Fourth Army.[40] These aircraft were to be protected in their tasks by continuous line patrols. Other squadrons were allocated to the subsidiary attacks by Third Army and to an organized offensive against enemy airfields, communication centers, and supply depots. It was hoped that the bombing raids, starting on the first day of the assault, would isolate the area by blocking railway cuttings and destroying bridges, so delaying reinforcements and ammunition supply. In order to maximize the effect of the bombing, it was decided to employ small groups of unescorted aircraft to carry out a program of continuous attacks across the whole front.[41]

A total of 183 airplanes were assigned to these initial tasks—a little over 40 percent of total frontline strength, although when the machines employed in bombing attacks are included this rises to over 50 percent. The RFC outnumbered the GAS on the Somme front, facing some 129 aircraft allocated to the German Second Army.[42] A substantial proportion of the GAS was still committed to the fighting at Verdun. Continuous bombardment of the German defenses began in the middle of June but the increase in intensity planned for 24 June was accompanied by poor weather that greatly impeded air observation. In the following days the RFC's observation aircraft and kite balloons played an important role in identifying German batteries and assessing the extent of the destruction inflicted on the defenses. In these tasks they were little troubled by enemy aircraft. A greater problem was the poor visibility caused by fog and low cloud. The weather on 1 July, the opening day of the offensive, was much improved but only served to allow the RFC's contact and counter-battery aircraft to observe the failure of many of the attacks and the loss to vigorous German counterattacks of much of the ground gained earlier in the day. Great difficulty was experienced in following the progress of the infantry, while the intensity of the bombardment denied accurate counter-battery fire.[43]

The bombing of railway stations and the lines of communication achieved mixed success and suffered heavy losses to ground fire and enemy fighters. The immediate results did not justify the casualties incurred and it was decided to halt individual bombing sorties and revert to escorted bomber formations. These attacks, and the continuous line patrols, did at least ensure that the artillery and contact aircraft were able to work virtually undisturbed, supporting the infantry's steady progress on the ground that resulted in the capture of the German first line by 4 July. Further heavy fighting cleared Mametz and Trones Woods. The latter was successfully held in the face of a German counterattack, disrupted by a counter-barrage called down from the air.[44]

Preparations for the attack on the second line were assisted by the RFC's continuing reconnaissance and photography and, in particular, registration of the enemy's new artillery positions. Meanwhile, bombing and machine-gun attacks continued against German reinforcements as they moved up by road and rail. The general assault between Longueval and Bazentin-le-Petit Wood commenced on 15 July.[45] Once again, the corps squadrons provided artillery observation and flew contact patrols—even though the weather was poor throughout the day. The initial success of this assault led to the (short-lived) hope that the cavalry could be deployed to exploit the weakened defenses. The village of Longueval was captured by the evening as was Bazentin-le-Petit. The fighting continued at a lower intensity over the next few days, but low-flying RFC aircraft were still able to engage the defending German infantry and artillery on several occasions, disrupting reinforcements and defensive positions. Poor weather, however, still interfered with the observation of artillery fire—an important factor in the failure to capture Pozières on 17 July. The importance of the RFC's role was underscored by General Sir William Pulteney (commanding III Corps) who wrote in his diary following this setback that "aeroplane observation now appears to be an essential preliminary to a successful attack."[46]

In the first phase of the battle, the RFC's observation and photography work had proved essential in the preparation and conduct of the attack. Low-flying contact aircraft had demonstrated an increasing ability to provide fire support to the infantry while disrupting the enemy's defenses. Although impeded by the weather, cooperation with the artillery had allowed trenches and strong points to be destroyed and German artillery to be neutralized. Just as importantly, the GAS had been kept away from the battle zone, allowing the corps squadrons to operate unmolested while denying German infantry the benefit of air support. In all of this, the RFC's ability to maintain adequate numbers of serviceable aircraft in the face of combat losses and other wastage provided the bedrock for success. "The enemy owed his success, first of all, to the daylong, overwhelming fire directed by aerial observation, especially to the heavy guns and mortars. The greatly inferior German batteries and aerial forces were, to all intents and purposes, eliminated. Accordingly, there could be no thought of meaningfully engaging the enemy artillery."[47]

The second phase of the battle continued until September. It began with the arrival of substantial German air reinforcements—a process that continued until the end of the fighting. The assault, delayed because of extremely poor weather and German counterattacks, was focused on the right of the British line around the village of Guillemont. The attack opened on 23 July, after two days of bombardment along the whole front.[48] The Germans had used the delay, however, to strengthen their defenses and the advance was largely halted. The poor weather continued to interfere with photography and artillery cooperation but improvements in August allowed more effective counter-battery fire. Nevertheless, the attack against Guillemont on 8 August failed in the face of strong enemy resistance. A combined attack along the whole line took place on 18 August but little progress was achieved, although Delville Wood was cleared on 24 August. The fighting continued throughout the remainder of the month in the face of increasingly poor weather.[49] A further general attack was launched along the line on 3 September after two days of artillery preparation. Significant gains were made, particularly around Ginchy and Guillemont, while Falfemont Farm was captured by 7 September and Ginchy itself two days later.[50] Throughout this period, the RFC continued to attack the enemy's lines of communication and airfields. Increasing opposition was encountered from enemy fighters but, although losses grew, artillery cooperation continued largely unaffected.[51]

The third and final phase of the battle opened on 15 September when the infantry attack was supported for the first time by a large number of tanks. The noise of the tanks coming up into the line the previous night was deliberately drowned by low-flying aircraft. The assault was preceded by a three-day artillery bombardment and met immediate success (albeit less extensive than had been hoped), including the capture of Courcelette, Martinpuich, High Wood, and Flers. The RFC provided invaluable support throughout the day's fighting with continuous contact patrols and artillery observation. The attack continued the next day with further slight gains, although a number of counterattacks were broken up with the assistance of air observation. Over the next few days, as the weather worsened, a reorganized and reequipped GAS was able to inflict increasing losses. Groups of German fighters sought to disrupt the RFC's operations but were unable to delay the preparations for the new general attack planned for 25 September. The assault was particularly successful, leading to the capture of Lesboeufs and Morval, once again supported by contact patrols and artillery observation—little affected by enemy aircraft. "Tanks and low-flying aircraft firing machine guns supported the enemy assault troops most effectively."[52] The next day saw the capture of Gueudecourt and Thiepval. Further successes followed in the succeeding days but so did the strength of the GAS. This was a cause for growing concern and led to Douglas Haig's request on 30 September for further fighter squadrons to reinforce the western front.[53] Although combat losses peaked in September (at just over one hundred aircraft), the flying hours achieved per aircraft lost steadily declined over the last three months of the battle—as did flying hours per aircraft struck off—confirming the basis for Haig's concerns.

While the offensive continued through October and into November, further gains were modest in the face of deteriorating weather conditions, which affected flying operations as much as they did the infantry's progress on the ground. Strong winds and poor visibility greatly reduced the effectiveness of artillery observation and contact patrols. Inadequate artillery preparation ensured that those attacks that were mounted met strong resistance and achieved little; moreover, enemy aircraft were increasingly able to interfere with the work of the RFC's corps squadrons while assisting their own artillery observation aircraft to operate freely for the first time since the offensive had begun. A number of large air fights took place, resulting in heavy RFC losses. The impact was mitigated, however, by the reinforcements that had arrived during October, including the redeployment of five squadrons from the northern brigades as well as three newly formed squadrons straight from England. Further support was provided by the detachment of a RNAS fighter squadron from Dunkirk. These additional units were absorbed with little trouble and were able to function effectively within a matter of days.[54] It is significant that these changes took place without any reduction in aircraft availability or operational output, indicating that the RFC's logistic system was able to absorb new units and meet their supply needs while coping with increased wastage rates.

The Somme fighting came to a close on 18 November when the western outskirts of Grandcourt were reached. Debate will no doubt continue regarding the conduct of the fighting, and particularly the shattering losses suffered on 1 July, but the RFC/RAF official history is justified in claiming that the RFC had won victory in the air. The organization emerged stronger at the end of the fighting than it had begun and could claim to have won the battle for air superiority. More importantly, it had used this advantage to telling effect, dropping 292 tons of bombs in nearly 300 raids, taking 19,000 photographs and registering over 8,600 targets.[55] All the German accounts of the Somme refer to the superiority of the British artillery assisted by air observation. "Gaining control of the air is a prerequisite to the battle of positional warfare for both short and long-range reconnaissance as well as for artillery observation from the air."[56]

These sentiments were echoed by Sir Henry Rawlinson, commanding Fourth Army, who commented that his experiences in the battle "had brought home to him the enormous importance of aeroplane and artillery co-operation and pointed to the necessity for a great future development in this branch of flying."[57] Some feel for the RFC's efficiency in delivering these effects can be gained from an analysis of the operational output (in flying hours and sorties flown) per frontline aircraft—recognizing that the number of the latter increased steadily throughout 1916.[58] As might be expected, the RFC's maximum effort occurred over the three months, July–September 1916, when each frontline aircraft flew on average for forty hours (or fifteen sorties). If aircraft in reserve or under repair are included, this ratio falls to just twenty-six hours for each deployed aircraft. Because of seasonal variations (particularly the effect of poor weather) it is difficult to ascertain a clear pattern, other than to note the relatively low utilization rate for individual aircraft—even in periods of high operational activity.

A more telling picture is provided by serviceability. Over the course of 1916, the RFC steadily improved the serviceability of its frontline aircraft—the average percentage of squadron machines available to fly daily. This reflects a combination of engineering effort (and diagnostic ability), as well as the timely provision of spares/replacements.[59] It is the single most important measure of overall logistic performance and continues to be employed to assess engineering and supply performance by the RAF. Analysis of the daily operational reports shows that the RFC was able to improve serviceability rates from 82 percent in January 1916 to over 90 percent by the end of the year, notwithstanding the significant losses experienced during the autumn and the heavy operational effort expended throughout the Somme offensive.[60] This applied across all aircraft types and roles.

The War Diary of No. 9 Squadron (equipped with the B.E.2 aircraft and employed on artillery cooperation duties) reveals a similar pattern.[61] Not only did the squadron's serviceability rate steadily improve over the course of 1916 (including the critical Somme period) but aircraft availability—the average number of machines available each month for operations—was increased to, and then maintained at, eighteen machines, indicating that the supply system was able to sustain the squadron at establishment irrespective of the flying rate or wastage.[62] This is particularly impressive given that three different versions of the B.E.2 were employed over this period. Anecdotal evidence from other squadrons supports this picture. Frederick Libby, a recently arrived observer with No. 11 Squadron operating the F.E.2b, recorded how as soon as one aircraft was lost "another is flown in from the base before you can turn round."[63]

Each sortie generated and every hour flown came at a price. There was, of course, the immediate cost in terms of consumables (fuel, oil, gases—mainly hydrogen and oxygen, and ordnance), and the engineering effort to prepare the machine for flight. On the aircraft's return there were checks to be made and repairs undertaken as well as refueling, replenishing, and rearming. Engine lives were short and, even when running reliably, engines had to be routinely replaced and sent for overhaul after some thirty to eighty hours of running.[64] Every squadron was provided with between three and nine replacement engines, depending on type, to meet planned removals (for overhaul) and unplanned removals (random failure, combat damage, poor running, etc.).[65] The RFC's maximum effort in September 1916 (some 22,000 flying hours) represented, therefore, a potential demand for at least four hundred engines.[66] Each hour in the air also added to the wear and tear on the airframe and especially its wooden and fabric components. Exposure to the elements—even if hangars were provided—took its toll and it was rare for an aircraft to achieve more than 150 hours' "war flying" before a squadron sought permission to strike it off strength.[67] These aircraft were often returned to Home Establishment where they fulfilled a useful role within the training system; however, they were still effectively lost to the front line. Crashed aircraft had to be recovered (if they fell on the Allied side of the lines) and replacement machines and engines collected from the aircraft parks or railheads. All of this represented a continuous effort on the part of the squadron's engineering personnel that was as unrelenting as it was critical. The evidence indicates that the RFC's supply system was able to respond to the changes in operational tempo (in terms of flying hours and sorties generated) and the vagaries of aircraft wastage while supporting a steadily expanding front line. In quantitative terms this was achieved because deliveries exceeded losses—from all causes.[68] On only one occasion (November) did deliveries fall below the number of machines lost through wastage. As a result, although more than 1,400 RFC aircraft were struck off on the western front during 1916, the front line more than trebled in strength.[69]

Of course, having sufficient aircraft and spares in the supply system was not the same as having them in the right place. It was the ready availability of equipment that gave the RFC the secure foundation needed to gain air superiority over the Somme. Key to the logistic pipeline's effectiveness was mechanical transport. The bulk of the RFC's stores (somewhere between five hundred and seven hundred tons each week at this stage of the war), were moved from the Channel ports by rail to the depots and Army air parks. Distribution from the railheads was executed by motor vehicle (primarily three-ton lorries).[70] Replacement aircraft were either flown directly to reception parks or delivered unassembled in crates and erected at the depots. So dependent were the frontline squadrons on this combination of road and rail that GHQ gave specific instructions about the supply arrangements for the RFC, stating bluntly that "a squadron without transport is useless as it cannot effect repair."[71]

The supply of aviation fuel was a major challenge, especially during periods of high operational tempo when the daily needs of individual squadrons could be as much as five hundred to six hundred gallons, all brought from the railhead in two- or four-gallon tins. The individual squadrons were capable of moving these volumes using organic transport, as long as their airfields were no more than twenty-five miles distant. Beyond this, they had to rely on the Army to bring up the fuel they needed. In June 1916, the RFC was consuming over 142,000 gallons of aviation spirit and some 13,000 gallons of lubricating oil every month.[72] Not surprisingly, the number of MT vehicles on charge on the western front grew rapidly, in line with frontline strength, such that by October 1916 there were more than 2,200 vehicles (lorries, tenders, and motorcycles) supporting over thirty service squadrons.[73]

In assessing the RFC's operational contribution to the Somme, it should be noted that the timetable for the air battle was not a mirror image of the BEF's assault. The air battle predated operations on the ground by several months and, arguably, continued beyond the last day of the offensive. The RFC's relentless effort was such that there were only two days in the whole of 1916 when low cloud, wind or heavy rain stopped all flying. Given the notoriously poor weather experienced by Europe during the summer this is a remarkable record.[74] The RFC's most obvious achievement, in the immediate weeks before the battle opened, was detailed reconnaissance, particularly aerial photography, of the German front line to assist the BEF's planning. In turn, this demanded an increased offensive effort by all squadrons to gain the air superiority needed to keep the GAS away from the vulnerable reconnaissance machines. This process commenced at the turn of the year and was increasingly successful, although the full impact was not understood (by either side) until the offensive had been under way for several weeks. Equal success was achieved in denying the GAS the opportunity to observe the BEF's preparations, although the RFC's ascendancy was not sufficient to stop all German aerial activity. As a result, they had become aware from April 1916 of the buildup in the Somme area.[75] At the heart of the RFC's battle, however, was artillery cooperation. Although the weight of the British bombardment was inadequate to destroy the German defenses, air observation enabled accurate and timely fire that took a heavy toll of the defending infantry and, in particular, the surviving German batteries. As a result of Trenchard's offensive policy, the losses suffered by the Army cooperation squadrons were light and, other than poor weather, there was little to impede their work through the summer and into the autumn—notwithstanding a resurgent GAS. Moreover, the proportion of successful artillery cooperation sorties (that is, targets successfully engaged for registration or destruction) actually grew throughout the fighting—only declining in the face of worsening winter weather. The reorganization of the German fighter arm during the Somme fighting was in direct response to the RFC's achievements. The German High Command, in observing the RFC's achievements, concluded that "in trench warfare to obtain air superiority is a prerequisite for long and near reconnaissance as well as for aerial direction of artillery fire. Next to the strength of the artillery and to the availability of ammunition, it is the decisive factor in the artillery combat. The struggle for supremacy in the air must, therefore, precede the artillery battle."[76] It has been argued, however, that the Germans failed to understand the strategic value of the RFC's bombing campaign in helping to secure air superiority: "We should note one failure of the German command to utilise completely the lessons of the Somme battles. While the importance of air superiority was recognised, the mission of securing it was left to the single-seat fighters. The Germans failed to see that bombing was not necessarily to be judged solely on material results. The British employed bombing to gain and maintain air superiority by carrying out a determined bombing offensive against vital German centres."[77]

Thus, although artillery cooperation and air observation were central to the RFC's operational contribution at the Somme, it was not the exclusive activity. The RFC was able to operate across a range of roles and to vary the balance and weight of its effort. This high degree of flexibility gave the organization both agility, in the face of unexpected demands, and responsiveness—qualities that would be tested to the full during 1917 and 1918. The bedrock for these substantial achievements was an effective and efficient logistic system. Although the RFC's efforts were compromised in some respects by equipment and tactical weaknesses, they were supported by a timely and generous supply of matériel that never faltered, irrespective of weather, wastage rates, or rapid changes in demand. During the course of the battle (1 July–17 November 1916), the RFC lost 972 machines, yet by the end of the year its frontline strength was stronger by nineteen squadrons and some four hundred aircraft compared to twelve months earlier. If the Somme was indeed a "battle of matériel," it was undoubtedly a battle that the RFC won.[78]

1917—ARRAS AND THIRD YPRES

THE THIRD BATTLE OF YPRES WAS THE BEF'S MAIN EFFORT IN 1917 AND provided the most significant test of the RFC's operational performance to date. In comparison to the Somme offensive, it involved more extensive and sustained air fighting by an organization that was twice the size it had been the previous summer. On 31 July 1917, the first day of the BEF's attack, the RFC on the western front comprised a total of 50 squadrons operating 858 aircraft compared to a front line of 27 squadrons operating just 421 aircraft on the eve of the Somme.[1]

Before turning to the detail of the offensive and the logistic contribution, two aspects of the RFC's operations earlier in 1917 are worthy of comment: Bloody April, when serious losses were suffered at the hands of a superior German fighter arm, and the aircraft reequipment program that reached its peak in the early summer, when the entire frontline inventory was exchanged for newer types with enhanced performance. These events tested the RFC's supply arrangements and engineering proficiency in different ways. Nothing encountered in 1916 had presaged Bloody April and its relentless consumption of matériel. Equally unprecedented, however, was the wholesale introduction of new aircraft, replacing familiar prewar designs and introducing more complex engineering and supply challenges, just as preparations for Third Ypres were being finalized. The way these challenges were handled provides a valuable perspective on the flexibility and resilience of the RFC's logistic arrangements after two years of fighting on the western front.

The story of Bloody April, the RFC's operations during the Battle of Arras between 9 April and 16 May 1917, has been the subject of frequent and critical study by historians, who have argued that the losses in aircrew and aircraft were unnecessary and achieved little.[2] The RFC/RAF official history, while not employing the term "Bloody April," does not try to disguise the attrition suffered by the RFC but presents it as the inevitable cost of providing effective support to the BEF.[3] Whatever view one takes about the conduct of the air offensive during Arras and the results achieved, the high wastage rate (both human and matériel) placed the RFC's logistic system under immense strain.

The British attack was aimed at capturing the German-occupied high ground that dominated the plain of Douai to the east of Arras. It was scheduled to distract the Germans from a much larger French offensive planned for the Aisne and to benefit from the latter's anticipated success. In the event, Arras, with its more limited objectives, was relatively successful—when compared to the tragedy that unfolded forty miles to the south. The main fighting fell to Third Army (with the capture of Vimy Ridge as their main objective), together with First Army and later Fifth Army, mounted over a front running from Vimy in the north to Bullecourt in the south—some twenty-four miles.[4]

The RFC contributed over 60 percent of its frontline strength (465 aircraft) comprising eighteen squadrons of I and III Brigades—supporting their "parent" armies—and seven squadrons of the Ninth (Headquarters) Wing.[5] Further aircraft were provided by II, IV, and V Brigades as part of a pooled resource, which was assembled to conduct a long-range bombing campaign intended to draw enemy fighters and anti-aircraft defenses away from Arras—hopefully easing the effort to gain air superiority over the battle area. The majority of the RFC's frontline aircraft were by this stage of the war significantly outclassed by the enemy's fighters.[6] This trend had become noticeable toward the end of the Somme, but the winter hiatus had mitigated the impact.

In an effort to redress the balance, a number of RNAS fighter squadrons were attached to the RFC, building on the successful employment of No. 8 Naval Squadron during the latter months of the Somme. During the course of 1917, up to five RNAS squadrons would be attached at any one time to the RFC. Although the numbers were modest, the additional fighter aircraft made an important contribution to the RFC's ability to counter the GAS. The day-to-day support of these units fell to the RFC's air parks, rather than the RNAS depot at Dunkirk. The relevant logistic arrangements were laid down in a detailed note prepared in advance by Brigadier-General Brooke-Popham.[7] In essence, the RFC was responsible, through its supply network, for all consumables, spares, replacement engines, machine guns, vehicle spares and repairs, and ordnance. Replacement aircraft were to be provided from Dunkirk, although in an emergency the RFC's depots would issue the required machines. This system appears to have worked well and certainly did not give rise to complaints similar to those raised by Officer Commanding (OC) No. 8 Naval Squadron in January 1917, about the failure of Dunkirk to deliver urgent spares in a timely manner. There is some evidence that the RNAS squadrons also found the RFC's supply arrangements superior—at least in the handling of consumable stores—and worthy of imitation.[8]

The RFC embarked on the battle confident that they enjoyed a significant numerical superiority, both locally and across the front as a whole, but in the knowledge that the qualitative advantage lay with the GAS.[9] The latter was expected to respond vigorously to the RFC's air offensive—unlike the opening weeks of the Somme. These concerns proved to be fully justified, although the heavy losses inflicted by German fighters were undoubtedly increased by poor RFC tactics. Like the Somme, the air campaign commenced well before the ground attack opened. From late March, the corps squadrons of I and III Brigades systematically registered the enemy's defenses.[10] This was critical to the preliminary bombardment that began from 2 April on the First Army front and from 4 April on the Third Army front. Other tasks included reconnaissance and photography, while the Army squadrons undertook offensive patrols and close escort to deter enemy fighters. The bombing program opened on 5 April, but was frequently interrupted by poor weather. Airfields, ammunition dumps, headquarters, and railway stations were all attacked, by day and night. The impact was limited, however, and any success came at a high price. Some bomber formations were wiped out while others were badly mauled.[11]

The weather on Monday 9 April, the opening day of the battle, was poor, with snow showers and low visibility.[12] Even so, the RFC was able to conduct artillery cooperation and to provide contact patrols in support of the advancing infantry. The neutralization of the enemy's batteries was extremely effective, but the weather meant that much of the bombing program had to be abandoned.[13] The contribution of the corps squadrons continued over the next few days but increasing numbers of machines were lost to ground fire and enemy fighters as the weather improved. The better conditions also allowed the bombing campaign to recommence, although once again with heavy losses. By 14 April the first phase of the offensive was over with many of the planned objectives captured—including Vimy Ridge. The RFC had played an important role in this achievement, particularly through the work of the corps squadrons, but had suffered significant attrition in the process. Operations resumed on 23 April with the aim of relieving pressure on the French army—which had struggled to make progress since the opening of its offensive on 16 April.[14] The attack was to have been renewed earlier, but poor weather restricted flying and, as a result, delayed the artillery preparations by several days. The initial assault resulted in further limited gains, but German counterattacks slowed progress. Great difficulty was experienced by the corps squadrons in calling down effective artillery support and, to make matters worse, German fighters continued to contest air superiority, countering the RFC's offensive patrols and disrupting artillery cooperation. Reconnaissance and bombing operations also fared badly, but the RFC's efforts continued to be sustained at high intensity. The improving weather led to ever-larger air fights and an ever-growing casualty list. By the end of the month, the RFC had lost 245 aircraft in combat and 319 aircrew killed or captured. As the RFC/RAF official history observed, "in no other month throughout the war was the Royal Flying Corps so hard pressed, nor were the casualties suffered so heavy."[15]

The fighting on the ground continued for the next fortnight in a series of smaller scale set-piece attacks designed to seize more of the German defenses. In the air, casualties began to fall as the RFC learned to counter the fighter threat by employing larger and more numerous formations, pushing the air battle further away from the front line and achieving local air superiority.[16] The improved protection enjoyed by the corps squadrons also saw a reduction in the loss of artillery cooperation machines. Progress on the ground was limited, however, by the German strategy of elastic defense coupled with vigorous counterattacks.[17] The RFC endeavored to neutralize these tactics by directing artillery fire against developing counter-attacks—a technique that would be deployed increasingly effectively in the succeeding months. The Battle of Arras formally ended on 16 May, by which time air superiority no longer lay with the Germans. "Enemy aircraft now enjoy significant numerical superiority. Our own, formerly superior, fighter pilots seem no longer to be able to make up for the enemy's numerical superiority."[18]

The air campaign had been as expensive as it was unstinting. If there was any consolation it was the knowledge that without the air effort there would have been no success on the ground. The Arras fighting had lasted just five weeks and cost the RFC a total of 263 aircraft and 430 aircrew killed, wounded, or prisoners of war.[19] This compares to 350 aircraft and 483 aircrew lost during the twenty weeks of the Somme. The RFC was a substantially larger organization than it had been the year before, but these losses were still severe. Combat casualties in April represented over 30 percent of available aircraft—the highest casualty rate suffered during the Somme never exceeded 19 percent (in September 1916). This was also the greatest monthly loss suffered during the whole of 1917 (including Third Ypres and Cambrai). Moreover, if other wastage is taken into account (accidents, aircraft struck off as beyond economic repair, or obsolete machines returned to Home Establishment) the total monthly loss in aircraft was the equivalent of nearly 50 percent of frontline strength.[20] It is interesting to note that the exceptional losses of Bloody April closely mirrored the experience on the ground. The BEF's daily loss rate at Arras proved greater than at the Somme, Third Ypres, or the Hundred Days.[21]

Notwithstanding these losses, the RFC still managed to generate a substantial operational output throughout April (in terms of total flying hours), a remarkable achievement given the relatively poor weather and the disruptive attacks of German fighters.[22] During the period April–May 1917 the frontline squadrons flew over 69,000 hours, the third highest total on the western front in any two-month period of 1917. In fact, the flying effort in May (39,409 hours) was the highest monthly total achieved in the war to date and would not be surpassed until March 1918. The ability to sustain operations on this scale was owed to several factors. Aircraft production had grown significantly since 1916, reflecting the higher priority assigned to aviation in the armaments program and the organizational improvements introduced by the Ministry of Munitions. The average monthly airplane output in 1917 was 1,100 machines compared to just 476 machines in the previous year.[23] While the western front was not the sole beneficiary (of the 10,593 machines supplied to the RFC in 1917, the largest allocation—4,763—went to the home-based Training Brigade), the BEF still took 40 percent of the total (4,227 aircraft)—equivalent to some 350 aircraft each month. This includes, however, 655 aircraft delivered directly to the RFC during the course of the year from French manufacturers.[24]

Since total aircraft wastage on the western front during 1917 amounted to some 4,300 machines, this suggests a rough parity between losses and supply.[25] Unfortunately, monthly production rates did not match the pattern of wastage. As a result, the cumulative balance between aircraft delivered to the western front and those struck off was much less healthy—with wastage exceeding deliveries in eight months of the year—creating a "deficit" equivalent to four hundred aircraft by August.[26] In reality, the RFC did enjoy a rough monthly parity—but only because of additional local production generated by salvaging and rebuilding wrecked machines retrieved from across the western front. As the RFC's operational efforts grew, so the work of repairing damaged aircraft played an ever more important part in sustaining the front line. The RFC's main depots at St-Omer and Candas reconstructed nearly nine hundred aircraft during 1917 from aircraft and engines that had been struck off strength. These "new" aircraft were then delivered back to the frontline squadrons. Since it took some two to four weeks to produce a serviceable aircraft from a salvaged wreck, there was an inevitable lag between wastage and reconstruction.[27] Nevertheless, the overall effect was to create a positive supply balance and, over the year, a net "surplus" of nearly six hundred machines, although there was a slight imbalance between April and July 1917. The latter was readily manageable by the depots, which were able to draw on their reserves to bridge any gaps.

It was this pragmatic strategy—combining external and internal supply with overseas purchase—that allowed the RFC to maintain aircraft availability during periods of high attrition, such as Bloody April. Reconstruction, driven in part by combat wastage rates, provided a "natural" compensating mechanism during periods of heavy fighting. The critical contribution of the depots in salvaging and repairing damaged machines was underscored by the special instructions issued to the front line in 1917 "to avoid the accumulation of a large number of derelict machines on the front and a waste of valuable material."[28] Advice was provided on liaison with Army formations, the composition of the salvage party, the supply of vehicles and specialist equipment, and recovery priorities. In this regard, "first consideration should be given always to the salvage of the engine, afterwards to wireless and photographic equipment when fitted, to instruments and to guns and ammunition." Strenuous efforts were made to recover crashed aircraft—even where they were under German fire. The work was particularly dangerous and a number of squadron tradesmen earned gallantry awards for their efforts.[29]

The success of the RFC's strategy can be seen in the number of aircraft available to the operational squadrons. Prior to the battle, production deliveries and the arrival of new units allowed the front line to grow to some nine hundred aircraft.[30] These numbers were sustained throughout the fighting, although the heavy losses suffered in the first week of the offensive did have a measurable, albeit short-lived, effect on availability. If the size of the front line determined the RFC's operational potential, serviceability determined the RFC's operational output. Numbers counted for little if the engineering and supply system was unable to maintain aircraft in a flying condition or provide the necessary spares and consumables—such as fuel, oil, and gases—to operate them. The intensive flying of Bloody April coupled with high wastage created a substantial engineering burden in the form of routine and unscheduled maintenance. Aircraft and engines had to be replenished, damage repaired, and new machines prepared (together with the necessary spares and piece-parts), yet daily serviceability remained extremely high, averaging 87 percent, and only once dropped below 80 percent throughout the battle.[31]

Firsthand evidence of what this involved is provided by Norman Macmillan, who served throughout the battle with No. 45 Squadron, where he flew the two-seat Sopwith 1½ Strutter in the fighter-reconnaissance role:

> Our rotary engines were heavily worked. They developed many minor troubles during flights—broken valve springs, valve rockers, and ignition wires, the last often causing additional shorting as the engine revolved and the broken wires fouled others; defective oil pumps, defective air pressure to the fuel system, blued cylinders denoting worn or broken obturator rings; magneto defects and faulty sparking plugs; the shearing of studs. Sometimes there were major troubles— broken pistons, a cylinder blowing off (and in its going damaging the aircraft), internal ball-races breaking. The engines required a great deal of attention to keep them going. Complete overhauls were frequent. Our mechanics worked splendidly to keep the aircraft in service, often working all night to change an engine or carry out some major airframe repair.[32]

There was a long-term price for these achievements. Individual squadron establishments could only be sustained by reducing the overall rate of expansion in front-line strength or by slowing the replacement program (of which more below). It was, therefore, only a matter of time before the strain began to show. The first indication occurred shortly after Bloody April when availability stagnated at around 850 aircraft for a period of four months.[33] Growth returned in August only to end abruptly in November when five operational squadrons were redeployed at short notice to the Italian front—discussed in more detail at the end of this chapter. This hiatus was exacerbated by the temporary withdrawal of two fighter squadrons in June, following the first German daylight raids on London. The impact of these events illustrates the fine balance that characterized the supply of aircraft and engines to the western front. The margin for error was so small that any unexpected occurrence or higher-than-planned wastage had a direct influence on frontline strength and hence on operational output—even when serviceability remained high.

During the course of 1917 over forty-five squadrons (effectively every service squadron serving on the western front at the end of 1916) exchanged their increasingly obsolete machines for the latest fighter and observation aircraft; designs incorporating lessons learned from the Somme fighting and all featuring more powerful and reliable aero-engines. These aircraft types, notably the R.E.8 (army cooperation), Armstrong Whitworth FK8 (army cooperation), DH4 (day-bomber), Sopwith Camel (single-seat fighter), and S.E.5a (single-seat fighter) would remain the mainstay of the RFC (and RAF) until the armistice. The rate of changeover peaked between July and August when sixteen squadrons were fully reequipped.[34] The speed of the program was undoubtedly hastened by a determination to place the RFC in the best possible position to support the Ypres offensive. However, the need to direct such a high proportion of new production to existing squadrons inevitably slowed the growth in the overall strength of the front line—particularly compared to the high rate of expansion enjoyed throughout 1916.

TABLE 4. REPLACEMENT OF OBSOLETE SQUADRON MACHINES, 1917

	JAN	FEB	MAR	APR	MAY	JUN	JUL	AUG	SEP	OCT	NOV	DEC
SQUADRONS REPLACED	0	2	4	3	4	6	8	8	1	5	3	3

As important as these changes were, they presented the RFC's logistic system with a major challenge. Spares for the older machines were largely incompatible with their successor types—even where the aircraft involved had emerged from the same design office (such as the Royal Aircraft Factory's B.E.2 and its successor design the R.E.8). The arrival of the R.E.8 required the depots and front line to relinquish their holdings of B.E.2-related spares—to be returned to Home Establishment where many of the ex-western front machines would be employed in training duties. However, the phased nature of the replacement program, and unpredictability in the demand for spares (by type and quantity) meant that the rate of drawdown was more a matter of judgment than a science. There was a risk, therefore, that stock levels would prove too low or the range of spares too narrow.

Each aircraft type employed by the RFC was provided with a specific schedule of spares—that for the R.E.8 comprised forty pages and two thousand parts. The schedule for its RAF4a engine comprised over one hundred individual components, each comprising some ten to one hundred parts (of which about 10 percent were AGS).[35] By comparison, the Rolls Royce Eagle aero-engine contained over three thousand parts, although the average for all types was two thousand.[36] The R.E.8 was not a particularly complex machine, compared to other aircraft employed on the western front, although it was larger than the single-seat fighters. If we use the R.E.8 as a yardstick, the twelve different aircraft types that formed the RFC's front line during 1917 represented around 24,000 separate stock items (the employment of standard AGS components—such as bolts, turnbuckles, and instruments—did not reduce this total significantly, although it did improve interchangeability), while the sixteen different engines employed represented around 24,000 separate stock items, creating a total holding of some 50,000 individual items. The efficient and effective handling of a large and complex inventory should not be taken for granted. The problems faced by the Tank Corps in implementing robust stores handling practices and sustaining adequate levels of availability underscore the RFC's relative proficiency in coping with both the mass and detail of industrial warfare.[37] While managing such a wide inventory range was in itself challenging, an even greater problem was obtaining the items in the first place.

For a variety of reasons, manufacturers found it easier to provide complete aircraft than to produce sets of spares. It was not until a new type was mature (and a representative set of drawings available) that a comprehensive spares package could be specified.[38] Contractual and financial imperatives encouraged manufacturers to produce complete aircraft rather than components or piece parts. As a result, the rate of spares production was always slower than the rate of aircraft production. This problem featured strongly in the deliberations of the Air Board's Progress and Allocation Committee. In June 1917 it was stated that "unless more spares were forthcoming it would be impossible to send out the replacement squadrons provided for in the programme. Spares were required for DH4, DH5, S.E.5, SPADs, Sopwith Camel, and Bristol Fighters."[39] It was further pointed out that all these machines were practically new types and that the supply of spares had not yet reached the maximum. In the case of the Sopwith Camel, the solution adopted required monthly production to be abated by twenty machines and the components turned into spares. To compound these difficulties, the prediction of failure modes and consumption rates (and hence the range and quantity to be provided) was an immature process in which the unknowns outnumbered the knowns (until practical experience was gained). If these were not problems enough, the loss of a well-understood aircraft type and its replacement by an unfamiliar (and untested) design inevitably created a knowledge gap across the entire engineering organization.

Some indication of the maturity of the RFC's logistic system and its responsiveness can be judged from the way that the front line's overall serviceability remained above 85 percent for most of 1917—throughout this period of major change.[40] It would be wrong to imply, however, that the re-equipment program did not have an impact on aircraft availability. At unit level the loss of experience and the need to learn the intricacies of a new design and its operating characteristics did reduce serviceability. A good example is No. 9 Squadron, which exchanged all of its B.E.2e aircraft for the newer R.E.8 between May and June 1917. From a peak of twenty-one B.E.2 machines on strength in March 1917, thirty-eight examples were struck off over the next two months as the changeover gathered pace. Twelve R.E.8s arrived from No. 1 Aircraft Depot in May, followed by a further sixteen in June and a final batch of twenty-three in July. On 1 August 1917, the squadron could boast a total strength of twenty-four R.E.8 aircraft. There was, nevertheless, a distinct learning curve reflected by reduced serviceability as both aircrew and engineers got to grips with the new type.[41]

The failure of the French spring offensive meant that the main Allied effort would now be in Flanders, where Sir Douglas Haig had long planned a major attack designed to break through the German defenses. However, before this could take place a preliminary operation was mounted in early June against the Messines-Wytschaete ridge to deny the enemy direct observation of the preparations for the forthcoming offensive. The assault was mounted along a front of some ten miles by three of the six corps forming Second Army.[42] The RFC contribution comprised II Brigade together with 9 (HQ) Wing—a total of some 375 aircraft—representing slightly less than 40 percent of the front line. The GAS could field six hundred aircraft but these were spread along the entire front of 4 Armee—that is, from Messines to the sea. Once again, the RFC enjoyed significant numerical superiority but, unlike Arras, the fighting would prove to be less one-sided.[43]

Success at Messines depended on dominating the defending German artillery. The concentration of British artillery was higher than anything previously attempted and relied on the RFC for its accurate direction. The air offensive began several weeks before the actual assault, subjecting German artillery positions and strong points to destructive fire. Systematic bombardment of the enemy's trenches began on 21 May in preparation for the main assault. The corps squadrons, some of which had been increased in establishment from eighteen to twenty-four machines in preparation for the battle, performed extremely effectively throughout this period, largely protected from enemy fighters by intense air activity in the form of offensive patrols and close escort. This "barrage line" was assisted by the employment of wireless detection to find and attack enemy artillery cooperation aircraft that crossed British lines.[44]

The attack on the morning of 7 June was preceded by the explosion of nineteen mines under Messines Ridge.[45] Although some difficulty was again experienced with contact patrols, the infantry had successfully secured all its objectives by the evening. The accuracy of the barrage and the rapid deployment of counter-battery fire weakened the German defenses such that there was little resistance. Enemy counterattacks were identified and eliminated while offensive patrols kept enemy fighters at bay—although not without losses. The opportunity was also taken to mount low-level attacks against the German rear area, including airfields, while bombing raids were mounted against railway stations and airfields, both day and night. There are numerous German accounts that testify to the RFC's effectiveness in these roles. "Those of us on the ground were frequently the targets of enemy aircraft: the boldest of these came down to twenty metres to fire at us. It went on like this day after day. By then we were worn down so much that, finally, careful watchfulness in the face of danger gave way to complete indifference." Another infantryman recorded how "swarms of enemy aircraft enhanced the efficiency of the artillery. They interdicted the rear areas by day and night, attacking all manner of live targets with bombs and machine-gun fire." Yet another wrote that "throughout the day British aircraft flew at extremely low level over the German positions and rear areas, directing the British artillery fire and dropping bombs on all identified targets . . . including Messines."[46] The German official history for 1917 states that the English "employed artillery that was far superior in number and calibre and aircraft that were easily three times superior to ours in number. No command post, no concrete construction, no tunnel entrance and hardly an isolated machine gun, light-signal or radio station escaped the enemy fliers, who worked without interference. In every instance artillery fire was immediately called in and the identified target was engaged with an expenditure of ammunition such as was never available to us."[47]

The defeat of a major German counterattack on the evening of 8 June effectively marked the end of the main phase of the battle. Although fighting continued until 17 June, the RFC's contribution was largely concluded. Some ninety-five aircraft and 106 aircrew had been lost in the three weeks of operations.[48] Wastage had been relatively low, but Major General Trenchard was driven to write to his brigade commanders on 10 June regarding the need to husband resources:

> I would ask that as far as possible you do your best to point out to your Armies that it is of the utmost importance that the Flying Corps should avoid wastage in both pilots and machines for some little time. My reserve at present is dangerously low, in fact, in some cases it barely exists at all, and the supply from home is not coming forward sufficiently freely to enable us to continue fighting an offensive in the air continuously. It is just as impossible for the air forces to fight a continuous offensive as it is for the infantry and as we have no reserve squadrons it is necessary to do everything to avoid losses.[49]

Indicative of the difficult supply position was the decision to reduce the establishment of the corps squadrons to eighteen aircraft once the battle was over. A further sign was the increase in the proportion of aircraft delivered by air rather than in crates. Delivery by air offered a faster response in providing replacement aircraft but it was not the most convenient way for the depots to handle or store machines, many of which needed modifications or new equipment before they could be issued (it was also a highly weather-dependent process). On the other hand, the work required to erect these aircraft took tradesmen away from other duties—such as reconstruction of salvaged airframes. Over the period January–March 1917, 46 percent of all aircraft supplied to the BEF were delivered to the depots in crates but this abruptly fell to 20 percent in April and as low as 12 percent in June. By comparison, the figure for June 1916 was 28 percent, suggesting that this was not simply a seasonal trend (reflecting the poor flying weather faced during a winter Channel crossing) but a conscious shift in policy.[50]

The rapid reduction in reserves helps explain the change in policy. Prior to Arras, the RFC's two depots held some 250 serviceable aircraft, but this fell to under two hundred by the end of Bloody April. The level grew over the next few

months, but Third Ypres saw the number fall again—only rising in December once
the fighting was over. This was not just a question of quantity but also one of detail.
With sixteen different aircraft/engine combinations in use, the 192 aircraft available
in the reserve on 1 May 1917 represented an average of twelve aircraft per type, substantially less than one squadron's worth (on an establishment of eighteen aircraft).

The RFC's ability to sustain superior numbers of aircraft provided an overwhelming advantage that could not be countered—other than for short periods
and by concentrating all forces at the combat front. The German official history,
while claiming that the GAS was superior from a tactical point of view, readily
acknowledged that the enemy's numerical superiority "was beyond overtaking."[51]
The concentration of squadrons for Third Ypres had begun even before the Arras
offensive concluded and developed independently of the reorganization required to
support the Messines attack. The new offensive was intended to capture much of
the Belgian coast and eliminate the German U-boat bases. The main thrust, to be
undertaken by Fifth Army (with support from Second Army and the French First
Army) along a front of seven and a half miles, was against the Passchendaele-Staden
ridge and the Roulers–Thourout railway. Supporting attacks, to be undertaken by
Fourth Army, were planned for the coast.[52] The core of the RFC's effort fell to IV
and V Brigades, supported by 9 (HQ) Wing. Additional aircraft were provided by
II Brigade, giving a total of 508 machines—or some 60 percent of the total RFC
strength on the western front. Progress with the re-equipment program meant that
many of these squadrons were flying the latest aircraft types, such as the R.E.8 and
Sopwith Camel. On the other hand, the supply of aircraft and pilots remained a
continuing concern particularly if the fighting were to prove long and intensive.
Accordingly, squadron establishments were reduced in I and III Brigades to provide a reserve pool to reinforce those units directly involved in the air offensive.[53]
These changes were prudent, but they also indicate how logistic constraints shaped
the RFC's operational posture. A less ambitious reequipment program would have
allowed a greater frontline strength to be fielded, but at the cost of fighting abilities and, ultimately, higher wastage rates (as Bloody April demonstrated). On the
other hand, allocating a higher proportion of aircraft production to the western
front would have reduced training capacity at home—and slowed the supply of
pilots. In fact, as the War Cabinet's reaction to the German daylight bombing of
London demonstrated, Home Defence could sometimes have an even greater call
on resources. Several fighter squadrons were withdrawn from France and promised
reinforcements were diverted to improve London's air defenses.[54]

Following the problems experienced in 1916 when an overly ambitious expansion plan had been agreed, there was a better understanding of the need to invest
in training and sustainability rather than blindly pursuing the chimera of frontline
numbers. Sefton Brancker, as director of air organization at the War Office, put it
quite succinctly: "The first and outstanding fact that I realised was that we had tried
to go too fast in our expansion and had outgrown our strength in both pilots and

aeroplanes." In his opinion, "the root of the trouble had been too much optimism, like many other troubles during the Great War."[55] One area where modest investment offered the prospect of significantly improving the supply position was repair capacity. The expansion of the depots and engine repair shops offered an effective route to sustaining the front line—without the need to withdraw men and machines from existing squadrons. This was partially self-balancing in that higher wastage created increased potential for reconstruction—as long as there was a comprehensive and widespread system for salvage and adequate repair capacity to handle the increased workload.

The air offensive in support of the Second and Fifth Armies was scheduled to begin on 7 July, some three weeks before the ground assault opened. The campaign comprised artillery cooperation, as well as reconnaissance, photography, and day and night bombing—together with offensive patrols. The initial focus was on countering the enemy's active patrolling while protecting the corps squadrons—a task facilitated by wireless intelligence. In the event, poor weather delayed operations by several days until 11 July. The German reaction was vigorous and on a large scale, substantial dogfights taking place all through the next day—indeed, air activity would remain intense until the end of the month. The RFC's success in helping register and destroy German batteries on the Fifth Army front forced many of them to be withdrawn. This delayed the offensive until the supporting artillery could be moved up and the enemy's new locations located. Bad weather further delayed the assault until the morning of 31 July.[56]

The main attack was undertaken by Fifth Army and was a partial success, although German counterattacks regained some lost ground. The supporting attacks by Second Army and the French First Army were more successful—securing the flanks of the main thrust. The RFC's close support activities were significantly handicapped throughout the day by poor weather. Numerous contact patrols were undertaken but, operating at low height, resulted in heavy attrition. The offensive campaign by the army squadrons was less constrained by the weather and targets were attacked across the German rear area. A new technique involved using single-seat fighters for low-level bombing. This appears to have been a late idea as the squadron engineers needed to jury-rig the necessary equipment literally the night before the attack.[57] The initiative greatly expanded the range and quantity of targets that could be attacked—albeit that the limited explosive power of the 25-lb Cooper bomb meant that serious damage was unlikely without a direct hit or a near-miss. Although these tactics attracted significant attrition, they improved the support afforded to the advancing infantry—when properly organized and coordinated. They were also capable of inflicting substantial casualties against troops in open ground—as would be demonstrated during the German 1918 offensive.[58]

Deteriorating weather over the next few days greatly interfered with the RFC's work such that the artillery program suffered major disruption. It was not until 16 August that the offensive was resumed, this time further north in the salient, against the German defenses at Langemarck. Yet again, low clouds and rain seriously impeded the RFC's efforts, restricting the program of offensive work and, more seriously, the ability of the corps squadrons to identify emerging counterattacks.[59] Offensive patrols largely kept enemy aircraft at a distance and those that broke through found the artillery cooperation machines well able to defend themselves. Artillery observation and counter-battery fire continued to prove effective, but progress on the ground was hampered by the presence of concrete pillboxes. These strong points were difficult to capture and slowed the advance, although it was the continuing poor weather that did most to hinder progress; indeed, little more was achieved during the rest of the month. Some minor operations mounted by Third Army did prove successful and in these the RFC was able to provide close support for the advancing infantry. A German infantryman reported how "the attack of the British infantry was very effectively supported by a large number of British aircraft. These circled very low overhead firing their machine guns."[60]

The rain began to ease at the beginning of September but the ground was not dry enough to mount a fresh attack until 20 September. The new objective was the Menin Road Ridge, to the southeast of Ypres, and involved corps from both Second and Fifth Armies. This phase of the offensive saw a change in tactics, instigated by General Sir Herbert Plumer who had replaced Sir Hubert Gough. A relatively short advance was planned, supported by a much higher concentration of artillery than employed on 31 July.[61] The RFC played an important part in accurately directing the bombardment and in the counter-battery task. In addition to its "usual" artillery cooperation and counterattack patrol work, the RFC also undertook a wide-ranging campaign against the German rear areas. This included day and night bombing of airfields, billets, and railway centers. Large numbers of low-flying fighter aircraft were employed to bomb and strafe any movement as well as engaging German contact patrol or other cooperation aircraft. Although the weather deteriorated on the eve of the battle, substantial progress was made and "under protection of a well-placed rolling barrage and supported by tanks, as well as by numerous low-flying aircraft they gained ground relatively rapidly."[62] German counterattacks continued over the next few days, but these were successfully broken up by artillery fire—employing information provided by RFC aircraft. Low-flying attacks against troops moving up to the front line were also judged to have been successful in blunting the German response. Meanwhile, regular offensive patrols meant that the corps squadrons were little troubled by fighters. Over the next few days the German road and rail network was bombed by day and night to impede the movement of reinforcements. The offensive was successfully concluded on 25 September.[63]

The advance continued the following day on the Second Army front, to the south of the Menin Road, where the remainder of Polygon Wood and numerous strongpoints were captured.[64] Throughout the attack, the RFC's corps squadron worked closely with the infantry, directing effective counter-battery fire and helping break up successive German counterattacks. Meanwhile, low-flying aircraft again hindered the progress of reinforcements. The bombing of airfields, transportation, and billeting centers was maintained over the next few days, together with reconnaissance and photography tasks. German counterattacks persisted until 3 October but all were repulsed.[65] The offensive now returned to the Fifth Army front where further advances were made against the enemy's defenses opposite Zonnebeke. Despite the poor weather and the state of the ground, all the main objectives were captured. These conditions hampered the corps squadrons but did not prevent counter-battery, contact patrol, and counterattack work. In the face of deteriorating weather, a further effort was made on 9 October to capture the remainder of Passchendaele ridge. This was successfully achieved, although the clouds and rain meant that very little flying was undertaken in support of the infantry attack.[66] What was achieved, however, comprised essential counter-battery registration tasks as well as contact patrols. Further limited attacks were carried out over the remainder of the month, supported by the RFC as weather permitted. On 30 October the advance resumed against Passchendaele itself. Little air opposition was experienced and the RFC was able to provide support unhindered by enemy fighters. The continuing effectiveness of the RFC was only too evident on the ground—when the weather permitted. A German officer wrote: "During the afternoon the sun broke through the heavy cloud cover and we were immediately plagued by enemy aircraft. Circling low, they were observing the exact line of our positions. They then fired off yellow flares and we were soon under fire from the British heavy guns. Finally, it was evening and the firing died away. By then, I had lost another twelve men killed and wounded."[67]

The attack was renewed on 6 November, resulting in the capture of Passchendaele village, although mist largely limited the RFC to strafing ground targets. Four days later, the Third Battle of Ypres was brought to a conclusion. Over the course of the offensive the RFC had generated over 118,000 operational flying hours, compared to the 83,000 hours flown during the Somme. Although this might not seem exceptional, given the substantial increase in frontline strength, the average hours flown per aircraft were actually higher—exceeding thirty hours in seven months of 1917, and in five months of 1916.[68] It should also be remembered that this was achieved against a GAS that had undertaken a substantial reorganization specifically to counter the dominance enjoyed by the RFC during the Somme offensive. As at Messines, however, the RFC's ability to sustain large numbers of aircraft over the battlefront meant that the GAS could barely hold its own and could only achieve air superiority by concentrating all of its forces—and then only temporarily.[69]

The RFC's superior operational output was built on improved logistic performance—in both engineering efficiency and supply chain effectiveness. Over the period 1916–1918, the number of tradesmen per frontline aircraft rose slightly but averaged around 25:1. The improvements achieved in 1917 were therefore not the result of "brute force" (in the form of more tradesmen) but of greater efficiency.[70]

Although the pattern of monthly flying hours achieved during 1917 dramatically illustrates the effect of winter weather, it also reveals the sustained engineering effort delivered between April and November—the start of Arras to the end of Third Ypres. As a result, the average monthly flying hours per tradesman rose from 1.0 in 1916 to 1.2 in 1917. This may seem a modest gain, but it generated an additional four thousand flying hours and was the equivalent of adding five squadrons to the front line.

Supply performance also showed a distinct improvement over the year, even though the supply chain had much to contend with. Combat losses experienced during Third Ypres comprised 765 aircraft and 1,000 aircrew (killed, wounded, and POW), compared to the 370 aircraft and 500 aircrew lost during the Somme. The pattern of wastage shows a strong correlation between aircraft and engines struck off, at least until the end of the year.[71] These averaged some 450–500 aircraft and engines each month during the height of the fighting—or approximately 50 percent of the available frontline strength. This level of attrition clearly presented a major challenge to the supply chain. However, a combination of direct deliveries and in-theatre repair actually enabled depot holdings to grow over this period, although much of the increase was owed to a rapid rise in unserviceable or under-repair aircraft.[72] The overall position, in terms of serviceable aircraft as a percentage of frontline strength, actually deteriorated over the course of 1917. Reserves fell from a peak of 38 percent in February 1917 (299 aircraft) to a low of 19 percent in November 1917 (193 aircraft), although the situation improved in the following month.

Of course, having the right spares or an adequate stock of replacement aircraft and engines was not the same thing as having them in the right hands at the front line. It was the last few miles of the supply chain that were critical. The high level of operational output sustained during Third Ypres provides prima facie evidence for the RFC's ability to move matériel between the depots and the squadrons in the required quantities and timescale. Individual testimony confirms this picture:

> As regards the damage done, it was surprising to see how often a pilot would come back with twenty bullet holes in his machine, not one of them having hit him or a vital part of the aircraft. Sometimes the fabric would be torn and we'd have to patch it up. On other occasions a pilot would get back all right, but with a dead engine, having managed to land at another aerodrome. Ordinary damage we used to repair by getting the spares from St-Omer, and we used to give the engines a minor overhaul but if it came to a big overhaul, the engine would be sent to the depot, repaired and returned to us. It was done very quickly indeed. I was always surprised at the speed with which the machines were replaced.[73]

The experience of No. 9 Squadron reinforces this picture at the micro level. The unit was heavily involved throughout Third Ypres (during which it lost sixty-six aircraft and fifty-eight aircrew). As a corps squadron it also undertook the artillery cooperation duties that were central to the RFC's contribution to the BEF's operations on the western front. From May 1917 (and well into 1918) the squadron was kept continuously supplied with R.E.8 aircraft. In general, deliveries matched wastage, enabling the number of available machines to stay at, or over, the full establishment of twenty-four aircraft for the duration of Third Ypres.[74] No. 9 Squadron's experience was not untypical of the other artillery cooperation squadrons in the XV Corps Wing, which operated nearly ninety R.E.8 aircraft throughout Third Ypres.[75]

Before concluding this chapter there is a final aspect of the RFC's operations on the western front that deserves comment. Although the Italian campaign lies outside the scope of this thesis, the deployment at short notice of five frontline squadrons to northern Italy is important because of the light it throws on the efficacy and flexibility of the logistic system as a whole.

On 24 October 1917 a German and Austro-Hungarian offensive broke through the Italian positions at Caporetto—a previously quiet section of the front (the campaign would officially be known as the Twelfth Battle of the Isonzo).[76] A general retreat followed that threatened the total collapse of the Italian armies. The Allies reacted quickly, deciding on 26 October to send immediate military aid. The British XIV Corps (comprising 7 and 23 Divisions) were ordered to move from France to Italy by train—together with two RFC squadrons (No. 28 and No. 34) forming 51 Wing. At a further meeting at Rapello on 5 November, it was agreed to send two more divisions (5 and 41) and three further squadrons (Nos. 42, 45, and 66) as part of No. VII Brigade.[77] A total of ninety aircraft had been allocated (comprising fifty-four single-seat fighters and thirty-six army cooperation). By deciding to standardize on two aircraft types (the Sopwith Camel and the R.E.8) the logistic and operational arrangements were made easier; however, the deployment of equipment and personnel over a distance of some one thousand miles represented a major challenge to an organization that had been fighting a largely static war for over three years.[78] Between 7 November and 12 December, all five squadrons, together with Headquarters VII Brigade, a dedicated aircraft park, and airplane supply depot left France by train for Italy.[79] According to one source, the personnel of the latter included a number of Coventry sheet-metal workers who had gone on strike for higher wages and were promptly drafted to Italy.[80] Only two of these squadrons would return before the armistice, the other three being lost permanently to the western front.

The initial warning order for the move of the first two squadrons was issued by HQ RFC on 28 October. When authorized, both units were to move to No. 2 AD at Candas, where they would be entrained for an unspecified location. The adjutant of the newly formed 51 Wing was impressed "by the smoothness with which the whole thing was done. Given the organisation, which of course existed at an immense depot like No. 2 AD, the entraining of a complete squadron is a comparatively simple matter."[81] Instructions were provided for the issue of additional transport as well as spare engines, hangars, and stores—sufficient for one month's operations. It was also directed that the first train would include the flat-bed lorries needed to unload these stores, including ten thousand gallons of petrol for each squadron.[82] Each train comprised thirty-six to thirty-nine trucks carrying personnel, vehicles, crated airplanes, hangars, fuel, oil, ammunition, and general stores. The tents alone required four 20-ton trucks, while the petrol and oil needed a further six.[83] In discussing these plans Trenchard estimated that it would take at least six days and four trains to load both squadrons and at least one week to erect and prepare the aircraft after arrival—warning that it took longer to transfer an RFC squadron than a division.[84] The following account by Norman Macmillan, who was personally involved in the move, provides some indication of the effort involved:

> No. 34 Squadron left France in two trains, one on 7 and the second on 8 November; 28 Squadron had followed on 9 and 10 November with 18 Camels and one spare. All aircraft were packed in crates. To aid off-loading and transportation at Milan, No. 2 Aircraft Depot (Candas) had sent ahead two flat-top trucks and a crocodile trailer. The standard equipment of both squadrons was increased by 18 canvas hangars and about a month's supply of petrol, oil, ammunition, and spares. The journey to Milan occupied about four days. There at the siding, each train was unloaded in about three hours using special cranes ordered in advance by telegram. Officers and men worked day and night shifts until every aircraft was erected at Milan airfield. In a little less than 48 hours the Camels were ready, tested in flight and passed for duty. The larger R.E.8s were ready by 17 November.[85]

The decision to move the squadrons by rail—even though the pilots were eager to fly direct to Italy—was sensible given the operational uncertainties and the danger that aircraft and pilots could become separated from their ground crew and stores. Nevertheless, the individual squadrons were ready for operations within eight and ten days respectively of their departure from Candas. The remaining three squadrons arrived considerably later—delayed by the opening of the Battle of Cambrai and higher priority railway traffic.[86] This did allow, however, for some additions to the original deployment instructions, such as the need to label each package and truck clearly with the name of the owning unit and the requirement to pack the train rations so they were readily available during the journey—presumably reflecting the experience of the first units to arrive in Italy.

Although this episode confirms that the frontline squadrons were indeed mobile, it is also evident that much depended on the availability of substantial numbers of vehicles and railway trucks. The first operational sorties were flown on 29 November—the day before the 23rd and 41st Divisions moved into position on the Montello sector and three weeks after the squadrons had left France. The flexibility and responsiveness of the depots in planning and implementing the move are also worthy of comment. The RFC's well-developed logistic arrangements and planning skills meant that the deployment proceeded much more smoothly than for other BEF units transported to Italy by rail.[87] However, the hiatus between the decision to move and the start of operations demonstrated that there were finite limits as to what could be achieved. The RFC's frontline squadrons could not operate without their logistic tail and the means to fight—in the form of fuel, oil, and ordnance. Unfortunately, the deployment of the five squadrons proved easier than maintaining their aircraft. Other than those supplies secured locally or sourced through the Army's separate arrangements, all stores—including replacement machines, engines, and technical spares—had to be sent by train from France. The presence of the Air Park, creating an in-theatre engineering capability, mitigated the impact on aircraft serviceability but average availability was still lower than the western front—even though the operational tempo was lower. It took some time before over 80 percent of the aircraft on squadron strength were regularly available for operations, a level routinely achieved in France.[88] Operating at the end of a long supply pipeline— regularly subject to delays because of overcrowding and weather—the RFC could not rely on an uninterrupted flow of spares and equipment.[89]

A more pervasive problem was the lack of logistic flexibility, not only because information took time to flow back to HQ RFC and the depots, but also because there was little margin for error. For example, on several occasions a replacement aircraft recently arrived from Candas was found to be deficient.[90] This was the result of an ex-squadron aircraft returned to store as "serviceable" that was then sent to Italy without inspection, creating considerable extra work on the part of 7 AP, who had little alternative but to spend several days rectifying worn controls and unserviceable engine components. In France such problems could be rapidly resolved but in Italy there was no safety net. These incidents also illustrate how the efficacy of the RFC's logistic system depended on common processes supported by accurate, comprehensive, and timely information. When these failed, the effectiveness of the entire supply chain was jeopardized.

A partial solution to these challenges was found by sending a weekly resupply train. Whereas the logistic system on the western front was demand-led (allowing the squadrons to "pull" replacement machines and stores as required), it was much easier to "push" material to the squadrons in Italy than wait for demands that would then take a finite time to satisfy. This was less efficient than a "pull" system but was probably the best arrangement in the circumstances. Even so, the inherent inefficiencies became apparent when Brigadier-General Tom Webb-Bowen, commanding VII Brigade, wrote to HQ RFC requesting that the special supply train be reduced to every alternate week. Storage accommodation was becoming problematic and the quantity of new machines needing to be erected meant that there was no capacity to work on existing aircraft, which otherwise would have to be returned to Candas for repair. It was agreed to reduce the level of resupply to six spare RAF4a engines and twelve Clerget engines every month, together with three replacement R.E.8s and six Camels every fortnight (all with engines). This would still leave six to seven weeks' reserve at the relatively low rates of attrition then being experienced.[91]

Serviceability rates did not markedly improve over the next few months; for example, only 65 percent of aircraft on the Italian front were serviceable in May 1918. However, this was not exceptional in that all the RAF's overseas service squadrons experienced substantially lower serviceability rates than the western front.[92] It is tempting to see a linear relationship between serviceability and distance (echoing Kenneth Boulding's "loss of strength gradient").[93] In reality, a combination of factors was involved, including extreme weather conditions, poor infrastructure, and limited local engineering capacity. Distance certainly was a factor, in as much as it made communication more difficult and delayed the flow of spares and replacements. On the other hand, serviceability levels on the western front were also higher than those experienced in England, suggesting that a concerted effort was made to sustain the highest level of aircraft availability on the most active front. Norman Macmillan certainly makes great play of the fact that the RFC in Italy demanded very few resources compared to the western front and still achieved significant results, a view echoed by the RFC's air commander in Mesopotamia: "The conditions on the Western Front were different. There an aeroplane could be replaced in a night; a wire was sent and a new pilot and machine would arrive next morning. In Mesopotamia there were a few reserve machines which could be flown up in, say, a couple of days by pilots sent back from the front; outside these the nearest source of supply was Egypt, three weeks away!"[94]

Looking at 1917 as a whole, it is evident that the RFC was able to grow substantially both as an organization and as a fighting service—without losing significant flexibility or responsiveness. While benefitting from increased aircraft production at home, it managed to re-equip the front line with more modern machines of superior fighting ability while delivering greater operational output. It was also able to cope with the dreadful attrition of Bloody April and handle a reenergized and better organized GAS. Notwithstanding the awful summer weather, the RFC provided an important—if not essential—contribution to the BEF's offensives at Messines and Third Ypres. The improved performance of the RFC's engineering and supply system played an essential role in all these achievements. Nevertheless, without such high wastage rates and the need to replace obsolete aircraft by newer types, the front line might have been expected to have grown to 1,800 aircraft and ninety squadrons on the western front by the end of 1917. In reality, it would only reach this size by the armistice. What is most striking, however, is the sheer persistence and ubiquity of the RFC. German accounts of Third Ypres repeatedly refer to the constant presence of British aircraft and their active role in supporting infantry attacks or directing artillery fire. Machine-gun fire and bombing from low-flying aircraft wore down morale, impeded communications, interdicted the movement of reserves, and played an important role in fragmenting the battlefield by isolating the front line. German counterattacks were disrupted through direct action or by bringing down artillery fire on the gathering forces. Such sustained and relentless effort—and the wastage it brought in men and machines—could only be maintained by a professional and responsive logistic organization underpinned by a well-resourced supply chain.

1918—LOGISTICS ON THE MOVE

CHAPTER

T HE LAST YEAR OF THE WAR PROVIDED MANY CHALLENGES FOR THE BEF, NOT least the need to adapt to mobile operations. The retreat precipitated by the German 1918 spring offensives and the continuous advance following the Battle of Amiens were far removed from the "static" warfare that had largely prevailed on the western front since late 1914. Under these circumstances it might be thought that the inherent mobility of aircraft—in terms of speed and reach—would provide the RFC with a logistic advantage compared to other parts of the BEF. "Where air forces had once operated simply to support army headquarters, their strategic mobility was now exploited and squadrons were switched across the front to act as aerial fire brigades in campaigns involving nearly 2,000 aeroplanes."[1]

Strategic mobility was not the same as operational sustainability. It is true that replacement machines could be moved rapidly by air (although this demanded a large pool of ferry pilots), but sustaining the RFC required a great deal more than a ready supply of new aircraft.[2] The ability of a squadron to travel faster than its ground-based organization meant that it ran a constant risk of outreaching its supplies.[3] Everything needed to maintain flying operations on the western front had to move by road, canal, or rail to a destination that might move in a matter of days by up to one hundred miles. The operation of the RFC's logistic system under these conditions provides an unprecedented opportunity to assess the overall effectiveness of the organization and to gain some feel for its responsiveness and resilience. As Liddell Hart observed, "Mobility is the true test of a supply system."[4]

The creation of the RAF on 1 April 1918, uniting the RFC and RNAS as a single service under a separate Air Ministry, had no immediate impact on the western front. The event has been described as a "formality," but the transition from RFC to RAF was more than simply an administrative exercise and had the potential to disrupt operations.[5] Although the handful of RNAS units based in France and Belgium (largely part of 5 Group) were already either integral to the RFC's order of battle or worked in close harmony, the organizational changes could still have proved problematic, as might have the requirement that GOC RAF, Major-General John Salmond, report to the chief of the Air Staff (CAS), Major-General Hugh Trenchard, while remaining under the command of CinC BEF. In the event, the relationship between the RAF and BEF was not weakened and any transitional problems were lost in the wider disruption caused by the German 1918 offensive. From the logistic perspective there was also little change. The staffs under Brigadier-General Robert Brooke-Popham oversaw the same arrangements that had supported the front line so effectively through Third Ypres. As previously noted, some duties were redistributed and new department titles were introduced, but the system and its enabling processes remained untouched—as did the sources of supply. Thus, the Army continued to provide rations, fuel, clothing, petrol, bombs, and ammunition while the depots and air parks supplied all other needs.[6] The most obvious changes were the reporting arrangements. No longer the responsibility of the Army, the RAF introduced new daily and monthly forms and altered both the detail and periodicity of returns. These developments were, however, essentially bureaucratic in nature.[7] The logistic system operated by the RAF during the remainder of 1918 was in effect the RFC logistic system, albeit under "new" management.

The RAF's logisticians would face two major challenges in 1918: the end of "static" warfare, and rapidly escalating attrition. An organization constructed around a largely immobile supply chain now had to sustain units on the move. At the same time, the rapid increase in operational wastage created unprecedented demands on the parks and depots. The losses experienced on the western front between January and November 1918 far exceeded anything previously seen. A total of 7,274 aircraft were struck off over the eleven months of fighting, compared to 4,290 for the whole of 1917 and just 1,462 for 1916.[8]

HQ RFC, during the last few months of 1917, engaged in a "lessons learned" exercise designed to build on the operational experience gained during Third Ypres and Cambrai. This mirrored a wider effort initiated by GHQ to review defensive measures and improve tactical training. Similar work had been undertaken after the Somme fighting, but there was a sense of urgency driven by the expected German assault (employing divisions redeployed from the eastern front) aimed at defeating the Allies before the arrival of substantial American forces on the western front. An early product was a general policy paper on defensive measures issued by GHQ on 14 December 1917. This was followed by a more detailed memorandum on the employment of the RFC in defense, distributed to all armies on 16 January 1918. The roles described for the RFC differed little from those undertaken during Third Ypres and Cambrai, but there was greater emphasis on identifying attacks and communicating the information as quickly as possible to the relevant army headquarters.[9]

Confident that there would be a German attack, GHQ was nevertheless uncertain about where it would occur. It was at this critical juncture that Trenchard left HQ RFC to join the Air Council as the first CAS.[10] Haig had been concerned that the departure of Trenchard would dilute the RFC's offensive spirit but his successor, John Salmond, was very much of the same mould and, although he would not enjoy the same close relationship with the CinC, Haig's concerns proved unfounded. Salmond was an able GOC and a highly effective leader during some "dreadful days in France."[11] Trenchard, as CAS, remained an influential figure, but Salmond did not lack initiative, overseeing a number of important developments designed to improve efficiency or to enhance operational capabilities. Some addressed tactical problems—such as the need to provide an additional aerodrome party for night-bombing squadrons—while others were aimed at improving mobility, including the creation of tent detachments, responsible for the erection and dismantling of tented accommodation.[12] Further changes were introduced to centralize airfield support tasks under dedicated maintenance sections responsible for maintaining existing landing grounds and protecting them from dilapidation or the unauthorized removal of material when unoccupied.[13] By August 1918, nearly 1,400 personnel were employed in a variety of ancillary units intended to improve the mobility of RAF squadrons, including tent detachments, maintenance sections, and dedicated construction parties (the latter responsible for preparing the ground of new aerodromes, erecting and maintaining hangars, and providing domestic accommodation).[14] The scale and importance of these tasks would later lead Salmond to set up a separate "air construction corps" (anticipating the RAF's Airfield Construction Branch of the Second World War), under a unified command and working directly to HQ RAF.[15]

One of Salmond's more significant and earliest decisions was to increase the establishment and number of Reserve Lorry Parks (RLPs) (created in 1917 to provide each brigade with a reserve of vehicles capable of moving up to half the brigade strength).[16] The RLPs were under the control of HQ RFC, but day-to-day management was exercised by their respective brigades.[17] It was Salmond's personal initiative to increase the RLP establishment by a further fifteen lorries and twelve trailers and also to create a dedicated headquarters lorry park.[18] By March 1918, there were five RLPs available, with a total establishment of over two hundred lorries and trailers, capable of supporting the move of up to thirty squadrons at any one time.[19] The expanded RLP system provided a much more flexible and capable reserve, but at some cost to the mobility of the individual squadrons. At least one squadron commander felt that the new policy was unhelpful:

> The transport allocated to the squadron was totally inadequate to cope with the work of transferring the squadron to a new aerodrome during a move, but a Reserve Lorry Park was attached to each Aircraft Park, where sufficient spare lorries and trailers were kept in reserve to be loaned to squadrons detailed to move. If only one squadron happened to be moving at the time, plenty of spare lorries were available, but when several squadrons in the same wing were moving together, the allotment of spare vehicles was very limited and sometimes totally inadequate.[20]

Such criticism aside, Salmond's insistence on these changes—initially against Trenchard's wishes—greatly helped the redeployment of the RAF's squadrons in the coming months:

> I had a long chat with him [Trenchard] about transport. He had cut down the transport with squadrons and other units to a minimum when static conditions on the front no longer necessitated the same mobile quota. Now we were anticipating great activity on our front by vastly superior forces and it was vital to be able to move squadrons at a moment's notice. I anticipated that we should have to move hurriedly when the attack was launched. He would not agree, [but] after returning home he must have changed his mind and the addition in all types of vehicles came pouring out in true Trenchard fashion.[21]

The value of these additional vehicles was confirmed by the experience of IX Brigade, operating under the direct control of HQ RAF. As the RAF's operational reserve, it was deployed on several occasions during 1918, notably in support of the French (in response to the agreement concluded in May between Douglas Haig and Ferdinand Foch that RAF squadrons would be made available in the event of a German attack). This provision was exercised by Foch on 2 June 1918 when eight RAF squadrons moved south from Hesdin to the Beauvais area:[22] "About 8 o'clock last night we got orders to move the brigade to the French area around Beauvais. Squadrons had transport and were prepared. The transport left at or about midnight. Machines left about 8 a.m. this morning . . . only one machine (a DH9 of No. 103 Squadron) crashed taking off, otherwise the brigade came down here complete: machines, transport, and personnel without any hitch whatever; quite a good performance."[23]

The deployment of approximately 160 aircraft and two thousand personnel (including air ammunition columns and an air park) over some one hundred miles was undoubtedly a major achievement, given that the brigade had only four days to prepare for the move. An equally significant step was Salmond's decision to expand the number of landing grounds in the rear area, to replace any forward airfields lost to the enemy and support additional squadrons flown in from other brigade areas as reinforcements. "After visiting the Army Commanders, I gave orders to the Chief of Works at HQ RFC to increase all landing grounds and establish sufficient [numbers] to take all RFC squadrons in case of an enforced retreat."[24] The expectation of a German offensive grew steadily and was not confined to the HQ staffs. A pilot with No. 52 Squadron recalled how "the cloud of the coming German attack was every day growing darker and darker."[25] The RFC did not remain passive in the face of the evident German preparations. A day-and-night bombing campaign was conducted from late February against enemy airfields and more distant targets, such as railheads. Convinced by the evidence provided by daily reconnaissance and photography that the assault would fall in the south, within the Third and Fifth Army areas, Salmond moved six squadrons of the newly formed IX Brigade to aerodromes behind the Fifth Army front. Even so, the GAS was able to assemble 730 aircraft against the 31 RFC squadrons and 579 aircraft based in the area of the Third and Fifth Armies.[26] For the first time, the GAS would outnumber the RFC during a major offensive.

The long-awaited attack opened on the early morning of 21 March 1918 and took place over fifty-four miles of the front, centered on the area between the Sensée and Oise rivers.[27] Fifty-six German divisions (with twelve more in reserve) faced fifteen divisions of the Third and Fifth Armies (with nine more in reserve). The initial bombardment was intense and caused widespread destruction and a rapid breakdown in communications. Poor weather, particularly fog, hindered the defenders and disguised the extent of the enemy's breakthrough, although it also hampered the efforts of the GAS to provide ground and artillery support.[28] Those RFC aircraft that were initially able to get airborne, and could see something on the ground, often found their wireless calls unanswered. As the weather improved, so the RFC mounted an increasing number of low-flying attacks, using bombs and machine guns against the advancing German infantry.[29] Artillery cooperation improved steadily through the day while organized bombing began against the German rear areas. There was also a great deal of confused fighting between the opposing air forces during the afternoon and evening. Despite some local setbacks, the German advance was rapid, particularly on the Fifth Army front, and it became necessary to withdraw all the squadrons in V Brigade (including the Fourth Aircraft Park) and some of the squadrons in III Brigade, before they were overrun.[30] The German assault resumed the next day with heavy fighting on the Third Army front. Fog again hampered the defenses. The RFC continued to mount low-flying attacks and to bomb targets in the German rear area. All the RFC's brigades were involved to some extent in trying to stem the enemy's advance, although the main burden fell on III, V, and IX Brigades. The effort was as relentless as it was expensive in aircraft and crews. It was not just the fighter squadrons that were thrown into the attack, but also the artillery cooperation squadrons, often unable to cooperate with the artillery but still able to bomb and strafe the enemy—as an R.E.8 pilot of No. 52 Squadron (V Brigade) recorded: "It is no exaggeration to say that for the next three or four days, during daylight hours, no machine of the squadron remained on the ground longer than was necessary to fill up, bomb up, and effect any necessary repairs or adjustments. Every machine and every crew was worked to the limit of capacity in bombing and ground strafing in a desperate attempt to stem the enemy advance."[31]

The problems in sustaining wireless communication with the army batteries had been anticipated, although the scale of the disruption would later give rise to criticism that resources were needlessly switched from artillery cooperation to low-flying attacks.[32] Salmond had anticipated that the air methods developed to suit static warfare—such as standing masts for counter-battery work—would be swept away in any German assault. In his opinion, the solution was "to bring to bear such a concentration of low-bombing aircraft on the front of the advancing infantry and back areas of the attack that the impetus must inevitably slacken and consequently relieve the pressure on our own troops."[33] Even so, it was not envisaged that every fighter available would need to carry out low-level bombing attacks and it was not until April that Brooke-Popham formally requested that S.E.5a, Camel, and Dolphin fighters were delivered from England with the necessary bombing fittings already installed—reducing the strain on squadron engineering resources and improving availability.[34]

By Sunday 24 March the position was extremely critical with the Germans threatening to drive a wedge between the Third and Fifth Armies. RFC aircraft continued to attack the enemy and to report on their advance. The 50th Infantrie Division, 18 Armee, unable to cross the Somme below Ham, reported serious losses, especially in horses, from low-flying enemy aircraft.[35] When the RFC was able to conduct artillery cooperation it proved effective in causing delays or breaking up attacks.[36] There was also a marked increase in air fighting, often lower than five thousand feet, but despite the attractive targets on the British side of the lines there was little interference from German aircraft. "The sight of our retreat is unforgettable; miles of road packed four abreast with vehicles, tired troops in the open regardless of cover—all affording a wonderful target for enemy low-flying aeroplanes. History will relate why there were so few."[37] The bulk of the RFC's effort focused on low-flying attacks with bombs and machine guns, pressed home with little regard for safety. A bugler in the German 8th Grenadier Regiment recorded that attacking aircraft flew so low that "my company commander had to fling himself flat on the ground, but for all that he was struck on the back by the wheels of the machine, thus being literally run over."[38] The German official history records that the initial German air superiority had been matched by 24 March and that "enemy wings of up to 60 aircraft dove down on the infantry with great zeal and strafed and bombed." XXXIX Reservekorps faced delays in moving forward on 23 March because of repeated low-level aircraft attacks, while LI Korps recorded serious losses (on 26 March) caused by strafing and bombing from low-flying aircraft. General Georg von der Marwitz, commanding 2 Armee, reported (28 March) that he was suffering logistic problems and attributed half his casualties to air attacks, while General Hermann von Kuhl (chief of staff to Prince Rupprecht's Army Group) referred to "extremely unpleasant enemy aerial activity."[39]

The RFC paid heavily for these efforts, losing fifty-one aircraft wrecked, shot down, or missing across the whole battle front. The following day was equally grave with the German advance threatening to split the British and French armies to the south while making strong progress against the Third Army in the north. Artillery cooperation was once again erratic with many calls being unanswered. The threat to the Third Army was so severe that Salmond directed additional squadrons from I and II Brigades to assist III and IX Brigades in low-flying attacks. "These squadrons will bomb and shoot up everything they can see on the enemy side of this line. Very low flying is essential. All risks to be taken. Urgent."[40] The day-bombing squadrons also participated in attacking the German lead elements, rather than the rear areas. The result of this unprecedented concentration was to "temporarily freeze up" the threatened breakthrough west of Bapaume.[41] Low-level attacks continued on 26 March in a desperate effort to slow the advance. By now, Salmond had concentrated 64 percent of his available squadrons behind Third Army.[42] During these critical hours, the RFC was largely able to operate without interference from the GAS. The latter's failure to provide effective ground support or to counter the RFC's operations is surprising given the detailed planning conducted prior to the offensive. Considerable effort was expended by the Germans to develop close air support tactics and assemble sufficient numbers of aircraft and trained crews. As with the RFC, fog denied the GAS a significant role in the initial assault, but the following days were not as successful as hoped for. Heavy casualties, supply problems, poor employment, and a breakdown of communications all contributed to this failure.[43] By contrast, the German official history records that enemy air formations pounced on the infantry "with great élan and attacked them with bombs and machine-gun fire . . . it was impossible to meet the demands of the troops for continuous air protection."[44] On the same day (26 March), Brigadier-General Rudolph Hogg, commanding IX Brigade, wrote in his diary that:

> The Huns are declaring that they have the supremacy of the air, yet our people have been out all day; many of them have done as many as five trips and all say they can't find a Hun in the air at all! Perhaps their advance has been too quick for them, perhaps they are out of petrol or perhaps they are trying to guard their back areas: anyway if any Huns are flying, they are miles behind where the fighting is. Our pilots have done splendidly, bombing from 1,000 ft firing with machine guns at infantry in trenches and in the open.[45]

The following day, the RFC's main effort shifted back to the Fifth Army area, where Amiens and its vital railway junction were threatened. The squadrons of V Brigade, together with aircraft from I, II, III, and IX Brigades, carried out continuous bombing and machine-gun attacks against a wide range of ground targets. From the RFC's perspective this marked the height of the battle—at least in terms of bombs dropped (by day and night) and machine-gun ammunition expended. Although such attacks came at a high price, they were particularly effective against troops in the open: "At Carrepuis we get our first dose of air bombing from an enemy squadron which has also been shooting away at us like mad with machine guns. . . . In an advance you are quite helpless against being bombed from the air, and it is a much more uncomfortable feeling than being bombed in static warfare when you have decent dug-outs. The casualties were correspondingly greater."[46]

The Germans now attempted (28 March) to open a new front at Arras (Operation Mars), but this time the weather was good and the assault was beaten off with the help of RFC-directed artillery fire and low-flying attacks against the assembling infantry. In the south, the fighting for Amiens intensified, with German troops infiltrating across the Somme during the night of 27–28 March and mounting a general assault on the Fifth Army and the French. There was little air fighting during the day, but the RFC's losses (largely from ground fire) still amounted to sixty-three aircraft destroyed or wrecked.[47] The RFC's efforts against ground targets continued unabated for the next three days as the Allied line began to stiffen. Artillery cooperation, bombing, and low-level attacks inflicted significant losses on German marching columns, assembling troops, and ammunition supplies, while night bombing of the rear area resumed with the improving weather.

There was little ground fighting on 1 April but considerable air activity. The newly constituted RAF continued to press home low-flying attacks, supporting counterattacks but also ranging well beyond the front line. Losses were again heavy, with fifty-two aircraft shot down or wrecked, although this included a high proportion of accidents owed, according to the RFC/RAF official history, to a combination of pilot exhaustion and bad airfields.[48] The weather over the next few days was poor, but it was clear that the German offensive was coming to a close. Final attacks north and south of the Somme failed to make progress and were defeated with heavy enemy losses. Once again, low-flying attacks by RAF squadrons contributed to the Allied success. By 5 April the German attacks had ground to a halt and the Somme battle was over.

The RFC's operational contribution during the offensive was not only substantial but also played a part in helping to slow and ultimately stop the German advance. It was, however, secured at considerable cost. Over 40,000 hours were flown during March—a total exceeding any previous month in the war, including Arras and Third Ypres. The RFC was almost 50 percent larger than it had been in March 1917 (when it had a frontline strength of 805 aircraft), but this was still an outstanding achievement. The wastage suffered was equally remarkable, with 839 aircraft lost across the entire front; once again the highest total in any month (only three hundred aircraft were lost in actual combat but, of these, 56 percent fell to ground fire).[49] Even when the increased number of squadrons is taken into account, this represented the worst attrition suffered by the RFC—including Bloody April— with total aircraft losses equivalent to over 70 percent of frontline strength.

The RFC/RAF official history makes light of this unprecedented level of wastage, stressing that "there was no difficulty with the supply of new aeroplanes to make good the losses." Much greater concern is expressed about the effect of the retreat on the overall functioning of the logistic system and, in particular, the disruption caused by the relocation of squadrons and air parks. Considerable emphasis is placed on the fact that the retreat exceeded anything anticipated, notwithstanding Salmond's efforts to mitigate the impact by expanding the lorry parks and creating additional aerodromes in the rear area. In fact, the demand for airfields was so high that forty-five new landing grounds had to be provided during the period of the offensive, often on unsuitable sites with little or no preparation. The greatest problem, however, was getting sufficient quantities of consumables (notably petrol, oil, lubricants, and ordnance) to the squadrons, together with replacement personnel and equipment. These difficulties were compounded by the need to relocate the aircraft parks supporting III and V Brigades (3 AP and 4 AP respectively), as well as the main depots serving the southern front—2 AD based at Candas and the adjacent 2 ASD at Fienvillers, some fifteen miles north-west of Amiens.[50]

Once the scale and direction of the German advance became clear, Brooke-Popham decided that both of the southern depots should be moved as a matter of urgency. The first to go was 2 ASD (employing nearly 1,600 personnel responsible for the receipt, preparation, and issue of aircraft to III and V Brigades), which started to pack on 25 March and within two days had relocated entirely to Verton (some six miles south of Étaples).[51] The Issues Section completed the move of 170 aircraft by the evening of 27 March, just before the sheds in which they had been housed were bombed and partly demolished.[52] Meanwhile, 2 AD at Candas (with over 1,500 personnel) moved to the vicinity of Rang-du-Fliers, also south of Étaples.[53] This was a more substantial operation as the depot had grown considerably during its time in France. The last remnants of 2 AD left Candas on 30 March, although its place was immediately taken by 3 AP. While these moves were under way, the frontline squadrons were instructed to return their damaged engines to Rang-du-Fliers, but were offered the option of burning their damaged airframes. Sufficient spares, fuel, and ammunition were left behind at Candas to sustain the squadrons of III, V, and IX Brigades for ten days—to be collected on a self-help basis.[54] The distribution of aircraft was little affected by these moves. The supply of new machines from the home-based AAP was continuous, and although there was a noticeable hiatus in the repair and reconstruction of damaged aircraft by 2 ASD, it was back in full production by May 1918. In the meantime, the shortfall was made up by further deliveries from England and increased production at 1 ASD.[55]

The difficulty of sustaining the frequently moving squadrons—at the same time that the depots and parks were themselves on the move—generated a radical response from HQ RAF. Brooke-Popham decided to suspend temporarily the existing demand-led system, in which squadrons "pulled" their supplies, and introduce a supply-led system in which the depots and parks "pushed" stores forward (similar to the technique adopted for the squadrons in Italy). By stockpiling petrol, oil, bombs, and ammunition on every airfield as soon as it was commissioned, sufficient stores were always available for incoming squadrons—allowing operations to continue while the supply chain was re-configured. Although this solution was undoubtedly inefficient (in that more stores were issued than strictly needed) it was certainly effective—while there were sufficient supplies available and as long as they could be delivered to the required locations quickly enough. At Brooke-Popham's instigation, therefore, two convoys were assembled (with eight light tenders each), one stocked with ammunition and 25-lb Cooper bombs and the other with aircraft and engine spares, for immediate deployment in support of any squadron that was short of stores—pending resupply from its parent air park.[56]

The selfless efforts of the ground crew in keeping the squadrons operating during these difficult days have been recorded in numerous accounts: "A tribute must be paid to the non-commissioned officers and to the air mechanics of the squadrons, parks and depots, on whom a great responsibility was thrown during the retreat. When all about them was uncertainty and confusion they proceeded, without fuss, to fulfil their duty of maintaining the squadrons as effective units, no matter how often or how much the situation changed."[57]

Guy Knocker, a pilot with No. 65 Squadron (II Brigade), equipped with the Sopwith Camel, wrote to his parents on 1 April 1918 that "the mechanics are working frightfully hard at present as there are beaucoup crashes and buses to repair and very little time to do it in. No workshop or anything and all work has to be done in the open or in a sort of extempore hangar."[58] The impact on the front line of this unprecedented effort was significant. Although the data is incomplete—the daily reporting regime faltered during the withdrawal—it indicates that serviceability rates began to fall, particularly in those brigades most closely involved in the fighting. Up to 21 March (and the opening of the German offensive) the proportion of serviceable aircraft in I, II, III, and V Brigades varied between 80 percent and 100 percent. Thereafter, it fluctuated between 70 percent and 90 percent. The impact was particularly marked on those units immediately in the path of the attack (III and V Brigades) and less so on those on the periphery (such as I and II Brigades), although within a week all brigades would be affected.

It is surprising that serviceability did not fall more quickly, given the "perfect storm" created by the rapid increase in flying rates (and the consequent rapid increase in the demand for spares), high operational attrition, frequent airfield moves (disrupting the squadron engineering effort), and the need to continuously reconfigure the supply pipeline.[59] The sheer scale of the challenge faced by the RFC logistic system is reflected in the number of airfield moves. The worst affected was V Brigade, with each of its squadrons occupying a minimum of three different airfields during March, although III and IX Brigades also had to relocate regularly, their squadrons moving eighty-three times in total during March 1918, compared to just ten moves the month before and twenty in April. Each change of airfield required a squadron to move 200–250 personnel and between thirty-five and forty-five vehicles (depending on role), together with equipment, spare engines, ammunition, bombs, hangars, and domestic supplies over a distance of ten to forty miles to an unfamiliar location, without technical or domestic accommodation, and begin operations as soon as possible.[60]

The main logistic challenge in March 1918 was therefore distribution rather than the supply. Indeed, Salmond wrote to Trenchard to express his "thanks for the supplies of machines which have kept us going very well." In meeting this challenge, the RFC's generous establishment of motor vehicles enabled the pipeline to adapt to the rapidly changing battlefield—an advantage that Salmond fully recognized. "The transport has stuck it all right so far, but I visualise a large number of moves in the future and shall be obliged for the extra vehicles of the extra Lorry Park." The RFC's inherent mobility was reflected in the relatively small quantity of matériel (other than aircraft) lost over this period. Units were largely able to pack up and move, notwithstanding the rapid German advance. By 25 March, 4,300 hydrogen tubes, 1,500 bombs, forty light aircraft tents, one car, two lorries, and two light tenders had been abandoned or destroyed—a relatively modest price considering the scale of resources available to the RFC.[61]

Even before the end of the Somme fighting, the Germans were already preparing for another offensive further north in the plain of the Lys, between La Bassée and Armentières, where the line had been weakened to reinforce the Somme position. The failed attack at Arras forced some changes to their original plans, but the Germans were able to assemble nine divisions for the assault with five in support and three more in reserve. Opposing them were four divisions (including a Portuguese division scheduled for imminent replacement) with two more divisions in reserve, many of them already tired from the recent Somme fighting. The squadrons of I Brigade had also been depleted to assist air operations in the Somme, but these had returned in early April. Together with reinforcements, the RAF had 390 aircraft available on the First Army front (comprising thirteen squadrons of I Brigade and eleven squadrons of IX Brigade). In comparison, the GAS was able to field 492 aircraft.[62]

Although no special offensive operations were mounted, the RAF was active throughout early April in artillery cooperation, reconnaissance, and day and night bombing against the German front line and rear areas, where air reconnaissance revealed significant preparations for the forthcoming offensive. The Battle of the Lys opened on the morning of 9 April 1918, following a short but intensive barrage. The initial assault swept away the Portuguese and made substantial gains everywhere along the line. Fog prevented flying until the afternoon and in the confusion No. 208 Squadron, based at La Gorgue some three and a half miles from the front line, had to abandon their airfield and burn all eighteen of their Sopwith Camels. The squadron relocated with all its equipment and transport to Serny, where they were fully equipped within forty-eight hours; yet another example of the efficiency and responsiveness of the RAF's logistic system.[63]

Visibility remained poor throughout the day, even after the fog had lifted. Contact patrols revealed the scale of the German advance that already extended beyond the Lys. Although a number of squadrons had to move airfields, the RAF was still able to mount energetic attacks on the enemy's forward elements. The next day, the fighting spread further north to the Second Army area. Once again, after a short but heavy preliminary bombardment the Germans made rapid gains, taking most of Messines by midday. At the same time, their advance continued further south on the original battlefront. The weather through the day was poor, consisting of low clouds and mist, but the squadrons of I and II Brigades continued to carry out low-flying attacks with machine guns and bombs. The impact was serious enough for 6 Armee, and later 4 Armee, to request additional fighter squadrons to counter the RAF's efforts.[64] The assault continued on 11 April with more ground lost and the furthest German troops reaching Merville. By this stage, matters were looking extremely serious with gaps appearing in the defensive line. The RAF's low-flying attacks were often the only means of slowing the German advance. The improving weather allowed the bombing of targets in the rear area, by both day and night. The twelfth of April proved critical with the squadrons of I and IX Brigades working together to help close the gap at Merville and prevent the Germans from taking Hazebrouck.[65] On this day, the RAF flew more hours, dropped more bombs, and took more photographs than on any day since the war had begun.[66] In its relentless attacks on the advancing German divisions, the RAF was judged to have rendered "splendid service."[67]

There was little flying over the next few days because of poor weather. In the meantime, the Germans took Bailleul on 15 April and made vigorous attempts to capture Kemmel Hill. When the conditions permitted, the RAF undertook artillery cooperation, together with contact and reconnaissance patrols as well as day and night bombing. An attack on 18 April toward Béthune was defeated with heavy enemy losses after which there was a lull in the fighting.[68] There were indications, however, that the Germans might resume their offensive in the Somme area in the vicinity of Villers-Bretonneux. The new assault opened on the morning of 24 April, after a short but intense bombardment. Under the cover of fog and using tanks, the Germans captured Villers-Bretonneux, only for it to be recaptured the next day following which the fighting died down. The weather was consistently poor over this period and very little flying was done. On 25 April, the Battle of the Lys was resumed with an attack by thirteen German divisions aimed at capturing Kemmel Hill. RAF squadrons once again participated in low-flying attacks. The GAS was also heavily involved and air fighting broke out between opposing formations. A number of further attacks took place over the next few days with some enemy success but at heavy cost. The weather over the last week of April was again poor with little flying by either side. The fighting flared up again on 29 April when the final German assault was beaten off, bringing an end to the offensive.[69]

The renewed German attacks had caused Brooke-Popham to plan for the evacuation of the northern depots—drawing on the lessons learned in moving the southern depots. These units were on the whole larger (comprising in total some 5,700 personnel) and had had more time to establish their roots. Brooke-Popham's over-riding aim was to ensure continuity of supply while safeguarding the immense range and quantity of stores that had accumulated over nearly four years of fighting.[70] On 4 April he ordered No. 1 AD at St-Omer to pack, for immediate removal, sufficient stores to provide a month's supply to the parks and squadrons of I and II brigades. If St-Omer was threatened, these were to be transferred to the site occupied by No. 4

ASD at Guines, previously a RNAS depot, some five miles from Boulogne. Work began immediately to prepare Guines, to be known as No. 1 AD (Reserve), for its new role. The aim was for Guines to issue stores to the squadrons while the main depot was packing up—avoiding the disruption that occurred when Candas and Fienvillers had to relocate at short notice. At this stage, it was not yet known where the main depot would go, but Brooke-Popham advised that it would "be on a railway and if possible on a canal as well." He further added that they should try to find some form of building where the stores could be placed straightaway, but marked off by group so that confusion did not occur. Brooke-Popham ended his instructions by saying, "There is not the slightest idea of your having to move at present or the slightest sign of your ever having to move. I only want you to make preparations in case the situation changes altogether."[71]

On 10 April, the day after the German offensive opened, the transfer of the emergency stores to Guines began. Although 1 AD (Reserve) was ready by 13 April, stores continued to be issued from St-Omer to avoid any unnecessary interruption to supply. In the meantime, the bulk stores were moved to Desvres, some twenty miles west, while 1 ASD Repair Section transferred to the reception park at Marquise.[72] The latter move was undertaken gradually to avoid interrupting the repair program. As a result, there was no significant fall in output, unlike 2 ASD's experience the previous month. The general situation on 13 April was so worrying that Brooke-Popham discussed whether the depot might actually have to move in the direction of Rouen rather than to Guines. Just two days later, on 15 April, it was clear that the German advance was slackening and the move was postponed. Once matters had settled down, it was decided to relocate the entire depot to Guines. Shortly after this was completed, on 18 May 1918, German aircraft attacked St-Omer over a period of four hours, dropping about one hundred bombs. One of the buildings that received a direct hit had previously held all the depot's engine spares. For the rest of the war, 1 AD would remain at Guines, with subsidiary depots at Desvres and Motteville (near Rouen). The latter provided an immediate dump for stores arriving from England and a potential fall-back location, if the Channel ports were once again threatened.[73]

Aircraft wastage during March and April 1918 was significant—almost four times the wastage experienced in the previous two months. Even so, these losses were rapidly made good through a combination of new supply and repair. Total losses of equipment and stores since the beginning of the German offensive (generally destroyed before being abandoned) amounted to 173 hangars and tents, 2 lorries, 4 light tenders, 6 motorcycles, 21 trailers, 37 machine guns, 1,738 bombs, 60 wireless receiving stations, 4,589 hydrogen tubes, 26,000 gallons of petrol, and 2,200 gallons of lubricating oil.[74] The consumables represented less than two days' consumption for the RAF in France, while the equipment was all readily replaced. It was Salmond's view, however, that "had I not been able to convince Trenchard of the necessity for more transport and provided landing grounds in our back area,

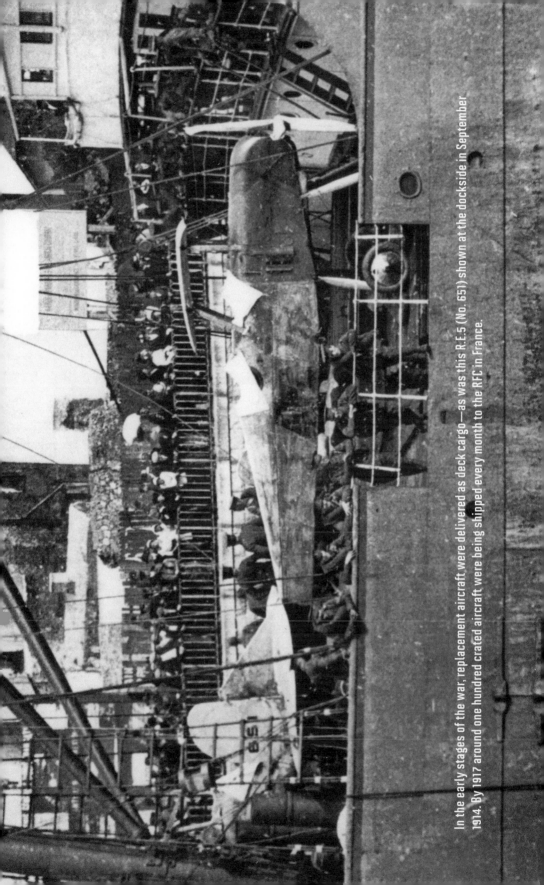

In the early stages of the war, replacement aircraft were delivered as deck cargo — as was this R.E.5 (No. 651) shown at the dockside in September 1914. By 1917 around one hundred crated aircraft were being shipped every month to the RFC in France.

No. 1 Aircraft Depot, St-Omer in November 1916. Four F.E.2b two-seat fighters, recently delivered from England, can be seen in the foreground alongside a line of Bessonneau hangars and, in the background, the buildings occupied by the depot's maintenance, repair, and manufacturing shops. The depot and airfield extended over most of the two hundred acres that made up the town's prewar race course, and would employ more than 2,700 technical and flying personnel by early 1918.

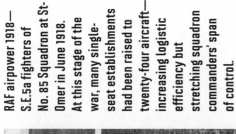

RAF airpower 1918—S.E.5a fighters of No. 85 Squadron at St-Omer in June 1918. At this stage of the war, many single-seat establishments had been raised to twenty-four aircraft—increasing logistic efficiency but stretching squadron commanders' span of control.

Air Commodore Robert Brooke-Popham, who created and led the RFC's logistic organization on the western front for more than four years. He was an inspirational, gifted, and innovative commander, but his reputation has suffered as a result of his involvement, as commander-in-chief, British Far East Command, in the loss of Singapore to the Japanese in 1942.

RAF airpower 1918—R.E.8 artillery cooperation aircraft of No. 15 Squadron in March 1918. Forced to relocate during the German spring offensive, the squadron operated from a series of temporary airfields. To sustain the supply chain, Headquarters RFC pre-positioned stores for the affected units, temporarily abandoning the longstanding "pull" arrangements under which squadrons only drew down stores when required. The R.E.8 (and Armstrong Whitworth FK8) provided the foundation for three-dimensional warfare on the western front—as long as wastage could be made good and air superiority maintained.

The aircraft spares section at "X" Depot, Aboukir, Egypt, in 1918, illustrating the immense range and quantity of holdings—including specialist tools—required to support flying operations.

A shortage of aero-engines constrained British aircraft production throughout the First World War. These completed airframes (Airco D.H.4, D.H.9, and Armstrong Whitworth FK8) await their engines. By August 1918, there were 4,200 aircraft in store without engines.

The Leyland 3-ton heavy tender provided the logistic foundation for British air operations on the western front. More than five thousand examples were procured by the RFC between 1914 and 1918. By 1914, each RFC squadron was equipped with twenty-six lorries and tenders as well as trailers and motorcycles. When in column of route, the convoy stretched for more than half a mile.

The end-user—No. 82 Squadron's Equipment Officer (Wireless) and section personnel in November 1918 with some of their specialist role equipment, including wireless sets (both ground and air for artillery cooperation) and klaxons (for infantry contact patrols).

Marquise became the new location for No. 1 ASD's repair activities when the depot at St-Omer was evacuated in March 1918. This oblique view shows the dispersed nature of the site, which also acted as the reception park for all aircraft travelling between the UK and France. Over 2,500 personnel were employed at Marquise by August 1918.

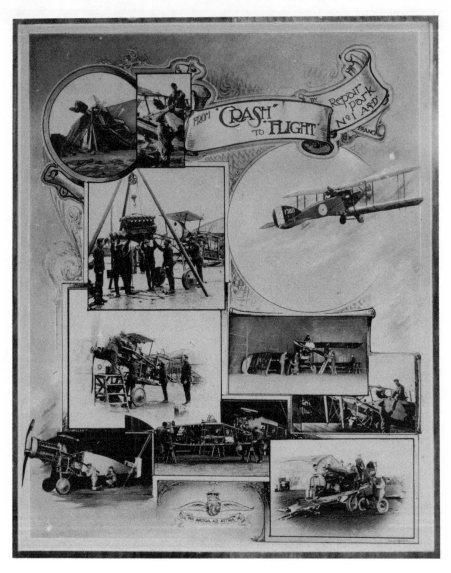

A contemporary photomontage depicting the work of No. 1 ASD Repair Park, Marquise. Nos. 1 and 2 ASD repaired or reconstructed more than 1,500 aircraft in 1918, making a vital contribution to air operations.

Engine recovery was an important activity for the depot's salvage section. Aero-engines were valuable but also suffered a higher number of arisings (from defects and damage) than airframes. As a result, the supply pipeline comprised almost twice as many engines as actually fitted to frontline aircraft.

No. 2 ASD Candas, not long before the site was evacuated as a precautionary measure in April 1918. More than thirty aircraft can be identified and, at the bottom, numerous aircraft containers adjacent to the sidings that linked the depot to the French railway system.

No. 2 AD Candas, Tinsmiths and Coppersmiths, 1916. A variety of fuel tanks and other metal components can be seen in the foreground. Mechanics worked an average of sixty-five hours each week.

The salvage yard at No. 2 ASD Repair Park, Le Bahot, in the summer of 1918. No. 2 ASD had relocated from Candas in April 1918. The depot's activities, involving more than two thousand personnel, were dispersed across several locations in the vicinity of the Rang-du-Fliers railhead, minimizing the potential loss from German night-bomber raids.

we should at this period of the war frequently been in severe difficulties."[75] One further aspect of the retreat was the impact on the movement of stores to and from the Channel ports. The German offensive largely curtailed the arrival of crated aircraft and engines.[76] The lack of the former was resolved by increasing the number of aircraft flown direct from England, but the supply of replacement aero-engines fell entirely on the ERS until the situation stabilized.[77] These problems aside, the key logistic challenge during this period was not the loss of stores (or the availability of replacement machines and equipment) but the frequent and short-notice moves of squadrons, parks, and depots. The interruption to the engineering and maintenance effort, coupled with the difficulty of reestablishing a functioning pipeline, posed major problems to a system optimized around a "static" front line. The efficient and effective way that these problems were overcome owes much to the energetic leadership of Brooke-Popham and his personal initiative and foresight. In adopting a "push" system to pre-position stores and by his willingness to learn from the difficulties experienced in attempting to relocate the southern depots, Brooke-Popham enabled the squadrons to sustain an exceptionally high operational tempo throughout the German 1918 offensive. When it came to selecting new locations for the main depots, proximity to the main ports and access to the railway were evidently regarded as more important than collocation. Indeed, there was a conscious effort to separate the issues, repair, and stores sections. Certainly, no attempt was made to re-create the large, comprehensive facilities previously enjoyed at St-Omer and Candas/Fienvillers. This more dispersed footprint not only facilitated mobility but also reduced vulnerability to enemy bombing. In view of the serious impact on the continued maintenance of a large proportion of the BEF's vehicles caused in August 1918 when the Calais MT depot was destroyed (together with all of its spares, including the stock recently evacuated from the Abbeville Advanced MT depot), this was a sensible and prescient step.[78] Brooke-Popham would later admit that "sufficient attention was not paid to laying out the depots to minimise the risk and effect of hostile bombing."[79]

The German attacks on the western front did not end with the Battle of Lys, but the remainder of this chapter will focus on the performance of the logistic system during the Hundred Days—the period starting with the Battle of Amiens in August and ending at the armistice in November. This is not to ignore the fighting that occurred between May and July, but it was the BEF's advance from August 1918 onwards that provided the greatest test of the RAF and resulted in the highest casualty and wastage rates of the entire war.[80] The RAF logistic organization, and particularly the depots, had settled into their new locations. No. 1 AD continued to operate from Guines, with 1 ASD Repair Section, Issues Section, and Reception Park at Marquise. No. 2 AD was based at Vron with 2 ASD Repair Section at Le Bahot and the Issues Section at Rely. This more extended network had no immediate impact on the supply pipeline, which largely depended on rail transport. The critical element was the movement of stores by road from the railhead to the air park and then from the air park to the squadron. If anything, following the withdrawal, the road element was reduced (with the BEF falling back toward the Channel ports). As a result, the logistic system was able to cope with the steadily growing front line, which had reached 1,565 aircraft by August, compared to 1,316 aircraft in April.

By June 1918 it was clear that the German attacks on the western front were fading. The final offensive on the Matz, in June and July, had seen some initial successes but these were soon reversed by the French, while further counterattacks between July and August (Second Marne) saw the Germans abandon all their gains. This effectively marked the turning point in the 1918 offensive; thereafter the German army was constantly on the defensive.[81] Meanwhile, planning had begun for a British offensive north of the Somme. Preparatory actions included a limited but highly successful attack on 4 July at Hamel that involved close cooperation between aircraft and tanks and the dropping of small-arms ammunition by parachute to the advancing infantry at pre-planned locations.[82]

The British offensive at Amiens was originally scheduled for 10 August but was brought forward to take advantage of the German withdrawal on the Marne. The immediate aim of the attack, to be undertaken by the Fourth Army supported by the First French Army, was to free Amiens and the Paris-Amiens railway. The RAF was to play a major role in the fighting although, as at Third Ypres, much of this came prior to the attack in the form of reconnaissance, photography, and registration—such that 503 out of 530 German guns in the attack sector had been accurately located.[83] Salmond's plans saw V Brigade reinforced with additional aircraft from IX Brigade. On the evening of 7 August, the RAF had eight hundred aircraft available to support the battle together with 1,104 French aircraft on the French First Army front. Against this unprecedented concentration (the largest seen on the western front to date), the Germans could only deploy 365 aircraft with 2 and 18 Armee.[84] That evening, RAF bombers flew up and down the line to cover the sound of tanks moving into position.

The Amiens offensive opened on 8 August with a short heavy bombardment. The enemy was taken by surprise and at the end of the day Australian, British, and Canadian troops had advanced about seven miles.[85] Such was the BEF's success that General Erich Ludendorff, the German army's quartermaster general, would describe the outcome as "the black day" of the German army.[86] Early mist limited the amount of air cooperation but by mid-morning RAF aircraft were engaged in low-flying attacks across the battlefield. The laying of smoke screens proved effective, but it was the machine-gun and bomb attacks on the German defenders that were most effective. "As visibility improved the massive enemy superiority in aircraft assumed importance as they directed artillery fire and strafed nests of resistance as well as battery positions."[87] During the afternoon it became clear that the roads leading to the Somme crossings were becoming increasingly crowded and that, if the bridges could be destroyed or badly damaged, there was an opportunity to cut off a large part of the German forces. At Salmond's direction, the RAF's main effort was directed at the Somme bridges, employing both day bombers and fighters. The GAS, alert to the danger and arriving in numbers from other parts of the front, fought hard to defend the bridges. The RAF made more than two hundred attacks and dropped twelve tons of bombs, albeit with minimal effect.[88] Casualties were heavy on both sides, particularly among the day bombers. The RAF lost ninety-seven aircraft, either shot down or struck off—an overall wastage rate of over 13 percent, while among the low-flying aircraft it was even higher at 23 percent.[89] Bombing attacks continued that night and for the next two days but, although combat losses fell, little damage was caused. Meanwhile, the Allied advance on the ground continued, but at a slower pace against stiffening German resistance and increasingly difficult terrain. The fighting was eventually called off on 16 August, by which time the advance had penetrated up to twelve miles, as far as the old Roye-Chaulnes defensive line. Amiens and its railway had been made safe from enemy artillery fire and, just as importantly, over 25,000 prisoners and more than four hundred guns had been captured.[90]

The RAF had made an important contribution to the first day's success and thereafter kept the GAS at bay, including conducting massed attacks against enemy airfields.[91] The RAF's presence was felt across 2 Armee; the officer in charge of aviation for the area reported on 15 August 1918:

> The British ground attacks were accompanied by numerous low-level flyers, who disrupted our troops with bombs and machine-gun fire. Strong reconnaissance groups of twenty units and more thrust deep into our rear areas to reconnoitre our troop transports . . . flights and groups of single-seat fighters flew almost without interruption at all altitudes along the entire Army Front and blockaded or impeded our aircraft in the fulfilment of their missions. Coming down to the lowest altitudes, they tried to force our aircraft away from the Front. The enemy bombing groups were extremely active. When it was overcast they pressed on under the protection of clouds, and during clear weather they were covered by groups of single-seat fighters as they pushed into our rear areas and dropped numerous bombs, which caused considerable damage.[92]

By contrast, the bombing of the Somme bridges had achieved little tactical effect, although there was strategic benefit in that it had kept the GAS away from the battle zone.[93] Although some of the German fighter units were so badly depleted they had to be withdrawn, the losses suffered by the RAF were particularly severe.[94] On 10 August 1918, IX Brigade (supplying most of the bombing force) recorded:

> Some of our bombing squadrons have suffered horribly: they have had to come down low over the Somme bridges and have had a bad time from AA fire and Hun scouts who were patrolling over their objectives

and coming down from the clouds which were only 2 or 3,000 feet. We shall want at least a fortnight to refit and train new pilots: in 107 Squadron some of them are quite considerably shaken by their losses.[95]

The BEF's next attack followed within a week, with the aim of recovering the Arras-Albert railway line. There was little redistribution or reinforcement of the RAF squadrons, but on the morning scheduled for the attack (21 August) ground mist and rain kept air activity to a minimum, although some counter-battery work was still possible in support of Third Army. Even so, considerable progress was made on the ground, reaching a depth of two to three miles. The advance continued the next day with the town of Albert captured. A German counterattack was seriously disrupted by RAF-directed counter-battery fire.[96] These successes paved the way for a larger offensive on 23 August by the Third and Fourth Armies, north of the Somme, along thirty-three miles of the front, in conjunction with a French attack on the right wing that extended as far as Soissons. The RAF's III, V, and IX Brigades were directly involved in supporting the attack. Learning from the opening day of the Battle of Amiens, special arrangements were made to identify suitable targets for low-flying attacks, particularly anti-tank guns. The assault made rapid progress and by the next day, 24 August, the whole of the Thiepval ridge had been cleared. The Allied advance continued steadily with the RAF providing support with low-level attacks and the bombing of ground targets by day and night. On 29 August, Bapaume was captured, followed by Mont St-Quentin on 30/31 August and Péronne on 1 September. In the meantime, the British First Army had launched an attack eastwards from Arras intended to turn the German position on the Somme. Poor weather restricted some of the RAF's planned contribution, but low-level attacks and artillery cooperation were successfully undertaken in support of the advance, which continued over the next four days.[97]

Ahead of the Third Army lay the heavily fortified Drocourt-Quéant switch line, regarded as the key to turning the Hindenburg Line—the last major organized German defensive line. The attack began on the morning of 2 September. Once again, night-flying RAF aircraft were employed to disguise the sound of tanks moving up, while selected villages forming the defensive line were bombed. When the attack was launched, low-flying aircraft attacked ground targets as specialist squadrons undertook close liaison with the tanks or focused on eliminating anti-tank guns. By noon, the whole of the defensive line had been captured. German air activity was spasmodic and although there was some heavy air fighting it did not diminish the RAF's support. During the night, the Germans retired east of the Canal du Nord where they intended to make a strong defense. Further south, the enemy was also in retreat, harried all the time by low-flying aircraft. By now, however, the strain of constant attacks was beginning to take its toll of men and machines. On 5 September, the opportunity was taken to reduce air activity and rest hard-pressed squadrons.[98]

In preparation for the assault on the Hindenburg Line, some preliminary actions were undertaken to capture outlying positions in the vicinity of Havrincourt and Épehy. These operations were opened on 12 September and successfully completed five days later. The weather was poor throughout this period and air support necessarily limited. The main assault on Havrincourt and Épehy took place on 18 September and over the next few days all the remaining strong points in advance of the Hindenburg Line were taken. German air activity continued to be intermittent, but large formations of enemy fighters were occasionally encountered, leading to heavy air fighting. The final Allied assault comprised four convergent simultaneous attacks. The entire RAF on the western front was involved in supporting the offensive. Five brigades were employed in support of the BEF, while II Brigade and 5 Group (Dunkirk) assisted Belgian, British, and French forces. The main air effort, however, was directed at the area of the Hindenburg Line, where 1,058 aircraft were available to support the Third, Fourth, and Fifth Armies in their advance on the St-Quentin–Cambrai front, where much of the German defensive position lay along the St-Quentin canal.[99] Such was the strength of the defenses, however, that prolonged artillery bombardment was necessary. The offensive opened on the morning of 27 September, with the First and Third Armies attacking toward Cambrai. Rapid progress was made and troops were soon across the Canal du Nord on a thirteen-mile front.[100] Ten thousand prisoners and two hundred guns were taken. Although the weather was poor, the advance was supported by low-flying attacks, artillery cooperation, and day and night bombing. Progress continued the next day, once again assisted by the RAF, although the weather remained poor. The Fourth Army's attack began on 29 September, after two days of artillery preparation and night bombing. By the evening, they had broken through the Hindenburg Line, although smoke, rain, and mist impeded air activity. Slow progress continued to be made over the next few days but the final battles of the war were approaching.

A multinational attack in Flanders, undertaken by a mixed Army Group that included the British Second Army supported by aircraft of II Brigade and 5 Group, was launched on 28 September and initially made rapid progress but then slowed because of logistical problems. The RAF's contribution was extensive and, in addition to bombing, artillery cooperation, and low-level attacks, included the dropping of rations to the forward Belgian elements. Meanwhile, the Allied advance continued across the entire front with the next major action on 8 October, south of Cambrai, where a combined British and French attack resulted in the capture of the remaining elements of the Hindenburg Line. The corps squadrons were particularly active, maintaining close contact with the advancing troops and providing smoke screens. By 9 October, Cambrai was three miles within British lines with the Germans in full retreat.[101] The advance also continued in Flanders, with Roulers captured on 15 October and Ostend abandoned by the Germans on 17 October. Lille fell the next day and by 22 October troops were on the general line of the Schelde River. Meanwhile, operations had resumed toward Le Cateau and by the evening of 19 October British forces had crossed the Sambre-Oise Canal against strong resistance. The next day, the Selle River was crossed north of Le Cateau. Operations continued over the next few days, although the variable weather meant that air support was reduced, as was German air activity. In addition to bombing railway communications, and harrying the retreating columns, further large-scale attacks were made against active enemy airfields. On the other hand, when enemy aircraft were encountered they were often in large formations, up to fifty aircraft strong. Some of the largest air combats seen on the western front occurred during these late October days as the RAF attempted to hasten the German retreat. The most intense fighting took place on 30 October when the RAF claimed sixty-seven German machines destroyed for the loss of forty-one aircraft in combat.[102] The RAF could make good these losses, the GAS could not. "Aerial combat with such a force-ratio took place, as always, almost exclusively behind and above the German lines where the German fighters dove on the intruding enemy wings. Although far more enemy aircraft were shot down in these actions, the numerical force-ratio did not in any way change in favour of the Germans. The fact that the enemy arma-ments industry had far greater production capacity and the enemy had a far greater number of men for the air force remained decisive."[103]

When the fighting ceased on 11 November, the RAF could properly claim to have played a major part in the BEF's success during the Hundred Days campaign. It had been in existence for just 225 days (14 percent of the war), but had contrib-uted over half the British air effort on the western front (in hours flown) and, in the process, experienced over 47 percent of all aviation casualties.[104] The RAF's opera-tional contribution to the western front was both substantial and relentless. Salmond believed in the "offensive" as passionately as Trenchard. No day passed without air operations of some form, irrespective of the weather. "Where the French bombed only by night, the RAF strafed and bombed marched troops and locations also by day. The British flew even on cloudy days!"[105]

The achievements of 1918 far exceeded any other year of the war. The RAF flew nearly 500,000 hours on the western front in 1918 (up to the armistice), compared to 309,000 hours in 1917 and 135,000 hours in 1916, reflecting not only a larger orga-nization but also a more intensive and sustained effort. In each of the last six (full) months of the war, the RAF flew over 50,000 hours. The previous highest monthly total was 39,000 hours in May 1917. Moreover, average monthly hours flown by each frontline aircraft rose from twenty-six hours in 1916 to twenty-nine hours in 1917 and thirty-three hours in 1918. Although poor weather severely affected flying operations, particularly in the winter months, there were eight occasions when forty hours or more were achieved: twice in 1916, twice in 1917, and four times in 1918. In terms of total output, therefore, the RFC and RAF achieved more per aircraft employed as the war progressed.

The RAF's focus throughout 1918 remained the support of the BEF, but there were significant changes in the range of roles undertaken and in the proportion of effort allocated to particular tasks as the year progressed. This was evident in artillery cooperation where, from a peak of over two thousand enemy batteries targeted each month in June and July, the number rapidly fell to less than two hundred a month in October. In comparison, the consumption of ammunition and bombs grew rapidly, reflecting the increasing effort expended on attacking ground targets—partly because of necessity (during the German 1918 offensive), and partly because of opportunity provided by mobile warfare, in the form of congested roads, busy rail communications, and infantry and artillery in the open or in hastily prepared defenses—where the RAF's light (25-lb) Cooper bombs were more effective.

The overall picture as the Hundred Days campaign progressed was of sustained operational effort, falling away slightly from a peak in August, with an increasing emphasis on ground targets as the opportunities for artillery communication diminished. The sheer scale of this achievement—in the three months, August to October, the RAF flew more hours (185,000) than in the whole of 1916—is all the more impressive given the very heavy losses experienced over the same period. Total wastage during the Hundred Days amounted to 2,981 aircraft, peaking in August when over 960 machines were struck off; equivalent to 62 percent of frontline strength. This was a smaller proportion than March 1918, but the three months from August to October 1918 still saw the highest wastage levels in the entire war and, in September 1918, the greatest monthly combat casualties (503 aircraft).

It is important, however, to look beyond these headline figures and consider how overall availability and serviceability fared over the same period. The RAF's frontline strength was sustained at around 1,500–1,550 aircraft from late July to late September. Notwithstanding the loss of over eight hundred aircraft each month, the first sign that wastage was beginning to have any impact was in late September, when frontline strength fell by over one hundred machines, although this picked up again in October. On the other hand, serviceability levels generally averaged over 90 percent, indicating that engineering effectiveness remained high—despite the frequent changes of airfield and the difficulties of getting supplies from the depots. However, the increasing variability (from a high of over 96 percent in late August to a low of 84 percent in early October) does hint at a system under stress.

There are a number of factors that might explain why the RAF logistic system faltered toward the end of the Hundred Days. The RFC/RAF official history, having been very positive about the overall supply position during the German 1918 offensive, is much less sanguine about the Hundred Days and highlights that some squadrons had to operate below strength because "aircraft production in August did not keep pace with the casualties on the Western Front."[106] The actual position is somewhat less clear. If the number of frontline aircraft available is compared with planned strength (calculated on the basis of squadron establishments) there is indeed a shortfall, but this is more evident in the months prior to, rather than during, the Hundred Days.[107] The decision to increase the establishment of single-seat fighter squadrons from nineteen to twenty-five machines in March 1918, and subsequently to increase the establishment of corps squadrons from eighteen to twenty-four machines, took five months to be fully realized because of production shortfalls; thereafter strength and establishment were fairly closely matched.

A more noticeable impact of the heavy attrition suffered by the RAF was on the level of reserves. The depots' aircraft holdings apparently grew by nearly two hundred aircraft during 1918 but this disguises the true position. If unserviceable machines and those without engines or under repair are removed, a rather different picture emerges. For example, the main depots held a total of 883 aircraft in January 1918, but only 391 of these were serviceable. By the end of March the serviceable reserve had fallen to just 258.[108] This was a cause for considerable concern as the number of aircraft at the depots was an important indicator of frontline sustainability. The high attrition experienced on the western front required a continuous supply of replacement aircraft, but production uncertainties and volatile wastage rates meant that it was virtually impossible to meet the front line's needs simply through production deliveries from England. As Robert Brooke-Popham later explained, "This heavy wastage means keeping a very large reserve in order to ensure that casualties are replaced at once and this is complicated by the fact that we always had a large number of different types of both machines and engines out in France."[109]

The aircraft held by the depots acted, therefore, as a buffer stock to make good unplanned and unexpected shortfalls. As such, they had to be ready to fly—that is, erected (not in cases), with engines and ancillary equipment fitted. Although this strategic reserve provided resilience, it also represented a wasted asset (the greater the reserve the fewer aircraft available for the front line). The risk could be mitigated by adjusting the depot's reconstruction program to generate aircraft types otherwise in short supply. An important step in this process was calculating both the overall size of the reserve and the composition (the balance between aircraft types). The logistic staffs developed a simple algorithm for this purpose, based on the number of squadrons equipped with the same type of aircraft and the average weekly wastage per squadron. This could only be an approximation, since wastage rates varied on a daily basis, but it suggests that a reserve of some 500 aircraft was needed in October 1918 to support a front line of 88 squadrons and 1,612 aircraft. The actual serviceable reserve was 221, distributed between 1 ASD and 2 ASD, with significant deficiencies in every type other than the Sopwith Camel and the Sopwith Snipe.[110]

The scale of the reconstruction effort undertaken by the depots during 1918 is impressive by any standard, but particularly so in view of the disruption created by the forced relocations of March and April. Reconstructions did falter, however, following an attack by German aircraft on the night of 23/24 September, when five and a half tons of bombs were dropped on Marquise. Twenty-seven airplanes were burnt and a further forty-six badly or slightly damaged. The number of rebuilt aircraft produced by 1 ASD fell by 34 percent compared to the previous month.[111] Such incidents aside, the scale and pace of the reconstruction program depended on the efficient salvage of aircraft from an increasingly distant battlefield. The salvage

Table 5. RAF Strategic Reserve, October 1918

AIRCRAFT TYPE	NO. OF SQNS	WEEKLY WASTAGE	REQD WEEKLY SUPPLY	WEEKS SUPPLY TO BE HELD IN RESERVE	QTY REQUIRED FOR RESERVE	ACTUAL RESERVE
AW FK8	5	3	15	3	45	11
BRISTOL FIGHTER	9	2	18	3	54	13
DH4	4	2	8	3	24	1
DH9	9	2	18	3	54	17
F.E.2	11	1	11	2	22	7
HANDLEY PAGE	1	5	5	4	20	0
R.E.8	15	2	30	2	60	22
S.E.5a	15	3	45	2	90	13
CAMEL	14	3	42	2	84	107
DOLPHIN	4	3	12	3	36	9
SNIPE	1	3	3	3	9	21
TOTAL	88		207		498	221

and rebuild process has already been described in detail. It suffices to say that recycling aeronautical material formed a critical element in the effort to sustain operations. The supply of damaged machines provided the essential raw material for the ASD repair sections. During 1918 some 5,800 aircraft were salvaged on the western front—representing nearly 80 percent of aircraft struck off. The ASD salvage sections could at times move forward but the nature of their work meant that they were effectively stationary units. As the armies advanced, therefore, and the fighting moved further away from the depots, it became increasingly difficult to locate and retrieve crashed machines. To cope with this growing problem, HQ RAF created two mobile advanced salvage parties (one for each ASD) allocated to the busiest brigades, and located near an advanced railhead. The salvage parties collected wrecked aircraft and moved them, using their own transport, to the railhead for shipping to the relevant salvage section, where they were sorted, the engines packed (to be repaired by the ERS or sent to England), and aircraft and instruments forwarded to the relevant ASD.[112] These changes appear to have been effective: whereas during the German 1918 offensive salvage lagged approximately one month behind wastage, during the Hundred Days campaign salvage largely matched the pattern of wastage.

As the squadrons moved forward to stay in touch with the front line, the increasing distance from the depots began to impede the movement of stores. A further difficulty was that the BEF's axis of advance drew the squadrons of I and II Brigades steadily south and east, disproportionately lengthening the supply pipeline from the northern depots and drawing the flow of matériel into a narrowing front alongside stores moving from the southern depots to III and IV Brigades. To compound this problem, the devastated landscape that the BEF had to cross meant that railheads could not be thrown forward fast enough, leading to significant delays in rail traffic and forcing the employment of motor transport to take up the strain.[113] Negotiating French roads was not easy at the best of times. Under good conditions, average speeds never exceeded 10 mph with stops every ten to fifteen miles.[114] The roads in the devastated area were already poor and deteriorated further under the weight of traffic.[115] Brooke-Popham's solution was to push forward advanced elements of the depots to provide more stock closer to the air parks.

The first units to move were the ASD issues sections (responsible for providing new aircraft direct to the squadrons). These were followed by advanced AD stores sections sent forward to the railheads, reducing the distance the APs had to travel to pick up stores.[116] These units held a month's supply of spares and were able to wait several weeks for replenishment from the main depots. All of this placed a large strain on motor transport and led to an increase in breakdowns.[117] A revised system of MT repair had already been introduced in July, based on a single MT depot established close to Rouen, combining the MT repair sections of both main depots.[118] The new depot was responsible for carrying out extensive repairs and the overhaul of "units" (principally engines and back-axles). Separate advanced sections were sent forward tasked with replacing unserviceable with serviceable "units"—so avoiding the need to send complete vehicles back to the depot. In Brooke-Popham's opinion this saved "a vast amount of road and rail transport. [The] advanced sections were not supposed to send vehicles back to the base unless they were completely smashed, i.e., required complete overhaul, and not merely the replacement of an engine or back axle. As a matter of fact, owing to the bad roads, the advanced sections were unable to cope with the work."[119]

The other major issue to be addressed were the APs themselves—the final link in the supply of matériel to the frontline squadrons and the route for all stores (other than aircraft) supplied from the depots. There is evidence to suggest that the mobility of the air parks was not as good as it might have been:

> I think that IX Brigade was the first and only RAF brigade in France to make any serious attempt to keep its aircraft park really mobile. During the long period of static warfare preceding the spring of 1918, Army Aircraft Parks had developed into miniature depots and were quite unable to move at short notice and still continue functioning. With the 9th Aircraft Park it was different. The entire unit could be moved in its own transport. Stores were properly binned in vehicles . . . there was no difficulty in issuing stores while the park was actually on the move, and this was frequently done.[120]

After the war, Brooke-Popham attempted to refute such criticism, arguing that: "I cannot agree that the [air] park was not really mobile. Certainly, whenever they could, they functioned in peace and comfort and practically always got to a building in order to protect their stores from damage, but they could move, and did move, at less than 24 hours' notice; in fact, there were several cases of air parks being actually packed up and on the move within six hours of the receipt of their orders."[121]

A further effect of the ever-lengthening supply chain was the increasing concentration of the RAF's brigades around their parks. As road movement became increasingly difficult, the squadrons fell back on the railheads (and their sources of supply). At the start of the Hundred Days roughly half of I Brigade's squadrons were located less than twelve miles from the front line (with the remainder between fifteen and twenty miles away). By November, every squadron in the brigade was at least twenty-eight miles from the front line.[122] This caused no significant operational impact—other than increased transit time. There was certainly no suggestion that the RAF's supply organization was on the brink of collapse, unlike the BEF. The increase in distance between the front line and the railheads (from fifteen to nearly thirty miles) placed considerable strain on the BEF's motor vehicles and the roads. As a result, the transport system became ever more difficult to maintain as the advance progressed. Unlike the RAF, the BEF's teeth arms could not fall back on the railheads, without compromising the speed of the advance and the pressure on the retreating German army.[123]

The Hundred Days saw a rapid increase in the number of aviation support units—rising from thirty-three in August to a total of forty-nine by the armistice (comprising advanced sections, salvage sections, lorry parks, and ammunition columns)—driven entirely by the need to sustain an ever-lengthening pipeline and mitigate the growing delays in the flow of matériel. Unprecedented operational tempo, high wastage, production shortfalls, enemy bombing raids, frequent moves, the poor state of the roads, delays in rail transport, and vehicle breakdowns made sustaining the RAF's front line increasingly problematic. The deteriorating situation is reflected in the number of aircraft issued to the squadrons compared to wastage. In the five months of May to September 1918, the depots issued more aircraft than were struck off, but in October there was a shortfall of more than one hundred. This was not an unprecedented situation (it also occurred in March and April 1918), but it reinforces the picture of a system under strain. The irony is that, without the impetus of the German 1918 offensive, the position might have been even worse—in the absence of the dispersed footprint that provided the RAF with enhanced mobility.[124]

The final part of this chapter will look at the experience of a discrete element of the front line—the fifteen R.E.8 squadrons that were the mainstay of the RAF's artillery cooperation effort on the western front—and whether it differed from the wider picture. It should be said immediately that the data is incomplete, with the weekly returns missing for some of September and all of October. Nevertheless, a clear picture does emerge. From June 1918 until the end of September, R.E.8 numbers were successfully maintained at over three hundred machines, that is, at the agreed establishment. Just as importantly, serviceability stayed above 90 percent until the end of September, although there was a decline over the summer. This echoes the wider picture but it also shows that the logistic staffs were largely successful in sustaining availability and serviceability through the Hundred Days (or at least until the end of September). There is no suggestion that the R.E.8 squadrons were in any way "protected" from the impact of the advance, having to relocate as frequently as other frontline units. Prior to 1918, the cadre of R.E.8 squadrons generated about five airfield moves each month, but this rose to twenty moves a month during the German 1918 offensive, before falling back in June and July only to rise rapidly between August and October to reach a peak of twenty-five airfield moves in the latter month.

The RAF was able to sustain high availability and good serviceability throughout the Hundred Days, notwithstanding high attrition and the increasing dislocation of the supply pipeline. This performance is all the more impressive when compared to the Tank Corps. Maintaining sufficient quantities of serviceable tanks during the advance was a continuous struggle, yet it was not too dissimilar from the problems faced by the RAF. Tanks and aircraft were high-technology weapons with poor reliability, needing constant engineering attention and a ready supply of spares.[125] Attrition was high and salvage—allied to a comprehensive in-theatre repair system— was essential to sustain frontline numbers. Breakdowns, limited reserves, and a lack of spares meant that frontline tanks were generally ineffective beyond seventy-two hours of continuous combat.[126] Unlike the RAF, however, the Tank Corps "was now becoming very weary—machines as fatigued as men—and very thin on the ground."[127] By 15 October 1918, out of the 1,232 tanks serving in France some 782 (63 percent) were recorded as unfit, leaving just 357 fighting machines.[128] Such was the level of attrition that 100 percent reserves were required in advance of an operation in order to cope with the resulting wastage. Between 8 August and 10 October 1918, 890 tanks were handed over to salvage—although frontline strength was never greater than around four hundred machines.[129] Unlike the RAF during the Hundred Days campaign, the Tanks Corps was unable to sustain combat operations in the face of substantial wastage and low repair rates.

In summing up the contribution of the RAF to the BEF's victory in 1918, we need look no further than Shelford Bidwell's analysis of the challenges faced in creating a huge citizen army while searching for technical solutions to the strategic deadlock created by trench warfare:

> The scientific and technological revolution on the Western Front,
> for it was nothing less, cannot be compressed in a paragraph or two,
> but a helpful way of understanding it is to note that it was not an

accumulation of "gadgets" but an almost automatic process of cross-fertilisation and linkages, contributing a rich mixture into tactical areas where they were badly needed. The most momentous contribution (in this writer's opinion)—greater than the tank—was from the maturing air force, the RFC/RAF, on its own initiative developing tactical air support and later strategic support, feeding reliable information to the intelligence staff and also enhancing the scope and accuracy of artillery fire.[130]

Bidwell went on to argue that the RAF's efforts were the genesis of the tactical air forces that played so decisive a part in the Allied victories of 1943 and 1944. John Terraine has offered equally positive words about the RAF's performance in 1918. "Both in the months of heavy defeat in the spring and in the sequence of brilliant offensive successes in the summer and autumn, the air role subject only (as always) to the iron rule of weather, grew steadily in importance."[131]

There are many examples during the Hundred Days of the direct physical effects of RAF operations as well as its role in reinforcing the German army's "sense of material inferiority."[132] Just as importantly, the record also shows an organization that continued to experiment and change as circumstances demanded and as new technology emerged. These outcomes were only possible because sufficient aircraft were available over the battlefront, day after day, in poor weather and in the face of relentless combat attrition, high wastage, and low reliability. The airpower enjoyed by the BEF was created through logistic excellence built on an organization imbued with an innovative spirit, a flexible approach, and a willingness to work hard to achieve results. Nothing could be in sharper contrast to the GAS, which experienced increasingly serious logistical problems as the German economy deteriorated.[133] Fuel rationing had been introduced as early as March 1918 and, by the beginning of June, fighter squadrons were restricted to 14,000 litres (3,000 gallons) per month and army cooperation squadrons to just 6,000 litres.[134] This compared to an average of 70,000 litres per month allocated to each RAF frontline squadron.[135] Although the RAF continued to lose aircraft at a higher rate than the GAS, the former enjoyed a continuous resupply of men and machines while German wastage exceeded new production. As a result, GAS frontline strength had fallen from 2,390 to 1,520 aircraft by the armistice.[136] The sense of overwhelming Allied logistic superiority is reflected in the comments of a German regimental historian (writing about the fighting in August): "What did it matter if here and there our guns blew up a tank, if our machine guns shot an attacking cavalry detachment to pieces, if our fighter aeroplanes shot down several hostile machines? The enemy filled the gaps in a twinkling of an eye."[137]

The German army's experiences in October were no less happy, with one regiment recording despondently that "during these days enemy aircraft participated with special intensity in the enemy infantry attacks . . . which was particularly depressing because no German planes could be seen and help or support from them was no longer expected."[138] Perhaps the final word on the performance of the RAF's logistic system in 1918 should be left to an anonymous German soldier who experienced the full fury of airpower and what seemed (to him) to be the relentless efforts of a single RAF fighter aircraft. "What a superabundance of men and matériel the enemy must have had that he could permit himself to hunt a single man from the air."[139]

CONCLUSIONS AND
ENDURING PRINCIPLES

THE PRECEDING CHAPTERS HAVE DESCRIBED THE SCALE AND EXTENT OF THE RFC's air operations on the western front and identified the critical importance of air superiority in enabling "three-dimensional" warfare (the employment of accurate, predicted, indirect artillery fire). Having established the importance of logistics in sustaining air operations, a quantitative and qualitative approach has been employed to determine the logistic contribution to strategic success. A range of performance indicators have been reviewed, capturing the logistic organization's achievements across a range of activities including: manpower utilization, sortie generation, maintenance, and fleet availability. Qualitative aspects have also been addressed, including: adaptability, agility, responsiveness, and leadership. Finally, this general analysis has been underpinned by an in-depth assessment of the logistic system's performance during four critical phases on the western front (the Somme, Third Ypres, the German 1918 offensive, and the Hundred Days), supplemented by data drawn from individual squadrons.

The evidence and supporting analysis have demonstrated that the RFC developed a highly sophisticated and comprehensive logistic system on the western front capable of supporting operations during sustained periods of intense fighting and strategic uncertainty, while coping with rapidly growing aircraft numbers and ever-increasing technical complexity. The logistic system's performance through the Somme, Third Ypres, and the Hundred Days can only be described as a success. Average monthly aircraft serviceability—a measure of both engineering effort and supply effectiveness—never fell below 80 percent and during the summer months was consistently above 88 percent.[1] Even today, this would be seen as a major achievement. There were frequent problems to be overcome, but at no stage of the war did the frontline squadrons suffer from want of aircraft, spares, or consumables.

While the Somme was in no sense the BEF's finest hour, the RFC's contribution was undoubtedly effective and provided a strong foundation for future success. If failure on the first day of the Somme can be attributed to any single factor it was the artillery plan—exacerbated by an inability to exploit success—rather than any failure on the part of the RFC. The difficulties experienced in maintaining contact with the advancing infantry and in directing counter-battery fire were of little relevance in the context of these wider, systemic problems. Irrespective, the RFC's logistic arrangements were more than adequate to meet operational demands, providing the necessary aircraft and crews during all phases of the battle. "The attacker—especially the English—by the employment of greater numbers of aircraft flying in tight formations and, at that very time, also with technically superior aircraft, fought his way to a perceptible superiority in the air."[2] At no point did the BEF lack for artillery cooperation aircraft or suffer from the attentions of the GAS. In as much as the RFC's supply system was able to function effectively, the Somme can be described as a logistic success.

In some ways, the RFC's logistic achievements at Third Ypres were even more impressive. While benefitting from an improved and more extensive system of depots, as well as the support of an expanded UK industrial base, the RFC faced a reorganized, revitalized, and better equipped enemy—as Bloody April revealed. Even so, the RFC's operations, notably its artillery cooperation efforts, were little affected and comprehensive support was provided to the BEF throughout the battle, notwithstanding substantial losses in aircraft and crews. Indeed, the logistic system was sufficiently resilient to be able to cope with the short-notice deployment of five squadrons to Italy—exhibiting a high degree of flexibility and mobility in the process.

The Hundred Days campaign, following the shock of the German 1918 offensive, demonstrated an inherent resilience on the part of the logistic organization as well as the ability to sustain operations in the mobile battle. The relocation of the major depots and the redeployment of squadrons did not cause the supply chain to falter, even though aircraft wastage was substantially higher than in any previous offensive. The Hundred Days, as with Third Ypres and the Somme, represented a significant logistic success, albeit that there is evidence the rapid advance and the heavy air fighting in the weeks immediately prior to the armistice did have an impact on frontline strength—such that the number of operational aircraft employed remained roughly constant over the last four months of fighting (even allowing for transfers to the Independent Force and U.S. Air Service), rather than continuing to expand as it had in the first part of 1918.[3]

In as much as 1918 represented the apogee of the RFC's logistic system, it is worth summarizing the front line's operational outputs during the final ten months of the war. Over this period, the RFC/RAF flew 484,000 hours and: engaged 12,000 hostile batteries for destruction, destroyed 1,150 gun pits and damaged 3,500, took 256,000 photographs, dropped 321,000 bombs, and fired 9.14 million rounds.[4] These achievements came at a substantial price, in both human and matériel terms, and depended on a complex and extensive military-industrial enterprise that drew heavily on modern management techniques. Business, bureaucracy, science, and the military worked collectively to mobilize national resources in support of the war effort, organized "as if it were a single firm designed to supply the armed forces with all they required."[5] By October 1918, the western front needed a monthly supply of nine hundred aircraft, one thousand tons of stores, and 1.5 million gallons of fuel (together with a ready supply of bombs and ammunition) in order to sustain a front line of some 1,500 aircraft (with another 1,500 in reserve), supported by 50,000 personnel and seven thousand vehicles—based at seventy-nine airfields, six depots, and eight aircraft parks.[6] Providing the necessary aircraft, aero-engines, and pilots required an unprecedented investment in manufacturing, support, and training facilities. A cottage industry with barely one thousand workers in 1914 was transformed by October 1918 into a business employing nearly 350,000 workers and producing approximately four thousand aircraft and 3,500 aero-engines each month.

Nearly 80,000 civilian and service personnel were engaged in repair and support activities, while just over 90,000 service personnel were employed on training activities, providing a combined output of some 400 aircraft, 2,000 aero-engines, 1,200 pilots, and 3,000 airmen each month. A further 91,000 service personnel

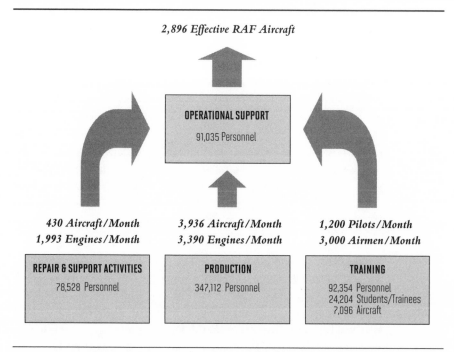

2,896 Effective RAF Aircraft

OPERATIONAL SUPPORT
91,035 Personnel

| 430 Aircraft/Month | 3,936 Aircraft/Month | 1,200 Pilots/Month |
| 1,993 Engines/Month | 3,390 Engines/Month | 3,000 Airmen/Month |

REPAIR & SUPPORT ACTIVITIES	PRODUCTION	TRAINING
78,528 Personnel	347,112 Personnel	92,354 Personnel
		24,204 Students/Trainees
		7,096 Aircraft

FIGURE 1. SUPPLY OF RAF AERONAUTICAL MATÉRIEL, OCTOBER 1918

were employed on frontline operations. The outcome of this immense national enterprise was a total front line (at home and overseas) of 2,896 aircraft—out of more than 22,000 held on strength.[7] In effect, just 13 percent of the total machines available to the RAF were employed on active operations and even this was only achieved because of a continuous supply of pilots, aircraft, aero-engines, stores, and consumables. There is no question that military aviation in the First World War was an expensive activity, but it was also one that demanded business skills and modern management techniques as much as tactical innovation and cutting-edge technologies.

The RAF's logistic operation on the western front was not simply a major national endeavor, but also part of a global supply network. Most of the materials needed in the manufacture and operation of aircraft (including aluminum, fabric, dope, petroleum products, and castor oil) had to be imported, although the special steels and forgings largely came from the UK—as did some of the wood (such as ash). This demanded the expansion of existing production facilities as well as the creation of new sources of supply. A portion of this material went straight to onshore manufacturing (as in North America where the RFC purchased aircraft directly), but the bulk was shipped to the UK to feed ever-larger production orders. Aircraft and aero-engine manufacture was also a global enterprise. Notwithstanding the expansion of the UK manufacturing base, substantial numbers of aircraft and engines had to be purchased overseas—primarily from France. However, such was the demand for aircraft that licensed production was also required—either British designs built by foreign manufacturers (in France and the United States) or foreign designs built by British manufacturers. In 1916, the British government even went so far as to fund an entire aero-engine plant in France to mass-produce the Hispano-Suiza design for both countries. More significantly, the high wastage experienced on the western front meant that manufacturing facilities (in the form of the RFC's depots) had to be created in France to make good the supply shortfalls by repairing and reconstructing aircraft and aero-engines. In effect, industry became part of the battle zone—shortening the supply chain, but blurring (permanently) the boundary between aviation support and air operations. The RFC was active in every theater of the First World War, from North America to India; however, flying aircraft at any distance from the home base represented a major logistic challenge, especially under climatic extremes. As a result, support units were established around the world to sustain air operations. Depots and parks were to be found in East Africa, Egypt, Canada, Russia, India, Iraq, and Italy, although the bulk of the logistic effort was focused on the western front.

The RFC's global presence also demanded a global transportation and distribution system to move raw materials and finished products to and within the operational theaters. The high number of vehicles employed by the RFC gave its supply chain substantial "velocity"—the speed at which items could move within the logistic system. Motorization—that is, the use of motor vehicles in support of operational functions—permeated every part of the RFC organization from the depots to the frontline squadrons.[8] Additional vehicles were allocated to specialist tasks (such as carrying ammunition) while others were held as a strategic reserve to deploy as required. These arrangements, along with a substantial inventory, allowed customer (frontline) needs to be met quickly under a wide range of conditions (static and mobile) at home and abroad. The global mobilization of supply, production, distribution, and transportation created a worldwide network of different companies producing, handling, and distributing goods, products, and services. However, as in today's global supply chain, this also created challenges in the form of increased uncertainty and variability, coupled with decreased control and visibility.[9] How the RFC coped with these issues is relevant to any assessment of logistic performance, if only to dispel the suspicion that success was as much about weight of numbers as managerial competence. John Ellis has argued—in the context of the Second World War—that Allied success was due to economic superiority and reliance on matériel and brute force, rather than on maneuver and adroit tactics.[10] Can the RFC's logistic success also be explained simply on the basis of superior industrial capacity and relative economic strength?

The effort to understand why the RFC was successful should perhaps start by examining what went wrong and, in particular, the criticisms leveled by Robert Brooke-Popham at the organization he led for much of the war.[11] One of his major concerns was the layout of the RFC's depots, an issue highlighted by the serious losses inflicted by German air attacks on the BEF's logistic infrastructure during 1918. At the beginning of the war, there was no appreciation of the size and extent of the in-theatre repair activities that would eventually be required. It was perhaps inevitable that the logistic system would develop around a few key (vulnerable) locations. It took the Germans, in the form of their 1918 offensive, to galvanize HQ RAF into adopting a more dispersed logistic footprint. By the time German air attacks began against the BEF's rear area in the summer of 1918, the RAF had already (but only just) reorganized and redeployed their main repair and supply depots in France.

A more serious challenge, and one that continues to dog contemporary military logisticians, was the problem of mobility—or rather immobility. While Brooke-Popham vigorously defended the air parks against the accusation that they were not properly mobile, he would later wonder whether the RAF was really serious about mobility when it insisted on being tied to dozens of heavy trucks.[12] In his view "squadron personnel must learn to improvise" rather than placing too much reliance on workshops and machine tools. The logistic staffs can certainly be criticized for failing to halt the creeping immobility that static warfare encouraged, but their response to the problems that emerged in 1918 demonstrated both agility and adaptability.

Another area of concern to Brooke-Popham was the decision to increase individual squadron establishments to more than twenty aircraft. This expansion certainly eased administration and effectively reduced the total overhead (in both personnel and support equipment) for a given number of frontline aircraft.[13] The downside was that the higher number of pilots severely stretched the squadron commander's span of control. In this instance, it could be argued that HQ RAF pursued logistic efficiency at some risk to operational effectiveness.

A more significant and deep-seated problem, given the BEF's increasing manpower difficulties as the war progressed, was the RFC's appetite for skilled personnel at home and abroad. Haig is reputed to have occasionally expressed the view that the RFC used manpower rather inefficiently.[14] To some extent, the situation was not of the RFC's making in that poor reliability and high wastage necessitated the employment of large numbers of tradesmen to keep squadrons operational, creating an unprecedented teeth-to-tail ratio. The number of support personnel per frontline aircraft gradually increased over the course of the war, rising from around twenty-two personnel per frontline aircraft to slightly below thirty personnel by the armistice. This was especially evident in the period December 1917 to March 1918 when the abrupt deployment of five squadrons to Italy saw frontline strength fall without any commensurate reduction in the support organization. At first glance, this pattern would seem to illustrate the "logistic snowball" at work—the tendency for logistic activities to grow out of all proportion to the tactical forces they support.[15] However, a rather different picture emerges if we consider the front line in isolation, excluding the depots and support units. Rather than showing a slight increase over time, the number of squadron personnel per frontline aircraft fell significantly over the last two years of the war—such that it required only half the manpower to support a single aircraft in November 1918 compared to January 1916.[16] It was the heavy investment in support units, and the expansion of the depots and parks required to sustain higher flying rates and cope with increased wastage, that drove the RFC's global manpower requirement, rather than the direct (on-aircraft) maintenance effort. In fact, of the 50,000 RAF personnel employed in France and Belgium at the armistice, only around 20,000 were engaged in first line (squadron) activities; the remainder being based in second line (air parks or ancillary support) or third line (depot) units.[17]

Manpower was not the only resource needed to sustain air operations on the western front. The demand for new or replacement aircraft and aero-engines required an ever-larger share of the nation's manufacturing capacity. If the war had continued into 1919, the total cost of the RAF would have been £370 million per year—some £1 million per day and a 150-fold increase since 1914.[18] Perhaps the most significant development was that, while the RAF represented just 11.6 percent of total defense expenditure in 1918–1919, aviation consumed nearly 25 percent of the total munitions budget, largely comprising aircraft and aero-engines.[19]

TABLE 6. WAR EXPENDITURE BY FISCAL YEAR, 1910–19 (£M – CURRENT PRICES)

	10/11	11/12	12/13	13/14	14/15	15/16	16/17	17/18	18/19
FIGHTING SERVICES	.63	68	71	73	362	739	815	952	1,161
MUNITIONS	-	-	-	-	-	242	534	647	461
TOTAL DEFENSE	63	68	71	73	362	981	1,349	1,599	1,622
AIR SERVICES	0	0	0	1	3	8	16	35	75
AERONAUTICAL SUPPLIES	-	-	-	-	-	4	12	72	113
TOTAL AVIATION	0	0	0	1	3	12	28	107	188
% TOTAL DEFENSE	0	0	0	2	0	1	2	7	12
% MUNITIONS	-	-	-	-	-	2	2	11	25

This was set to rise still further with £165m of outstanding aviation orders, more than half the production commitments of the Ministry of Munitions.[20] In other words, in less than a decade, UK spending on military aviation had grown from virtually zero to almost 12 percent of the defense and 25 percent of the equipment budgets. It was the scale of this investment, and the evident inefficiency in the allocation of aircraft and aero-engine production between the RFC and RNAS, that was one of the factors in the formation of the Air Council in 1916 and, ultimately, the creation of a separate Air Ministry in 1917 and an independent air service in 1918.

The share of national resources required to create and sustain the RAF on the western front can be estimated using the methodology developed by the Air Ministry shortly after the end of the war (in the context of the 1920 intervention in Somaliland).[21] At the armistice there were ninety-nine RAF squadrons based in France and Belgium (including the Independent Force and 5 Group), comprising thirty-nine single-seat fighter squadrons; fifty-two reconnaissance, day-, and night-bomber squadrons; and eight twin-engine bomber squadrons.[22] Each squadron represented an initial capital cost, a replacement cost (to make good wastage), and a running cost (consumables, spares, etc.). Using this yardstick, the RAF presence on the western front represented an annual cost of at least £120 million, excluding depot, training, and headquarters activities, or 67 percent of total expenditure on the Air Services.[23] Incidentally, this was also almost double what was spent annually on the Army and Navy (combined) prior to the war.

The high equipment cost encountered in sustaining air operations is reflected in the demand for spares and related consumables. Over 120,000 tons of aviation stores (excluding aircraft) were shipped to the western front during the course of the war.[24] The weekly rate of supply was largely constant through 1916 and 1917, averaging around five hundred tons (although it did exceed one thousand tons on occasion). However, the last nine months of 1918 saw a dramatic increase in the weight of stores shipped to the western front, which rose to over 3,500 tons per week in October, compared to a previous peak of 1,200 tons in April 1917.

In its analysis of the Somaliland Campaign, the Air Ministry advised that the initial equipment of a squadron deployed overseas required 900–2,800 tons of shipping (depending on aircraft type) and 300–930 tons annually (although these recurring costs excluded petrol, oil, and motor transport).[25] In the seven months (thirty weeks) from May to November 1918, seventeen squadrons joined the western front—representing an average shipping tonnage of 1,090 tons per week. The RAF squadrons already on the western front represented a weekly recurring cost of 768 tons—giving a total shipping requirement of nearly 1,900 tons per week. This is likely to be a cautious estimate as the operational tempo on the western front was clearly a great deal higher than that experienced in Somaliland, but it does suggest that the high demand for aviation stores experienced in the last six months of the war was destined to continue into 1919 and owed more to the overall size of the front line than to the particular conditions experienced during the Hundred Days. It also indicates that a significant proportion of the RAF's weekly stores requirement, from the summer of 1918 onwards, was driven by the deployment cost of the heavy bombers of the Independent Force—rather than simply the need to make good the wastage in aircraft and aero-engines.

Once in France, rail and motor transport were essential in keeping stores moving along the supply pipeline. Without a rapid and effective distribution system, the RFC could not have sustained the required levels of mobility and operational tempo. The importance of motor transport was such that by April 1918 the RAF possessed over 8,500 vehicles and motorcycles—compared to just seven hundred in 1915.[26] However, the Achilles' heel of motor transport was fuel. The greater the distance between the forward supply base and the front line, the less load-carrying capacity available—a problem rediscovered by Patton in his drive to the Meuse in 1944.[27] The RFC's squadrons could not be based farther than supply vehicles could travel from (and return to) the nearest railhead. Motor transport represented the RFC's "invisible tether" on the western front, sustaining the operational squadrons but also constraining their deployment. This paradox lay at the heart of motorized warfare. "A point constantly lost sight of is that the automobile in warfare is a factor of immobility."[28] The internal combustion engine certainly permitted large loads to be moved over short distances but venturing farther afield required a substantial and ready supply of fuel within a reasonable distance (perhaps no more than eighty miles) of a well-equipped and constantly replenished base.[29]

These problems aside, the RFC enjoyed a significantly more generous supply of motor vehicles than the BEF, and indeed, other Allied armies, including the American Expeditionary Force (AEF). This permitted the efficient and timely movement of stores between the air parks and the individual squadrons spread across more than one hundred miles of front. Moreover, the RFC's lorries, workshop vehicles, tenders, and motorcycles were a small part of a much wider Army transportation system that moved thousands of tons of stores from the Channel ports across a complex network of railways and inland waterways. Employing scientific management techniques, the BEF's Directorate of Transportation proved capable of meeting the BEF's substantial and ever-growing supply needs, using statistical analysis to predict future demands and to facilitate transport planning. The RFC's weekly requirement for around one thousand to two thousand tons of stores represented less than 2 percent of the BEF's total supply and was, therefore, well within the overall transport system's capacity.

For the RFC, however, the challenge was not capacity but complexity. Some feel for the immense range and scale of the aviation equipment and spares procured to support the RFC and RAF can be gauged from the postwar disposal program. By November 1918 the Air Ministry had over 20,000 airplanes and seaplanes on charge, with new machines being produced at a rate of four thousand per month. By March 1919, there were still 20,300 aircraft on inventory, notwithstanding a policy of scrapping the less valuable machines.[30] In March 1920, it was announced that the entire stock of surplus airplanes, seaplanes, aeronautical engines, and spares had been sold by the Ministry of Munitions to the Aircraft Disposal Company Ltd. for £1 million and 50 percent of the profits on reselling. The stock comprised: 10,000 airplanes and seaplanes, 35,000 aero-engines, and an immense quantity of spares and ground equipment (including hangars) together with 500 to 1,000 tons of ball-bearings, 350,000 spark plugs, and 100,000 magnetos. The correspondents who had an opportunity to view the surplus stock were clearly impressed: "It is impossible to convey in words all that was seen. Suffice to say that we passed through numerous sheds in which were stacked, packed and piled literally acres of aeroplanes, aero-engines, airscrews, landing gears, rev counters, compasses and other instruments, magnets and starters, carburetors, wire strainers, bolts, nuts, pins split and pins not, sundry other accessories not recognized at the moment, airship and kite balloon materials, etc., etc.—all to the Nth power!"[31]

Managing an inventory of this scale and detail had few if any prewar parallels. The nearest example was Sears Roebuck, founded in 1888, which grew into the largest retail firm in North America. By 1897, their mail-order catalogue comprised nearly seven hundred pages advertising over 20,000 items (including entire houses in kit form) supplied to thousands of customers in North America. However, in the absence of automatic data processing, such large inventories could only be managed by handwritten ledgers. This was a labor-intensive process that was prone to error. Indeed, Sears found increasing difficulties with shipping delays and damaged or duplicated orders—until it created a dedicated facility in 1906 to manage the inventory and assemble orders in a single location, rather than sending items direct to the customer from the factory.[32] The concept of central warehousing and integrated order control continues to underpin modern logistic systems.

The RFC's wartime inventory (50,000 line items) easily exceeded that managed by Sears Roebuck.[33] The challenge facing the RFC in managing thousands of delicate and expensive parts under wartime conditions was both significant and largely unprecedented. There were no tracking mechanisms allowing the movement of items to be followed and no real-time visibility of stock levels, other than information that could be provided on the telephone or by telegram. By any standard, therefore, the RFC's ability to sustain frontline serviceability at above 90 percent throughout the Somme, Third Ypres, and the Hundred Days is quite remarkable. It is interesting to note that despite advances in computerized inventories and item tracking, the Ministry of Defence (MOD) still finds it difficult to manage its current equipment inventory.[34]

Hoffman Nickerson described airpower as "a thunderbolt launched from an eggshell invisibly tethered to a base."[35] Although this observation was made in the context of his criticism of the Second World War strategic bomber offensive, it neatly contrasts the strengths and weaknesses of airpower—substantial offensive capabilities sustained through a fragile umbilical. Fragility arises because, to remain serviceable, aircraft demand a constant supply of spares and consumables. The provision of these items is a complex and intensive activity. Aircraft are sophisticated and delicate machines comprising multiple, interacting parts engineered to the highest standards. They operate across diverse and hostile environments and require constant attention to ensure continued operation in the face of wear or failure. In this sense, aviation logistics has always been more demanding than sea or land logistics, although increasing weapons complexity means that the distinction is steadily narrowing: "One of the key issues confronting U.S. and UK logisticians is that equipment has become increasingly complex and the logistics tail has grown accordingly. In many cases, following the entire chain from supplier to soldier is becoming more difficult because there are more things that can break, more things that do break, and replacements must be stockpiled and tracked."[36]

The use of term "supply chain" to describe the provision of aircraft, aero-engines, and spares to the western front is potentially misleading since it was a network rather than a series of sequential steps. As the war progressed, this involved an ever-growing number of suppliers and customers, as well as a greater range and quantity of parts. Every squadron that joined the BEF created an additional element in the system, as did every new logistic unit and the ever-widening UK-supplier base. Further complexity came from the increasing range of aircraft roles, the different types of aircraft and engines employed, and the range of parts to be procured and managed. These factors can be grouped into two broad categories: sources of network complexity (squadrons, aircraft and aero-engine firms, and logistic units), and sources of information complexity (lead times, aircraft and aero-engine types, inventory range, and

TABLE 7. SUPPLY CHAIN COMPLEXITY

TYPE OF COMPLEXITY	NOV 14	NOV 16	NOV 18
NETWORK NODES (deployed squadrons)	5	36	96
SUPPLIERS (UK aircraft firms)	9	27	64
SUPPLIERS (UK aero-engine firms)	5	114	323
ORGANIZATION (deployed logistic units)	2	8	32
NETWORK ELEMENTS (normalized against 1914)	1	9	25
RANGE (aircraft types employed on western front)	10	14	12
PRODUCT (individual parts in schedule)	67	2,000	2,234
PROCESS (lead time—months)	4	6	9
CUSTOMER (operational roles)	1	4	5
INFORMATION ELEMENTS (normalized against 1914)	1	250	443

operational roles). By 1918, sources of network complexity on the western front were twenty-five times greater than 1914, while sources of information complexity were more than four hundred times greater.[37]

Of course, this is not a precise measurement and it ignores equipment other than aircraft (including aero-engines), but it does indicate the increasing challenge faced by the RFC's logistic system as the front line expanded and air operations evolved. One effect of logistic complexity is to exacerbate the impact of distance. A good example is the Sopwith Dolphin when unexpected problems arose with various ancillary components as a result of engine vibration. By choosing a foreign engine design (and foreign manufacture involving several firms at different locations), the Air Board overcame a shortfall in British aero-engine production, only to discover that the subsequent design and production problems were much more difficult to resolve—because of distance (and to some extent language). In the end, it was found easier to undertake the necessary modifications at the RFC's own depots rather than incorporate them on the French production line; indeed, it was emphasized that, until these modifications were incorporated, such engines were "no better than spares."[38]

A further effect of complexity is process delay. A good example is the time elapsed between the first flight of a prototype aircraft and deliveries to the front line. The trend over the course of the war was for an increasing delay between prototype and production.[39] For example, the design of the Sopwith 1½ Strutter commenced in late 1915 with the first flight in January 1916. A production order for fifty RFC machines was placed in March 1916 with deliveries starting in May 1916 (admittedly diverted from existing RNAS orders). The first fully equipped RFC squadron reached France between May and June 1916. By comparison, the design of the

Sopwith Snipe commenced in August 1917 with the first flight in November 1917. Production orders were placed for 1,700 machines from seven manufacturers in March 1918. The first Snipe-equipped squadron on the western front became operational in July 1918. Interestingly, given the contemporary criticism, the evidence suggests that Factory-designed and -produced aircraft were generally deployed to the western front more quickly than commercial designs—a conclusion that supports Paul Hare's contention that "without the Royal Aircraft Factory, the evolution of the RFC would, inevitably, have been greatly retarded."[40]

Many of the logistic characteristics found on the western front continue to be integral to modern supply chains, including accelerating product life cycles, make-to-order strategies, and international sourcing. Indeed, the RFC pioneered processes that are only now being deployed by leading logistic organizations. The issue of network complexity has already been discussed but there are other elements—such as volatile demand and forecast uncertainty—that represent enduring problems.[41] Contemporary management practice provides a relevant yardstick for determining the RFC's logistic achievements on the western front and for understanding the techniques involved. The remainder of this chapter looks at the RFC logistic organization through the prism of modern supply chain theory, before concluding with an assessment of the long-term impact of the arrangements developed to support air operations on the western front.

How then does the RFC's logistic system compare to modern management practice? We have already touched on the increasing complexity of the RFC's supply chain and how this led to greater potential for delay or failure. Complexity, coupled with volatile demand, makes predicting spares requirements particularly difficult. Demand uncertainty was a permanent feature of the western front. Wastage (and hence demand) varied greatly from month to month—driven not only by operational tempo and enemy action but also by weather, accidents, unreliability, and obsolescence. Since air operations were continuous, the RFC's logistic system had to meet the front line's demand for replacement machines (and spares) on a daily basis. This meant that the depots needed to provide somewhere between twenty-five and thirty aircraft to the front line each day during the summer of 1918. The problem was that this was spread across some twelve types and there was no method of predicting in advance exactly what types would be needed or in what proportion. Determining the stores to procure, and the required quantities, relied on a combination of experience and guesswork; the relevant mathematical models to optimize spares procurement did not emerge until the 1960s when the necessary computational power was available.[42] A further difficulty was that, although the daily delivery in 1918 of new production aircraft averaged twenty-four machines (compared to an average demand of twenty-three aircraft per day), actual deliveries ranged from a low of twelve aircraft per day in February to a peak of thirty-one in November. Demand was equally variable, ranging from a low of six aircraft per day in January to a high of thirty-two aircraft per day in August. Thus, although there was some synchronization between supply and demand, this only existed at the macro level.

In modern supply chain theory, a key attribute in the marketplace is the ability to match supply with demand under volatile conditions. This is not so much about managing with fewer resources ("lean," in operations management terminology) as about meeting the customer's needs. Under the conditions present on the western front, agility was undoubtedly more significant than "lean." The uncertainty of demand, in both volume and detail, required a responsive and flexible supply system where the emphasis was on delivery rather than efficiency.[43] Since production generally takes longer than the customer is prepared to wait, the supply chain also needs to hold inventory. During the First World War it took an average of thirty-four weeks to take a new aircraft from design to mass production, and some sixty-four weeks for an engine.[44] Once a particular type was in production, contracts had to be set twenty-five to thirty weeks ahead of the required delivery. In other words, the western front's aircraft needs had to be estimated at least six to eight months ahead of actual demand, depending on whether it was a new or mature design. If anything, these lead times grew during the course of the war. As a result, there was a steady increase in reserves over the last two years of the war as air fighting became more intense and demand became ever more unpredictable. At the time of the Somme, the RFC's depot reserves equated to roughly 50 percent of frontline strength. This had increased to 100 percent by the beginning of 1918 and even slightly higher by the armistice—although this masks a major reduction during the German 1918 offensive when wastage grew rapidly and the depots' total reserves fell to a low of some 740 machines.[45]

Only a proportion of the depots' holdings were actually ready for immediate use; the remaining aircraft were a mixture of obsolete types or damaged and wrecked machines waiting for repair. The required level of reserves was calculated on the basis of two to four weeks' supply for each aircraft type, depending on the number of squadrons equipped with the same type of airplane.[46] For more than ten squadrons of the same type the reserve was set at two weeks, for under ten squadrons it was set at three weeks, and for a single squadron it was set at four weeks. As we have already noted, the weekly supply needs for each aircraft type varied according to wastage. Wastage rates during the period March–September 1918 ranged between 6.4 percent (R.E.8) to 12.3 percent (Sopwith Camel). For the majority of squadrons it was around 10 percent per week—the exceptions being those engaged in night operations such as the F.E.2b, where it was approximately 30 percent of squadron strength per month. Total wastage peaked in September 1918 at 218 aircraft per week, suggesting a "target range" of 436–654 machines (on the basis of two to three weeks' supply).[47] Although the number of aircraft held by the depots on 30 September 1918 totaled over 1,100 (out of 2,716 RAF machines on the western front), just 221 were serviceable.[48] This position was only manageable because the pool of aircraft available to meet immediate needs could be supplemented by the repair of damaged aircraft. By selecting which aircraft types to repair, from the stock of damaged airframes and aero-engines, the depots were able to overcome shortfalls in planned deliveries or to replenish the serviceable inventory depleted by high demand. Supply chain theory suggests that a key driver in determining the appropriate response to customer demands is the "supply characteristic"—the replenishment lead time. The longer the lead time and the more unpredictable the demand, the more agile the supply chain needs to be.[49] For the RAF, the lead time gap was around thirty weeks—or put another way, the supply of replacement aircraft (both quantity and type) was set at least six months ahead. In-theatre repair was, therefore, an essential element in sustaining the agility of the logistic system.

A review in the summer of 1917 suggested that although the overall level of losses could be predicted with some confidence (based on frontline strength), the proportion of losses could not be attributed with any confidence. Actual losses over the five months June–October 1917 were lower than predicted by more than four hundred machines.[50] However, this masked some significant variations. For example, R.E.8 losses had been predicted at 692 machines but the actual number was 443. On the other hand, Sopwith Camel losses were predicted at 111 but actual losses were 133. Of course, not all wastage was driven by attrition. Air superiority was a competitive business and a quantity could not compensate for a greatly inferior design. The pace of aeronautical development during the First World War, the "constant tactical factor," was so rapid that obsolescence was a permanent state of affairs. Failure to provide aircraft and aero-engines with adequate performance to counter continuing improvements in the fighting abilities of the GAS compromised the RFC's ability to achieve air superiority and led to a substantial increase in wastage. The "Fokker Scourge" in 1915–16 and Bloody April in 1917 are the most obvious examples of why quality mattered as much as quantity. The regular replacement of older aircraft types or time-expired machines was therefore a significant feature of RFC operations. Today, "new product introduction" is an increasingly important aspect of global logistics but, as on the western front, requires the careful management of the surge activity associated with the deployment and recovery of products from the field.[51] Sometimes, however, a change of role was all that was required. The transfer of the F.E.2 from daylight to night-bombing operations demonstrated how an old design could gain a new lease of life in a more benign environment.

Variable demand, erratic supply, and obsolescence created a high level of uncertainty but, by employing in-theatre repair to make good any deficiencies in supply, coupled with a strategic reserve to cope with excessive demand, the RFC created a system that combined the benefits of mass production with local responsiveness. This strategy echoes the conclusions reached by the controller of the Ministry of Aircraft Production during the Second World War regarding the economic benefits of repair compared to production. "Once you embark upon large-scale equipment with a high degree of wastage from battle causes, the maintenance of first-line strength can be achieved most economically if a properly balanced repair scheme is integrated with supply, so that both sources are available in order to maintain the serviceability of aircraft."[52]

The systems developed by the RFC in France to regulate the supply of aircraft to the front line are recognized as playing an important role in modern supply chains. If product configuration (make-to-order) can be postponed until as late as possible, the manufacturer can respond more rapidly to changing customer demands. Postponement not only saves time, but also allows production to be optimized, with a reduction in overall stock levels.[53] However, the ability to delay configuration requires the creation of a generic (or strategic) inventory that can be modified readily and quickly. By creating an in-theatre erection and repair facility—in the form of the RFC's engine and aircraft depots—equipment could be held close to the squadrons awaiting final configuration and "repair to order." The depots' reconstruction program was planned in advance (providing a "rough-cut" capacity plan), but amended in light of the supply position and "real" as opposed to "predicted" demand.[54] Without the depots and their ability to create additional aircraft and engines (beyond new supply from England), frontline availability would have fallen—unless a very much larger reserve had been created, with a commensurate reduction in the number of frontline squadrons. The depots were not only storage sites, therefore, but acted as strategic warehouses, synchronizing activities across the entire supply chain to meet the front line's daily needs—an increasingly important function in logistic operations since the Second World War.[55]

Forecasting future demand was central to the RFC logistic system, although a number of the variables, such as the weather or enemy action, were outside any direct influence. Forecasting the delivery of new aircraft was almost as challenging. Shortages in key components (particularly aero-engines), defective materials, industrial problems, and the inexperience of subcontractors meant that production targets were rarely met. As a result, there were significant discrepancies between what HQ RFC wanted, what the Ministry of Munitions agreed to provide, and what

TABLE 8. DEMAND FORECAST ACCURACY, JANUARY–MAY 1918

	JAN 18	FEB 18	MARCH 18	APRIL 18	MAY 18
MACHINES REQUESTED	471	550	581	890	972
MACHINES PROMISED	435	453	557	841	933
MACHINES DELIVERED	409	346	745	606	889
DEFICIT ON REQUIREMENT	−62	−204	164	−284	−83
WASTAGE	200	233	839	699	774
SUPPLY/DEMAND BALANCE	209	113	−94	−93	115
REBUILDS DELIVERED	92	89	117	130	148

was actually sent to the western front. In the first five months of 1918, the RFC's monthly requests for replacement aircraft routinely exceeded promised deliveries; moreover, in four of the five months deliveries were even lower than promised.[56]

On the positive side, wastage was higher than deliveries in only two of the five months (March and April 1918). With this level of uncertainty, the ability to produce aircraft in short supply by rebuilding or repairing damaged airframes in France—within a matter of weeks—was a vital tool in meeting frontline needs. The relationship between supply (in the form of production capacity and inventory) and demand can be represented as a fulcrum where demand is balanced by a combination of capacity and inventory. If the fulcrum can be moved closer to the customer, demand can be satisfied by a smaller inventory or less capacity, or both. This can be achieved either by increasing product velocity (the speed at which the product moves from the manufacturer to the customer) or by improving the demand horizon. This is exactly what the RFC implemented in France. By creating a network of depots and forward supply parks, linked by motor transport, the front line's demands were rapidly met—either from the immediate strategic reserve or by erecting cased aircraft. At the same time, the repair and reconstruction program focused on making good the shortfall. The RFC's depots represented what is known as the "decoupling point"—the point in the supply chain where supply meets demand.[57] Upstream of this point, the Ministry of Munitions was able to manage the production of new aircraft as efficiently as possible, while downstream the emphasis was on effectiveness rather than efficiency. In effect, the depots marked the transition from a lean to an agile system. This "hybrid" arrangement is recognized as best practice in supply chain management.

An essential element in the RFC's ability to make good any supply shortfall was the salvage program. Virtually every damaged or crashed aircraft and aero-engine within Allied lines was recovered to the depots as part of a determined effort to recycle materials and components for the home production program or for incorporation in the depots' own reconstruction program. As a result, the RFC's logistic system was not a one-way flow of matériel, but an arrangement where items moved in both directions. Known as "reverse logistics," this process is increasingly important in modern supply chains because of environmental legislation and the cost benefits of recycling. The application of reverse logistics also played a major role in sustaining RAF operations during the Second World War where salvage and repair were vital in maintaining frontline strength.[58]

Although the RFC benefitted from a substantial and rapidly growing industrial base and a generous supply of raw material and equipment, the effective management of the supply chain demanded considerable skill and a wide range of innovative techniques. The process may have been "brutal" in scale but it was sophisticated in delivery. It also depended on one essential lubricant—skilled manpower. Without the determination, flexibility, and professionalism of large numbers of skilled tradesmen, on the squadrons and in the depots and parks, the RFC could not have continued to operate. In recognizing the importance of the "human" as well as the "material," an important question arises: to what extent did the RFC's achievements benefit from good leadership?

Notwithstanding the danger of attempting to elevate a single individual above others, especially when reviewing the performance of a large and complex organization over an extended period, it is difficult not to applaud the achievements of Brigadier-General Robert Brooke-Popham. Brookham stands tall in any story of the RFC's logistic system on the western front. He led the earliest efforts to sustain air operations in support of the BEF and continued to play this vital role for a further four years—with hardly a break. There can be few British officers who were employed continuously on the western front, effectively in the same post, from August 1914 until well after the armistice. That he was retained in these duties, albeit rising in rank with his rapidly growing responsibilities, speaks volumes for Brooke-Popham's dedication, professional competence, and the enduring confidence of his superiors. Reviewing the key individuals and technologies that shaped the overall British air effort, J. M. Bruce provided the following assessment of Robert Brooke-Popham.

> With the growth of the RFC the Headquarters establishment was increased commensurately, and the new post of DA & QMG was filled by Brooke-Popham, promoted to Brigadier-General. From then until the end he oversaw, with extraordinary zeal and efficiency, virtually everything the Military Wing did and flew. It is doubtful whether any other British officer knew more about the aerial war than he did. What cannot be comprehensively or accurately assessed is the extent to which his individual influence and competence affected the RFC's and RAF's conduct of the war, but it must have been very substantial. It seems that he never received any very public recognition of his outstanding work.[59]

This study has striven to provide a better picture of Robert Brooke-Popham's achievements and his influence on the course of the air war. Although his career ultimately ended on a low note, Brooke-Popham had a seminal role in the development of the postwar RAF and, as the first commandant of the Staff College at Andover, was in a unique position to inculcate a generation of future RAF leaders with an understanding of the logistic foundations of airpower. The provision of data tables for students at the Staff College detailing wastage rates, the number of personnel required to man the depots on the western front, the output of repaired aircraft and engines, and the layout of squadron ground facilities suggests that he endeavored during his tenure to impart a proper understanding of the material basis of airpower. The RAF's focus on maintenance and training facilities, spelled out in Trenchard's

1919 Memorandum, reflects this broader perspective, as does the heavy investment in engineering and supply facilities represented by the RAF's expansion plans from 1934 onwards.[60] It should also be noted that this policy was distinctly different to the Royal Navy's attitude, which relegated aviation logistics to a subsidiary role when planning the expansion of the Fleet Air Arm (FAA), and to the Luftwaffe's strategy that placed proportionally more resources in the front line—only to find that operations could not be sustained in the face of the wastage rates that war brought.[61] It is not unreasonable, therefore, to view Brooke-Popham's legacy as extending beyond the First World War to the substantial and highly effective support arrangements that underpinned the RAF's operations in the Second World War.

Brooke-Popham did not work alone. Considerable credit must be given to his colleagues (and superiors). According to Williamson Murray, "one of the foremost attributes of military effectiveness must lie in the ability of armies, navies or air forces to recognize and adapt to the actual conditions of combat."[62] While the RFC's logistic system was never "perfect"—in the sense of delivering 100 percent serviceability while maintaining 100 percent of the frontline establishment for 100 percent of the time—it did demonstrate significant adaptability in sustaining air operations on the western front. In one sense, the very nature of First World War military aviation (without an established organizational culture or an agreed doctrine) created an ideal environment for innovation. No single branch of the Army dominated the senior leadership of the RFC or, indeed, the officer corps as a whole. Several factors are critical in the adaptation process, none more so than the role of military leaders in recognizing problems and instigating innovation. Asking the right question is not easy for leaders and subordinates "encumbered with their intellectual and historical baggage."[63] The RFC leaders most closely involved in maintenance and supply issues—Trenchard, Brooke-Popham, Salmond, and Brancker—were not afraid to ask questions or to innovate if this provided the necessary answers, however painful. The suggestion that rivalry and animosity between the senior leaders of the RFC adversely affected the conduct of the air war by restricting the supply of men and machines is not supported by the evidence.[64] The partial pooling of motor transport in late 1917, centralizing the management of a critical asset, is a good example of how tactical flexibility at unit level was consciously sacrificed for operational flexibility at the strategic. The instant decision to "push" supplies to squadrons during the German 1918 offensive—rather than relying on the well-established "pull" system—broke with all previous procedure, sacrificing efficiency for operational effect. Whether carefully considered or spontaneous, HQ RFC's decision making reveals an appetite for innovation and adaptation. This was not a series of revolutionary steps, but rather a continuous process whereby the logistic system evolved to cope with the uncertainty and urgency created by rapid technological progress and enemy action. "Adaptation demands constant, unceasing change because war never remains static but involves the complexities thrown up by humans involved in their effort to survive."[65] The personal involvement of Trenchard (and subsequently Salmond) in resolving supply and distribution issues suggests that they fully recognized the strategic importance of logistics and its contribution to air superiority. "Sound logistics forms the foundation for the development of strategic flexibility and mobility. If such flexibility is to be exercised and exploited, military command must have adequate control of its logistic support."[66] This perspective supports the view that the First World War RMA was not driven by radical transformation but by changes in the way that society organized warfare, and through the development of existing technologies in a process of evolution and innovation.[67]

How then does the RFC's logistic performance compare with other military systems—as defined by James Huston in his study of logistic best practice?[68] Of the sixteen areas identified as having general applicability, the RFC adhered to best practice in eleven (in three of the remaining five areas, the RFC adopted a different approach—but for reasons unique to aviation logistics):

1. *Equivalence*: The Headquarters' logistic staffs, led by Brooke–Popham, had equivalent status to the operations staffs. Logistic issues were considered alongside strategy and tactics, in both planning and execution.

2. *Feasibility*: Trenchard and Salmond both understood that their plans were constrained by the availability of matériel. The RFC's operational strategy could not be divorced from logistic feasibility.

3. *Unity of Command*: GOC RFC exercised full logistic authority, through the unified command of support and frontline units as well as controlling the means of supply—notably motor transport. The RFC undoubtedly enjoyed a significant advantage, compared to other elements of the BEF, in the scale of organic transport available.

4. *Matériel Precedence*: Although the mobilization of matériel (in creating and deploying new squadrons) did not always anticipate manpower, the relationship between the two was understood and priorities were largely balanced.

5. *Forward Impetus*: The emphasis on forward impetus (automatic supply from the rear, relieving commanders of detailed involvement in supply issues) was not adopted by the RFC. This underlines the most significant (and enduring) difference between aviation and ground logistic systems. The dynamic and complex nature of air warfare, and the high costs involved, require supplies be "pulled" rather than "pushed."

6. *Economy*: A distinctive characteristic of the RFC's logistic organization (and military aviation in general) was the ratio of secondary to primary requirements—the resources allocated to indirect support (the depots and parks) compared to direct support (the squadrons). This was extremely

high compared to the remainder of the BEF—an enduring characteristic of air forces, where the "tail to teeth" ratio is consistently larger than other operational environments.

7. *Mobility*: The RFC did largely maintain mobility within the logistic organization, despite the inevitable drift toward immobility fostered by trench warfare.

8. *Dispersion*: For a long time the RFC failed to take dispersion seriously—with near catastrophic consequences.

9. *Flexibility*: The overall system exhibited significant flexibility while balancing resources against competing needs, as demonstrated, for example, in the short-notice deployment of squadrons to Italy.

10. *Information*: The supply chain functioned effectively because of the innovative processes and techniques deployed to cope with uncertain production and variable demand. This was built on the continuous collection and analysis of timely and accurate information.

11. *Simplicity*: The RFC's logistic system could not be described as simple; however, this was, and continues to be, a defining characteristic of military aviation.

12. *Relativity*: Both Salmond and Trenchard recognized that there was a finite supply of resources and were willing to curtail frontline strength in order to create the necessary reserves (in aircraft or transport) to sustain operations. They also understood that the logistic needs of the home front were critical in sustaining air operations on the western front, and that investment in the former was essential if the front line was to grow.

13. *Continuity*: The question of continuity (in peacetime and wartime practice) is a moot point—since there was effectively no pre–First World War aviation logistic system. However, if we cast forward to the Second World War, it is evident that the logistic arrangements developed by the RAF during the expansion era (that mirrored those employed by the RFC on the western front) endured largely unchanged throughout the six years of fighting. In truth, the difference between wartime and peacetime aviation supply has always been a matter of tempo and scale, rather than of complexity or change.

14. *Timeliness*: The timely provision of resources was a principle fully understood by the RFC; witness the decision in April 1918 to abandon the "pull" system in order to pre-position supplies for the retreating squadrons. Timeliness could (and did) take precedence over efficiency, if the operational situation so demanded.

15. *Responsibility*: Procurement activity was coordinated with the needs of the civilian economy; indeed, the massive expansion of the British aircraft and aero-engine industry was built on a civil-military partnership. The role of the Royal Aircraft Factory, although considered controversial in some quarters, facilitated this transformation, and permitted quality and quantity to be balanced.

16. *Quality*: Although the outcome was not always satisfactory, the Air Ministry and Ministry of Munitions worked closely with GOC RAF to expand frontline strength while remaining competitive with the latest aircraft types deployed by the GAS.

Overall, therefore, the RFC's logistic system adhered to the majority of the principles advocated by Huston. Where this was not the case (forward impetus, teeth to tail ratio, and simplicity) the reasons were largely to do with the nature of air warfare and the different characteristics of aviation compared to army supply. Although the RFC demonstrated an impressive understanding of logistic principles, these achievements cannot be separated from the BEF's wider logistic excellence, which provided the foundation for Allied operational success—both physical and mental (created by the RAF's relentless air attacks on an enemy constantly in retreat)—during the Hundred Days.[69] The RFC relied on the Army Service Corps (ASC) for an extensive range of stores and consumables, as well as benefitting from the Inspector General Communications' (IGC) transportation and distribution network. The Army also assisted in other ways, including vehicle repair and the development of the depots and other fixed installations (undertaken by the RE Works Department), as well as the construction of airfield infrastructure. The RFC drew extensively on the BEF's supply capabilities and mirrored its procedures on those developed by the RE prior to the war to manage and distribute stores. It would be wrong to conclude that the RFC somehow stood separate from the BEF, uniquely blessed with exceptional strategic vision and an ability to adapt resources to the new paradigm of machine warfare. The reality is that the RFC operated within mainstream military leadership and benefitted greatly from the BEF's support organization and processes (including the employment of statistical forecasting). The RFC's increasing operational contribution confirms that GHQ was more than capable of coping with technological change (unlike the picture painted by Tim Travers).[70] Unfortunately, even when the BEF's logistic and technological abilities are recognized, they attract almost begrudging praise rather than being presented as an example of strategic awareness. "The victories from Amiens onwards, however ponderous, were genuine nonetheless, and the careful but unimaginative professionalism set the pattern for the British generalship until the Armistice, slowly grinding the enemy into submission by the inexorable logic of an attritional war of materiel."[71]

Niall Ferguson has argued that the Allies squandered their economic strength, yet the greater Allied capacity to solve the problems of supply and distribution placed Germany at an increasing disadvantage as the war progressed.[72] The airplane, as the most complex weapon deployed by either side, demanded the most advanced technical, scientific, and logistic techniques.[73] Turning airplanes into airpower required the creation of an extensive support network that married modern management methods with the exploitation of global resources and the development of worldwide manufacturing, supply, and transportation—key ingredients in the globalization process.[74] The First World War is often presented as marking the destruction of the first phase of globalization, but it is equally possible to see the conflict, depending as it did on industrial collaboration across national boundaries, as the culmination of a process that ended only with the Great Depression.[75] From this perspective, the RFC's logistic system was part of an economic, social, and industrial continuum. The complexity of the RFC's supply chain arose because of the need to balance mass production (and the standardization of design) with technical development.[76] In adapting to these circumstances, the RFC created arrangements that anticipated the most recent phase of globalization—characterized by dispersed production, extended distribution networks, short product lives, and rapid advances in technology. The RFC may not have been exceptional in its leadership or strategic vision, but in delivering airpower through the employment of advanced business and logistic techniques, it anticipated the global supply chain and foreshadowed the increasing complexity of modern warfare.

The extent to which the RFC's logistic experience was woven into the RAF's DNA is a matter for conjecture. Issues of supply certainly weighed heavily in the daily activities of the air staffs in France and London throughout 1918. The resource implications of further increases in the RAF's front line (had the war continued into 1919) was not lost on the War Cabinet, who nevertheless sanctioned a significant expansion. In reviewing this program, the chief of the Air Staff, Sir Frederick Sykes, dwelled at length on the resource requirements, particularly on the need to expand the "rearward" units—the range of in-theatre depots, parks, repair units, lorry parks, air ammunition columns, and so forth—that supported the flying squadrons. In France, the personnel employed in rearward services amounted to 47 percent of all deployed RAF personnel, the highest of any operational theater. To support the planned increase of fifty-seven frontline squadrons (including the Independent Force) by June 1919, a further twenty-six rearward units would be required. This in turn required an increase in the home organization to feed these formations "on a definite basis of wastage amongst the various categories of personnel, pilots, mechanics in squadrons and rearward service personnel."[77]

Unlike the Army that engaged in a (belated) "lessons learned" exercise, the RAF never commissioned a formal assessment of the lessons to be drawn from the First World War.[78] The critical role of logistics in sustaining airpower was not

specifically addressed in the British official histories, although the problems of supply and manpower were touched upon.[79] "Because the concept of airpower is so
easy—combat decisiveness is dramatic, after all, whereas supply and repair and facilities construction are not—the hard practical importance of logistics has been easy
to gloss over for both government and military planners alike."[80]

This was not just a contemporary perspective—subsequent historiography has
also tended to focus on the employment of aircraft rather than the enabling arrangements.[81] To be fair, the economic effort involved in creating and deploying airpower
was just one element in the nation's wider industrial mobilization and attracted no
particular comment. Moreover, despite the rapid expansion of the British air services
during the war, aviation still represented a relatively small proportion of the BEF at
the armistice (equivalent to less than 3 percent of personnel).[82] There was also no
reason to anticipate the immense expansion of the RAF in the Second World War.[83]
Under these circumstances, the logistic arrangements developed on the western
front did not present an obvious case for detailed study. However, it would be wrong
to conclude that the RAF forgot what had been learned—even if much of the organization's focus in the immediate postwar period was on the struggle to remain an
independent service. Air Commodore Robert Brooke-Popham, in a wide-ranging
lecture on the RAF delivered in 1919, addressed not only on the considerable operational and technical advances achieved during the war but also the "immense
importance of supply."[84] Despite the lack of a formal logistic doctrine, therefore, the
Air Ministry retained a sound understanding of supply and placed logistics at the
heart of its strategic planning both before and during the Second World War.[85] With
time, and the increasing complexity of warfare, these considerations have come to
underpin all military planning:

> The pace of military operations can be unpredictable and, as a conse-
> quence, the demands on the supply chain can ebb and flow. Moreover,
> the supply chain has to work in two directions, returning personnel
> and equipment from the frontline for rest, repair and replacement.
> Unlike the private sector, financial profit cannot be used as an indica-
> tor of success, and if the military supply chain fails the impact is not
> reduced profits, but increased risks to personnel and military tasks.[86]

This description could have been written about the RFC's logistic system on
the western front rather than the challenges faced by the MOD ninety years later
in maintaining combat capability in Afghanistan. The First World War, the first
major war between industrial nations, was in essence a war of matériel—a modern war conducted on an industrial scale. It was a war built on the management
methods, processes, and control systems that had created the global economy of the
late Victorian and Edwardian eras. On the other hand, mobilizing and managing
the nation's resources to deliver the necessary weapons, munitions, and manpower

required government involvement at every stage. "In view of the global propagation of managed economies in the second half of the twentieth century, this is likely to be seen as the major historical significance of World War 1 in time to come."[87]

Of course, the First World War was not the only factor in encouraging the development of state intervention. The impetus toward collectivism in economic planning existed well before 1914.[88] What was unprecedented, however, was the degree to which the state managed every aspect of the war. This blurred the distinction between waging war and producing the means to wage war, demanding new military competencies. "The skills that the war thereafter demanded of soldiers were organizational; and they pertained as much to questions of industrial management as they did to the movement of troops and supplies. Whether military officers oversaw railroad schedules, manpower allocations, labor relations, or the supply of fertilizer, they became central figures in the management of civilian economic affairs."[89]

The contribution of the RFC's logistic system in supporting air operations on the western front was significant and, in many ways, revolutionary. Airpower demanded very different logistic arrangements compared to previous military requirements. Sustaining the front line required substantial numbers of skilled and semiskilled personnel, located largely beyond the battle zone, capable of functioning at a continuously high tempo while coping with rapid technological change and substantial wastage. These support elements formed part of a complex, dynamic, and integrated network with the capacity to handle uncertainty while responding rapidly to unexpected demands. It was also partly self-sustaining, in that salvage and repair made a significant contribution to maintaining a continuous supply of aircraft and aero-engines. Van Creveld's assertion that the First World War was the first time in warfare that it was logistically easier to stay put than to move is an interesting observation but obscures a more important point.[90] The scale and intensity of fighting on the western front required all combatants to create complex networks capable of rapidly distributing large volumes of matériel that flowed both ways. What was significant about the First World War was that, whether the armies moved or not, their supplies were always on the move and none more so than the resources needed to sustain airpower. The German official history, while asserting the technical and tactical superiority of the GAS during 1917 and 1918, consistently highlights the impact of numerical inferiority. "The fact that the enemy armaments industry had far greater production capacity and the enemy had a far greater number of men for the air force remained decisive."[91] This imbalance had an increasing impact on operations as the war progressed. On 16 and 17 August 1918, four squadrons of the RAF's 80th Wing raided Haubourdin and Lomme airfields, near Lille, causing considerable damage and destroying perhaps as many as fifty aircraft. It would be three weeks before the GAS supply system could provide replacements. By comparison, the RAF was able to replace the entire inventory of No. 208 Squadron (eighteen Sopwith Camels), lost on 9 April 1918, in less than twenty-four hours.[92]

The RFC's logistic system was modern both in its needs and in the processes developed to meet these needs. In this effort, a variety of logistic techniques were pioneered (supply chain integration, strategic warehousing, velocity management, postponement and make-to-order, new product introduction, international sourcing, hybrid and reverse logistics) that provide the basis for global supply chain logistics management. The RFC, led by a new breed of soldier-technocrat, who combined military values, managerial competence, and business skills, was the epitome of an "entrepreneurial military organization," characterized by intellectual honesty, imagination, and the courage to exploit historical failure.[93] The outcome was a new style of warfare that wove together "industrial mobilization, national resources, morale and operational art."[94] The RFC's logistic system on the western front was the bedrock for this achievement, delivering strategic success, facilitating "modern warfare," and anticipating the management practices that form the global supply chain—an immense legacy for a small military organization that flourished for just five years at the beginning of the last century. In providing the foundation for air operations, and sustaining the RFC's efforts to achieve air superiority, logistics was the bridge between the nation's economy and airpower. It is a relationship that continues to this day.

APPENDIX A: LOGISTIC DATA

RFC/RAF Manpower Strength

MONTH	MANPOWER (ALL RANKS)	FRANCE (ALL RANKS)	MONTH	MANPOWER (ALL RANKS)	FRANCE (ALL RANKS)
Aug 14	1,200	0	Oct 16	51,061	13,610
Sep 14	1,585	860	Nov 16	53,345	15,193
Oct 14	1,653	911	Dec 16	54,731	16,885
Nov 14	1,888	1,046	Jan 17	55,931	18,167
Dec 14	2,280	1,077	Feb 17	59,610	19,007
Jan 15	2,559	1,116	Mar 17	65,349	21,380
Feb 15	3,224	1,240	Apr 17	72,249	22,733
Mar 15	3,666	1,287	May 17	76,794	23,884
Apr 15	4,316	1,605	Jun 17	82,121	25,093
May 15	4,859	· 2,014	Jul 17	85,163	25,610
Jun 15	5,662	2,096	Aug 17	87,603	25,995
Jul 15	6,526	2,250	Sep 17	92,970	25,990
Aug 15	7,234	2,819	Oct 17	97,857	27,674
Sep 15	8,014	2,865	Nov 17	105,185	27,384
Oct 15	9,087	3,141	Dec 17	111,955	30,419
Nov 15	11,243	3,611	Jan 18	121,518	31,758
Dec 15	15,023	4,502	Feb 18	132,751	33,930
Jan 16	16,299	4,787	Mar 18	144,078	33,976
Feb 16	19,503	5,810	Apr 18	*188,000*	*34,826*
Mar 16	22,980	6,506	May 18	*192,000*	*35,676*
Apr 16	25,436	8,458	Jun 18	*196,000*	*36,526*
May 16	26,884	8,488	Jul 18	*200,000*	*37,376*
Jun 16	29,570	10,074	Aug 18	206,599	38,241
Jul 16	35,819	10,665	Sep 18	229,394	40,568
Aug 16	42,185	11,500	Oct 18	258,126	41,854
Sep 16	46,951	13,198	Nov 18	270,329	44,290

(Source on following page)

Source: War Office, *Statistics of the Military Effort of the British Empire* (London: HMSO, 1922), p. 227, supplemented by the original monthly army returns for 1914–1918 (WO73/97-108, *Army Monthly Manpower Return*) detailing the disposition of all RFC manpower. Both these sources cease (for the RAF) from April 1918 and are replaced by the Air Ministry's *Monthly Return of Personnel of the Royal Air Force* (Home & Overseas). The Air Historical Branch holds copies of this document, however, the earliest example dates from August 1918, indicating that there was a hiatus of some four months between the two reporting systems. The data for these "missing" months (shown in italics) has been calculated using the establishment tables available in TNA AIR10/65. A further complication (in determining the RAF's strength in France) was the creation in June 1918 of the Independent Force (reporting directly to the Air Ministry), which was not under the command of GOC RAF and not included in the returns provided from the western front. By November 1918, the strength of Independent Force had risen to some 6,100 personnel. Excludes the Independent Force and 5 Group.

Operational Squadrons—Western Front

MONTH	RFC SQNS ON WESTERN FRONT	MONTH	RFC/RAF SQNS ON WESTERN FRONT
Aug 14	4	Oct 16	35
Sep 14	4	Nov 16	36
Oct 14	5	Dec 16	38
Nov 14	5	Jan 17	41
Dec 14	6	Feb 17	44
Jan 15	6	Mar 17	49
Feb 15	7	Apr 17	50
Mar 15	8	May 17	51
Apr 15	9	Jun 17	51
May 15	9	Jul 17	51
Jun 15	9	Aug 17	51
Jul 15	11	Sep 17	54
Aug 15	11	Oct 17	58
Sep 15	12	Nov 17	55
Oct 15	13	Dec 17	54
Nov 15	14	Jan 18	58
Dec 15	16	Feb 18	59
Jan 16	18	Mar 18	69
Feb 16	20	Apr 18	76
Mar 16	23	May 18	79
Apr 16	24	Jun 18	77
May 16	26	Jul 18	83
Jun 16	27	Aug 18	82
Jul 16	29	Sep 18	83
Aug 16	31	Oct 18	88
Sep 16	31	Nov 18	86

Source: Jones, *War in the Air*, Appendices, Appendix XXVIII. The total includes attached RNAS squadrons (varying in number between October 1916 and March 1918 as the operational situation demanded), but not the Independent Force that comprised ten squadrons by November 1918. The fall in frontline strength during June 1918 reflects the transfer of two squadrons to the Independent Force, while the reduction in November 1918 reflects the transfer of two squadrons (17 Squadron USAS and 148 Squadron USAS) from GOC RAF to the full control of the AEF. Also excluded is 5 Group, although squadrons did transfer frequently between the two organizations.

Flying Hours—Western Front

MONTH	OPERATIONAL FLYING HOURS— WESTERN FRONT	FLYING HOURS PER FRONTLINE AIRCRAFT	MONTH	OPERATIONAL FLYING HOURS— WESTERN FRONT	FLYING HOURS PER FRONTLINE AIRCRAFT
Jan 16	2,910	14	Jul 17	32,754	38
Feb 16	3,842	16	Aug 17	31,792	36
Mar 16	6,063	22	Sep 17	38,405	40
Apr 16	8,526	28	Oct 17	31,042	31
May 16	11,264	35	Nov 17	17,702	19
Jun 16	12,303	31	Dec 17	17,943	19
Jul 16	17,374	40	Jan 18	21,262	19
Aug 16	19,561	40	Feb 18	20,406	19
Sep 16	21,889	40	Mar 18	40,218	34
Oct 16	13,709	24	Apr 18	31,323	24
Nov 16	11,656	19	May 18	63,325	45
Dec 16	6,043	10	Jun 18	63,053	44
Jan 17	10,378	15	Jul 18	62,537	42
Feb 17	12,144	17	Aug 18	70,485	45
Mar 17	14,716	18	Sep 18	61,945	40
Apr 17	29,599	33	Oct 18	53,296	34
May 17	39,409	45	Nov 18	15,490	10
Jun 17	33,602	39	Dec 18		

Source: Jones, *War in the Air*, Appendices, Appendix XXXVII, listing operational hours flown by the RFC and RAF on the western front from July 1916 up to August 1918 (excluding the Independent Force and 5 Group). The "missing" hours for January–June 1916 and September–November 1918 can be established from TNA AIR1/759/204/4/139-140—Summary of Work, TNA AIR1/760/204/4/141-144—Summary of Work, and TNA AIR1/2129/207/82/1—Operations on the Western Front. Although excluded from this analysis, the Independent Force flew two to three thousand hours per month over the period June-October 1918 (TNA AIR69/41—Reports on Operations Carried out by VIII Brigade and Independent Force October 1917–November 1918).

Aircraft Strength and Serviceability—Western Front

MONTH	AVAILABILITY (AVERAGE FRONTLINE AIRCRAFT STRENGTH)	AVERAGE AIRCRAFT SERVICEABILITY (PERCENT)	MONTH	AVAILABILITY (AVERAGE FRONTLINE AIRCRAFT STRENGTH)	AVERAGE AIRCRAFT SERVICEABILITY (PERCENT)
Jan 16	206	82	Jul 17	861	90
Feb 16	244	85	Aug 17	884	92
Mar 16	271	86	Sep 17	952	90
Apr 16	303	88	Oct 17	994	90
May 16	324	88	Nov 17	954	90
Jun 16	394	89	Dec 17	927	87
Jul 16	439	89	Jan 18	965	83
Aug 16	516	89	Feb 18	1,074	86
Sep 16	544	90	Mar 18	1,170	87
Oct 16	569	92	Apr 18	1,314	92
Nov 16	613	90	May 18	1,415	90
Dec 16	624	91	Jun 18	1,430	92
Jan 17	674	86	Jul 18	1,498	92
Feb 17	714	80	Aug 18	1,565	90
Mar 17	805	86	Sep 18	1,537	90
Apr 17	889	88	Oct 18	1,555	90
May 17	886	88	Nov 18	1,524	87
Jun 17	858	89	Dec 18		

Source: This table is based on the daily returns prepared by HQ RFC from 1916 until March 1918, comprising: TNA AIR1/759/204/4/139-140, TNA AIR1/760/204/4/141-144, TNA AIR1/762/204/4/165-170, TNA AIR1/837/204/5/278-279, TNA AIR1/837/204/5/278-279, and TNA AIR1/838/204/5/280-290—Summaries of Work 1916–1918. There are difficulties in establishing similar data for the period April–November 1918, partly because of the disruption caused by the German 1918 offensive and partly because of the organizational changes that followed the creation of the RAF. The most comprehensive data series (excluding the Independent Force and 5 Group) is provided by TNA AIR1/1073/204/5/1655—Weekly Returns. Strength and serviceability data have been averaged across the month to provide a more reliable assessment of the RFC/RAF's sustained performance. The Independent Force comprised some 140 frontline aircraft by the armistice, while No. 5 Group possessed a little over sixty frontline aircraft. The total number of frontline RAF aircraft in France and Belgium was therefore approximately 1,750 by the end of the war.

Aircraft Held by Depots

MONTH	TOTAL HOLDINGS	AT DEPOTS	RESERVE	MONTH	TOTAL HOLDINGS	AT DEPOTS	RESERVE
Jan 16	230	47		Jul 17	1,357	511	278
Feb 16	238	53		Aug 17	1,356	496	215
Mar 16	287	67		Sep 17	1,433	517	238
Apr 16	325	125		Oct 17	1,548	551	208
May 16	418	137		Nov 17	1,682	624	193
Jun 16	444	164		Dec 17	1,752	729	298
Jul 16	533	223		Jan 18	1,837	883	391
Aug 16	633	257		Feb 18	2,052	978	431
Sep 16	712	240		Mar 18	2,102	932	455
Oct 16	777	269		Apr 18	2,142	828	238
Nov 16	817	316		May 18	2,152	737	277
Dec 16	930	316		Jun 18	2,337	907	371
Jan 17	980	336	237	Jul 18	2,563	1065	
Feb 17	1,069	355	299	Aug 18	2,563	998	
Mar 17	1,123	368	264	Sep 18	3,032	1,495	
Apr 17	1,267	400	303	Oct 18	2,608	1,053	236
May 17	1,348	472	200	Nov 18	3,522	1,998	
Jun 17	1,383	492	222	Dec 18			

Source: From late 1914, HQ RFC provided a monthly return to the War Office detailing aircraft held by the frontline squadrons and the depots—the latter grouped into machines comprising the Reserve (both serviceable and unserviceable) and those under reconstruction. This series is incomplete and is spread over several files in the TNA but still provides a reasonably clear picture of the growth in overall aircraft inventory and the varying size of the (serviceable) reserve during the last two years of the war. Details can be found in TNA AIR1/926/204/5/915—Aeroplane and Engine Casualties, TNA AIR1/998/204/5/1242—Duplicate Returns, TNA AIR1/1128/204/5/2160—Aeroplanes Flown from France, and TNA AIR1/1042/204/5/1494—Duplicate Returns. All figures are at the first of the month. Attached RNAS squadrons are included, but not the Independent Force or 5 Group.

Aircraft and Engines Repaired by Depots

MONTH	AIRCRAFT REBUILT	ENGINES REPAIRED	MONTH	AIRCRAFT REBUILT	AIRCRAFT WRECKS SALVAGED	ENGINES REPAIRED
Dec 16	48		Dec 17	118		179
Jan 17	10	97	Jan 18	92	205	271
Feb 17	16	149	Feb 18	89	229	176
Mar 17	36	202	Mar 18	117	491	269
Apr 17	77	229	Apr 18	130	885	285
May 17	71	232	May 18	148	605	292
Jun 17	90	249	Jun 18	149	593	327
Jul 17	86	227	Jul 18	179	485	388
Aug 17	122	251	Aug 18	186	562	408
Sep 17	116	253	Sep 18	145	535	409
Oct 17	59	253	Oct 18	233	531	495
Nov 17	96	242	Nov 18	38	168	

Source: There is no single, consistent data series that captures the comprehensive work undertaken by the depots on the western front. This table is based on a variety of documents held by the TNA. Details of aircraft reconstructed and salvaged can be found in TNA AIR1/1111/204/5/1895-1—Work Summary Aircraft Parks, TNA AIR1/1110/204/5/1893—Work Summary Aircraft Depots, and TNA AIR1/1084/204/5/1721—Reorganisation of Aircraft Depots. Engines repaired are recorded at TNA AIR1/942/204/5/976—Reports on Work at Aircraft Parks and Depots, together with a useful summary in Brooke-Popham 1/4—Staff College Notes: Miscellaneous Statistics, Liddell Hart Centre for Military Archives. Data prior to December 1916 is not available. Details of engines repaired in December 1916 and November 1918 are not available.

Aircraft and Engine Wastage—Western Front

MONTH	AIRCRAFT STRUCK OFF	AVERAGE DAILY AIRCRAFT WASTAGE	ENGINES STRUCK OFF	MONTH	AIRCRAFT STRUCK OFF	AVERAGE DAILY AIRCRAFT WASTAGE	ENGINES STRUCK OFF
Jan 16	45	1	43	Jul 17	496	16	465
Feb 16	45	1	49	Aug 17	471	15	417
Mar 16	65	2	60	Sep 17	435	16	448
Apr 16	74	2	74	Oct 17	442	14	530
May 16	106	3	117	Nov 17	338	11	567
Jun 16	94	3	94	Dec 17	114	4	498
Jul 16	187	6	225	Jan 18	200	6	
Aug 16	208	7	244	Feb 18	233	8	
Sep 16	199	7	259	Mar 18	839	27	
Oct 16	166	5	185	Apr 18	696	23	
Nov 16	173	6	183	May 18	774	25	360
Dec 16	98	3	64	Jun 18	763	25	270
Jan 17	149	5	114	Jul 18	785	25	425
Feb 17	149	5	117	Aug 18	965	31	526
Mar 17	272	9	215	Sep 18	904	30	
Apr 17	446	15	466	Oct 18	835	27	549
May 17	498	16	480	Nov 18	338	31	470
Jun 17	480	16	462	Dec 18			

Source: There are a variety of sources on aircraft and aero-engines struck off. It should be noted that wastage includes not only combat losses but also aircraft lost in accidents and struck off because of age or replacement by newer types. The relevant data can be found in TNA AIR1/9/15/1/31/1—A Programme of Development for the RAF, TNA AIR1/998/204/5/1242—Duplicate Returns, TNA AIR1/926/204/5/915—Aeroplane and Engine Casualties, and TNA AIR1/474/15/312/185—Statistical Reports. No data for engines struck off is available for January–April 1918.

Aircraft Deliveries—Western Front

MONTH	BY AIR	IN CASES	AVERAGE DAILY DELIVERIES	MONTH	BY AIR	IN CASES	AVERAGE DAILY DELIVERIES
Jun 16	122	48	6	Sep 17	370	104	16
Jul 16	140	60	6	Oct 17	375	118	16
Aug 16	158	38	6	Nov 17	288	119	14
Sep 16	149	74	7	Dec 17	264	131	13
Oct 16	112	49	5	Jan 18	263	146	13
Nov 16	73	49	4	Feb 18	219	129	12
Dec 16	37	51	3	Mar 18	522	223	24
Jan 17	79	82	5	Apr 18	594	12	20
Feb 17	63	86	5	May 18	782	112	29
Mar 17	166	96	8	Jun 18	707	80	26
Apr 17	297	73	12	Jul 18	842	81	23
May 17	301	92	13	Aug 18	760	143	29
Jun 17	321	43	12	Sep 18	689	175	29
Jul 17	392	68	15	Oct 18	655	284	30
Aug 17	310	67	12	Nov 18	278	68	31

Source: Aircraft deliveries to the western front (including those from French sources) are detailed in TNA AIR1/2302/215/12. This includes, from April 1918, deliveries to 5 Group and from July 1918, deliveries to the Independent Force. The data runs from June 1916 to the armistice.

Engine Strength—Western Front

MONTH	ENGINES ON STRENGTH	MONTH	ENGINES ON STRENGTH	ENGINES UNDER REPAIR
Jan 16	468	Jul 17	2,167	
Feb 16		Aug 17		
Mar 16		Sep 17		
Apr 16	663	Oct 17		
May 16		Nov 17	2,717	498
Jun 16		Dec 17		
Jul 16		Jan 18		
Aug 16		Feb 18		
Sep 16		Mar 18		
Oct 16		Apr 18	3,508	
Nov 16		May 18	3,698	756
Dec 16		Jun 18	4,124	735
Jan 17	1,608	Jul 18	4,614	1,024
Feb 17		Aug 18	4,492	853
Mar 17		Sep 18	4,908	1,018
Apr 17	2,159	Oct 18	5,257	1,272
May 17		Nov 18	5,540	1,109
Jun 17		Dec 18	3,508	842

Source: Engine records for the western front are fewer and less frequent than comparable data for airplanes (particularly prior to the formation of the RAF in April 1918). Sources include: TNA AIR1/1128/204/5/2159—Various Returns, TNA AIR1/162/15/124/9 Part 1—Periodical Engine Returns, TNA AIR1/1155/204/5/2429—Quarterly Returns of Engines held by RAF, and TNA AIR1/2302/215/12—Correspondence: Department of Aircraft Production. Engine strength (installed and uninstalled, as well as both serviceable and unserviceable) is recorded as at the first of the month and includes 5 Group (from 1 April 1918) and the Independent Force.

Vehicle Strength—Western Front

MONTH	TOTAL HOLDINGS	VEHICLES ON WESTERN FRONT	MONTH	TOTAL HOLDINGS	VEHICLES ON WESTERN FRONT
Jan 16			Jul 17		
Feb 16			Aug 17	8,584	
Mar 16			Sep 17		
Apr 16			Oct 17		3,807
May 16			Nov 17		
Jun 16	3,360	1,921	Dec 17	8,173	
Jul 16			Jan 18		
Aug 16	5,282		Feb 18		
Sep 16	5,151	2,267	Mar 18		
Oct 16			Apr 18	8,500	
Nov 16			May 18		
Dec 16			Jun 18		
Jan 17	5,796		Jul 18		
Feb 17			Aug 18	15,584	
Mar 17	6,985	2,932	Sep 18		
Apr 17			Oct 18		
May 17			Nov 18	17,704	6,768
Jun 17			Dec 18		6,216

Source: Vehicle records for the western front are few and generally record transactions (vehicles acquired or struck off) rather than inventory holdings or repair output. A further difficulty is that the distinction between vehicles, lorries, motorcycles, side-cars, and trailers is often unclear and can create an inflated view of the number of motor vehicles actually available to the RFC. The strength figures include motorcycles and vehicles under repair but exclude trailers. Sources include: TNA AIR1/1155/204/5/2429—Quarterly Returns of Engines Held by RAF, TNA AIR1/109/15/30—Mechanical Transport—Statistics, and TNA AIR1/953/204/5/1025—Mechanical Transport Returns.

APPENDIX B: LOGISTIC UNITS, 1914–18

OVERSEAS

Aircraft Depots

The St-Omer and Candas Aircraft Depots started life as Aircraft Parks, being renamed Aircraft Depots on 15 December 1915, responsible for fixed supply and repair duties while separate Army Aircraft Parks were created to provide mobile support to individual RFC brigades.

No. 1 AD St-Omer: The basis for No. 1 AD was the RFC Aircraft Park that deployed to France in August 1914. This arrived at St-Omer in late October 1914 via Le Havre, Le Mans, and Juvisy. The depot remained at St-Omer until the German offensive of March 1918, when, as a temporary measure, No. 1 AD Reserve was set up at Guines (effective 10 April 1918) and bulk stores at Desvres (effective 15 April 1918). However, by 18 May 1918, these arrangements became permanent with the main depot at Guines and sub-sites at Desvres, No. 1 AD (D), and Motteville, No. 1 AD (M), where they remained until the armistice.

No. 2 AD Candas: Relocated to Groffliers in March 1918, occupying disused farm buildings at Le Bahot (effective from 30 March 1918). The depot had moved to Vron by the armistice (with an advanced section at Cambrai).

No. 3 AD Courban: Created in March 1918 to serve the Independent Force.

No. 4 AD Balinghem: Created on 21 August 1918 but not completed by the armistice.

Kite Balloon Factory Arques: A sub-site of No. 1 AD, engaged in the repair of balloons, production of hydrogen, and so forth.

Engine Repair Shops Pont de l'Arche: The origin of the ERS can be traced back to October 1914 and the establishment at Rouen of a base echelon to serve the Aircraft Park at St-Omer.

MT Repair Depot Motteville: First formed to hold stores for the Rouen and Le Havre Port Depots and subsequently the site of a MT Repair Depot constructed from June to December 1918.

"X" AD Aboukir

"X" Engine Repair Depot Abbassia

"X" Balloon Repair Depot Abbassia

Army Aircraft Parks

First formed in December 1915, to support individual RFC brigades, each AAP comprised a HQ, plane repair, stores, and MT sections. Renamed Aircraft Parks from 1 January 1918.

No. 1 AP Aire: Created 15 December 1915. Relocated to Lillers by 12 January 1917, Houdain by 31 July 1917, Ouve-Wirquin by 8 June 1918, Lugy by August 1918, and Somain by the armistice.

No. 2 AP Hazebrouck: Created 15 December 1915. Relocated to Droglandt by January 1918, Eecke by March 1918, Houlle by August 1918, and Bisseghem by the armistice. Disbanded 18 July 1919.

No. 3 AP Beauval: Created 15 December 1915. Relocated to Frévent by 1 July 1916. Split into Northern (Puchevillers) and Southern (Eterpigny) in June 1917 but rejoined at Puchevillers in November 1917.

No. 4 AP Daours: Relocated to Beauval by 1 July 1916, Daours by 17 February 1917, Harbonnières by April 1917, Eterpigny by 19 June 1917, Couderkerque by 11 July 1917, Villers-Carbonnel by March 1918, Guillaucourt by 7 March 1918, Vron by 29 March 1918, St. Riquier by 11 April 1918, Villers-Carbonnel by 27 September 1918, and Premont by the armistice. Disbanded 15 February 1919.

No. 5 AP Puchevillers: Relocated to Herzeele by July 1917, Arnke by June 1918, and Menin by the armistice.

No. 6 AP Vézelise: Created November 1917 to support the Independent Force.

No. 7 AP Italy: Created November 1917 to support VII Brigade in Italy, initially at Poggio Renatico and Campoviampiero. Relocated to Ospitaletto by March 1918, later to San Pelagio, Padova, and Verona. Reduced to cadre and disbanded at Blandford 4 June 1919.

No. 8 AP Ambouts-Capelle: Created March 1918. Relocated to Wevelghem by the armistice.

No. 9 AP Vacquerie-le-Boucq: Relocated to Noyelles-sur-L'Escaut by the armistice.

No. 10 AP Ouve-Wirquin: Relocated to Faubourg-des-Postes (Fonderie Daniel Butin, Rue Marquillies) by the armistice.

No. 11 AP Coudekerque: Relocated to Wirquin by 10 June 1918, Rambervillers by November 1918.

No. 12 AP Rambervillers: To support the Independent Force.

Airplane Supply Depots

First formed in November 1917 to help expedite the supply of airplanes to the front-line squadrons, each ASD comprised a repair park and an issues section. No. 1 ASD was additionally provided with a reception park. Later in the war, dedicated salvage sections were also established within each ASD, as well as advanced issues sections.

No. 1 ASD St-Omer: Formed November 1917, with repair park at St-Omer, issue section at Serny, and reception park at Marquise. During the German March 1918 offensive, it was relocated to Marquise (as of 22 April 1918) where it remained until the armistice, with the issue section at Fienvillers and repair park at Le Bahot. It had moved to Merheim by 18 July 1919 and was disbanded on 30 September 1919.

No. 2 ASD Fienvillers: Formed November 1917. During the German March 1918 offensive, the repair park was relocated to Verton (as of 25 March 1918) and the issue section to St. André-aux-Bois. It had moved to Hesdin by 31 May 1918 and Berck-sur-Mer by 8 June 1918.

No. 3 ASD Courban: Formed March 1918, to support Handley Page aircraft of the Independent Force.

No. 4 ASD Guines: Formed 24 March 1918 to support the RNAS. Repair park at Guines with issues and reception sections at Audembert from May 1918. Joined in April 1918 by elements of No. 1 AD relocated from St-Omer.

Salvage Sections

No. 3 Salvage Section

No. 4 Salvage Section

No. 5 Salvage Section: Formed June 1918 at Motteville to support 1 ASD.

No. 6 Salvage Section Les Fontainettes: Formed June 1918 to support 2 ASD. At Cayeux by the armistice.

No. 7 Salvage Section Bohain: At the armistice.

No. 8 Salvage Section Wevelghem: At the armistice.

No. 9 Salvage Section Caudry: At the armistice.

Port Detachments

Port Detachment Rouen

Port Detachment Boulogne

No. 6 Port Detachment: 82nd Wing.

No. 7 Port Detachment: 14th Wing.

RFC Brigade Ammunition Columns

Placed under RFC control in 1917, renamed Air Ammunition Columns (AAC) from 1 January 1918. The AAC supplied all armament to the squadrons, drawing on the Army for standard bombs and the main depots for non-standard bombs and ammunition.

No. 1   AAC Lillers: At Sautrecourt by August 1918, Ferme du Muid by the armistice.

No. 2   AAC Abeele: At Boisdinghem by August 1918, Menin by the armistice.

No. 3   AAC Savy: At Bois au Bois by August 1918, Ribécourt by the armistice.

No. 4   AAC Villers-Bretonneux: At Conteville by August 1918, Premont by the armistice.

No. 5   AAC Puchevillers: At Estrées-en-Chaussee by the armistice.

No. 7   AAC Armbouts Capelle: By August 1918, Wevelghem by the armistice.

No. 8   AAC Vézelise: To support the Independent Force.

No. 9   AAC Fienvillers: At Willeman by armistice.

No. 10 AAC Lesquin: At Willeman by armistice.

No. 11 AAC: To support the Independent Force.

No. 12 AAC: To support the Independent Force. Proceeded overseas 31 October 1918.

Reserve Lorry Parks

Created in September 1917 as a strategic reserve for each brigade.

No. 1   RLP Sautrecourt: At Ferme du Muid by the armistice.

No. 2   RLP Arneke: At Menin by the armistice.

No. 3   RLP Candas: By August 1918, Bihucourt by the armistice.

No. 4   RLP Conteville: At August 1918, Premont by the armistice.

No. 5   RLP Vézelise: To support the Independent Force.

No. 6   RLP Willeman: At the armistice.

No. 7   RLP St Pol: Wevelghem by the armistice.

No. 9   RLP Wavrans: At August 1918, Faubourg-des-Postes by the armistice.

No. 10 RLP Bulgnéville: To support the Independent Force.

No. 11 RLP Houlle: At Ferme du Muid by the armistice.

No. 12 RLP Premont: At the armistice.

No. 13 RLP Dunkirk.

No. 14 RLP: Not brigaded.

No. 15 RLP: Attached 89th Wing HQ.

No. 16 RLP: Attached 90th Wing HQ.

No. 18 RLP: To support the Independent Force.

No. 19 RLP Bihucourt: At the armistice. Attached 91st Wing HQ.

No. 20 RLP Willeman: At the armistice.

Miscellaneous Units

RAF Electrolytic Gas Plant Rouen: Construction commenced in July 1918 (Route de Caen), completed December 1918.

Nos. 1–27 Tent Detachments France and Belgium

Central Repair Depot, St. Pol: Originally part of No. 1 (RNAS) Wing.

German East Africa AP Mbuyuni: Formed 4 February 1916 from a section of No. 26 (South African) Squadron, having arrived at Mombasa on 31 January 1916. An advanced Aircraft Park was later established at Korogwe on 23 July 1916 while the main section moved to Dar-es-Salaam on 6 December 1916.

India AP Risalpur: Nucleus left South Farnborough for India in November 1915, arriving on 26 December 1915 and moving initially to Nowshera before arriving at Risalpur in March 1916.

Mesopotamia AP Amarah: Formed December 1915, to Baghdad March 1918.

Salonika AP Mikra Bay: Formed September 1916.

Composite Repair Depot Mudros

Malta Repair Depot

Stores Park Malta

"X" AP Abbassia: Formed November 1915. To Qantara in January 1918 as part of the Palestine Brigade. Facilities at Abbassia taken over by Engine Repair Section.

Eastern Aircraft Factory Egypt

Stores Distributing Park Egypt

"Z" AP Milan: Formed November 1917.

"X" Aircraft Park Palestine

Engine Repair Park Toronto

Aircraft Repair Park Toronto

Composite Repair Depot Toronto

HOME

Aircraft Repair Depots

Home-based equivalents of the Aircraft Depots.

No. 1 ARD (Southern) South Farnborough

No. 2 ARD (Northern) Coal Aston, Sheffield

No. 3 ARD (Western) Yate, Bristol

No. 4 ARD Ebury Road, Chelsea

No. 5 ARD (Eastern) Henlow: From October 1918.

No. 6 ARD (Scottish) Renfrew: From December 1918.

No. 7 ARD (North West) Shrewsbury: From September 1918, later the MT Repair Depot.

No. 8 ARD (Irish) Baldonell: From October 1918.

No. 9 ARD Edmonton: From April 1918.

No. 10 ARD Wormwood Scrubs: For MT repair only.

Salvage Sections

No. 1 Salvage Section Southampton: Southampton as at 1 November 1918.

No. 2 Salvage Section Richborough: Richborough as at 1 November 1918.

Port Detachments

No. 1 Port Detachment Folkestone

No. 2 Port Detachment Newhaven

No. 3 Port Detachment Southampton

No. 4 Port Detachment Avonmouth

No. 5 Port Detachment Richborough

No. 8 Port Detachment London

No. 9 Port Detachment Aberdeen

Wing Airplane Repair Sections

Created in 1916 to undertake centralized repair for individual RFC wings.

6th Wing Dover

7th Wing Thetford

8th Wing Catterick

17th Wing Gosport

18th Wing Hounslow

19th Wing Turnhouse

21st Wing Yatesbury

23rd Wing Waddington

24th Wing Spittlegate

25th Wing Castle Bromwich

CFS Netheravon

Aircraft Acceptance Parks

First formed 1917.

No. 1 AAP Coventry: Formed 1917 at Radford, restyled No. 1 AAP 10 December 1917, closed 1919.

No. 2 AAP Hendon: Restyled No. 2 AAP 10 December 1917, closed 1919.

No. 3 AAP Norwich: Formed 1917 at Mousehold Heath, restyled No. 3 AAP 10 December 1917.

No. 4 AAP Lincoln: Formed 1917 at West Common racecourse, restyled No. 4 AAP 10 December 1917.

No. 5   AAP Bristol: Formed at Filton, restyled No. 5 AAP 10 December 1917.

No. 6   AAP Glasgow: Formed 10 March 1918 at Renfrew.

No. 7   AAP Kenley: Formed June 1917.

No. 8   AAP Lympne

No. 9   AAP Newcastle on Tyne: Formed 1 August 1917 at Tower Moor, opened 25 August 1917.

No. 10 AAP Brooklands: Formed 1 August 1917, opened 2 September 1917.

No. 11 AAP Southport: Formed 15 September 1917 at Hesketh Park Sands.

No. 12 AAP Hawkinge: Formed 27 August 1917.

No. 13 AAP Telscombe: Formed 27 August 1917 at Telscombe Cliffs.

No. 14 AAP Castle Bromwich: Formed July 1918.

No. 15 AAP Manchester: Formed at Didsbury/Alexandra Park in 1918, closed 1919.

No. 16 AAP Aldegrove: Formed 1918, closed 1921.

The following Acceptance Parks were under construction at the time of the armistice and were not officially numbered:

Birmingham

Bracebridge

Brockworth

Eastleigh: To support the USAS.

Feltham

Inchinan

Oldham: To support the USAS.

Sherburn-in-Elmet

Shrewsbury

South Shotwick

Whitley Abbey: Formed as an Aircraft Acceptance Storage Park.

Stores Depots

Stores Depots differed in the stock ranges held. Milton was responsible for Section 51 while Regents Park held Section 63. Individual items were issued to home-based squadrons through the Stores Distributing Parks or, in the case of overseas units, through the Aircraft Depots and appropriate Army Air Park.

No. 1   SD Kidbrooke: Originally a sub-site of the OASD at Farnborough, established in October 1915, it became a separate unit in June 1916, the bulk of the stores being transferred to a purpose-built site at Kidbrooke from September 1918 with Greenwich as a sub-depot.

No. 2   SD Regents Park: Formed 1 June 1917 out of the former OASD depot (engines and engine spares) at the Clement Talbot Works, North Kensington, later relocated to Regents Park.

No. 3 SD Milton

No. 4 SD Albany Street: HQ relocated to Ickenham, Ruislip, in October 1918.

No. 5 SD Earls Court: Holding balloon stores.

No. 6 SD Ascot: Sub-site at Hammersmith.

No. 7 SD Mexborough

Stores Distributing Parks

Formed in 1917 to support home training units, established on a regional basis, and drawing on the Stores Depots as required for stock.

No. 1 SDP Bradford

No. 2 SDP Newcastle

No. 3 SDP Edgware Road

No. 4 SDP Ely

No. 5 SDP Edgbaston

No. 6 SDP Lincoln

No. 7 SDP Westbury: Construction completed in December 1918.

No. 8 SDP Eastleigh

No. 9 SDP Edinburgh

No. 10 SDP Canterbury

No. 11 SDP Dublin

Airship Depots

Airship Constructional Station Barlow

Airship Constructional Station Barrow

Airship Constructional Station Bedford

Airship Constructional Station Inchinnan

Airship Constructional Station Kingsnorth

Airship Constructional Station Wormwood Scrubs

Airship Storage Depot Shepherd's Bush

Airship Fabric Works Shepherd's Bush

RNAS/Miscellaneous Depots

RNAS Service Repair Depot Isle of Grain: Renamed The RN Aeroplane Repair Depot (Port Victoria) in 1915. However, during the course of the war it was gradually transformed into a purely experimental workshop, ultimately becoming the Naval Aircraft Experimental Depot.

Fleet Aircraft Repair Depot Donibristle: Established for ship's airplanes, construction commenced in September 1918. Later retitled the Coastal Area Depot.

No. 1 Marine Acceptance Depot (Southern) Hamble

No. 2 Marine Acceptance Depot (Northern) Brough

Seaplane Refueling Station Flamborough

Repair Depot and Store Base South Shields

Repair Depot and Store Base Peterhead

Plane Repair Park Islington

Clothing Salvage Park South Farnborough

Clothing Acceptance Depot London

No. 1 (POW) MT Repair Depot Buckminster

No. 2 (POW) MT Repair Depot Shrewsbury

No. 1 MT Depot Hurst Park

MT Issue Park (Northern) Manchester

Balloon Acceptance and Testing Station Richmond Park (Kingston Hill)

 **NOTES**

Preface

1. P. Dye, "The Royal Flying Corps Logistic Organisation," *RAF Air Power Review* 1, no. 2 (1998): 42–58; "Logistics and Air Power Doctrine," *RAF Air Power Review* 2, no. 1 (1999): 80–90; "Logistics and the Battle of Britain," *Air Force Journal of Logistics*24, no. 4 (2000): 1, 31–39; "Logistics Doctrine and the Impact of War" in *Air Power History*, ed. S. Cox (London: Frank Cass, 2002), 207–223; and "Logistics and the Falklands Campaign," *RAF Historical Society Journal*, no. 30 (2003): 85–96.

2. P. Dye, "Sustaining Air Power: The Influence of Logistics on RAF Doctrine," *RAF Air Power Review* 9, no. 2 (2006): 41–51.

3. It appears that John Slessor was the first to employ "three-dimensional" warfare. J. Slessor, *Air Power and Armies* (London: Oxford University Press, 1936), 200; as defined by J. Bailey, *The First World War and the Birth of the Modern Style of Warfare* (Camberley, UK: Strategic and Combat Studies Institute, 1996).

4. B. Holden Reid, *J. F. C. Fuller: Military Thinker* (London: Macmillan, 1987), 137–138; J. Bailey, "The First World War and the Birth of Modern Warfare," in *The Dynamics of Military Revolution 1300–2050*, ed. M. Knox and W. Murray (Cambridge, UK: Cambridge University Press, 2001), 132–53. This analysis is largely supported by C. Gray, *Strategy for Chaos* (London: Frank Cass, 2002), 170–202, and G. Sheffield, *Forgotten Victory* (London: Headline, 2001), 140–41.

5. The concept of a "military revolution" in early modern Europe was first proposed by Michael Roberts in 1955. He postulated that there had been a revolution in military practice arising from changes in tactics, a marked growth in army size, more ambitious enabling strategies, and a greater impact of war on society. In the years that followed, the concept was refined and developed while alternative timelines were offered. Much of the argument revolves around the nature of state-organized supply that permitted significant changes in the scale, intensity, and duration of warfare. These ideas were first presented to the general public in Geoffrey Parker's *The Military Revolution* (Cambridge, UK: Cambridge University Press, 1988) and expanded upon by Clifford Rogers, ed., *The Military Revolution Debate* (Boulder, CO: Westview, 1995).

6. J. Black, *The Battle of Waterloo* (London: Icon Books, 2010), 202.

7. See Michael Howard's description of the use of military history in creating an image through careful selection and interpretation to sustain certain emotions or beliefs. Michael Howard, "The Use and Abuse of Military History," in *The Causes of Wars* (London: Temple Smith, 1983), 188.

8. Delbrück quoted in Howard, *The Causes of Wars*, 191. It is ironic, therefore, that Delbrück should have been heavily criticized for his methodology and willingness to overlook evidence, particularly about the logistic competence of early armies; see B. S. Bachrach, "From Nicaea to Dorylaion" in *Logistics of Warfare in the Age of the Crusades*, J. H. Pryor, ed. (Aldershot, UK: Ashgate, 2006), 46–48.

9. T. Kane, *Military Logistics and Strategic Performance* (London: Routledge, 2001), 13.

10. Howard, *The Causes of Wars*, 195–96.

Introduction

1. H. Eccles, *Logistics in the National Defense* (Harrisburg, PA: Stackpole, 1959), 10. According to the *Oxford Dictionary of Etymology* the word "logistics" originates from either the French *logis* (lodgings) or the Greek *logos* (calculate).

2. A. Jomini, *The Art of War* (Philadelphia: Lippincott, 1862), reprinted with new introduction (London: Greenhill Books, 1992). Jomini was a Swiss citizen who served in both the French and later Russian armies during the Napoleonic Wars, retiring as a full general in 1829.

3. M. Howard and P. Paret, eds., *Carl von Clausewitz on War* (Princeton, NJ: Princeton University Press, 1976), 330–41.

4. The unfinished nature of Clausewitz's work has allowed selective interpretation and questionable interpolation to support a variety of strategic perspectives over the past 150 years. For example, Delbrück argued that Clausewitz would have gone on to develop a system that recognized a second form of strategy designed to wear the enemy out; see H. Strachan, *Carl von Clausewitz's On War* (London: Atlantic Books, 2007), 17. It has even been claimed that Clausewitz might have assigned logistics an important role had he had more time to revise his manuscript; see J. Thompson, *The Lifeblood of War* (London: Brassey's, 1991), 5.

5. Howard and Paret, *Clausewitz*, 133–47. The question of how logistics might be included within the framework of Clausewitz's theory presents an enduring challenge to military writers. D. Proenca and E. Duarte, "The Concept of Logistics Derived from Clausewitz," *Journal of Strategic Studies* 28, no. 4 (2005): 645–77.

6. Howard, M. "The Forgotten Dimensions of Strategy," *The Causes of Wars* (London: Temple Smith, 1983), 101–5. G. Perjes, "Army Provisioning, Logistics and Strategy in the Second Half of the 17th Century," *Acta Historica Academiae Scientiarum Hungaricae* 16, nos. 1–2 (1970): 1–51, goes further and accuses Clausewitz of fundamentally misunderstanding Napoleon's system of supply and erroneously concluding that he broke with the past in meeting the supply needs of his armies through requisitioning—rather than relying on depots to his rear. In reality, Napoleon employed both methods.

7. E. Luttwak, "Logistics and the Aristocratic Idea of War," in *Feeding Mars*, ed. J. A. Lynn (Boulder, CO: Westview Press, 1993), 3–7.

8. G. Shaw, *Supply in Modern War* (London: Faber & Faber, 1938), 23.

9. J. Hackett, *The Profession of Arms* (London: Sidgwick & Jackson, 1982); Obituary, J. Hackett, *Times* (London), 10 September 1997.

10. S. J. Simon, "The Art of Military Logistics," *Communications of the Association for Computing Machinery* 44, no. 6 (2001): 62.

11. W. Allen, "The Logistics Revolution and Transportation," *The Annals of the American Academy of Political and Social Science* 553, no. 1 (1997): 107; P. Drucker, "The Economy's Dark Continent," *Fortune*, April 1962, 72.

12. Ministry of Defence, *British Defence Doctrine* (London: Joint Warfare Publication 0–01, 1996), 22–23.

13. NATO, *NATO Logistics Handbook* (Brussels: Logistics Secretariat, 1997).

14. K. Macksey, *The Penguin Encyclopaedia of Weapons and Military Technology* (London: Viking, 1993). Macksey sidesteps the argument about whether logistics is a science or an art—unlike the *Oxford English Dictionary*, which defines logistics as "the art of moving, lodging and supplying troops and equipment." On the other hand, the American Production and Inventory Control Society has defined logistics as "the art *and* science of obtaining, producing and distributing material and product in the proper place and in proper quantities." Also see D. Krumwiede and C. Sheu, "A Model for Reverse Logistics Entry by Third-Party Providers." *The International Journal for Management Science* 30 (2002): 325.

15. Ministry of Defence, *Defence Costs Study No. 10: Repair, Spares, Storage and Distribution* (London: Ministry of Defence, 1994), 1–15. Complexity is assessed on the basis of the cost of spares and repairs, the operating environment, the fragility of the systems involved, and the support facilities required. In 1994 (shortly before the creation of the Tri-Service Defence Logistic Organisation) it was reported that the Air Force Department spent as much on spares as the other two service departments combined and spent twice as much effort on repair activities.

16. W. Manship, "Air Force Supply Measures," in *Today's Logistics*, ed. J. Rainey (Maxwell AFB, Montgomery, AL: Air Force Logistics Management Agency, 2001).

17. NOA, Comptroller and Auditor General, *The Use of Information to Manage the Logistics Supply Chain* (London: House of Commons, HC 827, Session 2010–2011), 4–5.

18. See, for example, D. Chandler, *Blenheim Preparation* (Stroud, UK: Spellmount, 2004), 161–184; H. C. B. Rogers, "Logistics in the Peninsula War," *British Army Review* 62 (1979): 15–20; and J. Weller, *On Wellington* (London: Greenhill Books, 1978), 60–72. The late-Victorian military strategist, Edward Hamley, addressed aspects of supply and administration in his highly influential *The*

Operations of War (London: Blackwood & Sons, 1867), 20, as well as warning that recent developments had greatly increased the quantity and weight of stores required by modern armies.

19. G. Bannerman, *Merchants and the Military in Eighteenth Century Britain* (London: Pickering & Chatto, 2008), 144; 139–40.

20. R. A. Bowler, *Logistics and the Failure of the British Army in America 1775–1783* (Princeton, NJ: Princeton University Press, 1975); R. Morriss, "Colonization, Conquest, and the Supply of Food and Transport: The Reorganization of Logistics Management 1780–1795," *War in History* 14, no. 3 (2007): 310–24.

21. A. Frost, *The First Fleet: The Real Story* (Collingwood, Victoria, Australia: Black, 2011), 214.

22. J. Riley, *Napoleon as a General* (London: Continuum, 2007), 113–29. However, D. Chandler, *The Campaigns of Napoleon* (London: Weidenfeld & Nicolson, 1966), 366–367, has argued that logistical support was one of the least efficient branches of the Imperial Army.

23. I. M. Brown, *British Logistics on the Western Front 1914–1919* (Westport, CT: Praeger, 1998), 110.

24. H. S. G. Miles, "Army Administration," *Royal United Services Institution Journal* 68, no. 469 (1923): 29–44, conceded that this might have been helpful in small wars—given the greater prominence of transport and supply.

25. R. Ruppenthal, *Logistical Support of the Armies*, vol. 1, *May 1941–September 1944*, and vol. 2, *September 1944–May 1945* (Washington, DC: Center of Military History, 1995).

26. G. Thorpe, *Pure Logistics: The Science of War Preparation* (Washington, DC: National Defense University Press, 1986). Thorpe was a forty-two-year-old lieutenant colonel in the United States Marine Corps who had served in the Spanish-American War. He retired for reasons of ill health in 1924 and died in 1936. His book continues to be a recommended text at the U.S. National Defense University and the service staff colleges.

27. W. Kobbe, *Notes on Strategy and Logistics* (Fort Munroe, VA: Artillery School Press, 1896).

28. P. Crowl, "Alfred Thayer Mahan: The Naval Historian," in *Makers of Modern Strategy: From Machiavelli to the Nuclear Age*, ed. P. Paret (Princeton, NJ: Princeton University Press, 1986), 456.

29. E. Hagerman, *The American Civil War and the Origins of Modern War* (Indianapolis, IN: Indiana University Press, 1992), xl.

30. C. King, W. Robertson, and S. Clay, *Staff Ride Handbook for the Overland Campaign: A Study in Operational Command* (Fort Leavenworth, KS: Combat Studies Institution, 2006), 28–29.

31. N. Trudeau, *Southern Storm: Sherman's March to the Sea* (New York: Harper, 2008), 538; B. Liddell Hart, *Sherman* (New York: Praeger, 1958), 234–36.

Liddell Hart has described Sherman's management of supply issues in this campaign as "brilliantly orthodox."

32. Martin van Creveld, *Supplying War: Logistics from Wallenstein to Patton* (Cambridge, UK: Cambridge University Press, 1977). A summary of van Creveld's main arguments appeared as "Supplying an Army: An Historical View," *Royal United Services Institute Journal* 123, no. 2 (1978): 56–63.

33. D. Engels, *Alexander the Great and the Logistics of the Macedonian Army* (Berkeley, CA: University of California Press, 1978); S. R. Waddell, *United States Army Logistics—The Normandy Campaign* (Westport, CT: Greenwood Press, 1994).

34. J. Lynn, ed., *Feeding Mars: Logistics in Western Warfare from the Middle Ages to the Present* (Boulder, CO: Westview Press, 1993).

35. Thompson, *Lifeblood of War*.

36. K. Macksey, *For Want of a Nail* (London: Brassey's, 1989).

37. P. Meilinger, "The Historiography of Airpower: Theory and Doctrine," *Journal of Military History* 64, no. 2 (2000): 467–501.

38. Robin Higham, "Air Power in World War 1, 1914–1918," in *The War in the Air 1914–1994*, ed. A. Stephens (Canberra, Australia: RAAF Air Power Studies Centre, 1994), 1–20. In reviewing the development of airpower in the First World War, Higham has written that "air superiority was also closely linked to the logistics organisation including that of salvage and repair, a topic very largely neglected in the literature."

39. R. Higham, *Bases of Air Strategy* (Shrewsbury, UK: Airlife, 1998) and "Revolutionary Innovation and the Invisible Infrastructure: Making Royal Air Force Bomber Command Efficient, 1939–1945," in *Innovation and the Development of Flight*, ed. R. D. Launius (College Station, TX: Texas A&M Press, 1999), 235–62.

40. R. Miller, "Maintenance and Supply at the Signal Corps Logistic School," *Air Force Journal of Logistics* 19, no. 4 (1995): 36–40; "What to Do with the Truck?—The Air Service of the AEF and the Limits of Organic Transport 1917–1919," *Air Force Journal of Logistics* 21, no. 1 (1997): 35–41; and "The Teeth to Tail Ratio: Royal Flying Corps and Air Service Co-operation in Maintenance Training During WW1," *Air Force Journal of Logistics* 28, no. 3 (2004): 22–33. Miller follows his colleague, Robert Smith, who provided an earlier series of articles on First World War aviation logistics for the *Air Force Journal of Logistics*.

41. R. Overy, *The Air War 1939–1945* (London: Europa, 1980).

42. J. F. C. Fuller, in *Supply in Modern War*, ed. G. C. Shaw (London: Faber & Faber, 1938).

43. B. Liddell Hart, *Thoughts on War* (London: Faber & Faber, 1944), 77–78.

44. T. Travers, *The Killing Ground* (London: Allen & Unwin, 1987) and *How the War Was Won* (London: Routledge, 1992).

45. For example, J. Bourne, "Haig and the Historians," in *Haig: A Re-appraisal 80 Years On*, ed. B. Bond and N. Cave (Barnsley, UK: Pen & Sword, 1999), 6–8; and Sheffield, *Forgotten Victory*, 135.

46. W. Murray, *Military Adaptation in War* (Cambridge, UK: Cambridge University Press, 2011), 116.

47. S. Bidwell and D. Graham, *Fire-Power: British Army Weapons and Theories of War 1904–1945* (London: Allen & Unwin, 1982).

48. P. Griffith, *Battle Tactics of the Western Front* (London: Yale University Press, 1994).

49. T. Finnegan, *Shooting the Front: Allied Aerial Reconnaissance in the First World War* (Stroud, UK: Spellmount, 2011).

50. P. Chasseaud, *Artillery's Astrologers* (Lewes, UK: Mapbooks, 1999). A previous book, *Topography of Armageddon* (Lewes, UK: Mapbooks, 1991), provides a brief survey of extant British maps from the western front.

51. Chasseaud, *Artillery's Astrologers*, 196.

52. P. Mead, *The Eye in the Air* (London: HMSO, 1983).

53. "The Air Force Estimates" *Flight*, 20 March 1919, 377–78; annual expenditure on the RAF was the equivalent of £200 million a year by the armistice compared to £1 million in 1914. H. A. Jones, *War in the Air*, Appendix XXXI (Oxford, UK: Clarendon Press, 1937), 154–57; T. Mason, "RNAS Order of Battle," *Cross & Cockade International Journal* 3, no. 4 (1972): 137–42, and "RFC Aeroplanes," *Cross & Cockade International Journal* 8, no. 4 (1977): 145–67. The RAF comprised a total of 22,171 aircraft at the armistice, compared to a total of 242 aircraft held by the RFC and RNAS in August 1914.

54. J. Terraine, "World War One and the RAF," *Royal Air Force Historical Society Proceedings*, no. 12 (1994): 16; D. J. Jordan, "The Army Co-operation Missions of the Royal Flying Corps/Royal Air Force 1914–1918," (PhD thesis, University of Birmingham, 1997), 343–44.

55. An excellent overview of the corps reconnaissance role and the techniques involved is provided by C. G. Jefford, "Corps Reconnaissance 1914–1918," *RAF Historical Society Journal*, no. 54 (2013): 8–35.

56. Bidwell and Graham, *Fire-Power*, 101–13. By 1917, 90 percent of counter-battery observation was done by aircrew using wireless.

57. This sort of activity is now described as "reverse" logistics, to distinguish it from "traditional" unidirectional logistics. The BEF's supply pipeline, largely comprising consumables, involved little return flow.

58. Eccles, *Logistics in the National Defense*, 141–42. Eccles, who is otherwise critical about the excessive growth in military logistic activities, recognizes that the basic reason for the increasing ratio in service to combat troops is ever-greater mechanization.

59. Air Historical Branch (RAF), *Monthly Return of Personnel of the Royal Air Force [Overseas] from Returns Dated 1 November 1918*, Part II, Ser. No. 457.

60. TNA WO 394/20 "Statistical Abstracts of Information Regarding the Armies at Home and Abroad." The data provided covers the BEF's operations from the summer of 1916 until the armistice.

61. TNA AIR69/41, Air Warfare Lecture Notes, 94.

62. H. A. Jones, *War in the Air*, vol. 3 (Oxford, UK: Clarendon Press, 1931); and Appendices VIII and XLI (Oxford, UK: Clarendon Press, 1937).

63. In announcing the RAF Estimates for 1919–20, General Jack Seely stated that by the armistice expenditure on the RAF was running at the equivalent of £200 million a year (*Flight*, 20 March 1919). Of this total, some £121 million was allocated for aeronautical supplies provided by the Ministry of Munitions; TNA MUN4/4693, "Air Force: Expenditure on Aeronautical Supplies, 1916–1919."

64. Van Creveld, "Supplying an Army," 56.

65. Prior to 1914, demand for anything other than provisions was miniscule, yet by 1916 the quantity of supplies needed to fight exceeded those required to be able to eat.

66. Van Creveld, "Supplying an Army," 60.

67. R. G. Miller, "The Logistics of the British Expeditionary Force: 4 August to 5 September 1914," *Military Affairs* 43, no. 3 (1979): 133–38.

68. Brown, *British Logistics on the Western Front*.

69. K. Grieves, *Sir Eric Geddes: Business in War and Peace* (Manchester, UK: Manchester University Press, 1990).

70. J. Morrow, *German Air Power in World War One* (Lincoln, NE: University of Nebraska Press, 1982), 2–3.

71. This has a modern parallel in the challenge faced by NATO logistic planners in the post–Cold War era. Simon, "The Art of Military Logistics," 64.

72. W. Raleigh, *The War in the Air*, vol. 1 (Oxford, UK: Clarendon Press, 1922); H. A. Jones, *The War in the Air*, vols. 2–4 (Oxford, UK: Clarendon Press, 1928–34).

73. M. Paris, "The Rise of the Airman: The Origins of Air Force Elitism, c. 1890–1918," *Journal of Contemporary History* 28, no. 1 (1993): 138.

74. RAF Museum, X003–8803, Correspondence 1926–27.

75. T. Biddle, *Rhetoric and Reality in Air Warfare* (Princeton, NJ: Princeton University Press, 2004), 70–81; and G. Williams, "Statistics and Strategic Bombardment: Operations and Records of the British Long-Range Bombing Force during World War 1 and their Implications for the Development of the Post-War Royal Air Force, 1917–1923" (PhD thesis, University of Oxford, 1987).

76. D. French, "Official but No History?" *Royal United Services Institute Journal* 131, no. 1 (1986): 58–63, and "Sir James Edmonds and the Official History: France and Belgium," in *The First World War and British Military History*, ed. B. Bond

(Oxford, UK: Clarendon Press, 1991), 69–86; A. Green, *Writing the Great War: Sir James Edmonds and the Official Histories* (London: Frank Cass, 2003).

77. Reichsarchiv, *Der Weltkrieg 1914 bis 1918: Bearbeitet im Reichsarchiv*, published in fourteen volumes (Berlin: Mittler und Sohn, 1925–44).

78. J. E. Edmonds, *Military Operations France and Belgium, 1916*, vol. 1 (London: Macmillan & Co, 1932).

79. A. M. Henniker, *Transportation on the Western Front* (London: Macmillan & Co., 1937).

80. War Office, *Report of the Military Board of Allied Supply—The Allied Armies under Marshal Foch in the Franco-Belgian Theater of Operations* (Washington, DC: War Office, 1924).

81. Ministry of Munitions, *History of the Ministry of Munitions*, twelve volumes (London: HMSO, 1919–22).

82. A good overview of the writing of the history is provided by D. Hay, "The Official History of the Ministry of Munitions 1915–1919," *The Economic History Review* 14, no. 2 (1944): 185–190.

83. Higham, "Revolutionary Innovation," 246.

84. TNA AIR1/1112/204/5/1895–1, "Work Summary and Statistical Returns: Aircraft Parks and Supply Depots," describes the monthly work of the two main aircraft supply depots, including numbers of aircraft issued, repaired, and reconstructed for the period December 1917 to December 1919.

85. Each RFC brigade completed a daily report, Army Form W3359 (France), at 6 p.m. covering the previous twenty-four hours. This recorded the effort by individual wing and detailed serviceable and unserviceable aircraft, the number of pilots available, and the flying hours achieved. Additional detail included hostile batteries engaged for destruction, reconnaissance, photography, and patrols.

86. The records for April 1917 are also strangely thin.

87. Somewhat surprisingly, there has never been a biography of Robert Brooke-Popham. Born in 1878, he was commissioned in the Oxfordshire Light Infantry in 1898. He gained his aviator's certificate in 1911 before joining the Air Battalion in 1912, transferring to the RFC on its formation. Brooke-Popham remained in the peacetime RAF, becoming commandant of the RAF Staff College (1922–26) and the Imperial Defence College (1931–32). He retired in 1937, but rejoined the RAF in 1939. He retired again in 1942. Brooke-Popham's considerable achievements in the First World War have been overshadowed by his perceived failings as CinC Far East (1940–41). Recent scholarship, such as Henry Probert's *The Forgotten Air Force* (London: Brassey's, 1995) and Ong Chit Chung's *Operation Matador* (Singapore: Times Academic Press, 1997), has been more sympathetic about his role in the fall of Singapore. The only (albeit brief) account of Brooke-Popham's career to date was published in the RAF Staff College journal: G. Evans, "70 Years of

Brooke-Popham," *The Hawk* (Bracknell, UK: Royal Air Force Staff College, 1992): 83–92.

88. TNA AIR1/8/15/1/7, "Notes on System of Supply for the RAF in France during the War."

89. These include Cross & Cockade (in the UK, Australia, and the United States), The Royal Air Force Historical Society, The Western Front Association, and the Canadian Aviation Historical Society.

90. D. S. Ballantine, *U.S. Naval Logistics in the Second World War* (Princeton, NJ: Princeton University Press, 1947), 3.

91. L. Neal, ed., *War Finance from Antiquity to the Present* (Cheltenham, UK: Edward Elgar, 1994).

92. D. Stevenson, *Armaments and the Coming of War* (Oxford, UK: Clarendon Press, 1996); N. Ferguson, *The Pity of War* (London: Allen Lane, 1999); K. Stubbs, *The Race to the Front* (Westport, CT: Praeger, 2002).

93. H. Strachan, *Financing the First World War* (Oxford, UK: Oxford University Press, 2004). This was originally published as part of Strachan's *To Arms* (Oxford, UK: Oxford University Press, 2001).

94. This data has been drawn from a variety of sources including *History of the Ministry of Munitions*, *War in the Air* (which contains priced tables for all aircraft and engines procured for the Air Services), *Flight*, and *Hansard*.

95. J. Ellis, *Brute Force: Allied Strategy and Tactics in the Second World War* (London: Andre Deutsch, 1990).

96. K. Grieves, *The Politics of Manpower* (Manchester, UK: Manchester University Press, 1988), 8.

97. TNA AIR1/678/21/13/2138, "Development of Aircraft Production."

98. D. Winter, *The First of the Few* (London: Allen Lane, 1982), 36–37; C. Hobson, *Airmen Died in the Great War 1914–1918* (Suffolk, UK: J. B. Hayward, 1995), and C. Hobson, "The First Air War: The Casualty Records," *Cross & Cockade International Journal* 30, no. 4 (1999): 204–9. A total of 6,933 British airmen (including observers and air gunners) were killed while flying in the First World War, rather than the 14,166 pilots claimed. This may have been a transcription error, but there is no credible explanation as to why Winter adds that eight thousand died in training. In fact, the number of pilots killed in training accidents between 1914 and 1918 was just over two thousand.

99. This includes Ian Beckett, *The Great War* (London: Pearson Education, 2007), 256, and more recently, Joshua Levene, *On a Wing and a Prayer* (London: Collins, 2008), 63.

100. D. Reiter and A. Stam, "Democracy and Battlefield Military Effectiveness," *Journal of Conflict Resolution* 42, no. 3 (1998): 271.

101. J. Stockfish, *Linking Logistics and Operations: A Case Study of World War II Air Power* (Santa Monica, CA: RAND Corporation, 1991), 52–3.

102. These are drawn from a variety of studies, including Stockfish, *Linking Logistics*; Miller, "Logistics of the BEF"; and Brown, *British Logistics*.

103. D. Bowersox, D. Closs, M. Cooper, and J.C. Bowersox, *Supply Chain Logistics Management* (New York: McGraw-Hill, 2010), 382–404.

104. Bachrach, "From Nicaea to Dorylaion," 45.

105. Miller, "Logistics of the BEF," 138.

106. TNA AIR1/678/21/13/2138, "Development of Aircraft Production 1917–1918."

107. T. Gabreski, *Maintenance Metrics* (Maxwell AFB, Montgomery, AL: Air Force Logistics Management Agency, 2001).

108. J. Huston, *Sinews of War: Army Logistics 1775–1953* (Washington, DC: Center of Military History, 1966). In subsequent articles these were expanded from fourteen to sixteen principles: J. Huston, "16 Principles of Logistics," *Army Logistician*, September–October 1988, 14–16.

Chapter 1. Royal Flying Corps Operations on the Western Front

1. J. Morrow, *The Great War in the Air* (Washington, DC: Smithsonian Institution Press, 1993), xiii–xv. Morrow has suggested that this perspective emerged from a natural tendency to emphasize the heroic and a desire to affirm the importance of the individual.

2. J. Terraine, "World War 1 and the Royal Air Force," *Royal Air Force Historical Society Journal*, no. 12 (1994): 10–22.

3. Jones, *War in the Air*, Appendices XXXI and XXXV.

4. Jones, *War in the Air*, Appendix XXXI. Although it has often been stated that the RAF was the world's largest air force at the end of the First World War, it is arguable that this honor should go to the French, who deployed a total first-line strength of 4,511 airplanes compared to the RAF's 3,300 (although the RAF was deployed over one hundred miles of front and the French some two hundred miles).

5. War Office, *Report of the Military Board of Allied Supply*, Chapter XVIII, Section II, 1.

6. Biddle, *Rhetoric and Reality in Air Warfare*, 12–20. Biddle provides an excellent summary of these views, placing them in their contemporary social and cultural context while noting that, in England, aviation was "a very public technology."

7. The War Office was sufficiently impressed to start discussions with the Wright brothers in 1904 for the employment of their services; however, negotiations proved difficult and were terminated in 1906.

8. F. Sykes, *From Many Angles* (London: George Harrap, 1942), 87–88.

9. P. Brooks, "Why the Airship Failed," *Aeronautical Journal*, October 1975, 439–49. It was not until the 1930s, and following two disastrous accidents (the

British R-101 in 1930 and the German *Hindenburg* in 1937), that the continued development of rigid airships was abandoned.

10. S. Kandebo, "The Wright Brothers and the Birth of an Industry," *Aviation Week & Space Technology*, 30 December 2002, 17–44; Terraine, "World War 1," 11.

11. These contrasting views are offered by D. Edgerton, *England and the Aeroplane: An Essay on a Militant and Technological Nation* (London: Macmillan, 1991), and H. Driver, *The Birth of Military Aviation* (Woodbridge, UK: Boydell, 1997).

12. P. W. L. Brooke-Smith, *The History of Early British Military Aeronautics* (Bath, UK: Cedric Chivers, 1968), 1.

13. Ibid., 12.

14. Ibid., 30–32.

15. Ibid., 32–33.

16. A. Gollin, *No Longer an Island* (London: William Heinemann, 1984), 399–401.

17. A. Gollin, "The Mystery of Lord Haldane and Early British Military Aviation," *North American Conference on British Studies* 11, no. 1 (1979), 46–65.

18. Brooke-Smith, *Early British Military Aeronautics*, 38.

19. Ibid., 41.

20. Ibid., 60.

21. According to General Sir William Nicholson, chief of the Imperial General Staff, in Driver, *Military Aviation*, 262–63.

22. G. Sheffield, *The Chief* (London: Aurum Press, 2011), 62; A. Whitmarsh, "British Army Manoeuvres and the Development of Military Aviation, 1910–1913," *War in History* 14, no. 3 (July 2007): 310–25. Just as importantly, a number of up-and-coming officers, such as Douglas Haig, were enthusiastic about the potential of aviation.

23. Brooke-Smith, *Early British Military Aeronautics*, 55. A separate War Office committee, chaired by Lord Kitchener, had already concluded in August 1911 that aeronautics should no longer be included in the functions of the RE.

24. RAF Museum MFC77/13, Sykes Papers.

25. Sykes, *From Many Angles*, 93–96.

26. E. Ash, *Sir Frederick Sykes and the Air Revolution 1912–1918* (London: Frank Cass, 1999), 24.

27. Driver, *Military Aviation*, 244.

28. *Flight*, 21 September 1912, 859.

29. Edgerton, *England and the Aeroplane*, 10. This is based on a comparison of front-line aircraft numbers—as presented in Jones, *War in the Air*, Appendix XXXI. However, the figure quoted for France (120 airplanes) is too low (it was 141 airplanes) and, more importantly, excludes the general reserve (126 airplanes), while the figure quoted for Germany (232 airplanes) is also low (it was 245); Morrow, *The Great War in the Air*, 35–45.

30. S. W. Roskill, *Documents Relating to the Naval Air Service 1908–1918* (London: Naval Records Society, 1969); and Charles Grey, "The Supplementary Estimate," *The Aeroplane*, 26 February 1914, 209.

31. Driver, *Military Aviation*, 26; Sykes; *From Many Angles*, 88.

32. J. T. C. Moore-Brabazon, *Flight*, 2 January 1909, 13–14.

33. A. Gollin, *The Impact of Air Power on the British People and their Government, 1909–14* (London: Macmillan, 1989), 22.

34. George Holt Thomas, Letter to the *Daily Mail*, 17 September 1910.

35. R. Dallas Brett, *History of British Aviation 1908–1914* (London: John Hamilton, 1933), 2:149.

36. Jones, *War in the Air*, 3:255.

37. Raleigh, *War in the Air*, 1:177–81.

38. Brett, *History of British Aviation*, 1:124–25.

39. TNA AIR1/785/204/4/565, "Attendance of RFC Officers at French manoeuvres;" J. N. Pugh, "The Conceptual Origins of the Control of the Air: British Military and Naval Aviation, 1911–1918" (PhD thesis, University of Birmingham, 2012), 98–99. The *Training Manual* (Part 2), sometimes known as the *War Book*, described the functions of the RFC, including its strategic and tactical employment. The *Training Manual* was conceived by Sykes in February 1913 to provide guidance on how the Military Wing should operate in war.

40. TNA AIR1/783/204/4/515, "Report by RFC Officers on Visit to French Aeroplane Works." This included Major Herbert Musgrave, assistant commandant and officer in charge of experiments who attended the Army maneuvers of 1912, expressing great admiration for all that he saw, and Major Robert Brooke-Popham who toured French aviation establishments in May 1914.

41. B. H. Barrington-Kennett, "Military Aeronautics in France," *Royal United Services Institution Journal* 56 (February 1912): 171–78. Barrington-Kennett later became the RFC's first adjutant.

42. Jones, *War in the Air*, Appendix XXXI.

43. Ministry of Munitions, *Ministry of Munitions, The Supply of Munitions*, I:177.

44. TNA AIR1/625/17/11, "Report on Meeting of Representatives of French Aviation Service, RFC and RNAS." At a meeting between the French Aviation Service and the RFC, held in London on 15 December 1915, it was agreed that the British would provide Sopwith 1½ Strutters, as well as hydrogen bottles and an example of the CFS Mk4 bombsight.

45. Excluding the Independent Force and 5 Group.

46. Ministry of Munitions, *Ministry of Munitions, The Supply of Munitions*, I:174.

47. Chasseaud, *Artillery's Astrologers*, 26, 52.

48. RAF Museum MFC/76/1/66, "Relationships with the French."

49. H. Probert, *High Commanders of the Royal Air Force* (London: HMSO, 1991), 1–2. Colonel Hugh Trenchard arrived in France in November 1914 to take

command of Third Wing. In August 1915 he replaced Brigadier-General David Henderson as GOC RFC in France, commanding the RFC through both the Somme and Third Ypres, before returning to London in January 1918 to become the RAF's first chief of the Air Staff. He resigned after three months and later commanded the Independent Force, tasked with conducting a strategic bombing campaign against Germany.

50. Commandant Paul du Peuty was a prewar cavalry officer who joined the aviation service early in the war. He commanded Escadrille MS 48 on its formation in March 1915 and subsequently a Groupe de Chasse on the Artois front before being appointed to the French Tenth Army in the autumn of 1915—at that time located between the British First and Third Armies. Following General Robert Nivelle's arrival as CinC in December 1916, du Peuty replaced Colonel Joseph-Edouard Barès as head of the Service Aéronautique. He resigned his post in August 1917 to return to the army, being killed in action in March 1918.

51. RAF Museum MFC76/1/66, "Relations with the French," letter from Major-General Hugh Trenchard to Colonel Duval, Head French Air Services in the Field, January 1918.

52. Jones, *War in the Air*, 2:164–66.

53. A. Boyle, *Man of Vision* (London: Collins, 1962), 166–68.

54. *Fighting in the Air*, issued by the General Staff, April 1918, 2.

55. Pugh, "The Conceptual Origins," 246–47.

56. Lieutenant G. de G. Ferriere and Captain A. H. Cooper respectively.

57. Conclusions of the report by Commandant du Peuty, forwarded to Brigadier-General Trenchard, "The Working of Aviation in the Vaux-Douaumont Sector," RAF Museum MFC76/1/66.

58. Jones, *War in the Air*, 3:167–68.

59. RAF Museum MFC76/1/66, "Secret Memorandum on the French Air Services."

60. Letter from Major-General Hugh Trenchard to Colonel Duval, Head French Air Services in the Field, dated January 1918, RAF Museum MFC76/1/66.

61. War Office, *Statistics of the Military Effort of the British Empire* (London: HMSO, 1922), 495–506.

62. War Office, *Statistics*, 441–43; Jones, *War in the Air*, Appendices. There were five frontline aircraft per division in January 1916 and over twenty per division at the armistice (compared to sixty-four guns per division in January 1916 and 105 per division at the armistice).

63. Slessor, *Air Power and Armies*, 1.

64. P. Dye, "RFC Bombs and Bombing 1912–1918," *RAF Historical Society Journal*, no. 54 (2009): 8–14.

65. TNA AIR69/31, "The Development of Aeroplane Co-operation with the Army."

66. Ibid.

67. J. Terraine, "World War One and the RAF," 14.

68. TNA AIR69/31, "The Development of Aeroplane Co-operation with the Army."

69. P. Dye, "No. 9 (Wireless) Squadron 1914–1915," *Cross & Cockade International Journal* 35, no. 2 (2004): 106–20.

70. TNA AIR69/31, "The Development of Aeroplane Co-operation with the Army."

71. Bidwell and Graham, *Fire-Power*, 103.

72. TNA AIR69/31, "The Development of Aeroplane Co-operation with the Army."

73. Bidwell and Graham, *Fire-Power*, 143.

74. A long series of postwar articles describing the evolution of the BEF's artillery techniques was provided by Lieutenant-Colonel (later Field Marshal) Alan Brooke, "The Evolution of Artillery in the Great War," *The Journal of the Royal Artillery*, vol. 51, Parts I and II, 250–67 and 359–72; vol. 52, Parts III and IV, 37–51 and 385–87; and vol. 53, Parts V, VI, VII, and VIII, 76–93, 233–49, 320–38, and 469–82; 1925–27. P. Strong and S. Marble, *Artillery in the Great War* (Barnsley, UK: Pen & Sword, 2011) provide a more recent assessment on the artillery tactics of the major belligerents (in all theaters).

75. Brooke, "The Evolution of Artillery," Part III, 92.

76. Ibid., Part VII, 321–22.

77. Jonathan Bailey, "The First World War and the Birth of the Modern Style of Warfare," *Strategic and Combat Studies Institute Occasional Paper* (Camberley, UK: Staff College, 1996). A version of this paper with some changes appeared as "The First World War and the Birth of Modern Warfare," in *The Dynamics of Military Revolution*, ed. M. Knox and W. Murray (Cambridge, UK: Cambridge University Press, 2001).

78. G. P. Neumann, *The German Air Force in the Great War* (London: Hodder & Stoughton, 1921), 202.

79. P. Hart, *Bloody April* (London: Weidenfeld & Nicolson, 2005), 33.

80. C^3I: Command, Control, Communications and Information. S. Bidwell, "After the Wall Came Tumbling Down: A Historical Perspective," *Royal United Services Institute Journal*, Autumn 1990, 57–59.

81. John Terraine, "Lessons of Air Warfare," *Royal United Services Institute Journal*, August 1992, 53–57

82. Neumann, *The German Air Force*, 201–2.

83. Jones, *War in the Air*, Appendix XXVIII.

84. There were nineteen corps (army cooperation) squadrons with the RFC in January 1917 and twenty by the armistice.

85. M. Cooper, "Blueprint for Confusion: The Administrative Background to the Formation of the Royal Air Force 1912–19," *Journal of Contemporary History* 22, no. 3 (July 87): 441.

86. This included both day and night squadrons as well as the aircraft of the Independent Force, tasked with the strategic bombing of Germany. By the armistice, there were twenty-one RAF bombing squadrons on the western front (as well as three with 5 Group and nine with the Independent Force), compared to just one in January 1917.

87. Peter Dye, "9 Squadron RFC/RAF: An Analysis," *Cross & Cockade International Journal* 28, no. 2 (1997): 78.

88. Ibid.

89. Brooke, "The Evolution of Artillery," Part III, 49

90. Hobson, "The First Air War," 207.

91. TNA AIR1/926/204/5/915, "Aeroplane and Engine Casualties," and TNA AIR1/998/204/5/1242–1243, "Duplicate Returns."

92. Liddell Hart Centre for Military Archives, Brooke-Popham Papers 1/4, "Staff College Notes."

93. Brooke, "The Evolution of Artillery," Part VIII, 469–82.

94. Terraine, "Lessons of Air Warfare," 57.

95. A. Liaropoulos, "Revolutions in Warfare: Theoretical Paradigms and Historical Evidence," in *War Studies Reader*, ed. G. Sheffield (London: Continuum, 2010), 148.

96. T. Wilson and R. Prior, "Conflict, Technology and the Impact of Industrialization 1914–1918," *Journal of Strategic Studies* 24, no. 3 (2001): 128–57.

97. Gray, *Strategy for Chaos*, 185.

Chapter 2. The Royal Flying Corps' Logistic System, 1914–18

1. Raleigh, *War in the Air*, 1:206–208.The Royal Navy was never a strong supporter of the organization and engineered a separation of the Naval Wing to create the Royal Naval Air Service in July 1914, although the Central Flying School based at Upavon remained (for a while) as a joint unit.

2. Raleigh, *War in the Air*, 1:201. A personal account of the rationale behind this system is provided by Sykes, *From Many Angles*, 94–95.

3. TNA AIR1/785/204/4/558, *RFC Training Manual*, Pt. II, "Correspondence and Proofs."

4. Brancker, "The Aeroplane in War," *Flight*, 12 June 1914, 632–33. Major Sefton Brancker, in a lecture given in 1914, commented that the difficulties of maintenance were sometimes lost sight of—the airplane and its engine being both flimsy and fragile—necessitating the provision of large quantities of spare parts

and portable tents for housing machines. As a result, only a small proportion of airplanes in the field would be fit to take to the air at any given moment.

5. TNA AIR1/785/204/4/558, *RFC Training Manual*; Liddell Hart Centre for Military Archives, Brooke-Popham Papers 1/4; Pugh, "The Conceptual Origins," 113. The need for a training manual to regularize the organization, procedures, and employment of the RFC was identified by the Military Wing in February 1913. Major Robert Brooke-Popham may have written substantial sections of the manual; he was certainly actively involved in editing the final draft.

6. Ministry of Munitions, *Ministry of Munitions, The Supply of Munitions*, IV:3.

7. Jones, *War in the Air*, 3:252; WO24/899, "War Establishment: Part 1: Expeditionary Force 1914," 115–19. The full establishment comprised: one Crossley touring car for the commanding officer; six Crossley light tenders for the conveyance of tradesmen and boxes; six heavy tenders for the transport of large spare parts and camp equipment; three reserve equipment lorries; three shed lorries; three flight repair lorries fitted with hand-power tools, electric lighting plant, and raw materials; one heavy repair lorry fitted with machine tools; one lorry carrying spare parts and stores for the mechanical transport; one baggage lorry; one lorry for petrol, oil, and lubricants (POL); six motor-cycles; and six aircraft trailers.

8. Major F. H. Sykes, "Military Aviation," *Flight*, 8 March 1913, 280. An analysis of the Army's 1912 maneuvers showed that eight steam lorries, ten heavy tenders, twelve light tenders, and eight motor cars had been required to keep two airships and fourteen airplanes in commission.

9. A. Wakefield, "Subvention, Impressment and Mass Production—The 'Standard' Lorry and British Military Logistics 1912–1918," *Stand To!*, September 1997, 12–14.

10. B. Robertson, *Wheels of the RAF* (Cambridge, UK: Patrick Stephens, 1983), 2–3.

11. Raleigh, *War in the Air*, 1:287; Roger G. Miller, "What to Do with the Truck?" *Air Force Journal of Logistics*, Winter 1997. In this respect, the experience of the Air Service of the AEF mirrors the RFC's, although an overall shortage of trucks forced the AEF to centralize the management of all motor transport, much to the chagrin of the Air Service, who envied the RFC's independence.

12. Liddell Hart, *Thoughts on War*, 160. Employing Liddell Hart's definition of "motorization," as distinct from "mechanization"—the employment of armored fighting vehicles.

13. TNA AIR1/1155/204/5/2428, "Quarterly Returns of Engines and Vehicles held by the RAF in the Field."

14. TNA WO394/20, "Statistical Abstracts of Information."

15. Ministry of Munitions, *Ministry of Munitions, The Supply of Munitions*, IV:19.

16. Care needs to be taken as the term "vehicles" can include motorcycles and even trailers, while "lorries" can be divided into heavy trucks, light trucks, repair trucks, and trailers.

17. D. Stevenson, *With Our Backs to the Wall* (London: Allen Lane, 2011), 242; M. McCoy, "Grinding Gears: The AEF and Motor Transportation in the First World War," *War in History* (2004): 194–208. The AEF (approximately 2 million strong) possessed some 40,000 vehicles by the armistice.

18. J. Winter, "1918: The Road to Victory," in *1918: Year of Victory*, ed. A. Elkins (Auckland, New Zealand: Exisle, 2010), 38.

19. M. Baring, *Flying Corps Headquarters 1914–1918* (Edinburgh: Bell & Sons, 1920), 69.

20. Liddell Hart, *Thoughts on War*, 192.

21. E. Carter, "The New Transport System—Its Principles and their Application," *Royal United Services Institution Journal* (1912): 611–702.

22. Robertson, *Wheels of the RAF*, 4–5. Major repairs on the western front were initially undertaken by the AOD but the ASC assumed this task from October 1916. For general histories of the ASC, see R. H. Beadon, *The Royal Army Service Corps—A History of Transport and Supply in the British Army* (Cambridge, UK: Cambridge University Press, 1931); G. Crew, *The Royal Army Service Corps* (London: Leo Cooper, 1970); and M. Young, *Army Service Corps 1902–1918* (Barnsley, UK: Leo Cooper, 2000).

23. TNA AIR1/793/204/4/795, "Notes on the Provision of Spare Parts for Mechanical Transport."

24. Raleigh, *War in the Air*, 1:213.

25. Ibid., 1:283. The mobilization plan required twenty-four aircraft to be crated. In the event, the balance was flown direct to France or used to make up deficiencies on the squadrons.

26. Ibid., 1:284–85.

27. P. Dye, "The Royal Flying Corps and Royal Air Force at St-Omer," *Cross & Cockade International Journal* 35, no. 2 (2004): 71–88.

28. G. P. Bulman, "Early Days," *Journal of the Royal Aeronautical Society* 70 (1966): 177.

29. N. Macmillan, *Sir Sefton Brancker* (London: Sir William Heinemann, 1935), 62. The "bad results" were the lack of inter-service cooperation over the allocation of resources and the management of production contracts, which followed the departure of key individuals who had formed the Air Committee.

30. J. Cuneo, *Winged Mars: The Air Weapon 1914–1916* (Harrisburg, PA: Military Service Publishing Company, 1947), 143.

31. Ibid., 147.

32. Ibid., 151.

33. No. 6 Squadron joined the original four squadrons at St-Omer in October 1914.

34. Baring, *Flying Corps Headquarters*, 145–46, describes the problems faced by the operational squadrons arising from the confusion between English and French spares.

35. For a general history of the AOD, see A. Forbes, *A History of the Army Ordnance Services*, vol. 3, *The Great War* (London: The Medici Society, 1929), and H. Harris, *The First Five Hundred Years* (Aldershot, UK: RAOC School, 1962), 98–103.

36. The supply of complete machines and vehicles was in the hands of the director of Military Aeronautics at the War Office.

37. TNA AIR1/2398, "Notes on the History of the RAF Stores Branch."

38. Ministry of Munitions, *Ministry of Munitions, The Supply of Munitions*, I:49.

39. Jones, *War in the Air*, 2:188.

40. In August 1914, the Air Park was responsible for just sixty-three aircraft in the field, but by May 1915 this had risen to 156.

41. Once the Air Park became firmly established at St-Omer it became easier and quicker to ship stores via Boulogne rather than Rouen. The latter port continued to serve the southern depots and parks.

42. TNA AIR1/529/16/12/75, "Organisation and Establishment of Aircraft Parks and Depots." The ERS output in August 1916 was roughly one hundred engines per month with an establishment of ten officers and 406 other ranks. It was agreed to increase this in two stages until, by May 1917, the output reached four hundred engines per month with an establishment of thirty-two officers and 1,702 other ranks. The total output for the last year of the war (ten months) of repaired or rebuilt engines reached 3,196 from an establishment of 4,532 personnel of all ranks. TNA AIR1/686/21/13/2252, Statistical Data.

43. Ministry of Munitions, *Ministry of Munitions, The Supply of Munitions*, I:79–81. The perceived advantages arising from this policy were: immunity from civilian labor troubles, the training potential to the Service in undertaking the work, and the reduced turnaround time because of the proximity of service workshops to the frontline. However, there was also recognition that industry could not keep pace with repair requirements. In June 1918, for example, there was a total outstanding deficiency of 1,491 repaired engines from civilian firms as compared with the scheduled output. Please see H. A. Jones, *War in the Air*, vol. 6 (Oxford, UK: Clarendon Press, 1937), 99.

44. Jones, *War in the Air*, 2:188–90.

45. Ibid., 1:189.

46. RAF Museum MFC76/1/25, "Orders for Aircraft Parks issued by Lt-Col Brooke-Popham."

47. The balance between Army-supplied and RFC-supplied stores is detailed (by section) in Appendix B.

48. By early 1916, the Army's total petrol consumption had risen to over 2 million gallons a month, of which at least 200,000 gallons was aviation spirit. Edmonds, *Military Operations France and Belgium, 1916*, 1:102–4.

49. TNA AIR1/139/15/40/295, DAQMG to ADMA, 10 May 1915.

50. TNA AIR1/530/16/12/86, DDMA to GOC RFC, 12 April 1916.

51. Jones, *War in the Air*, 4:358.

52. TNA AIR1/366/15/231/6, Correspondence, vol. 6.

53. TNA AIR1/1291/204/11/83, "War Establishments." Two grades of equipment officers were initially established: equipment officer (with the rank of captain) for wings, and assistant equipment officer (with the rank of second lieutenant) for squadrons.

54. TNA AIR10/65, "RAF War Establishments in France." Comprising one Equipment Officer (Grade 3) Squadron and three Equipment Officers (Grade 3) Wireless.

55. *Army List*, July 1916. The Monthly Army List was published by His Majesty's Stationery Office, London.

56. Ministry of Munitions, *Ministry of Munitions, The Supply of Munitions*, I:173.

57. Ibid., 12:79. In August 1918, there were more than 4,200 machines in store without engines.

58. AW FK8 Ser No B273, Aircraft Logbook held by RAF Museum.

59. TNA AIR1/1139/204/5/2305, "Visits to Paris."

60. C. G. Jefford, *RAF Squadrons* (Shrewsbury, UK: Airlife, 1988), 27.

61. TNA AIR1/1245/204/6/56–57, "No. 9 Squadron Record Book."

62. TNA AIR69/41, "Air Warfare Lecture Notes."

63. In contemporary RAF terminology, "first line" comprises those engineering and maintenance activities carried out by a squadron; "second line" are those activities beyond squadron capability conducted at station level; and "third line" are those activities beyond station capability conducted at the depot.

64. "No. 253 RFC—An Interview with Mr. W Smyrk," *The 1914–1918 Journal*, 1970, 55–61.

65. F. M. Cutlack, *Official History of Australia in the War of 1914–1918* (Sydney: Angus & Robertson, 1938), 440.

66. TNA AIR8/1, "Personnel Establishment Figures for RAF in France." For fighter squadrons, the formal establishment was smaller, comprising 149 ground crew and 35 vehicles.

67. TNA AIR1/1084/204/5/1721, "Reorganisation of Aircraft Depots." The new organization came into effect on 1 November 1917, comprising No. 1 Northern ASD (Reception Park at Marquise, Repair Park at St-Omer, and Issue Section at Serny) and No. 2 Southern ASD (Repair Park and Issue Section at Fienvillers). The strength of the former was 92 officers and 2,235 other ranks and the latter, without a reception park, 50 officers and 1,905 other

ranks—based on 80 squadrons employed on the western front. The strengths of Nos. 1 and 2 Aircraft Depots were adjusted accordingly, both units comprising 43 officers and 1,697 other ranks.

68. TNA AIR1/520/16/12/1 Part III, "Air Policy Expansion and Organisation of the RFC and RAF;" Jones, *War in the Air*, 4: 353. RLPs were initially established with thirty lorries and twenty-four trailers, but an additional section of fifteen lorries and twelve trailers was authorized in February 1918.

69. RAF Museum MFC76/1/40, Brooke-Popham to Trenchard, 28 October 1920.

70. TNA AIR1/1072/204/5/1643, "Casualty and Replacements of Aircraft and Engines."

71. RAF Museum MFC76/1/40, Brooke-Popham to Trenchard, 28 October 1920.

72. TNA AIR1/1159/204/5/2459, "Distribution of Duties Chart: HQ RAF Equipment Branch." His responsibilities embraced the supply and allotment of engines, mechanical transport, all record work, returns, estimates and statistics, electric lighting sets, movements of transport and units arriving in France, and methods of dispatch of stores to and from England.

73. TNA AIR1/8/15/1/7, "Notes on the System of Supply for the RAF in France."

74. TNA AIR1/1157/204/5/2474, "Reports and Miscellaneous Correspondence."

75. Baring, *Flying Corps Headquarters*, 145–46.

76. TNA AIR1/2390/228/11/124, "Wing Commander E. W. Havers, War Experiences," 3.

77. TNA AIR1/2430/305/30/16, "Report by Deputy Assistant Director RFC on Visits to Aircraft Depots and Remarks by General Brooke-Popham."

78. TNA AIR1/8/15/1/7, "Notes on the System of Supply for the RAF in France."

79. TNA AIR69/31, "Air Cdre Brooke-Popham: The Development of Aeroplane Co-operation with the Army during the War."

80. Jones, *War in the Air*, 3:253.

81. Ibid., 6:92–93.

82. Ibid., 4:202.

83. TNA AIR1/1111/204/5/895–1, "Work Summary and Statistical Returns: Aircraft Parks and Supply Depots."

84. T. Henshaw, *The Sky Their Battlefield* (London: Grub Street, 1995), 132–455.

85. TNA AIR1/1157/204/5/2474, "Reports and Miscellaneous Correspondence."

86. TNA AIR1/2423/305/18/29, "Report on Aircraft Salvage and Repair Depot."

87. Ibid.

88. TNA AIR1/1111/204/5/1895, "Work Summary and Statistical Returns."

89. Ibid.

90. TNA WO394/1–20, "Statistical Abstracts of Information."

91. Air Commodore R. Brooke-Popham, "The Air Force," *Royal United Services Institution Journal* 65 (1920): 43–70.

92. TNA AIR1/763/204/4/197, "Replacements: Spare Parts of Aeroplanes," 27 June 1913. David Henderson, the director of military training and GOC RFC, was in many ways the father of the RFC and still awaits a full biography; however, a good account of his life and achievements can be found in: François Prins, "Forgotten Founder," *Air Enthusiast Quarterly* 47, September–November 1992, 1–8.

93. TNA AIR10/774, "Schedule for RAF Aeroplanes, Type R.E.8."

94. TNA AIR1/823/204/5/68, "RFC Squadron Mobilization Store Table."

95. War Office, *Statistics*, 521. From 9 August 1914 up to 1 May 1920.

96. TNA AIR1/8/15/1/7, "Notes on System of Supply for RAF in France."

97. TNA AIR1/1139/204/5/2305, "Shipping and Tonnage."

98. TNA WO394, "Statistical Abstracts of Information."

99. I. M. Brown, "The Evolution of the British Army's Logistical and Administrative Infrastructure and its Influence on GHQ's Operational and Strategic Decision-Making on the Western Front, 1914–1918" (PhD thesis, King's College London, 1996), 196–97.

100. TNA AIR1/1139/204/5/2305, "Shipping and Tonnage;" K. Grieves, "The Transport Mission to GHQ, 1916," in *Look to Your Front*, ed. B. Bond et al. (Stroud, UK: Spellmount, 1999), 63–78.

101. C. G. G. Grey, "Good Technical Work," *The Aeroplane*, 15 January 1919, 212.

102. TNA WO394/1–5, "Statistical Abstracts of Information."

103. The empty weight of aircraft employed on the western front in 1917 ranged from the Sopwith Camel (1,000 lb) to the F.E.2b (2,000 lb). For planning purposes, a figure of 2.5 tons per aircraft was used (TNA AIR1/1139/204/5/2305, "Shipping and Tonnage"). On this basis, the 1,079 aircraft shipped in crates from England represented some 2,500 tons, or 50 tons per week.

104. TNA AIR1/1139/204/5/2305, "Shipping and Tonnage."

105. Over the period 31 March–30 June 1917, 10,676 tons of aviation stores were shipped to France. In the same three months, 208 aircraft (some 500 tons) were shipped to France in crates, representing approximately 5 percent of all stores shipped.

106. TNA AIR1/1139/204/5/2304, "Shipping and Tonnage: Stores to and from England and France." For most of the war, the bulk of supplies for the RFC were shipped through Rouen and Boulogne. As of May 1917, the total had been less than three thousand tons per month (excluding petrol, ordnance stores, etc.).

107. TNA AIR1/1112/204/5/1898, "Work Summary and Statistical Returns at Port Depot, Rouen."

108. I. M. Brown, "Feeding Victory: The Logistic Imperative behind the Hundred Days," in *1918: Defining Victory*, ed. P. Dennis and J. Grey (Canberra, Australia: Army Historical Unit, 1999), 2–3.

109. These issues are explored in Ian Brown's "The British Expeditionary Force and the Difficult Transition to Peace 1918–1919," *Journal of Strategic Studies* 19, no. 4 (1996): 89–104.

110. TNA AIR1/1112/204/5/1898, "Work Summary and Statistical Returns at Port Depot, Rouen." The Rouen Port Detachment comprised 5 officers and 126 other ranks (including twenty-two Women's Royal Air Force) as of 15 May 1919.

111. TNA AIR1/1112/204/5/1896, "Work Summary and Statistical Returns: Aeroplane Supply Depots."

112. *RFC Technical Notes 1916* (London: Arms and Amour Press, 1968); A. Judge, *Automotive and Aircraft Engines* (London: Pitman, 1924). The 50 hp Gnome engine, employed widely by the RFC in the first years of the war, had a petrol consumption of around five gallons per hour and an oil consumption of three-quarters of a gallon per hour. The Bentley BR1, introduced in 1917 and also a rotary engine, was rated at 150 hp with a petrol consumption of some thirteen gallons per hour and an oil consumption of two gallons per hour. Stationary engines, air- and water-cooled, although generally exhibiting higher petrol and lower oil consumption, also saw a similar increase in power and overall consumption rates during the course of the war.

113. C. E. Fayle, *Seaborne Trade*, vol. 3 (London: John Murray, 1924). Annual imports of petroleum rose from 1.8 million tons in 1913 to 4.1 million tons in 1917 and were approaching 5.2 million tons in 1918.

114. The four-gallon tin was thin, cheap, and non-returnable but the two-gallon tin was capable of being refilled several times, although wastage of the latter amounted to 20 percent through loss or damage. On the whole, however, the two-gallon tin was found to be more economical and practical for use in France.

115. Edmonds, *Military Operations France and Belgium, 1916*, 1:103–104. By early 1916, the Army's total petrol consumption had risen to over 2 million gallons a month, of which at least 200,000 gallons was aviation spirit. By 1918, the RAF required at least 600,000 gallons per month to sustain operations.

116. Ibid., 102–3.

117. War Office, *Statistics*, 847.

118. TNA AIR1/1124/204/5/2101, "Bulk Supply of Petrol." It was initially estimated that the southern aerodromes of the Independent Force would require 200,000 gallons per month. A total of forty-five petrol tank wagons were ordered to supply this requirement, based on a fifteen-day turnaround time. However, by June 1918 the forecast consumption had risen to 600,000 gallons

with the expectation that it would rise still further, to about 1 million gallons per month, by April 1919. Consumption by the remainder of the RAF in France was predicted to be 2 million gallons per month at this date, or some 3 million gallons in total.

119. Morrow, *The Great War in the Air*, 300–301. Monthly consumption in Italy, Egypt, Mesopotamia, Palestine, Canada, and Salonika amounted to a minimum of 500,000 gallons, making a total of 3.3 million gallons (or 10,500 tons) per month. In comparison, the GAS had been rationed to just seven thousand tons a month by August 1918. The price of petrol varied as the war progressed. In 1915 it was of the order of 2 shillings per gallon but by 1918 was a little over 1 shilling per gallon.

120. J. E. Tennant, *In the Clouds above Baghdad* (London: Cecil Palmer, 1920), 190–91.

121. Ministry of Munitions, *Ministry of Munitions, The Supply of Munitions*, I:145–46.

122. *The Aeroplane*, 2 June 1920, 1069–70. The conduct and outcome of the two enquiries held in 1916 to examine the administration of the RFC have been described in Chapter 2. Charles Grey, the long-serving editor of *The Aeroplane*, described himself as the "chief instigator of the said agitation" in an editorial review of Maurice Baring's *Flying Corps Headquarters*.

123. Baring, *Flying Corps Headquarters*, 191–92.

124. *The Aeroplane*, 10 January 1917, 118.

125. Evans, "70 Years of Brooke-Popham," 83.

126. Liddell Hart Centre for Military Archives, Brooke-Popham Papers 1/4, "Lecture to Staff College by Captain H. R. M. Brooke-Popham," November 1911.

127. W. R. Read, "Cavalryman in the Clouds," in *People at War*, ed. M. Moynihan (Newton Abbott, UK: David & Charles, 1973), 23. Read arrived in France with No. 3 Squadron on 13 August 1914.

128. RAF Museum B2621/4, "Sir John Salmond (Draft) Autobiography;" Baring, *Flying Corps Headquarters*, 27–28. According to Maurice Baring, Brooke-Popham purchased supplies in gold that he carried in a portmanteau—much to the surprise of the French.

129. J. T. B. McCudden, *Flying Fury* (London: Hamilton, 1930), 32.

130. Brooke-Popham was awarded the Distinguished Service Order on 23 June 1915 for his leadership of III Wing during Neuve Chapelle and Aubers Ridge.

131. TNA AIR1/529/16/12/70, "Organisation and Establishment of RFC Headquarters." Brooke-Popham's responsibilities ranged from the posting of officers and the handling of casualties to the supply of matériel and the allotment of airplanes.

132. Festing was first appointed DAA & QMG at HQ RFC in March 1915, on transfer from the Northumberland Fusiliers. He chose not to serve in the

postwar RAF (joining Sefton Brancker at the Department of Civil Aviation). His son, Field Marshal Sir Francis Festing, later served as chief of the Imperial General Staff. Personnel issues in the headquarters became the responsibility of Brigadier-General Phillip Game.

133. TNA AIR1/1159/204/5/2459, "Distribution of Duties Chart: HQ RAF Equipment Branch."

134. Brooke-Popham was appointed controller, Technical Department, Ministry of Munitions, on 1 March 1919.

135. Major General John Salmond replaced Hugh Trenchard as GOC RFC on 20 January 1918, remaining in command until the armistice.

136. RAF Museum B2621/4, "Sir John Salmond (Draft) Autobiography."

137. J. M. Bruce, *The Aeroplanes of the Royal Flying Corps* (London: Putnam, 1982), xiii.

138. Evans, "70 Years of Brooke-Popham," 91; Ong Chit Chung, *Operation Matador* (Singapore: Times Academic Press, 1997), 226. Duff Cooper's views hastened Churchill's decision to replace Brooke-Popham with a younger officer.

139. *News Review*, August 1941, 10–11; *Northern Daily Telegraph*, 4 March 1941.

140. Peter Wykeham, "Popham, Sir (Henry) Robert Moore Brooke- (1878–1953)," *Dictionary of National Biography* (London: Oxford University Press, 1971), 144–46. This account, as with others, is in error over the details of his employment on the western front.

141. *The Aeroplane*, 30 October 1953, 591.

142. RAF Museum DC76/74/130, "Air Chief Marshal Sir Robert Brooke-Popham, Record of Service."

143. L. Fell, "The Engine Repair Shops Pont de l'Arche," *Journal of the Royal Aeronautical Society* 70 (1966): 168.

144. Bulman, "Early Days," 176–77.

145. TNA AIR1/2390/228/11/124, "War Experiences," 1–13.

146. Ibid., 9–10. These comments were penned at the RAF Staff College, but after Robert Brooke-Popham's tenure as commandant.

Chapter 3. The Supply of Aircraft and Aero-Engines, 1914–18

1. Ministry of Munitions, *Ministry of Munitions, The Supply of Munitions*, I:173. This total includes seaplanes and ship airplanes. From May 1917, the output figures represent the number of machines handed to the services. Thereafter, they record the number "passed inspection" at the manufacturers. This did not require the fitting of government furnished equipment—such as engines, instruments, and armament.

2. Jones, *War in the Air*, Appendix XXXI.

3. TNA AIR1/678/21/13/2138, "Development of Aircraft Production 1917–1918"; Ministry of Munitions, *Ministry of Munitions, The Supply of Munitions*, I:174. It was calculated, in the spring of 1917, that it took an average of

thirty-four weeks between the start of an aircraft design to bulk production, compared to sixty-four weeks for an aero-engine.

4. Ministry of Munitions, *Ministry of Munitions, The Supply of Munitions*, I:173.

5. TNA AIR1/2429/305/30/1, "Memorandum of Visit to France August 1915." The ERS was the RFC's main engine repair facility on the western front. No full history of the ERS has been produced but several short articles have appeared over the years: Fell, "The Engine Repair Shops Pont de l'Arche," 167–68; A. Williams, "The RFC/RAF Engine Repair Shops," *Cross & Cockade International Journal* 17, no. 4 (1986): 154–61, and "The RFC/RAF Engine Repair Shops Revisited," *Cross & Cockade International Journal* 23, no. 1 (1992): 42–46.

6. The Admiralty was responsible for the design and production of RNAS aircraft.

7. The full story of British aircraft and aero-engine production lies outside the scope of this study; however, it is covered in some detail in: Ministry of Munitions, *Ministry of Munitions, The Supply of Munitions*, I:39–186; Jones, *War in the Air*, 3:251–301; TNA AIR1/678/21/13/2186, "Aircraft Design and Production 1914–1918;" and TNA AIR1/678/21/13/2138, "The Development of Aircraft Production."

8. TNA AIR1/678/21/13/2186, "Design and Supply of Aircraft."

9. P. Hare, *Aeroplanes of the Royal Aircraft Factory* (Marlborough, UK: Crowood Press, 1999), 35.

10. The Burbidge Committee was instigated by the Army Council following allegations made in Parliament by Noel Pemberton Billing, a recently elected MP and the founder of Pemberton-Billing Ltd. (later Supermarine Aviation Works Ltd.), about the Royal Aircraft Factory and the unsuitability of the B.E.2 design for employment on the western front.

11. The Bailhache Committee was established to investigate Pemberton Billing's further allegations about the deficient management of the RFC.

12. Macmillan, *Brancker*, 123. The report of the Burbidge Committee, together with the Air Board's response, was published in *Flight*, 3 August 1916, 650–53. The Interim Report of the Bailhache Committee was published in *Flight*, 17 August 1916, 696–99, and the Final Report in *Flight*, 28 December 1916, 1145–47, 4 January 1917, 15–18, and 11 January 1917, 39–45. According to Brancker, "Never was there a more useless waste of time and energy in the middle of a great war."

13. Hare, *Aeroplanes of the Royal Aircraft Factory*, 135.

14. IWM73/183/1, Papers of Sir Sefton Brancker, "Some Notes on Supply." Brancker spent much of the war in a variety of senior appointments within the War Office, initially as deputy director of Military Aeronautics and later as director of Air Organisation, responsible for the support of the RFC in the

field, including the supply of aircraft and pilots. As such, he had an extremely close and productive working relationship with Trenchard during the most critical periods of 1916 and 1917.

15. Macmillan, *Brancker*, 100.

16. Ibid., 146.

17. Ibid., 150.

18. Ibid., 78–79. Brancker alleged that this led to some parts, rejected as unfit for War Office contracts, being incorporated in naval machines.

19. TNA AIR1/678/21/13/2138, "Development of Aircraft Production." At that time (June 1917) there were just forty-six service squadrons in France.

20. TNA AIR1/520/16/11/1, "Organisation and Expansion of the RFC and RAF in France." In accordance with General Haig's submissions of 15 June and 16 November 1916, this comprised seventy-six squadrons in France, ten squadrons in other theaters of war, ten long-range bombing squadrons, and ten Home Defence squadrons. It was assessed that there would need to be a corresponding increase in the number of reserve squadrons (for training purposes) from thirty-two to ninety-five.

21. AIR1/686/21/13/2252, "Statistical data of the R.F.C. and R.A.F." By October 1918, monthly production was slightly more than 3,800 airplanes but only 3,400 aero-engines.

22. TNA AIR1/678/21/13/2138, "Development of Aircraft Production," 147. In August 1916 the works strength of Rolls Royce was 3,276 with 24 percent dilution. By the armistice the dilution rate had increased to 39 percent on a total complement of 8,342.

23. Ministry of Munitions, *Ministry of Munitions, The Supply of Munitions*, I:79.

24. "History of the Aeronautical Inspection Department 1914–1918," RAF Museum TH/81/50; B. Robertson, "An AID to Quality," *Aeroplane Monthly*, November 1993, 4–66.

25. Bernard Isaac, "On the Standardisation of Aircraft Parts," *The Aeroplane*, 20 December 1916, 1188–89.

26. TNA AIR1/1284/204/11/27, "AID Report on Visit to Squadrons in France, 26 April 1916."

27. TNA AIR1/2302/215/12, "Correspondence and Data: Department of Aircraft Production." The other four most numerous types delivered in 1917 and 1918 were Sopwith Camel (2,116); S.E.5a (1,998); Bristol Fighter (934); and DH9 (789).

28. Bruce, *The Aeroplanes*, 458.

29. J. M. Bruce, *AW FK8—Windsock Data File 64* (Berkhamsted, UK: Albatros Publications, 1997), 7–8.

30. TNA AIR1/731/176/6/18, "Work Completed for Year." The R.E.8 was similar in configuration to the B.E.2c, albeit that the observer sat behind the pilot

with a much improved field of fire. A two-seat, single-bay tractor biplane, the R.E.8 had a faster top speed (102 mph compared to 72 mph), substantially greater payload, and higher operational ceiling. It was a robust and reliable design that gave good service, although it was not a forgiving aircraft in the hands of a novice pilot.

31. Bruce, *The Aeroplanes*, 459. Brigadier-General Brooke-Popham wrote to the director of Aviation Equipment on 11 August 1916 listing twelve modifications that had been made at Candas and identifying twelve more that were considered necessary.

32. TNA AIR1/731/176/6/18, "Work Completed for Year." The order also required the Factory to provide twenty-five sets of spares, the intention being to provide sufficient machines and spares to get the first squadron overseas while providing sufficient machines to train pilots for the machines being produced on contract.

33. Bruce, *The Aeroplanes*, 460.

34. TNA AIR1/731/176/6/18, "Work Completed for Year."

35. TNA AIR1/1144/204/28, "Minutes of the Progress & Allocation Committee, 26 Feb 17."

36. TNA AIR1/2101/207/28/19, "Department of Aeronautical Supplies Tenth Report, 12 May 1917."

37. Bruce, *The Aeroplanes*, 458–64. A total of 4,278 R.E.8s were built by seven manufacturers.

38. Jones, *War in the Air*, Appendix XLI, 162–63. A total of 1,913 R.E.8s were recorded on RAF strength at the armistice, together with 2,996 RAF4a engines. Some two thousand R.E.8s and six hundred RAF4as had therefore been struck off in two years.

39. Williams, "The Engine Repair Shops," 61.

40. TNA AIR1/678/21/13/2138, "Development of Aircraft Production 1917–1918," 47–48.

41. Ministry of Munitions, *Ministry of Munitions, The Supply of Munitions*, I:69.

42. Data drawn from C. G. Jefford, *RAF Squadrons* (Shrewsbury, UK: Airlife, 1988), and TNA AIR1/1155/204/5/2429, "Quarterly Returns of Engines Held by RFC in the Field."

43. TNA MUN4/6650, "Aeronautical Supplies: Output of Aeroplanes, August 1914–1919." The RAF4a was also fitted to the R.E.7 and B.E.12, but not in any significant numbers.

44. TNA AIR1/2101/207/28/19, "Department of Aeronautical Supplies 16th Report, 23 June 1917, and 18th Report, dated 7 Jul 1917."

45. Bruce, *The Aeroplanes*, 174–79. The 8-cylinder, 200 hp Arab featured a cast aluminum engine case and aluminum cylinders. Considerable manufacturing problems were experienced with these castings. In addition, it was found

necessary to make a substantial number of modifications to the gear wheels, propeller shafts, pump, and cylinder blocks. The Bristol Fighters allocated to the army reconnaissance squadrons were equipped with the Rolls Royce Falcon, which had fewer manufacturing or reliability problems, although production consistently lagged demand.

46. TNA AIR1/2101/207/28/19, "Department of Aeronautical Supplies 12th Report, 26 May 1917."

47. This was still the view as late as August 1917 when the Fifth Sea Lord commented that "we had no right to produce 1,400 R.E.8s if Bristol Fighters could be made available." TNA AIR1/678/21/13/2138, "Development of Aircraft Production 1917–1918," 61–64.

48. TNA MUN4/6650, "Aeronautical Supplies: Output of Aeroplanes August 1914–1919."

49. TNA AIR1/2101/207/28/19, "Department of Aeronautical Supplies 12th Report, 11 October 1917."

50. TNA AIR 1/2304/215/13, "Minutes of Progress & Allocation Committee."

51. Ibid.

52. RAF Museum B2045, "Index to DMA Alteration Sheets."

53. TNA AIR1/678/21/13/2138, "Development of Aircraft Production 1917–1918," 47–48.

54. Liddell Hart Centre for Military Archives, Brooke-Popham Papers 1/4, "Staff College Notes."

55. TNA AIR1/2302/215/12, "Correspondence and Data: Department of Aircraft Production."

56. TNA AIR1/3/4/26/18, "Operations Correspondence."

57. Ibid.

58. Johns flew as a pilot with No. 55 Squadron on the western front before being shot down and captured in September 1918. He is better known, of course, as the author of *Biggles*. The debate erupted in 1933, following Johns' favorable review of the type under the title "Planes of History." This led to a heated exchange of correspondence both for and against the aircraft. The debate was renewed by Trevor Mellor-Ellis, "Four Thoughts: In Praise of Harry Tate," *Over the Front* 12, no. 2 (Summer 1997): 166–67 and Alan Rowe, "The RE8 Controversy Revisited," *The 1914–1918 Journal*, 2001, 64–70. In general, those who had flown the aircraft operationally spoke more favorably than those who had encountered it only in the training environment.

59. Jones, *War in the Air*, 6:99.

60. "No. 253 RFC—An Interview with Mr. W. Smyrk," *The 1914–1918 Journal*, 1970, 55–68.

61. Liddell Hart Centre for Military Archives, Brooke-Popham 1/4, "Staff College Notes: Miscellaneous Statistics." Of this total, the RAF4a represented 14 percent in 1917 and 11 percent in 1918.

62. Henshaw, appendix II to *The Sky*.

63. TNA AIR1/1112/204/5/1897, "Work Summary and Statistical Returns: Aeroplane Supply Depots."

64. Bruce, *The Aeroplanes*, 543.

65. Judge, *Automobile and Aircraft Engines*, 396, Table LXXV. For example, the 200 hp Hispano-Suiza was rated at 2.67 lb per bhp compared to 4.17 lb for the RAF4a.

66. TNA AIR1/2302/215/10, "Output Figures for Airframes and Engines." In addition to complete engines, engine parts were produced by at least eleven French manufacturers, including Brasier, Peugeot, SCAP, Aries, Chenard & Walcker, Mayen, Fives Lilles, Le Flaive, Hispano-Suiza, Delaunay-Belleville, and Salmson.

67. On 30 June 1918 there were 500 Wolseley Viper and 772 Hispano-Suiza 200 hp engines (657 French-built and 115 English-built) on the western front. TNA AIR1/1155/204/5/2428–2429, "Quarterly Returns of Engines."

68. Jones, *War in the Air*, Appendix XXXII.

69. TNA AIR10/249, "Instruction Book for the Hispano-Suiza."

70. Jones, *War in the Air*, 3:266.

71. Jones, *War in the Air*, 6:31–37. Of the 8,000 engines, 3,500 were to be allocated to Britain, 3,000 to France, and 1,500 to Russia.

72. A. Lumsden, *British Piston Aero-Engines and Their Aircraft* (Shrewsbury, UK: Airlife, 1994), 232.

73. Ibid., 156–57.The most common gearing was 1,500, which meant that the propeller turned at 1,500 rpm when the engine was turning at 2,000 rpm. The type 8B was commonly known by the RFC as the "French 1500 Geared Engine."

74. TNA MUN4/6650, "Aeronautical Supplies: Output of Aeroplanes, August 1914–1919."

75. TNA AIR1/1145/204/5/2355, "Minutes of Meetings of Progress and Allocation Committee, 11 March 1918."

76. Jones, *War in the Air*, 6:32.

77. Lumsden, *British Piston Aero-Engines*, 157.

78. TNA AIR1/1100/204/5/1798–1808, "Reports on Hispano-Suiza Engines."

79. TNA AIR1/1411/204/28/43, "Minutes of Second Monthly Hispano-Suiza Meeting."

80. TNA AIR1/1411/204/28/43, "Miscellaneous Technical Correspondence."

81. TNA AIR1/1100/204/5/1799, "Reports and Miscellaneous Correspondence."

82. TNA AIR1/1100/204/5/1800, "Reports and Miscellaneous Correspondence." Of this total, 13.6 percent had broken connecting rods—indicative of lubrication failure.

83. TNA AIR1/1100/204/5/1802, "Reports and Miscellaneous Correspondence on Hispano-Suiza Aero-engines, 1 August 1918."

84. Many of these measures were incorporated in a Ministry of Munitions Confidential Document, "Hispano-Suiza – Notes for Squadrons in the Field," issued in September 1918, TNA AIR1/1590/204/82/83.

85. TNA AIR1/1100/204/5/1798, "Reports and Miscellaneous Correspondence on Hispano-Suiza Aero-engines, HQ RAF correspondence with ERS, 23 April 1918."

86. Liddell Hart Centre for Military Archives, Brooke-Popham Papers 1/4, "Staff College Notes."

87. TNA AIR1/37/15/1/250, "Expeditionary Force Engine Returns." By October 1918, there were over 450 unserviceable Hispano-Suiza engines awaiting repair at the ERS. The previous month just over 170 repaired Hispano-Suiza were issued but more than 280 engines were received for repair.

88. TNA AIR1/1158/204/5/2483, "Reports and Miscellaneous Correspondence." The oil tank was rigidly fixed to a portion of the fuselage that was constantly being warped by the engine's torque, causing the seams to break and the tank to leak. The vent pipe from the top of the radiator frequently froze, creating a steam lock and consequent overheating. The gear wheels and pipelines of the Constantinesco gear were exposed to the cold and airflow, impeding lubrication and straining the mechanism.

89. Ibid.

90. TNA AIR1/1101/204/5/1806, "Reports and Miscellaneous Correspondence."

91. Ministry of Munitions, *Ministry of Munitions, The Supply of Munitions*, I:77.

92. TNA AIR1/1831/204/205/2, "No. 87 Squadron Record Book."

93. TNA AIR1/1101/204/5/1808, "Reports and Miscellaneous Correspondence, Brooke-Popham to Air Ministry, 26 October 1918."

94. Ibid.

95. TNA AIR1/2411/303/4/28, "Minutes of Progress & Allocation Committee, 9 August 1918."

96. TNA AIR1/1101/204/5/1808, "Reports and Miscellaneous Correspondence."

97. "The Hispano-Suiza Aeroengine," (Farnborough, UK: Royal Aircraft Establishment, 1968)—based on a translation of articles originally published in *Zeitschrift fur Flugtechnik und Motorluftschiffart*, vol. VIII (1917) and vol. IX (1918).

98. TNA AIR1/2423/305/18/28, "Charts Showing Distribution of Aeroplanes."

99. Ibid.

100. TNA AIR1/9/15/1/31/1, "Loose Minute, 21 May 1918."

101. Ibid.

Chapter 4. 1916—The Somme

1. This analysis focuses on the RFC as a whole, rather than individual squadrons. Throughout the fighting, new units joined—and others rotated out of—the line as required. In addition, a number of squadrons, although not directly based on the Somme, undertook diversionary attacks to draw German aircraft away from the area.

2. BEF, *SS 515, Extracts From German Documents and Correspondence No. 2* (BEF: Central Distribution System, 1916).

3. J. Sheldon, *The German Army on the Somme* (Barnsley, UK: Pen & Sword, 2005), 339.

4. BEF, *SS 564, Extracts From German Documents and Correspondence* (BEF: Central Distribution System, 1916).

5. Reichsarchiv, *Der Weltkrieg 1914 bis 1918: Band X, Die Operationen des Jahres 1916 bis zum Wechsel in der Obersten Heeresleitung* (Berlin: Mittler und Sohn, 1936), 374–75.

6. P. Hart, *Bloody April* (London: Weidenfeld & Nicolson, 2005), 32. These changes, intended to wrest air superiority from the RFC, included a substantial reinforcement in the number of German aircraft on the Somme, the regrouping of fighter assets into dedicated units (Jagdstaffel), and the introduction of new types—such as the Albatros DII, which rapidly proved a match for the RFC's DH2 and F.E.2b fighters.

7. BEF, *SS 553, Experience of the German First Army in the Somme Battle 24 June–26 November 1916* (BEF: Central Distribution System, 1917).

8. Jones, *War in the Air*, 2:252. Authors detailing the RFC's successful contribution to the Somme offensive include P. Mead, *The Eye in the Air* (London: HMSO, 1983), 73–85; R. Barker, *The Royal Flying Corps in France: from Mons to the Somme* (London: Constable, 1994), 156–225; C. Duffy, *Through German Eyes: The British and The Somme 1916* (London: Weidenfeld & Nicolson, 2006), 305–19; and W. Philpott, *Bloody Victory* (London: Little Brown, 2009), 268–71.

9. D. Pisano and T. Dietz, *Legend, Memory and the Great War in the Air* (Seattle, WA: University of Washington Press, 1992), 54–60.

10. Including, for example, P. Hart, *Somme Success* (Barnsley, UK: Pen & Sword, 2001) and, most recently, E. R. Hooton, *War over the Trenches* (Horsham, UK: Ian Allen, 2010).

11. G. Sheffield, *The Somme* (London: Cassell, 2003), 157–60.

12. Edmonds, *Military Operations France and Belgium, 1916*, 1:25–27.

13. TNA AIR1/520/16/11/1, "Organisation and Expansion of the RFC and RAF in France."

14. This data is drawn largely from War Office, *Statistics,* and the original data summaries (issued from late 1916 until the armistice) available in TNA WO394/1–20, "Statistical Abstracts."

15. Hart, *Bloody April*, 33–34.

16. War Office, *Statistics*, and TNA WO 394/1–20, "Statistical Abstracts of Information." This excludes the single RNAS fighter squadron (No. 8) attached to the RFC from October 1916.

17. This data is drawn from a variety of sources including War Office, *Statistics*, and TNA AIR1/926/204/5/915, "Aeroplane and Engine Casualties: Return of RFC in France."

18. TNA AIR1/759/204/4/139, "Summary of Work Carried Out by RFC Wings and Squadrons."

19. War Office, *Statistics*, and TNA AIR1/926/204/5/915, "Aeroplane and Engine Casualties: Return of RFC in France."

20. RAFM/Trenchard 76/1/6, Loose Minute, Trenchard to Brancker, dated 30 May 1916.

21. F. Sykes, "Developments of Military Aviation," *Flight*, 14 February 1914, 170–73.

22. Jones, *War in the Air*, 2:253.

23. Macmillan, *Brancker*, 117–18.

24. A. Bott, *An Airman's Outings with the RFC, June–December 1916* (London: William Blackwood, 1917), 6–7.

25. P. Dye, "Logistic Lessons from the Past," *Air Clues*, September 1996, 347–51.

26. TNA AIR1/942/204/5/975, "Organisation of and Personnel for Aircraft Depots"; Macmillan, *Brancker*, 117.

27. TNA AIR1/960/204/5/1043, "Reports of RFC Manpower in France." The majority of personnel employed by the RFC on the western front belonged to the technical trades. Data prepared for Lieutenant-General Sir Henry Lawson's review in November 1916 of men employed in the fighting area revealed that there were over 11,000 engineering and logistic tradesmen in a total RFC strength of slightly over 17,000 (officers and other ranks) on the western front.

28. This data is drawn from a combination of places including War Office, *Statistics* (for overall RFC manpower figures), TNA AIR1/927/204/5/916, Part I and Part II, "Squadron Ration Field Returns," TNA AIR1/915/204/5/862–867, "Monthly and Fortnightly Returns Rendered to War Office of RFC Casualties and Strengths, Units in France," and TNA AIR1/1022/204/5/1400, "Fortnightly Casualty and Monthly Trade Strength Returns." Aircraft strength is drawn from the Daily Returns held in TNA AIR1/759/204/4/139–140, "Summary of work carried out by RFC Wings and Squadrons," and TNA AIR1/837/204/5/279, "Summary of RFC Work and Operations in France."

29. TNA AIR1/678/21/13/2/38, "Development of Aircraft Production," 1–3.

30. Baring, *Flying Corps Headquarters*. Baring, Trenchard's personal assistant, recorded numerous visits by Trenchard to the frontline squadrons and depots

and the high level of effort directed at solving various technical and supply problems.

31. RAFM MFC/76/1/4, Trenchard Memorandum, dated 17 Apr 18.

32. TNA AIR1/529/16/12/75. These changes were first proposed by the then Brigadier-General Trenchard in September 1915 in order to create a decentralized supply organization with the flexibility to support mobile operations.

33. Jones, *War in the Air*, 2:148–49. These changes came about on 12 March 1916.

34. Ibid., 2:189.

35. TNA AIR1/911/204/5/832, "Assistant Director of Aeronautical Equipment."

36. Ibid.

37. This data is drawn from the RFC Daily reports held in TNA AIR1/759, AIR1/760, and AIR1/762. "Flying Hours" includes all flying—both operational and training—conducted on the western front.

38. TNA AIR1/759–762, "RFC Work Summaries 1916."

39. Edmonds, *Military Operations France and Belgium, 1916*, 1:304–5.

40. Jones, *War in the Air*, 2:198.

41. Ibid., 199; R. Prior and T. Wilson, *The Somme* (New Haven, CT: Yale University Press, 2005), 68. A problem that was exacerbated by the bad weather immediately prior to the assault, poor maps, and the limited priority allocated to counter-battery fire.

42. Jones, *War in the Air*, 2:201.

43. Ibid., 2:210.

44. Ibid., 2:224.

45. J. E. Edmonds, *Military Operations France and Belgium, 1916*, (London, Macmillan, 1938) 2:90–93.

46. Jones, *War in the Air*, 2:234.

47. Reichsarchiv, *Die Operationen des Jahres 1916*, 386.

48. Edmonds, *Military Operations France and Belgium, 1916*, 2:141–48.

49. Jones, *War in the Air*, 2:245–46.

50. Edmonds, *Military Operations France and Belgium, 1916*, 2:250–65.

51. Jones, *War in the Air*, 2:268.

52. Edmonds, *Military Operations France and Belgium, 1916*, 2:373–75; Reichsarchiv, *Der Weltkrieg 1914 bis 1918: Band XI, Die Kriegführung im Herbst 1916 und im Winter 1916/17; vom Wechsel in der Obersten Heeresleitung bis zum Entschluss zum Rückzug in die Siegfried-Stellung* (Berlin: Mittler und Sohn, 1938), 75.

53. Jones, *War in the Air*, 2:296.

54. Ibid., 2:313–14.

55. Edmonds, *Military Operations France and Belgium, 1916*, 2:514–26; Jones, *War in the Air*, 2:323–24, 2:471–72.

56. Reichsarchiv, *Die Kriegführung im Herbst 1916 und im Winter 1916/17*, 109–10.

57. Ibid., 324–25.

58. TNA AIR1/759–762, "RFC Daily Returns."

59. The RFC also benefitted from a rigid policy of standardization that ensured each squadron was only equipped with a single type or model of aircraft— unlike both the French and the Germans, who frequently mixed the types operated by an individual unit, greatly complicating the supply and engineering challenges.

60. Hooton, *War over the Trenches*, 104. By comparison, on 7 August 1916, the serviceability of aircraft attached to the German First Army was 88 percent and those with the Second Army only 77 percent.

61. Data taken from TNA AIR1/1233/204/6/12, "No. 9 Squadron Record Book."

62. This was part of a wider policy to increase all squadron establishments during June and July 1916.

63. F. Libby, *Horses Don't Fly* (New York: Arcade Publishing, 2012), 167.

64. TNA AIR1/29/15/1/142, "Life of Engines."

65. TNA AIR1/8/15/1/7, Brooke-Popham, "Notes on System of Supply," 3.

66. Calculated on the basis that an average aero-engine would be replaced after fifty flying hours. This is a conservative figure, as many engines would be replaced earlier than this because of technical failure or other causes of wastage.

67. TNA AIR1/911/204/5/832, "Assistant Director of Aeronautical Equipment." An analysis provided by Brigadier-General Brooke-Popham in April 1916 showed that the average life of a B.E.2c in the field struck off through all causes was 71 flying hours (132 days), while the average life of an aircraft struck off through deterioration only was 127 flying hours.

68. TNA AIR1/998/204/5/1242–1243, "Duplicate Returns"; TNA AIR1/2302/215/12, "Correspondence: Department of Aircraft Production."

69. Frontline strength grew from 206 aircraft in January to 624 aircraft by December.

70. TNA WO394/1, "Statistical Abstracts." By 1 October 1916, over 23,000 tons of airplane parts and associated equipment (less complete aircraft) had been shipped to France since August 1914. By the end of 1916 the total shipped since the start of the war amounted to more than 30,000 tons.

71. RAF Museum MFC/76/1/26, "Preparatory Measures to be Taken by Armies and Corps before Undertaking Offensive Operations on a Large Scale, 24 November 1916."

72. TNA AIR1/1122/204/5/2097, "Petrol & Oil Supplies." In the first months of the war the RFC's consumption of aviation spirit was no more than ten thousand gallons per month.

73. TNA AIR1/529/16/12/70, "Organisation and Establishment of RFC Headquarters France."

74. Prior and Wilson, *The Somme*, 302.

75. Sheffield, *The Somme*, 27.

76. Quoted in Cuneo, *Winged Mars*, 266.

77. Ibid., 284

78. Jones, *War in the Air*, vol. 2, Appendix VIII; Sheffield, *The Somme*, 7.

Chapter 5. 1917—Arras and Third Ypres

1. Jones, *War in the Air*, vol. 2, Appendix IV, 457–59, and vol. 3, Appendix V, 414–18. The total for Third Ypres does include, however, five attached naval squadrons (ninety single-seat fighters).

2. For example, A. Morris, *Bloody April* (London: Jarrolds, 1967); N. Franks, R. Guest, and F. Bailey, *Bloody April, Black September* (London: Grub Street, 1995); and P. Hart, *Bloody April: Slaughter in the Skies over Arras* (London: Weidenfeld & Nicholson, 2005).

3. Jones, *War in the Air*, 3:332–79.

4. C. Falls, *Military Operations France and Belgium, 1917* (London: Macmillan, 1940), 1:171–79.

5. Jones, *War in the Air*, 3:332–34.

6. Ibid., 3:320.

7. TNA AIR1/68/15/9/109, "Stores, Transport and Armament Correspondence."

8. TNA AIR1/68/15/9/109, "OC No. 8 Squadron to HQ RNAS Dunkerque, 12 January 1917;" TNA AIR1/68/15/9/109, "OC No. 8 Squadron to HQ RNAS Dunkerque, 29 December 1916." The system of providing small consumable spares in steel bins, delivered routinely to the squadron from the main stores, was still in use with the RAF eighty years later.

9. Jones, *War in the Air*, 3:332.

10. Ibid., 3:343–44.

11. Ibid., 3:341–42. Such as the attack mounted against the Ath railway junction on 6 April, when all three aircraft were shot down, or the bombing of Prince Rupprecht's headquarters on 8 April when four out of the six aircraft involved were brought down.

12. Falls, *Military Operations France and Belgium, 1917*, 1:300.

13. Jones, *War in the Air*, 3:345.

14. R. Doughty, *Pyrrhic Victory: French Strategy and Operations in the Great War* (Cambridge, MA: Harvard University Press, 2005), 352–54. The failure of General Robert Nivelle's offensive had become apparent by 20 April. Although some gains were achieved, the extravagant expectations of success were not realized.

15. Jones, *War in the Air*, 3:370. Of course, this needs to be set against the more than 150,000 casualties suffered by the British Army over the same period.

16. Reichsarchiv, *Der Weltkrieg 1914 bis 1918: Band XII, Die Kriegführung im Frühjahr 1917* (Berlin: Mittler und Sohn, 1939), 262.

17. Falls, *Military Operations France and Belgium, 1917*, 1:471–81.

18. Reichsarchiv, *Die Kriegführung im Frühjahr 1917*, 265–66.

19. Henshaw, *The Sky*, 150–74.

20. Data taken from TNA AIR1/2302/215/10, "Output Figures for Airframes and Engines," and TNA AIR1/998/204/5/1242–1243, "Duplicate Returns."

21. G. Sheffield, *Forgotten Victory* (London: Headline, 2001), 190.

22. Data taken from TNA AIR1/509/16/3/54, TNA AIR1/613/16/15/305, and War Office, *Statistics*.

23. TNA AIR1/686/21/13/2248, "Various Air Statistics." It should be noted that the 1916 figures represent complete aircraft (with engines), whereas from June 1917 they represent aircraft "passed test."

24. TNA AIR1/686/21/13/2248, "Various Air Statistics." This total excludes aircraft for new squadrons.

25. Wastage figures are drawn from TNA AIR1/998/204/5/1242–1243, "Duplicate Returns."

26. Data from TNA AIR1/998/204/5/1242–1243, "Duplicate Returns."

27. Jones, *War in the Air*, 4:202. Reconstruction data from TNA AIR1/1084/204/5/1721, "Reorganisation of Aircraft Depots," and TNA AIR1/29/15/1/142, "Life of Engines." Combat wastage from Henshaw, Appendix II to *The Sky*.

28. M. Davis, "Salvage: 1917 Orders, 2 Brigade RFC," *Cross & Cockade International Journal* 39, no. 1 (2008): 23–24. Orders issued by HQ II Brigade, 30 May 1917.

29. N. J. Severs, "Courage on the Ground," *Cross & Cockade International Journal* 39, no. 2 (2008): 90–93.

30. TNA AIR1/837/204/5/279, "Summary of RFC Work & Operations."

31. Serviceability data from TNA AIR1/837/204/5/279, "Summary of RFC Work & Operations."

32. N. Macmillan, *Into the Blue* (London: Jarrolds, 1969), 77.

33. Data drawn from RFC daily returns held in TNA AIR1/837/204/5/279 and TNA AIR1/759/204/4/139—AIR1/762/204/4/170. An indication of the difficult supply situation was the decision to issue No. 45 Squadron with Nieuport two-seaters (previously withdrawn from frontline service as obsolete) when it proved impossible to sustain the established number of Sopwith 1½ Strutters. (Macmillan, *Into the Blue*, 71.)

34. TNA AIR1/8/15/1, "Progress of the RAF: Secretary of State's Statement to the House of Commons."

35. TNA AIR10/774 and RAF Museum, RAFM 002811, "Spare Parts for Aeroplane Engines—Types RAF4a."

36. "An RAF Engine Hospital," *Flight*, 3 July 1919, 882–84.

37. D. Childs, "British Tanks 1915–1918, Manufacture and Employment" (PhD thesis, University of Glasgow, 1996), 122.

38. Ministry of Munitions, *Ministry of Munitions, The Supply of Munitions*, I:61.

39. TNA AIR1/1144/207/28, "93rd Meeting," 12 June 1917.

40. TNA AIR1/837/204/5/279, "Summary of RFC Work."

41. TNA AIR1/1242/204/6/55, "No. 9 Squadron Record Book January–December 1917."

42. J. E. Edmonds, *Military Operations France and Belgium, 1917* (London: Macmillan, 1948), 2:32–35.

43. Jones, *War in the Air*, vol. 4, Appendix III; Edmonds, *Military Operations France and Belgium, 1917*, 2:109–12.

44. Edmonds, *Military Operations France and Belgium, 1917*, 2:115–17.

45. Ibid., 2:54.

46. Quoted in J. Sheldon, *The German Army at Passchendaele* (Barnsley, UK: Pen & Sword, 2007), 4–11.

47. Reichsarchiv, *Die Kriegführung im Frühjahr 1917*, 438–39.

48. Henshaw, *The Sky*, 185–90.

49. Jones, *War in the Air*, 4:134.

50. Data drawn from TNA AIR1/2302/215/12, "Correspondence: Department of Aircraft Production."

51. Reichsarchiv, *Die Kriegführung im Frühjahr 1917*, 529–36.

52. Edmonds, *Military Operations France and Belgium, 1917*, vol. 2; P. Liddle, ed., *Passchendaele in Perspective* (London: Leo Cooper, 1997); R. Prior and T. Wilson, *Passchendaele: The Untold Story* (New Haven, CT: Yale University Press, 1996).

53. Jones, *War in the Air*, 4:142. The reduction in capability that this created was met by the French Air Service.

54. Jones, *War in the Air*, 4:152–55.

55. Macmillan, *Brancker*, 117–18.

56. Jones, *War in the Air*, 4:158–59.

57. Ibid., 4:163.

58. Described in more detail in Chapter 6.

59. Jones, *War in the Air*, 4:172.

60. Quoted in Sheldon, *The German Army at Passchendaele*, 124–25.

61. Edmonds, *Military Operations France and Belgium, 1917*, 2:383–85.

62. Reichsarchiv, *Der Weltkrieg 1914 bis 1918: Band XIII, Die Kriegführung im Sommer und Herbst 1917. Die Ereignisse ausserhalb der Westfront bis November 1918* (Berlin: Mittler und Sohn, 1942), 63–64.

63. Jones, *War in the Air*, 4:180–90.

64. Ibid., 4:190–196.

65. Edmonds, *Military Operations France and Belgium, 1917*, 2:289–95.

66. Jones, *War in the Air*, 4:204–6.

67. Quoted in Sheldon, *The German Army at Passchendaele*, 292–93.

68. Data drawn from TNA AIR1/837/204/5/279, "Summary of RFC Work."

69. Reichsarchiv, *Die Kriegführung im Sommer und Herbst 1917*, 309–13.

70. Flying hour data drawn from TNA AIR1/837/204/5/279, manpower data drawn from TNA WO73/97–108.

71. Data drawn from TNA AIR1/998/204/5/1242–1243, "Duplicate Returns."

72. TNA AIR1/29/15/1/142, AIR1/1084/204/5/1721, and AIR1/998/204/5/1242–1243, "Duplicate Returns."

73. F. Archer, "Sergeant Observer Frederick Archer," in *Voices in Flight*, ed. A. Malinovska and M. Joslyn (Barnsley, UK: Pen & Sword, 2006), 112–13.

74. TNA AIR1/1242/204/6/55, "9 Squadron Record Book."

75. Jones, *War in the Air*, 4:417.

76. J. E. Edmonds and H. R. Davies, *Military Operations Italy, 1915–19* (London: HMSO, 1949), 300–301.

77. Jones, *War in the Air*, 6:273–76.

78. N. Macmillan, *Offensive Patrol* (London: Jarrolds, 1973), 57. There were two main reasons for not sending the squadrons by air: first, the lack of prepared aerodromes en route, particularly from the French frontier to Milan; and secondly, the fact that it was quicker to rail the stores than send them by road (recognizing that operations could not commence until the stores and mechanics arrived). Squadron Leader J. J. Breen, "War Experiences," in *AP 1308* (London: Air Ministry, 1926–27), 21–22.

79. No. 28 Squadron (Sopwith Camel), No. 34 Squadron (R.E.8), No. 42 Squadron (R.E.8), No. 45 Squadron (Sopwith Camel), and No. 66 Squadron (Sopwith Camel).

80. J. De La Ferte, *The Forgotten Ones* (London: Hutchinson, 1961), 78–79.

81. Breen, *AP 1308*, 22.

82. TNA AIR1/1072/204/5/1644, "Supply of Aeroplanes for Italy."

83. Liddell Hart Centre for Military Archives, Brooke-Popham Papers 1/8.

84. TNA AIR1/1072/204/5/1644, "Supply of Aeroplanes for Italy."

85. Macmillan, *Offensive Patrol*, 58. The excellent performance of the squadrons in emptying each train in an average of three hours was confirmed by Webb-Bowen in a personal memo to Trenchard: TNA AIR1/1072/204/5/1644, "Supply of Aeroplanes for Italy."

86. Macmillan, *Offensive Patrol*, 57–58.

87. J. R. Farmer, "What approach did the British Army take to solving the logistic problems related to operations on the Italian Front between deployment in 1917 and the conclusion of hostilities in 1918?" (MA dissertation, University of Birmingham, UK, 2006).

88. TNA AIR1/1664/204/98/33, "51 Wing Summary of Work 1917–1918."

89. Macmillan, *Offensive Patrol*, 87. The resources allocated to 51 Wing were modest by the standards of the western front, even allowing for lower wastage rates (in aircrew and machines).
90. TNA AIR1/1664/204/98/33, "HQ RFC/VII Brigade Correspondence, January 1918."
91. Ibid.
92. War Office, *Statistics*, 506.
93. K. E. Boulding, *Conflict and Defense: A General Theory* (New York: Harper & Rowe, 1962), 245–47. Kenneth Boulding argued that the amount of power that a nation could bring to bear in any part of the world depended on geographic distance.
94. Macmillan, *Offensive Patrol*, 87; Tennant, *In the Clouds*, 59–60.

Chapter 6. 1918—Logistics on the Move

1. Hooton, *War over the Trenches*, 198.
2. TNA AIR1/942/204/5/975, "Organisation of and Personnel for Aircraft Depots."
3. Air-based supply would not be a practical proposition for many decades until aircraft with the necessary load-carrying capacity emerged. Even in the Second World War, the volume of matériel involved was too high for air supply to be routinely employed.
4. Liddell Hart, *Thoughts on War*, 78.
5. Cooper, "Blueprint for Confusion," 440.
6. TNA AIR1/8/15/1/7, "Notes on System of Supply for RAF in France."
7. TNA AIR10/84, "RAF Periodical Strength Returns." This details the periodical strength returns required by the Air Ministry following the cessation of the Army reporting system.
8. TNA AIR1/926/204/5/915, "Aeroplane and Engine Casualties"; TNA AIR1/998/204/5/1242–1243, "Duplicate Returns." The 1917 total was inflated to some extent by the frontline replacement program, which saw most squadrons re-equip with new types.
9. Jones, *War in the Air*, vol. 4, Appendix XIV, 260–61.
10. Ibid., 266. Salmond was appointed GOC RFC on 18 January 1918.
11. Jones, *War in the Air*, 6:23–24; Sheffield, *The Chief*, 152; M. Dean, *The Royal Air Force and Two World Wars* (London: Cassell, 1979), 32.
12. TNA AIR1/533/16/12/118, "War Establishment of RAF Parks and Depots." GOC RAF wrote to GHQ on 25 May 1918, asking for additional manpower (now that bombing operations were almost nightly), since working all day to prepare aircraft and then through the night to launch and recover them proved too great a strain.

13. These maintenance parties (comprising six tradesmen each) were first proposed in April 1918, on the basis of five for each depot.

14. These units were directly managed by the aircraft depots.

15. The units involved also included Lighthouse Sections employed to guide night bombers.

16. TNA AIR1/520/16/12/1, Part III, "Air Policy: Expansion and Organisation of the RFC and RAF"; Jones, *War in the Air*, 4:353. The original establishment comprised thirty lorries and twenty-four trailers drawn from vehicles allocated to the frontline squadrons.

17. TNA AIR1/520/16/12/1, Part III, "Air Policy: Expansion and Organisation of the RFC and RAF."

18. Jones, *War in the Air*, 4:353.

19. TNA WO73/108, "Distribution of Monthly Army Returns, March 1918."

20. Major W. A. McClaughry writing in *Australian Airmen—History of the 4th Squadron Australian Flying Corps*, ed. E. J. Richards (Melbourne: Bruce & Co., 1922), 53–58.

21. RAF Museum B2621/4, "Sir John Salmond (Draft) Autobiography," 201.

22. Jones, *War in the Air*, 4:272, 401–2.

23. RAF Museum X006–3371, Brigadier-General R. E. T. Hogg, Commander IX Brigade, Personal Diary, 3 June 1918.

24. RAF Museum B2621/4, "Sir John Salmond (Draft) Autobiography," 202.

25. Anon., "With an Army Co-operation Squadron during the German Attacks of 1918," *The Hawk*, 1931, 20–27.

26. Jones, *War in the Air*, 4:271–73.

27. Ibid., 4:292–93.

28. J. E. Edmonds, *Military Operations in France and Belgium, 1918* (London: Macmillan, 1935), 1:161–69; Reichsarchiv, *Der Weltkrieg 1914 bis 1918: Band XIV, Die Kriegführung an der Westfront im Jahre 1918* (Berlin: Mittler und Sohn, 1944), 106.

29. Reichsarchiv, *Die Kriegführung an der Westfront im Jahre 1918*, 132.

30. Jones, *War in the Air*, 4:301.

31. Anon., "With an Army Co-operation Squadron," 20.

32. Jones, *War in the Air*, 4:358–61.

33. RAF Museum B2621/4, "Sir John Salmond (Draft) Autobiography, 201."

34. TNA AIR1/1042/204/5/1495, "Reports and Supply of Bomb Carriers."

35. Reichsarchiv, *Die Kriegführung an der Westfront im Jahre 1918*, 158. The German 18 Armee lost over five thousand horses from 21 March to 31 March 1918.

36. Jones, *War in the Air*, 4:315.

37. B. E. Smythies, "War Experiences," *AP 956* (London: Air Ministry, 1923), 82.

38. Jones, *War in the Air*, 4:316.

39. Reichsarchiv, *Die Kriegführung an der Westfront im Jahre 1918*, 196–97, 184, 192, 220.

40. Ibid., 320.

41. Slessor, *Air Power and Armies*, 105.

42. Hooton, *War over the Trenches*, 208.

43. J. Cuneo, "Preparation of German Attack Aviation for the Offensive of March 1918," *Military Affairs* 7, no. 2 (1943): 69–78.

44. Quoted in B. Greenhous, "Evolution of a Close Ground-Support Role for Aircraft in World War 1," *Military Affairs* 39, no. 2 (1975): 28.

45. RAF Museum X006–3371, Brigadier-General R. E. T. Hogg, Personal Diary.

46. H. Sulzbach, *With the German Guns* (London: Leo Cooper, 1973), 154.

47. Jones, *War in the Air*, 4:338.

48. Ibid., 4:346.

49. Hooton, *War over the Trenches*, 215.

50. Jones, *War in the Air*, 4:354–55.

51. TNA WO73/108, "Manpower Return, March 1918." The Issues Section (responsible for issuing airplanes to the squadrons) was now located at St. André-aux-Bois and the Repair Section (responsible for salvage and reconstruction of airplanes and aero-engines) at Le Bahot.

52. Jones, *War in the Air*, 4:356.

53. The main stores were later relocated to a larger site at Vron.

54. Jones, *War in the Air*, 4:358.

55. TNA AIR1/1114/204/5/1950, "Monthly Demands by RFC/RAF Units in France."

56. Jones, *War in the Air*, 4:355.

57. Ibid., 4:358.

58. C. M. Burgess, *The Diary and Letters of a Fighter Pilot* (Barnsley, UK: Pen & Sword, 2008), 180.

59. Smythies, "War Experiences," 83. At least one squadron commander felt that the frequent moves over this period were injurious to efficiency, adding that that "pilots and mechanics work better when comfortable."

60. Liddell Hart Centre for Military Archives, Brooke-Popham Papers 1/4, "Staff College Notes."

61. TNA AIR1/475/15/312/201, "Letters from General Salmond to General Trenchard."

62. Jones, *War in the Air*, vol. 4, Appendix XVI; Hooton, *War over the Trenches*, 215.

63. Jones, *War in the Air*, 4:375.

64. Hooton, *War over the Trenches*, 216.

65. Jones, *War in the Air*, 4:380.

66. Ibid., 4:381–82. The RAF squadrons flew 3,240 hours, dropped 2,548 bombs, took 3,358 photographs, and fired 114,904 rounds on 12 April 1918.

67. J. E. Edmonds, *Military Operations France and Belgium, 1918* (London: Macmillan, 1937), 2:273–74.

68. Ibid., 2:358–69.

69. Ibid., 2:442–59.

70. TNA WO73/108, "Army Monthly Returns, March 1918."

71. TNA AIR1/1/4/11, "Letters Written by General Brooke-Popham." The stores represented 250 lorry-loads (approximately 750 tons).

72. Jones, *War in the Air*, 4:400–401.

73. TNA AIR1/1/4/11, "Letters Written by General Brooke-Popham."

74. Jones, *War in the Air*, 4:402–3.

75. RAFM B2621/4, "Sir John Salmond (Draft) Autobiography," 209.

76. The volume of aviation stores arriving in France, which had been growing throughout March, fell rapidly during April to half its previous level. The number of crated aircraft received in April 1918 (twelve) was by far the lowest of any month since January 1916.

77. Fell, "The Engine Repair Shops," 166.

78. TNA AIR1/678/21/13/2137, "German Night Bombing over the British Areas of the Western Front." The spares lost represented 55 percent of all holdings of cars and ambulances and 40 percent of lorries.

79. TNA AIR69/41, "Air Warfare Lecture Notes (Fourth Course)."

80. J. E. Edmonds, *Military Operations France and Belgium, 1918*, vol. 3 (London: Macmillan, 1939); Franks, Guest, and Bailey, *Bloody April*, 3.

81. M. S. Neiberg, *The Second Battle of the Marne* (Bloomington, IN: Indiana University Press, 2008), 1–7.

82. Jones, *War in the Air*, 4:415–16.

83. D. Stevenson, *With Our Backs to the Wall* (London: Allen Lane, 2011), 208.

84. Jones, *War in the Air*, 6:435–36.

85. J. P. Harris, *Amiens to the Armistice* (London: Brassey's, 1998), 87–108.

86. Jones, *War in the Air*, 6:437.

87. Reichsarchiv, *Die Kriegführung an der Westfront im Jahre 1918*, 555.

88. The relatively low explosive power of the bombs employed, coupled with the small size of the bridges involved and the nature of their construction, made it unlikely that anything other than a direct hit would be successful.

89. Reichsarchiv, *Die Kriegführung an der Westfront im Jahre 1918*, 445–46.

90. J. E. Edmonds, *Military Operations France and Belgium, 1918*, vol. 4 (London: HMSO, 1947),154–55; Harris, *Amiens to the Armistice*, 116.

91. S. F. Wise, *Canadian Airmen and the First World War* (Toronto: Toronto University Press, 1980), 135–36. On 17 August 1918, 80 Wing RAF conducted a devastating raid on Lomme airfield (occupied by Jasta 40), bombing and strafing aircraft, hangars, and personnel.

92. P. Kilduff, *Over the Battlefronts* (London: Arms & Armour Press, 1996), 133–34.

93. Slessor, *Air Power and Armies*, 184.

94. Jones, *War in the Air*, 6:456–57.

95. RAF Museum X006–3371, Brigadier-General R. E. T. Hogg, Personal Diary, 10 August 1918. No. 107 Squadron lost six DH9 aircraft on 9 August in a series of attacks on the Somme bridges.

96. J. Boff, *Winning and Losing on the Western Front* (Cambridge, UK: Cambridge University Press, 2012), 151, 163.

97. Harris, *Amiens to the Armistice*, 153–57.

98. Jones, *War in the Air*, 6:500.

99. Ibid., 512–13.

100. J. E. Edmonds, *Military Operations France and Belgium, 1918*, vol. 5 (London: HMSO, 1946), 30–45.

101. Ibid., 5:227.

102. Henshaw, *The Sky*, 447.

103. Reichsarchiv, *Die Kriegführung an der Westfront im Jahre 1918*, 720–24.

104. C. Hobson, "The First Air War: The Casualty Record," *Cross & Cockade International* 30, no. 4 (1999): 205.

105. J. Boff, "Air/Land Integration in the 100 Days: The Case of Third Army," *RAF Air Power Review*, Autumn 2009, 77–88.

106. Jones, *War in the Air*, 6:491.

107. TNA AIR1/676/21/13/1880, "Statistics of Aircraft Despatched to France."

108. TNA AIR1/35/15/1/229, "Return of Serviceable Machines in France;" TNA AIR1/1114/204/5/1950, "Monthly Demands." The size of the reserve required by 1 May 1918 was assessed to be 571 machines.

109. Brooke-Popham, "The Air Force," 49.

110. Liddell Hart Centre for Military Archives, Brooke-Popham Papers 1/4, "Staff College Notes."

111. TNA AIR69/41, "Air Warfare Lecture Notes (Fourth Course)."

112. TNA AIR1/1153/204/5/2408, "Salvage of Aeroplanes."

113. Brown, *British Logistics*, 202–3.

114. Air Ministry, *Air Publication 48—RAF Field Service Pocket Book* (London: Air Ministry, 1918), 31–32.

115. Edmonds, *Military Operations France and Belgium, 1918*, 5:245–46.

116. TNA AIR1/8/15/1/7, "Notes on System of Supply for the Royal Air Force," 3.

117. Henniker, *Transportation on the Western Front*, 461.

118. TNA AIR1/533/16/12/118, "War Establishment."

119. TNA AIR1/8/15/1/7, "Notes on System of Supply for the Royal Air Force," 2.

120. Breen, "War Experiences," 25.

121. TNA AIR1/8/15/1/7, "Notes on System of Supply for the RAF in France," 2.

122. TNA AIR1/1130/204/5/2171, "Location Lists."

123. J. Boff, "Logistics during the Hundred Days Campaign, 1918: British Third Army," *Journal of the Society for Army Historical Research* 89 (2011): 321.

124. Brown, *British Logistics*, 197.

125. J. F. C. Fuller, *Tanks in the Great War* (London: John Murray, 1920), 125–129. The logistic system developed to support the Tank Corps was similar to the RFC's and comprised a combination of forward crew-based maintenance, mobile salvage companies (equivalent to the ASD repair sections), advanced stores (equivalent to the AP), Central Workshops (equivalent to the ASD), and Central Stores (equivalent to the AD).

126. Fuller, *Tanks*, 228.

127. J. Terraine, *To Win a War: 1918 The Year of Victory* (London: Sidgwick & Jackson, 1978), 89.

128. Ministry of Munitions, *Ministry of Munitions, The Supply of Munitions*, I:69.

129. C. Williams-Ellis, *The Tank Corps* (London: George Newnes, 1919), 261.

130. Bidwell, "After the Wall Came Tumbling Down," 58.

131. J. Terraine, "The Royal Air Force," *RAF Historical Society Journal*, no. 12 (1994): 18.

132. Boff, "Air/Land Integration in the 100 Days," 77–88.

133. J. Morrow, "Defeat of the German and Austro-Hungarian Air Forces in the Great War," in *Why Air Forces Fail*, ed. R. Higham and S. Harris (Lexington, KY: University of Kentucky, 2006), 99–133.

134. Wise, *Canadian Airmen*, 516.

135. A. Mahncke, *For Kaiser and Hitler* (Pulborough, UK: Tattered Flag Press, 2011), 68. The RAF's monthly fuel consumption by the armistice had reached 1.5 million gallons—or approximately 500 gallons (2,300 litres) per frontline squadron per day.

136. Hooton, *War over the Trenches*, 245.

137. Quoted in Wise, *Canadian Airmen*, 551.

138. Ibid., 565.

139. Ibid.

Chapter 7. Conclusions and Enduring Principles

1. A consistent feature of the western front was the fall in serviceability that accompanied the winter months (December–February), when the weather adversely affected both ground crew and machines.

2. Reichsarchiv, *Die Kriegführung im Herbst 1916 und im Winter 1916/17*, 109–12.

3. Jones, *War in the Air*, Appendices, 129. The Independent Force and 5 Group comprised some 203 aircraft by the armistice.

4. TNA AIR1/9/15/1/32/1, "Work in the Field, Consolidated Weekly Statements."

5. W. McNeill, *The Pursuit of Power* (Chicago: University of Chicago Press, 1982), 345.

6. TNA AIR1/686/21/13/2252, "Statistical Data of the RFC and the RAF."

7. Ibid.

8. The RAF fielded 3 percent of the BEF's personnel but 12 percent of its vehicles.

9. M. Christopher, *Logistics and Supply Chain Management* (London: Pearson, 2011), 189; R. Alfalla-Luque and C. Medina-Lopez, "Supply Chain Management," *Business History* 51, no. 2 (2009), 209; Bowersox, *Supply Chain Logistics Management*, 290.

10. Ellis, *Brute Force*, 538–39.

11. TNA AIR69/41, "Air Warfare Lecture Notes, Brooke-Popham, Fourth Course (1925–26)."

12. Ibid.

13. Potentially equivalent to some three thousand personnel—based on the squadron establishment for an average strength of twenty aircraft—as well as significant savings in vehicles and support equipment.

14. Harris, *From Amiens to the Armistice*, 51.

15. Eccles, *Logistics in the National Defense*, 102–14.

16. TNA WO73 and TNA AIR1/1242/204/6/55–57.

17. Air Ministry, *RAF Overseas Manpower Survey, November 1918* (London: Air Ministry, 1918).

18. "Major-General Seely's Statement on the Air Estimates," *Hansard*, 13 March 1919, Col 1501. Real GDP grew rapidly during the war, reaching a peak in 1917–18 when government spending accounted for 38.7 percent of GDP.

19. S. Broadberry and P. Howlett, "The United Kingdom in World War I," in *The Economics of World War I*, ed. S. Broadberry and M. Harrison (Cambridge, UK: Cambridge University Press, 2005), 216. "Fighting Services" includes the cost of munitions until 1916 and the cost of aeronautical supplies until March 1917. FY 15/16, FY 16/17, and FY 17/18 have been estimated on the basis of the total number of personnel and squadrons employed (including consumables and infrastructure but less aeronautical supplies). The figures for FY 18/19 are taken from Seely, *Hansard*, "Statement on Air Estimates," 13 March 1919.

20. Seely, *Hansard*, 13 March 1919, "Statement on the Air Estimates."

21. RAF Museum A790, "Cost of the Somaliland Campaign." This data is largely replicated in the 1923 Confidential Annex (Appendix 20) prepared by Air Commodore Brooke-Popham, AIR 69/41, "Air Warfare Lecture Notes."

22. Jones, *War in the Air*, Appendices, Appendix XXX.

23. On the basis of the ninety-nine squadrons serving on the western front on 11 November 1918, as detailed in Jones, *War in the Air*, Appendices, Appendix XXX; RAF Museum A790, "Cost of the Somaliland Campaign." All prices as of 1920.

24. TNA WO/394, "Statistical Abstracts of Information."

25. RAF Museum A790, "Cost of the Somaliland Campaign."

26. War Office, *Statistics*.

27. P. Dye, "Patton's Culmination on the Meuse in 1944," *USAF Logistic Journal* 23, no. 2 (Summer 1999): 30–32.

28. M. Harris, *Lifelines of Victory* (New York: Putnam's Sons, 1942), 7.

29. Ibid., 8. The range of a fully laden 3-ton Leyland Lorry was some eighty miles (based on an average fuel consumption of six miles per gallon): Air Ministry, *Air Publication 48—RAF Field Service Pocket Book*, 34. This was equivalent to a day's travel as convoys moved no faster than six to eight miles an hour (with stops every ten to fifteen miles) to reduce damage to the springs and excessive tire wear: "Despatches from the Front," *The Commercial Motor*, 1 February 1917, 20.

30. Statement by Major-General Seely, *Flight*, 22 May 1919.

31. *Flight*, 29 April 1920.

32. M. Raff and N. Temin, "Sears Roebuck in the Twentieth Century," in *Learning by Doing in Markets*, ed. N. Lamoureaux, M. Raff, and N. Temin (Chicago: University of Chicago Press, 1999), 221–25.

33. Sears Roebuck 1912 catalog; Air Historical Branch, *Maintenance* (London: Air Ministry, 1954), 160; J. Reichert, *IKEA and the Natural Step* (Washington, DC: World Resources Institute, 1998), 5; A. Eaves and B. Kingsman, "Forecasting for the Ordering and Stock-holding of Spare Parts," *Journal of the Operational Research Society*, no. 55 (2004): 431–37; Defence Storage and Distribution Agency (DSDA), *Annual Report and Accounts 2008–2009* (London: Stationery Office, 2010), 15; TESCO, *Annual Report and Accounts 2011* (Cheshunt, UK: Tesco plc, 2011), 28.

34. "Alarming MOD Accountancy to Blame for £6bn of Missing Kit, MPs say," *Times* (London), 5 July 2011.

35. Hoffman Nickerson, *Arms and Policy 1939–1944* (New York: Putnam's Sons, 1945), 267. Nickerson was an early critic of strategic bombing, which he referred to as "baby killing." He was equally skeptical of the claims made by the USAS for the destructive power of aerial bombing.

36. *Jane's Defence Weekly*, 17 November 2004, 17–18.

37. Jones, *War in the Air*, Appendices. This table records the number of the separate organizations involved in the movement of aircraft and aircraft-related stores on the western front (network elements) and the number of individual items managed by the network (information elements). Aero-engines are excluded for simplicity.

38. TNA AIR1/1101/204/5/1803, "Reports on Hispano-Suiza Aero-Engines."

39. Examples of individual aircraft (including the S.E.5a and R.E.8) were routinely deployed to France for evaluation at an early stage; however, these

timescales refer to the date when the first fully equipped squadron deployed to the western front.

40. Hare, *Aeroplanes of the Royal Aircraft Factory*, 6.
41. Christopher, *Logistics and Supply Chain Management*, 189–95.
42. J. Adams and J. Abell, *Modelling and Forecasting Aircraft Recoverable Spare Parts*, RAND Report R-4211 (Washington, DC: Department of Defense, 1993), 4–20.
43. Christopher, *Logistics and Supply Chain Management*, 99–100.
44. TNA AIR1/678/21/13/2138, "Development of Aircraft Production," 5.
45. Data compiled from TNA AIR1/926/204/5/915, "Aeroplane and Engine Casualties," TNA AIR1/998/204/5/1242, "Duplicate Returns," TNA AIR1/1128/204/5/2160, "Aeroplanes Flown From France," and TNA AIR1/1042/204/5/1494, "Duplicate Returns."
46. Liddell Hart Centre for Military Archives, Brooke-Popham Papers 1/4, "Staff College Notes."
47. TNA/AIR1/1114/204/5/1950, "Monthly Demands." The required level of reserves (as calculated by HQ RAF) rose from 492 aircraft in April 1918 to 649 in September.
48. TNA AIR1/1128/204/5/2159, "Various Returns."
49. Christopher, *Logistics and Supply Chain Management*, 101.
50. TNA AIR1/2/4/26/8, "Aeroplane Wastage."
51. Bowersox et al., *Supply Chain Logistics Management*, 405–6.
52. TNA AVIA46/168, "Repair & Maintenance of Aircraft," H. M. Fraser to E. Bridges (Official Historian Branch), 12 December 1950.
53. Christopher, *Logistics and Supply Chain Management*, 114.
54. Ibid., 91. Rough-cut planning activity is a central feature of contemporary demand management.
55. Bowersox et al., *Supply Chain Logistics Management*, 246–68.
56. Aircraft (asked and promised) from Liddell Hart Centre for Military Archives, Brooke-Popham Papers 1/4, "Staff College Notes: Miscellaneous Statistics."
57. Christopher, *Logistics and Supply Chain Management*, 85.
58. P. Dye, "Royal Air Force Repair and Salvage, 1939–1945," *Royal Air Force Historical Society Journal*, no. 51 (2011): 111–23.
59. J. M. Bruce, "The War in the Air: The Men and Their Machines," in *Facing Armageddon*, ed. H. Cecil and P. Liddle (London: Leo Cooper, 1996), 195; P. Leaman, "J. M. Bruce: An Appreciation," *Cross & Cockade International Journal* 33, no. 3 (2002): 139. Jack Bruce died in 2002 having written extensively on First World War aviation for nearly fifty years.
60. Dye, "Logistics Doctrine and the Impact of War," 211–19; Air Historical Branch, *Maintenance*, 1–16.

61. B. Jones, "Ashore, Afloat and Airborne: The Logistics of British Naval Airpower, 1914–1945" (PhD thesis, Kings College London, 2007). The Royal Navy's neglect of aviation logistics handicapped the FAA throughout the entire Second World War; indeed, much of the engineering task in support of the FAA fell to the RAF, as did the training of aviation technicians, even after the ending of dual control in 1939.

62. Murray, *Military Adaptation in War*, 1.

63. Ibid., 311.

64. M. Cooper, "A House Divided: Policy, Rivalry and Administration in Britain's Military Air Command 1914–1918," *Journal of Strategic Studies* 3, no. 2 (1980): 178–201. Cooper highlights the poor relationships between Henderson, Sykes, Brancker, and Trenchard, but then goes on to assert that this compromised decision making while ignoring the wider factors involved in expanding the RFC's capabilities.

65. Murray, *Military Adaptation*, 310.

66. Eccles, *Logistics in the National Defense*, 10.

67. Liaropoulos, "Revolutions in Warfare," 129–57.

68. Huston, *The Sinews of War*, 656–68.

69. Brown, "Feeding Victory," 9.

70. Travers, *The Killing Ground*, 262.

71. S. Robbins, *British Generalship on the Western Front 1914–1918: Defeat into Victory* (Abingdon, UK: Frank Cass, 2005), 140.

72. Ferguson, *The Pity of War*, 248–81; J. Winter, "1918: The Road to Victory," in *1918, Year of Victory*, ed. A. Elkins (Auckland: Exisle, 2010), 29.

73. Ministry of Munitions, *Ministry of Munitions, The Supply of Munitions*, I:67–68.

74. M. Albrow and E. King, eds., *Globalization, Knowledge and Society—Readings from International Sociology* (London: Sage Publications, 1990), 9.

75. P. Stearns, *Globalization in World History* (London: Routledge, 2010), 1–10; N. Ferguson, "Sinking Globalization," *Foreign Affairs* 84, no. 2 (2005): 64–77; S. Horowitz, "Reversing Globalization: Trade Policy Consequences of World War 1," *European Journal of International Relations* (2004), 10:33.

76. J. Buckley, *Air Power in the Age of Total War* (London: UCL Press, 1999), 68.

77. TNA AIR1/9/15/1/31/1, "A Programme of Development for the RAF, 17 October 1918."

78. TNA WO33/1297, "Committee on the Lessons of the Great War." The Army did commission such a study (in 1932) under the chairmanship of Lieutenant-General Sir Walter Kirke.

79. The role of logistics in supporting the BEF was also largely ignored—the one exception being transportation, which was the subject of a dedicated history.

80. R. Higham and S. Harris, *Why Air Forces Fail* (Lexington, KY: University of Kentucky, 2006), 351.

81. Typical of this approach is John Terraine's "Lessons of Air Warfare," 53–58.

82. War Office, *Statistics*, 64 (iii). There were some 50,000 personnel serving with the RAF on the western front in November 1918, compared with more than 1.86 million serving in the BEF.

83. *Flight*, 18 December 1919, 1622–24. Trenchard's 1919 Memorandum on the Air Force identified the need for investment in technical training and a (modest) network of repair and stores depots (all service-manned).

84. Brooke-Popham, "The Air Force," 49–50.

85. Dye, "Logistics Doctrine and the Impact of War," 207–33.

86. Comptroller and Auditor General, *HC 287—The Use of Information to Manage the Logistics Supply Chain* (London: National Audit Office, March 2011).

87. McNeill, *The Pursuit of Power*, 344.

88. J. Black, *The Great War and the Making of the Modern World* (London: Continuum, 2011), 260–61.

89. R. Chickering, *Imperial Germany and the Great War* (Cambridge, UK: Cambridge University Press, 2004), 191.

90. Van Creveld, *Supplying War*, 233.

91. Reichsarchiv, *Die Kriegführung an der Westfront im Jahre 1918*, 720–24.

92. M. Molkentin, *Fire in the Sky* (Crow's Nest, New South Wales, Australia: Allen & Unwin, 2010), 294–301; Jones, *War in the Air*, 4:375.

93. J. Shimshoni, "Technology, Military Advantage and World War 1," *International Security* 15, no. 3 (Winter, 1990–91): 187–215.

94. Liaropoulos, "Revolutions in Warfare," 155–57.

● SELECTED BIBLIOGRAPHY

PRIMARY SOURCES

Private Papers

Imperial War Museum. IWM73/183/1—Sir Sefton Brancker Papers.

Liddell Hart Centre for Military Archives. Sir Robert Brooke-Popham Papers.

RAF Museum. A790—Cost of the Somaliland Campaign.

———. B2045—Index to MAD Alteration Sheets.

———. B2621/4—Salmond (Draft) Autobiography.

———. DC76/74/130—ACM Sir Robert Brooke-Popham, Record of Service.

———. MFC76/1/4—Trenchard Memorandum.

———. MFC76/1/25—Orders for Aircraft Parks.

———. MFC76/1/66—Relations with the French.

———. RAFM 002811—Spare Parts for Aeroplane Engines.

———. TH/81/50—History of AID.

———. X003–8803—*War in the Air* Correspondence (1926–1927).

———. X006–3371—Brigadier-General R. E. T. Hogg Papers.

Official Papers

Air Historical Branch (RAF). *Monthly Return of Personnel of the Royal Air Force at Home and Overseas,* August–November 1918.

Army List. London: His Majesty's Stationery Office, July 1916.

The National Archives. AIR1/1/4/11—Letters Written by General Brooke-Popham.

———. AIR1/2/4/26/8—Aeroplane Wastage.

———. AIR1/3/4/26/18—Operations Correspondence.

———. AIR1/8/15/1—Progress of the RAF.

———. AIR1/8/15/1/7—Notes on System of Supply for RAF in France.

———. AIR1/9/15/1/31/1—A Programme of Development for the RAF.

———. AIR1/9/15/1/32/1—Work in the Field, Consolidated Weekly Statements.

———. AIR1/29/15/1/142—Life of Engines.

———. AIR1/35/15/1/229—Return of Serviceable Machines in France.

———. AIR1/37/15/1/250—Expeditionary Force Engine Returns.

————. AIR1/68/15/9/109—Stores, Transport and Armament Correspondence.

————. AIR1/109/15/30—Mechanical Transport—Statistics.

————. AIR1/139/15/40/295—DAQMG to ADMA, 10 May 1915.

————. AIR1/162/15/124/9 Part I—Periodical Engine Returns.

————. AIR1/366/15/231/6—Correspondence Vol. VI.

————. AIR1/474/15/312/185—Statistical Reports.

————. AIR1/475/15/312/201—Letters from General Salmond to General
Trenchard.

————. AIR1/509/16/3/54—Air Casualties.

————. AIR1/520/16/11/1—Organisation and Expansion of the RFC and RAF.

————. AIR1/520/16/12/1 Part III—Expansion and Organisation of the RFC
and RAF.

————. AIR1/529/16/12/70—Organisation and Establishment of RFC
Headquarters.

————. AIR1/529/16/12/75—Organisation and Establishment of Aircraft Parks.

————. AIR1/530/16/12/86—DDMA to GOC RFC.

————. AIR1/533/16/12/118—War Establishment of Parks and Depots.

————. AIR1/613/16/15/305—Contract for Supply of Petroleum Spirit.

————. AIR1/625/17/11—Report on Meeting with French Aviation Service.

————. AIR1/676/21/13/1880—Statistics of Aircraft Despatched to France.

————. AIR1/678/21/13/2/38—Development of Aircraft Production.

————. AIR1/678/21/13/2137—German Night Bombing.

————. AIR1/678/21/13/2138—Development of Aircraft Production 1917–1918.

————. AIR1/678/21/13/2186—Aircraft Design and Production 1914–1918.

————. AIR1/686/21/13/2248—Various Air Statistics.

————. AIR1/686/21/13/2252—Statistical Data of the RFC and RAF.

————. AIR1/731/176/6/18—Work Completed for Year.

————. AIR1/759/204/4/139–140—RFC Work Summaries 1916.

————. AIR1/760/204/4/141–144—RFC Work Summaries 1916.

————. AIR1/762/204/4/164–170—RFC Work Summaries 1916.

————. AIR1/763/204/4/197—Replacements: Spare Parts of Aeroplanes.

————. AIR1/783/204/4/515—Reports on Visits to French Aircraft Works.

————. AIR1/785/204/4/558—RFC Training Manual, Part II, Correspondence.

————. AIR1/785/204/4/565—Attendance of RFC Officers at French
Manoeuvres.

————. AIR1/793/204/4/795—Notes on the Provision of Spare Parts for MT.

————. AIR1/823/204/5/68—RFC Squadron Mobilization Store Table.

————. AIR1/837/204/5/278–279—Summary of RFC Work and Operations in
France.

————. AIR1/838/204/5/280–290—Daily Summary.

————. AIR1/911/204/5/832—Assistant Director of Aeronautical Equipment.

————. AIR1/912/204/5/846—Programme of RFC and RAF Developments.

———. AIR1/915/204/5/862–867—Monthly and Fortnightly Returns.

———. AIR1/926/204/5/915—Aeroplane and Engine Casualties.

———. AIR1/927/204/5/916 Part I and Part II—Squadron Ration Field Returns.

———. AIR1/942/204/5/975—Organisation and Personnel for Aircraft Depots.

———. AIR1/942/204/5/976—Reports on Work at Aircraft Parks and Depots.

———. AIR1/947/204/5/1011&1012—Weekly Engine Returns.

———. AIR1/953/204/5/1025—Mechanical Transport Returns.

———. AIR1/960/204/5/1043—Reports of RFC Manpower in France.

———. AIR1/998/204/5/1242–1243—Duplicate Returns.

———. AIR1/1022/204/5/1400—Fortnightly Casualty and Monthly Trade Returns.

———. AIR1/1042/204/5/1494—Duplicate Returns.

———. AIR1/1042/204/5/1495—Reports and Supply of Bomb Carriers.

———. AIR1/1072/204/5/1643—Casualty and Replacements of Aircraft and Engines.

———. AIR1/1072/204/5/1644—Supply of Aeroplanes for Italy.

———. AIR1/1073/204/5/1655—Weekly Returns.

———. AIR1/1084/204/5/1721—Reorganisation of Aircraft Depots.

———. AIR1/1100/204/5/1798–1802—Reports on Hispano-Suiza Aero-engines.

———. AIR1/1101/204/5/1803–1809—Reports on Hispano-Suiza Aero-engines.

———. AIR1/1110/204/5/1893–1894—Work Summary Aircraft Depots.

———. AIR1/1111/204/5/1895—Work Summary Aircraft Parks.

———. AIR1/1112/204/5/1896–1898—Work Summary Aeroplane Supply Depots.

———. AIR1/1114/204/5/1950—Monthly Demands by RFC/RAF Units in France.

———. AIR1/1122/204/5/2097—Petrol and Oil Supplies.

———. AIR1/1124/204/5/2101—Bulk Supply of Petrol.

———. AIR1/1128/204/5/2159—Various Returns.

———. AIR1/1128/204/5/2160—Aeroplanes Flown From France.

———. AIR1/1139/204/5/2304—Shipping and Tonnage.

———. AIR1/1139/204/5/2305—Visits to Paris.

———. AIR1/1144/204/5/2352–2354—Minutes of Progress and Allocation Committee.

———. AIR1/1145/204/5/2355—Minutes of Progress and Allocation Committee.

———. AIR1/1153/204/5/2408—Correspondence on Salvage of Aeroplanes.

———. AIR1/1155/204/5/2428–2429—Quarterly Returns of Engines Held by RAF.

———. AIR1/1157/204/5/2474—Reports and Miscellaneous Correspondence.

———. AIR1/1158/204/5/2483—Reports and Miscellaneous Correspondence.

———. AIR1/1159/204/5/2459—Distribution of Duties Chart.

———. AIR1/1233/204/6/12—No. 9 Squadron Record Book.

———. AIR1/1245/204/6/55–57—No. 9 Squadron Record Book.

———. AIR1/1284/204/11/27—AID Report on Visit to Squadrons in France.

———. AIR1/1291/204/11/83—War Establishments.

———. AIR1/1411/204/28/43—Minutes of Second Monthly Hispano-Suiza Meeting.

———. AIR1/1664/204/98/33—51 Wing Summary of Work 1917–1918.

———. AIR1/1831/204/205/2—No. 87 Squadron Record Book.

———. AIR1/2101/207/28/19—Department of Aeronautical Supplies Reports.

———. AIR1/2129/207/82/1—Operations on Western Front.

———. AIR1/2302/215/10—Output Figures for Airframes and Engines.

———. AIR1/2302/215/12—Correspondence: Department of Aircraft Production.

———. AIR1/2304/215/13—Minutes of the Progress and Allocation Committee.

———. AIR1/2390/228/11/124—Wing Commander E. W. Havers, War Experiences.

———. AIR1/2398—Notes on the History of the RAF Stores Branch.

———. AIR1/2423/305/18/28—Charts Showing Distribution of Aeroplanes.

———. AIR1/2423/305/18/29—Report on Aircraft Salvage and Repair Depot.

———. AIR1/2429/305/30/1—Memorandum of Visit to France August 1915.

———. AIR1/2430/305/30/16—Report by Deputy Assistant Director RFC.

———. AIR2/939—Weekly Reports on Pilots and Aeroplanes.

———. AIR10/65—RAF War Establishments in France.

———. AIR10/84—RAF Periodical Strength Returns.

———. AIR10/249—Instruction Book for the Hispano-Suiza.

———. AIR10/774—Schedule for RAF Aeroplanes, Type R.E.8.

———. AIR69/31—The Development of Aeroplane Co-operation with the Army.

———. AIR69/41—Air Warfare Lecture Notes, AVM Brooke-Popham.

———. AVIA46/168—Repair and Maintenance of Aircraft.

———. MUN4/4693—Air Force: Expenditure on Aeronautical Supplies, 1916–1919.

———. MUN4/6650—Aeronautical Supplies: Output of Aeroplanes.

———. WO24/899—War Establishment, Part 1: Expeditionary Force 1914.

———. WO73/97–108—Army Monthly Manpower Return, 1914–1918.

———. WO394/1–20—Statistical Abstracts of Information.

Books

Air Ministry. *Air Publication 48—RAF Field Service Pocket Book*. London: Air
Ministry, 1918.

———. *RAF Overseas Manpower Survey, November 1918*. London: Air Ministry,
1918.

Archer, F. "Sergeant Observer Frederick Archer." In *Voices in Flight*, edited by A.
Malinovska and M. Joslyn, 108–18. Barnsley, UK: Pen & Sword, 2006.

Baring, M. *Flying Corps Headquarters 1914–1918*. Edinburgh: Bell & Sons, 1920.

BEF. *SS 515, Extracts from German Documents & Correspondence No 2*. BEF: Central
Distribution System, 1916.

———. *SS 553, Experience of the German First Army in the Somme Battle 24 June–26
November 1916*. BEF: Central Distribution System, 1917.

———. *SS 564, Extracts From German Documents and Correspondence*. BEF: Central
Distribution System, 1916.

Bott, A. *An Airman's Outings with the RFC, June–December 1916*. London: William
Blackwood, 1917.

Breen, J. J. "War Experiences." In *AP 1308: A Selection of Lectures and Essays from
the Work of Officers Attending the Fifth Course at the Royal Air Force Staff
College, 1926–1927*. London: Air Ministry, 1926–27.

Burgess, C. M. *The Diary and Letters of a Fighter Pilot*. Barnsley, UK: Pen & Sword,
2008.

General Staff. *Fighting in the Air*. London: War Office, April 1918.

Libby, F. *Horses Don't Fly*. New York: Arcade Publishing, 2012.

Macmillan, N. *Into the Blue*. London: Jarrolds, 1969.

———. *Offensive Patrol*. London: Jarrolds, 1973.

Mahncke, A. *For Kaiser and Hitler*. Pulborough, UK: Tattered Flag Press, 2011.

McClaughry, W. A. "A Squadron Commander's Perspective." In *Australian
Airmen—History of the 4th Squadron Australian Flying Corps*, edited by E. J.
Richards, 53–58. Melbourne: Bruce & Co., 1922.

McCudden, J. T. B. *Flying Fury*. London: Hamilton, 1930.

Ministry of Munitions. *Hispano-Suiza: Notes for Squadrons in the Field*. London:
Ministry of Munitions, 1918.

Read, W. R. "Cavalryman in the Flying Machines." In *People at War*, edited by
M. Moynihan, 19–41. Newton Abbott, UK: David & Charles, 1973.

Roskill, S. W. *Documents Relating to the Naval Air Service 1908–1918*. London:
Naval Records Society, 1969.

Smythies, B. E. "War Experiences." In *AP 956*, 74–90. London: Air Ministry,
1923.

Sulzbach, H. *With the German Guns*. London: Leo Cooper, 1973.

Sykes, F. *From Many Angles*. London: George Harrap, 1942.

Tennant, J. E. *In the Clouds above Baghdad*. London: Cecil Palmer, 1920.

War Office. *Report of the Military Board of Allied Supply—The Allied Armies under Marshal Foch in the Franco-Belgian Theater of Operations.* Washington, DC: War Office, 1924.

———. *RFC Technical Notes 1916.* London: Arms and Amour Press, 1968.

———. *Statistics of the Military Effort of the British Empire.* London: HMSO, 1922.

Articles

Anon. "Despatches from the Front." *The Commercial Motor,* 1 February 1917, 494.

———. "With an Army Co-operation Squadron during the German Attacks of 1918." *The Hawk,* 1931, 20–27.

Barrington-Kennett, B. H. "Military Aeronautics in France." *Royal United Services Institution Journal* 56 (February 1912): 171–76.

Brancker, S. "The Aeroplane in War." *Flight,* 12 June 1914, 632–33.

Brooke, A. "The Evolution of Artillery in the Great War." *The Journal of the Royal Artillery* 51, Parts I and II; 52, Parts III and IV; 53, Parts V, VI, VII, and VIII (1925–27).

Brooke-Popham, R. "The Air Force." *Royal United Services Institution Journal* 65 (1920): 43–70.

Bulman, G. P. "Early Days." *Journal of the Royal Aeronautical Society* 70 (1966): 176–78.

Carter, E. E. "The New Transport System—Its Principles and their Application." *Royal United Services Institution Journal* 56 (1912): 671–702.

Fell, L. "Aero-engine Repair in War-time." *The Aeroplane,* 17 May 1940, 676–77.

———. "The Engine Repair Shops Pont de l'Arche." *Journal of the Royal Aeronautical Society* 70 (1966): 167–68.

Grey, C. G. G. "Good Technical Work." *The Aeroplane,* 15 January 1919, 212.

Isaac, Bernard. "On the Standardisation of Aircraft Parts." *The Aeroplane,* 20 December 1916, 1188–89.

Miles, H. S. G. "Army Administration." *Royal United Services Institute Journal* 68 (1923): 23–24.

Smyrk, W. "No. 253 RFC—An Interview with Mr. W. Smyrk." *The 1914–1918 Journal* (1970): 55–68.

Sykes, F. "Developments of Military Aviation." *Flight,* 14 February 1914, 170–73.

———. "Military Aviation." *Flight,* 8 March 1913, 277–81.

Official Histories

Air Historical Branch. *Maintenance.* London: Air Ministry, 1954.

Cutlack, F. M. *Official History of Australia in the War of 1914–1918.* Sydney: Angus & Robertson, 1938.

Edmonds, J. E. *Military Operations France and Belgium, 1916.* Vol. 1. London: Macmillan, 1932.

———. *Military Operations France and Belgium, 1916.* Vol. 2. London: Macmillan, 1938.

———. *Military Operations France and Belgium, 1917*. Vol. 2. London: Macmillan, 1948.

———. *Military Operations France and Belgium, 1918*. Vol. 1. London: Macmillan, 1935.

———. *Military Operations France and Belgium, 1918*. Vol. 2. London: Macmillan, 1937.

———. *Military Operations France and Belgium, 1918*. Vol. 3. London: Macmillan, 1939.

———. *Military Operations France and Belgium, 1918*. Vol. 4. London: HMSO, 1947.

———. *Military Operations France and Belgium, 1918*. Vol. 5. London: HMSO, 1946.

Edmonds, J. E., and H. R. Davies. *Military Operations Italy, 1915–19*. London: HMSO, 1949.

Falls, C. *Military Operations France and Belgium, 1917*. Vol. 1. London: Macmillan, 1940.

Fayle, C. E. *Seaborne Trade*. Vol. 3. London: John Murray, 1924.

Henniker, A. M. *Transportation on the Western Front, 1914–1918*. London: Macmillan, 1937.

Jones, H. A. *The War in the Air*. Vol. 2. Oxford, UK: Clarendon Press, 1928.

———. *The War in the Air*. Vol. 3. Oxford, UK: Clarendon Press, 1931.

———. *The War in the Air*. Vol. 4. Oxford, UK: Clarendon Press, 1934.

———. *The War in the Air*. Vol. 5. Oxford, UK: Clarendon Press, 1935.

———. *The War in the Air*. Vol. 6. Oxford, UK: Clarendon Press, 1937.

———. *The War in the Air*. Appendices. Oxford, UK: Clarendon Press, 1937.

Ministry of Munitions. *History of the Ministry of Munitions 1915–1919*. 12 vols. London: HMSO, 1919–22.

Office of Air Force History. *The U.S. Air Service in World War 1*. 4 vols. Washington, DC: Headquarters USAF, 1978.

Raleigh, Sir Walter. *The War in the Air*. Vol. 1. Oxford, UK: Clarendon Press, 1922.

Reichsarchiv. *Der Weltkrieg 1914 bis 1918:*

———. *Band X, Die Operationen des Jahres 1916 bis zum Wechsel in der Obersten Heeresleitung*. Berlin: Mittler und Sohn, 1936.

———. *Band XI, Die Kriegführung im Herbst 1916 und im Winter 1916/17; vom Wechsel in der Obersten Heeresleitung bis zum Entschluss zum Rückzug in die Siegfried-Stellung*. Berlin: Mittler und Sohn, 1938.

———. *Band XII, Die Kriegführung im Frühjahr 1917*. Berlin: Mittler und Sohn, 1939.

———. *Band XIII, Die Kriegführung im Sommer und Herbst 1917. Die Ereignisse ausserhalb der Westfront bis November 1918*. Berlin: Mittler und Sohn, 1942.

———. *Band XIV, Die Kriegführung an der Westfront im Jahre 1918*. Berlin: Mittler und Sohn, 1944.

Royal Engineers. *The Work of the Royal Engineers in the European War 1914–1918*. 9 vols. Chatham, UK: Royal Engineers Institution, 1921.

Ruppenthal, R. *Logistical Support of the Armies*. Vol. 1, *May 1941–September 1944*, and Vol. 2, *September 1944–May 1945*. Washington, DC: Center of Military History, 1995.

Wise, S. F. *Canadian Airmen and the First World War*. Toronto: Toronto University Press, 1980.

SECONDARY SOURCES

Books and Pamphlets

Adkin, F. J. *From the Ground Up—A History of RAF Ground Crew*. Shrewsbury, UK: Airlife, 1983.

Albrow, M., and E. King, eds. *Globalization, Knowledge and Society—Readings from International Sociology*. London: Sage Publications, 1990.

Ash, E. *Sir Frederick Sykes and the Air Revolution 1912–1918*. London: Frank Cass, 1999.

Bachrach, B. S. "From Nicaea to Dorylaion." In *Logistics of Warfare in the Age of the Crusades*, edited by J. H. Pryor, 43–62. Aldershot, UK: Ashgate, 2006.

Bailey, J. *The First World War and the Birth of the Modern Style of Warfare*. Camberley, UK: Strategic and Combat Studies Institute, 1996.

———. "The First World War and the Birth of Modern Warfare." In *The Dynamics of Military Revolution 1300–2050*, edited by M. Knox and W. Murray, 132–53. Cambridge, UK: Cambridge University Press, 2001.

Ballantine, D. S. *U.S. Naval Logistics in the Second World War*. Princeton, NJ: Princeton University Press, 1947.

Bannerman, G. *Merchants and the Military in Eighteenth Century Britain*. London: Pickering & Chatto, 2008.

Barker, R. *The Royal Flying Corps in France: From Mons to the Somme*. London: Constable, 1994.

Beadon, R. H. *The Royal Army Service Corps—A History of Transport and Supply in the British Army*. Cambridge, UK: Cambridge University Press, 1931.

Beckett, I. *The Great War*. London: Pearson Education, 2007.

Biddle, T. *Rhetoric and Reality in Air Warfare*. Princeton, NJ: Princeton University Press, 2004.

Bidwell, S., and D. Graham. *Fire-Power: British Army Weapons and Theories of War 1904–1945*. London: Allen and Unwin, 1982.

Black, J. *The Battle of Waterloo*. London: Icon Books, 2010.

———. *The Great War and the Making of the Modern World*. London: Continuum, 2011.

———. *A Military Revolution? Military Change and European Society 1550–1800*. London: Macmillan, 1991.

Boff, J. *Winning and Losing on the Western Front*. Cambridge, UK: Cambridge University Press, 2012.

Boulding, K. E. *Conflict and Defense: A General Theory*. New York: Harper & Rowe, 1962.

Bourne, J. "Haig and the Historians." In *Haig: A Re-appraisal 80 Years On*, edited by B. Bond and N. Cave, 1–11. Barnsley, UK: Pen & Sword, 1999.

Bowersox, D. J., D. J. Closs, M. B. Cooper, and J. C. Bowersox. *Supply Chain Logistics Management*. New York: McGraw-Hill, 2010.

Bowler, R. A. *Logistics and the Failure of the British Army in America 1775–1783*. Princeton, NJ: Princeton University Press, 1975.

Boyle, A. *Trenchard: Man of Vision*. London: Collins, 1962.

Broadberry, S. "The United Kingdom in World War I: Business as Usual?" In *The Economics of World War I*, edited by S. Broadberry and M. Harrison, 206–34. Cambridge, UK: Cambridge University Press, 2005.

Brooke-Smith, P. W. L. *The History of Early British Military Aeronautics*. Bath, UK: Cedric Chivers, 1968.

Brown, I. M. *British Logistics on the Western Front 1914–1919*. Westport, CT: Praeger, 1998.

———. "Feeding Victory: The Logistic Imperative behind the Hundred Days." In *1918: Defining Victory*, edited by P. Dennis and J. Grey, 130–47. Canberra, Australia: Army Historical Unit, 1999.

Bruce, J. M. *The Aeroplanes of the Royal Flying Corps*. London: Putnam, 1982.

———. *AW FK8—Windsock Data File 64*. Berkhamsted, UK: Albatros Publications, 1997.

———. "The War in the Air: The Men and Their Machines." In *Facing Armageddon*, edited by H. Cecil and P. Liddle, 193–217. London: Leo Cooper, 1996.

Buckley, J. *Air Power in the Age of Total War*. London: UCL Press, 1999.

Chandler, D. *The Campaigns of Napoleon*. London: Weidenfeld & Nicolson, 1966.

———. "Supply: Logistical Support in War." Ch. 9 in *Blenheim Preparation*. Stroud, UK: Spellmount, 2004.

Chasseaud, P. *Artillery's Astrologers*. Lewes, UK: Mapbooks, 1999.

———. *Topography of Armageddon*. Lewes, UK: Mapbooks, 1991.

Chickering, R. *Imperial Germany and the Great War*. Cambridge, UK: Cambridge University Press, 2004.

Christopher, M. *Logistics and Supply Chain Management*. London: Pearson, 2011.

Cohen, E. A., and J. Gooch. *Military Misfortunes: The Anatomy of Failure in War*. New York: Free Press, 1990.

Crew, G. *The Royal Army Service Corps*. London: Leo Cooper, 1970.

Crowl, P. "Alfred Thayer Mahan: The Naval Historian." In *Makers of Modern Strategy: From Machiavelli to the Nuclear Age*, edited by P. Paret, 444–77. Princeton, NJ: Princeton University Press, 1986.

Cuneo, J. *Winged Mars: The Air Weapon 1914–1916*. Harrisburg, PA: Military Service Publishing Company, 1947.

Dallas Brett, R. *History of British Aviation 1908–1914*. Vol. 1. London: John Hamilton, 1933.

Dean, M. *The Royal Air Force and Two World Wars*. London: Cassell, 1979.

De La Ferte, J. *The Forgotten Ones*. London: Hutchinson, 1961.

Dennis, P., and J. Grey. *1918: Defining Victory*. Canberra, Australia: Army Historical Unit, 1999.

Dictionary of National Biography. London: Oxford University Press, 1971.

Doughty, R. *Pyrrhic Victory: French Strategy and Operations in the Great War*. Cambridge, MA: Harvard University Press, 2005.

Dreisziger, N. F. *Mobilization for Total War*. Waterloo, Ontario, Canada: Laurier University Press, 1981.

Driver, H. *The Birth of Military Aviation*. Woodbridge, UK: Boydell, 1997.

Duffy, C. *Through German Eyes: The British and the Somme 1916*. London: Weidenfeld & Nicolson, 2006.

Dye, P. J. "Logistics Doctrine and the Impact of War: The Royal Air Force's Experience in the Second World War." In *Air Power History: Turning Points from Kitty Hawk to Kosovo*, edited by S. Cox and P. Gray, 207–23. London: Frank Cass, 2002.

Eccles, E. *Logistics in the National Defense*. Harrisburg, PA: Stackpole, 1959.

Edgerton, D. *England and the Aeroplane: An Essay on a Militant and Technological Nation*. London: Macmillan, 1991.

Ellis, J. *Brute Force*. London: Andre Deutsch, 1990.

Engels, D. *Alexander the Great and the Logistics of the Macedonian Army*. Berkeley, CA: University of California Press, 1978.

Farndale, M. *History of the Royal Regiment of Artillery, Western Front 1914–1918*. Woolwich, UK: The Royal Artillery Institution, 1986.

Ferguson, N. *The Pity of War*. London: Allen Lane, 1999.

Finnegan, J. *Shooting the Front: Allied Aerial Reconnaissance in the First World War*. Stroud, UK: Spellmount, 2011.

Forbes, A. *A History of the Army Ordnance Services*. Vol. 3, *The Great War*. London: The Medici Society, 1929.

Franks, N., R. Guest, and F. Bailey. *Bloody April, Black September*. London: Grub Street, 1995.

French, D. "Sir James Edmonds and the Official History: France and Belgium." In *The First World War and British Military History*, edited by B. Bond, 69–86. Oxford, UK: Clarendon Press, 1991.

Frost, A. *The First Fleet: The Real Story*. Collingwood, Victoria, Australia: Black, 2011.

Fuller, J. F. C. *Tanks in the Great War*. London: John Murray, 1920.

Gabreski, T. L. *Maintenance Metrics*. Maxwell AFB, Montgomery, AL: Air Force Logistics Management Agency, 2001.

Gollin, A. *The Impact of Air Power on the British People and their Government, 1909–14.* London: Macmillan, 1989.

———. *No Longer an Island.* London: William Heinemann, 1984.

Gray, C. *Strategy for Chaos: Revolutions in Military Affairs and the Evidence of History.* London: Frank Cass, 2002.

Green, A. *Writing the Great War: Sir James Edmonds and the Official Histories 1915–1948.* London: Frank Cass, 2003.

Grieves, K. *The Politics of Manpower.* Manchester, UK: Manchester University Press, 1988.

———. *Sir Eric Geddes: Business in War and Peace.* Manchester, UK: Manchester University Press, 1990.

———. "The Transport Mission to GHQ, 1916." In *Look to Your Front,* edited by B. Bond, 63–78. Stroud, UK: Spellmount, 1999.

Griffith, P. *Battle Tactics of the Western Front.* London: Yale Press, 1994.

Hackett, J. *The Profession of Arms.* London: Sidgwick & Jackson, 1982.

Hagerman, E. *The American Civil War and the Origins of Modern War.* Indianapolis, IN: Indiana University Press, 1992.

Hamley, E. *The Operations of War.* London: Blackwood & Sons, 1867.

Hare, P. *Aeroplanes of the Royal Aircraft Factory.* Marlborough, UK: Crowood Press, 1999.

Harris, H. *The First Five Hundred Years.* Aldershot, UK: RAOC School, 1962.

Harris, J. P. *Amiens to the Armistice.* London: Brassey's, 1998.

Harris, M. *Lifelines of Victory.* New York: Putnam's Sons, 1942.

Hart, P. *Bloody April: Slaughter in the Skies over Arras.* London: Weidenfeld & Nicolson, 2005.

———. *Somme Success.* Barnsley, UK: Pen & Sword, 2001.

Hartup, G. *The War of Invention: Scientific Developments 1914–1918.* London: Brassey's, 1988.

Henshaw, T. *The Sky Their Battlefield.* London: Grub Street, 1995.

Higham, R. "Air Power in World War 1, 1914–1918." In *The War in the Air 1914–1994,* edited by A. Stephens, 23–45. Canberra, Australia: RAAF Air Power Studies Centre, 1994.

———. *Bases of Air Strategy: Building Airfields for the RAF 1914–1945.* Shrewsbury, UK: Airlife, 1998.

———. "Revolutionary Innovation and the Invisible Architecture: Making Royal Air Force Bomber Command Efficient, 1939–1945." In *Innovation and the Development of Flight,* edited by R. Launius, 235–62. College Station, TX: Texas A&M University Press, 1999.

Higham, R., and S. Harris. *Why Air Forces Fail.* Lexington, KY: University of Kentucky, 2006.

Hobson, C. *Airmen Died in the Great War 1914–1918.* Suffolk, UK: J. B. Hayward, 1995.

Holden Reid, B. *J. F. C. Fuller: Military Thinker*. London: Macmillan, 1987.

Hooton, E. R. *War over the Trenches*. Horsham, UK: Ian Allen, 2010.

Howard, M. *The Causes of Wars*. London: Temple Smith, 1983.

Howard, M., and P. Paret. *Carl von Clausewitz on War*. Princeton, NJ: Princeton University Press, 1976.

Hull, I. *Absolute Destruction: Military Culture and the Practices of War in Imperial Germany*. Ithaca, NY: Cornell University Press, 2005.

Huston, J. *The Sinews of War: Army Logistics 1775–1953*. Washington, DC: Center of Military History, 1966.

Imlay, T.C., and M. D. Toft. *The Fog of Peace and War Planning: Military and Strategic Planning under Uncertainty*. London: Routledge, 2006.

Jefford, C. G. *RAF Squadrons*. Shrewsbury, UK: Airlife, 1988.

Jomini, A. H. *The Art of War*. London: Greenhill Books, 1992.

Judge, A. W. *Automotive and Aircraft Engines*. London: Pitman, 1924.

Kane, T. M. *Military Logistics and Strategic Performance*. London: Routledge, 2001.

Kilduff, P. *Over the Battlefronts*. London: Arms & Armour Press, 1996.

King, C. S., W. Robertson and S. Clay. *Staff Ride Handbook for the Overland Campaign: A Study in Operational Command*. Fort Leavenworth, KS: Combat Studies Institute, 2006.

Knox, M., and W. Murray. *The Dynamics of Military Revolution*. Cambridge, UK: Cambridge University Press, 2001.

Kobbe, W. *Notes on Strategy and Logistics*. Fort Monroe, VA: Artillery School Press, 1896.

Kramer, A. *Dynamic of Destruction*. Oxford, UK: Oxford University Press, 2007.

Levene, J. *On a Wing and a Prayer*. London: Collins, 2008.

Liaropoulos, A. "Revolutions in Warfare: Theoretical Paradigms and Historical Evidence." In *War Studies Reader*, edited by G. Sheffield, 129–57. London: Continuum, 2010.

Liddell Hart, B. H. *Sherman*. New York: Praeger, 1958.

———. *Thoughts on War*. London: Faber & Faber, 1944.

Liddle, P., ed. *Passchendaele in Perspective*. London: Leo Cooper, 1997.

Lumsden, A. *British Piston Aero-Engines and Their Aircraft*. Shrewsbury, UK: Airlife, 1994.

Luttwak, E. "Logistics and the Aristocratic Idea of War." In *Feeding Mars*, edited by J. A. Lynn, 3–7. Boulder, CO: Westview Press, 1993.

Lynn, J. A., ed. *Feeding Mars: Logistics in Western Warfare from the Middle Ages to the Present*. Boulder, CO: Westview Press, 1993.

Macksey, K. *For Want of a Nail: The Impact on War of Logistics and Communications*. London: Brassey's, 1989.

———. *The Penguin Encyclopaedia of Weapons and Military Technology*. London: Viking, 1993.

Macmillan, N. *Sir Sefton Brancker*. London: Sir William Heinemann, 1935.

Manship, W. "Air Force Supply Measures." In *Today's Logistics*, edited by J. Rainey, 50–67. Maxwell AFB, Montgomery, AL: Air Force Logistics Management Agency, 2001.

McNeill, W. H. *The Pursuit of Power.* Chicago: University of Chicago Press, 1984.

Mead, P. *The Eye in the Air: History of Air Observation and Reconnaissance for the Army 1785–1945.* London: HMSO, 1983.

Ministry of Defence. *British Defence Doctrine.* London: Ministry of Defence, Joint Warfare Publication 0–01, 1996.

———. *Defence Costs Study No. 10: Repair, Spares, Storage and Distribution.* London: Ministry of Defence, 1994.

Molkentin, M. *Fire in the Sky.* Crow's Nest, UK: Allen & Unwin, 2010.

Morris, A. *Bloody April.* London: Jarrolds, 1967.

Morrow, J. H. "Defeat of the German and Austro-Hungarian Air Forces in the Great War." In *Why Air Forces Fail*, edited by R. Higham and S. Harris, 99–134. Lexington, KY: University of Kentucky, 2006.

———. *German Air Power in World War One.* Lincoln, NE: University of Nebraska Press, 1982.

———. *The Great War in the Air: Military Aviation from 1908–1921.* Washington, DC: Smithsonian Institute Press, 1993.

Murray, W. *Military Adaptation in War.* Cambridge, UK: Cambridge University Press, 2011.

NATO. *NATO Logistics Handbook.* Brussels: Logistics Secretariat, 1997.

Neal, L., ed. *War Finance from Antiquity to the Present.* Cheltenham, UK: Edward Elgar, 1994.

Neumann, G. P. *The German Air Force in the Great War.* London: Hodder & Stoughton, 1921.

Nickerson, H. *Arms and Policy 1939–1944.* New York: Putnam's Sons, 1945.

Ong, C. *Operation Matador.* Singapore: Times Academic Press, 1997.

Overy, R. J. *The Air War 1939–1945.* London: Europa, 1980.

Parker, G. *The Military Revolution.* Cambridge, UK: Cambridge University Press, 1988.

Philpott, W. *Bloody Victory.* London: Little Brown, 2009.

Pisano, D., and T. Dietz. *Legend, Memory and the Great War in the Air.* Seattle, WA: University of Washington Press, 1992.

Prior, R., and T. Wilson. *Passchendaele: The Untold Story.* New Haven: Yale University Press, 1996.

———. *The Somme.* New Haven, CT: Yale University Press, 2005.

Probert, H. *The Forgotten Air Force.* London: Brassey's, 1995.

———. *High Commanders of the Royal Air Force.* London: HMSO, 1991.

Raff, M., and N. Temin. "Sears Roebuck in the Twentieth Century." In *Learning by Doing in Markets*, edited by N. Lamoureaux, M. Raff, and N. Temin, 219–52. Chicago: University of Chicago Press, 1999.

Rainey, J., and B. Scott. *The Logistics of War*. Maxwell AFB, Montgomery, AL: Air Force Logistics Management Agency, 2000.

Riley, J. *Napoleon as a General*. London: Continuum, 2007.

Robbins, S. *British Generalship on the Western Front 1914–1918: Defeat into Victory*. Abingdon, UK: Frank Cass, 2005.

Robertson, B. *Wheels of the RAF*. Cambridge, UK: Patrick Stephens, 1983.

Rogers, C., ed. *The Military Revolution Debate*. Boulder, CO: Westview, 1995.

Roth, J. P. *The Logistics of the Roman Army at War*. Boston: Brill, 1999.

Shaw, G. C. *Supply in Modern War*. London: Faber & Faber, 1938.

Sheffield, G. *The Chief*. London: Aurum Press, 2011.

———. *Forgotten Victory*. London: Headline, 2001.

———. *The Somme*. London: Cassell, 2003.

Sheldon, J. *The German Army at Passchendaele*. Barnsley, UK: Pen & Sword, 2007.

———. *The German Army on the Somme*. Barnsley, UK: Pen & Sword, 2005.

Sinclair, J. *Arteries of War: A History of Military Transportation*. Shrewsbury, UK: Airlife, 1992.

Slessor, J. *Air Power and Armies*. London: Oxford University Press, 1936.

Stearns, P. N. *Globalization in World History*. London: Routledge, 2010.

Stevenson, D. *Armaments and the Coming of War*. Oxford, UK: Clarendon Press, 1996.

———. *With Our Backs to the Wall*. London: Allen Lane, 2011.

Strachan, H. *Financing the First World War*. Oxford, UK: Oxford University Press, 2004.

———. *Carl von Clausewitz's On War*. London: Atlantic Books, 2007.

Stockfish, J. A. *Linking Logistics and Operations: A Case Study of World War II Air Power*. Santa Monica, CA: RAND Corporation, 1991.

Strong, P., and S. Marble. *Artillery in the Great War*. Barnsley, UK: Pen & Sword, 2011.

Stubbs, K. *The Race to the Front*. Westport, CT: Praeger, 2002.

Sturtivant, R. *Royal Air Force Flying Training and Support Units*. Tunbridge Wells, UK: Air Britain Historians, 1997.

Terraine, J. *To Win A War: 1918 The Year of Victory*. London: Sidgwick & Jackson, 1978.

Thompson, J. *Lifeblood of War: Logistics in Armed Conflict*. London: Brassey's, 1991.

Thorpe, G. C. *Pure Logistics: The Science of War Preparation*. Washington, DC: National Defense University Press, 1986.

Toulmin, H. A. *Air Service: American Expeditionary Force 1918*. New York: Van Nostrand, 1927.

Travers, T. *How The War Was Won: Command and Technology in the British Army on the Western Front*. London: Routledge, 1992.

———. *The Killing Ground: The British Army, the Western Front and the Emergence of Modern Warfare*. London: Allen & Unwin, 1987.

Trudeau, N. A. *Southern Storm: Sherman's March to the Sea.* New York: Harper, 2008.

van Creveld, M. *Supplying War: Logistics from Wallenstein to Patton.* Cambridge, UK: Cambridge University Press, 1977.

Waddell, S. R. *United States Army Logistics—The Normandy Campaign.* Westport, CT: Greenwood Press, 1994.

Weller, J. *On Wellington.* London: Greenhill Books, 1978.

Williams-Ellis, C. *The Tank Corps.* London: George Newnes, 1919.

Winter, D. *The First of the Few.* London: Allen Lane, 1982.

Winter, J. "1918: The Road to Victory." In *1918, Year of Victory,* edited by A. Elkins, 29–44. Auckland: Exisle, 2010.

Young, M. *Army Service Corps 1902–1918.* Barnsley, UK: Leo Cooper, 2000.

Articles

Alfalla-Luque, A., and C. Medina-Lopez. "Supply Chain Management." *Business History* 51, no. 2 (2009): 202–21.

Allen, W. B. "The Logistics Revolution and Transportation." *The Annals of the American Academy of Political and Social Science* 553, no. 1 (1997): 106–16.

Bidwell, S. "After the Wall Came Tumbling Down: A Historical Perspective." *Royal United Services Institution Journal* 135 (1990): 57–59.

Boff, J. "Air/Land Integration in the 100 Days: The Case of Third Army." *RAF Air Power Review* 12, no. 3 (2009): 77–88.

———. "Logistics during the Hundred Days Campaign, 1918: British Third Army." *Journal of the Society for Army Historical Research* 89 (2011): 326–21.

Brooks, P. W. "Why the Airship Failed." *Aeronautical Journal* 79, October 1975, 439–49.

Brown, I. M. "The British Expeditionary Force and the Difficult Transition to Peace 1918–1919." *Journal of Strategic Studies* 19, no. 4 (1996): 89–104.

Cooper, M. "Blueprint for Confusion: The Administrative Background to the Formation of the Royal Air Force 1912–19." *Journal of Contemporary History* 22, no. 3 (1987): 437–53.

———. "A House Divided: Policy, Rivalry and Administration in Britain's Military Air Command 1914–1918." *Journal of Strategic Studies* 3, no. 2 (1980): 178–201.

Cuneo, J. "Preparation of German Attack Aviation for the Offensive of March 1918." *Military Affairs* 7, no. 2 (1943): 69–78.

Davis, M. "Salvage: 1917 Orders, 2 Brigade RFC." *Cross & Cockade International Journal* 39, no. 1 (2008): 23–24.

Drucker, P. F. "The Economy's Dark Continent." *Fortune,* April 1962, 103, 265–70.

Dye, P. J. "9 Squadron RFC/RAF: An Analysis." *Cross & Cockade International Journal* 28, no. 2 (1997): 78.

———. "Logistic Lessons from the Past." *Air Clues,* September 1996: 347–51.

———. "Logistics and Air Power Doctrine." *RAF Air Power Review* 2, no. 1 (1999): 80–90.

———. "Logistics and the Falklands Campaign." *RAF Historical Society Journal*, no. 30 (2003): 85–96.

———. "Logistics and the Battle of Britain." *Air Force Journal of Logistics* 24, no. 4 (2000): 1, 31–39.

———. "No. 9 (Wireless) Squadron 1914–1915." *Cross & Cockade International Journal* 35, no. 2 (2004): 106–20.

———. "Patton's Culmination on the Meuse in 1944." *USAF Logistic Journal* 23, no. 2 (1999): 30–32.

———. "RFC Bombs and Bombing 1912–1918." *RAF Historical Society Journal*, no. 54 (2009): 8–24.

———. "Royal Air Force Repair and Salvage, 1939–1945." *Royal Air Force Historical Society Journal*, no. 51 (2011): 111–23.

———. "The Royal Flying Corps and Royal Air Force at St-Omer." *Cross & Cockade International Journal* 35, no. 2 (2004): 1–18.

———. "The Royal Flying Corps Logistic Organisation." *RAF Air Power Review* 1, no. 2 (1998): 42–58.

———. "Sustaining Air Power: The Influence of Logistics on RAF Doctrine." *RAF Air Power Review* 9, no. 2 (2006): 41–51.

Eaves, A., and B. Kingsman. "Forecasting for the Ordering and Stock-holding of Spare Parts." *Journal of the Operational Research Society* 55, no. 4 (2004): 431–37.

Evans, G. "70 Years of Brooke-Popham." *The Hawk*. Bracknell, UK: Royal Air Force Staff College, 1992, 83–92.

Ferguson, N. "Sinking Globalization." *Foreign Affairs* 84, no. 2 (2005): 64–77.

French, D. "Official but No History?" *Royal United Services Institute Journal* 131 (1986): 58–63.

Gollin, A. "The Mystery of Lord Haldane and Early British Military Aviation." *North American Conference on British Studies* 11, no. 1 (1979): 46–65.

Goodall, M. "RNAS Order of Battle." *Cross & Cockade International Journal* 3, no. 4 (1973): 137–46.

Greenhous, B. "Evolution of a Close Ground-Support Role for Aircraft in World War 1." *Military Affairs* 39, no. 1 (1975): 22–28.

Hay, D. "The Official History of the Ministry of Munitions 1915–1919." *Economic History Review*, October 1944: 185–90.

Hobson, C. "The First Air War: The Casualty Records." *Cross & Cockade International Journal* 30, no. 4 (1999): 204–9.

Horowitz, S. "Reversing Globalization: Trade Policy Consequences of World War 1." *European Journal of International Relations* (2004) 10:1, 33–60.

Jefford, C. G. "Corps Reconnaissance 1914–1918." *RAF Historical Society Journal*, no. 54 (2013): 8–35.

Kandebo, S. "The Wright Brothers and the Birth of an Industry." *Aviation Week & Space Technology* 157, no. 27 (30 December 2002): 17–22.

Krumwiede, D., and C. Sheu. "A Model for Reverse Logistics Entry by Third-Party Providers." *Omega, The International Journal for Management Science* 30, no. 5 (2002): 325–33.

Leaman, P. "J. M. Bruce: An Appreciation." *Cross & Cockade International Journal* 33, no. 3 (Autumn 2002): 139.

Mason, T. "RFC Aeroplanes." *Cross & Cockade International Journal* 8, no. 4 (1977): 145–67.

McCoy, M. "Grinding Gears: The AEF and Motor Transportation in the First World War." *War in History* 11, no. 2 (April 2004): 193–208.

Meilinger, P. S. "The Historiography of Airpower: Theory and Doctrine." *Journal of Military History* 64, no. 2 (2000): 467–501.

Mellor-Ellis, T. "Four Thoughts: In Praise of Harry Tate." *Over the Front* 12, no. 2 (1997): 166–67.

Miller, R. G. "The Logistics of the British Expeditionary Force: 4 August to 5 September 1914." *Military Affairs* 43, no. 3 (1979): 133–38.

———. "Maintenance and Supply at the Signal Corps Logistic School." *Air Force Journal of Logistics* 19, no. 4 (1995): 36–40.

———. "The Teeth to Tail Ratio: Royal Flying Corps and Air Service Co-operation in Maintenance Training During WW1." *Air Force Journal of Logistics* 28, no. 3 (2004): 22–33.

———. "What to Do with the Truck? The Air Service of the AEF and the Limits of Organic Transport 1917–1919." *Air Force Journal of Logistics* 21, no. 1 (1997): 35–41.

Morriss, R. "Colonization, Conquest and the Supply of Food and Transport: The Reorganization of Logistics Management 1780–1795." *War in History* 14, no. 3 (July 2007): 310–24.

Paris, M. "The Rise of the Airman: The Origins of Air Force Elitism, c. 1890–1918." *Journal of Contemporary History* 28, no. 1 (1993): 123–41.

Perjes, G. "Army Provisioning, Logistics and Strategy in the Second Half of the 17th Century." *Acta Historica Academiae Scientiarum Hungaricae* 16, nos. 1–2 (1970): 1–51.

Prins, F. "Forgotten Founder." *Air Enthusiast Quarterly* 47, September–November 1992, 1–8.

Proenca, D., and E. Duarte. "The Concept of Logistics Derived from Clausewitz." *Journal of Strategic Studies* 28, no. 4 (2005): 645–77.

Reiter, D., and A. C. Stam. "Democracy and Battlefield Military Effectiveness." *Journal of Conflict Resolution* 42, no. 3 (1998): 259–77.

Robertson, B. "An AID to Quality." *Aeroplane Monthly*, November 1993, 64–66.

Rogers, H. C. B. "Logistics in the Peninsula War." *British Army Review*, August 1979, 15–20.

Rowe, A. "The RE8 Controversy Revisited." *The 1914–1918 Journal*, 2001, 64–70.

Severs, N. J. "Courage on the Ground." *Cross & Cockade International Journal* 39, no. 2 (2008): 90–97.

Shimshoni, J. "Technology, Military Advantage and World War." *International Security* 15, no. 3 (Winter, 1990–91): 187–215.

Simon, S. J. "The Art of Military Logistics." *Communications of the Association for Computing Machinery* 44, no. 6 (2001): 62–66.

Smith, R. P. "Maintenance on the Cheap: Air Force Logistics 1907–1917." *Air Force Journal of Logistics*, Spring 1987, 17–20.

———. "Unprepared for War: Aviation Logistics and the Home Front 1917–1918." *Air Force Journal of Logistics*, Fall 1987, 8–12.

Terraine, J. "Lessons of Air Warfare." *Royal United Services Institute Journal* 137 (1992): 53–58.

———. "World War One and the Royal Air Force." *Royal Air Force Historical Society Proceedings*, no. 12 (1994): 10–22.

van Creveld, M. "Supplying an Army: An Historical View." *Royal United Services Institute Journal* 123 (1978): 56–63.

Wakefield, A. "Subvention, Impressment and Mass Production—The 'Standard' Lorry and British Military Logistics 1912–1918." *Stand To!*, September 1997, 12–14.

Whitmarsh, A. "British Army Manoeuvres and the Development of Military Aviation." *War in History* 14, no. 3 (July 2007): 325–26.

Williams, A. J. "The Engine Repair Shops Revisited." *Cross & Cockade International Journal* 23 (1992): 42–46.

———. "The RFC/RAF Engine Repair Shops." *Cross & Cockade International Journal* 17, no. 4 (1986): 154–61.

Williamson, G. W. "Some Problems of a Technical Service." *Royal United Services Institution Journal* 79 (1934): 780–800.

Wilson, T., and R. Prior. "Conflict, Technology and the Impact of Industrialization 1914–1918." *Journal of Strategic Studies* 24, no. 3 (2001): 128–57.

OTHER WORKS

Adams, J., and J. Abell. *Modelling and Forecasting Aircraft Recoverable Spare Parts.* RAND Report R-4211. Washington, DC: Department of Defense, 1993.

Brown, I. M. "The Evolution of the British Army's Logistical and Administrative Infrastructure and its Influence on GHQ's Operational and Strategic Decision-Making on the Western Front, 1914–1918." PhD thesis, King's College London, 1996.

Childs, D. "British Tanks 1915–1918, Manufacture and Employment." PhD thesis, University of Glasgow, 1996.

Defence Storage and Distribution Agency (DSDA). *Annual Report and Accounts 2008–2009.* London: Stationery Office, 2010.

Farmer, J. R. "What approach did the British Army take to solving the logistic problems related to operations on the Italian Front between deployment in 1917 and the conclusion of hostilities in 1918?" MA dissertation, University of Birmingham, 2006.

Jones, B. "Ashore, Afloat and Airborne: The Logistics of British Naval Airpower 1914–1945." PhD thesis, Kings College London, 2007.

Jordan, D. J. "The Army Co-operation Missions of the Royal Flying Corps/Royal Air Force 1914–1918." PhD thesis, University of Birmingham, 1997.

Kane, T. M. "Getting It There: The Relationship between Military Logistics and Strategic Effectiveness." PhD thesis, University of Hull, 1998.

NAO. *The Use of Information to Manage the Logistics Supply Chain.* London: House of Commons, HC 827 Session 2010–2011.

Pugh, J. N. "The Conceptual Origins of the Control of the Air: British Military and Naval Aviation, 1911–1918." PhD thesis, University of Birmingham, 2012.

TESCO. *Annual Report and Accounts 2011.* Cheshunt, UK: Tesco plc, 2011.

Williams, G. "Statistics and Strategic Bombardment: Operations and Records of the British Long-Range Bombing Force during World War 1 and their Implications for the Development of the Post-War Royal Air Force, 1917–1923." DPhil thesis, University of Oxford, 1987.

Zabecki, D. T. "Operational Art and the German 1918 Offensives." PhD thesis, Department of Defence Management, Cranfield University, UK, 2003.

INDEX

administrative excellence, 16

Admiralty, 24, 62, 63, 70, 211n6

aero-engines: average life of, 89, 220n66; delivery of, 53, 71, 75–76; design, production, and supply of, 8, 60–65, 70–76, 142, 212n21, 215n71, 215n73, 215n82, 215nn65–67, 216nn87–88; design-to-production timeline, 61, 210–11n3; French-made engines, 25, 26–27, 40, 61, 62, 70–76, 142, 215n71, 215n73, 215n82, 215nn65–67, 216nn87–88; inspection and testing of, 64–65; maintenance of, 36–37, 61, 89, 97, 201–2n4; manpower for building, 15; number needed for each squadron, 66–67; official designs, 61–62; possession of and operational success, 6; powerful engines, failure to develop, 62; private designs, 61–62; rebuilt engines, number of, 69, 171, 214n61; records and writings about, 11–12; reliability of, 60, 73–76; replacement of, 89, 220n66; shortage of, 8, 15, 62–64, 75–76, 205n57; spares for, 75–76, 98, 110, 213n32; standardization policy, 64; strength of, 174; struck off, number of, 172; trouble associated with, 97

aeronautics: American Civil War use of military aeronautics, 4; military use of, 23–24, 197n22; research on, 23

l'Aéronautique Militaire. *See* French Air Services (l'Aéronautique Militaire)

Aeroplane General Sundries (AGS), 51, 53, 64

Air Ammunition Columns (AAC), 41, 180

Air Battalion, 23–24

Air Board, 63, 64

air construction corps, 114

Air Force, U.S. (USAF), 2, 17

Air Services, U.S. (USAS), 12

air superiority: achievement of, 31–32, 35; Arras operations, 94–95; communications and, 32–33; importance of, 139; logistics and, 31–32, 35, 191n38; modern style of warfare and, xiii, 31; operational success and, 6–7; RAF capabilities and, 32–33; Somme operations, 87–91; Third Ypres operations, 105, 110–11

aircraft: advantages of, debate about, 22; average life of, 89, 220n67; budget allocation for, 9, 14–15, 193n63; challenges of maintaining, xiii; delivery of, 40, 42–43, 46, 52, 53, 66, 68, 80–81, 89, 101, 125, 149–55, 173, 207n103, 207n105, 228n76; design and production of, 8, 42–43, 60–65, 75–76, 95–96, 142, 210n1, 211nn6–7, 212n21, 222nn23–24; design-to-production timeline, 61, 79, 149–50, 151, 210–11n3, 232–33n39; development of and experimentation with by British Army, 22–24; fragility of, 36–37, 79–80; French development of, 23, 26; French-made aircraft, 25, 26–27, 40, 142; German development and production, 23, 60; inactive aircraft, 79–80; inspection and testing of, 40, 62, 63, 64–65, 109, 210n1, 212n18; issuing of, 46–47, 206n72; loss rates, 34, 35; manpower for building, 15; military use of, 23–24, 197n22;

operations: boundary between aviation support and air operations, 142; complexity of, 34; logistical capabilities and campaign outcomes, 4, 190–91n31; mission analysis, 17; supply chain performance and operational capabilities, 3

Ordnance Aeronautical Stores Department (OASD), 40, 43, 83, 183

Overy, Richard, 5–6, 16

Paine, Godfrey, 24

Passchendaele operations, 102, 105

patrols and observation: air war victory and, 35; Arras operations, 94; contact patrols to support infantry, 27, 29, 34; counter-battery observation and wireless communications, 192n56; employment of squadrons for, 34; offensive patrols, 34; RFC role in, 7; Somme operations, 84–87, 90–91; target identification and engagement, 24, 34, 35

Pemberton Billing, Noel, 211nn10–11

personnel. See manpower/personnel

photography: aerial photography for mapping, 7, 8; aerial photography, RFC role in, 7; employment of squadrons for, 34; French influence on practices for, 27, 29; importance of capabilities, 34–35; improvements in equipment and practices, 30–31; intelligence from aerial photographs, 30–31; interest in and writings about, 7; number of photos taken, 123, 140, 227n66; number of photos taken and efficiency, 17; number of photos taken and printed, 30; records about western front operations, 194n85; RFC organization for, 27; Somme operations, 84–86, 90–91

pilots and aircrew: accommodations for, 83, 114; availability of trained pilots, 15; combatant to noncombatant ratio, 9, 192n58; expansion of force strength and, 102–3; losses during combat, 15, 195n98; losses during training, 15, 195n98; records about western front operations, 194n85; shortage of pilots, 15, 63; supply of, 8; training of, 15; victories by, focus of literature on, 21, 196n1

Pont de l'Arche Engine Repair Shops, 40–41, 53, 61, 177, 204nn42–43, 211n5

Port Detachments, 53, 179, 182, 208n110

primary requirements, ratio of secondary requirements to, 18, 157–58

procurement: civilian economy, coordination with, 19, 159; logistics activities, 2

pull systems, 109, 120, 156

Pulteney, William, 85

push systems, 109–10, 120–21, 125, 156

quality, 19, 159

RAF1a engines, 62, 63, 64–65

RAF4a engine: B.E.12 use of, 213n43; development of, 62; number built and delivered, 66–67, 213n38; R.E.7 use of, 213n43; R.E.8 use of, 65, 66–67, 69–70, 213n38; repair of, 69–70, 214n61; spares for, 98, 110

railroads: American Civil War use of, 4; Italy operations and transport of stores, 107–10, 224n85; motor transport and support from, 38; movement of stores by, 125–26, 135, 146; Somme operations and transport of stores, 89–90, 220n70

Raleigh, Walter, 10–11

Rawlinson, Henry, 88

R.E.7 aircraft, 213n43

R.E.8 aircraft, 133; aero-engines for, 65, 66–67, 213n38; artillery cooperation role of, 34, 135–36; delivery of, 53, 66, 68; design, development, and deployment of, 65–70, 75, 212–13nn30–31, 232–33n39; Italy operations, 108, 110, 224n79; modifications program, 65–66, 68; number built and delivered, 65, 66,

ABOUT THE AUTHOR

PETER DYE is a graduate of Imperial College and Birmingham University. He served in the Royal Air Force for more than thirty-five years and was awarded the OBE for his work in support of the Jaguar Force during the First Gulf War, retiring as an air vice-marshal. He was appointed director general of the Royal Air Force Museum in 2008.